MICRO CONCEPT

Micro Concept

Copyright © 2015 Seong-Ju Choi
Book Cover Picture Artist by Ki-Ho An

Published in the Republic of korea by Publishing Jisikgonggam,
112, Gyeondalsan-ro 225beon-gil, Ilsandong-gu, Goyang-si, Gyeonggi-do, Korea.

Web: www.bookdaum.com
Email: bookon@daum.net
Tel: +82 2 3141 2700

Paperback ISBN: 979-11-5622-072-5 (03100)
CIP 2015002828
First published in paperback February 2015.

MICRO CONCEPT

SEONG-JU CHOI

Jisik Gonggam Publishing Company

Micro Concept

This is my excitement gift; I have to be excitement in my daily living.
It helps macro concept actor righteous living to be blessed from
micro righteous souls. This excitement will lead to the perfection

_Author: **CHOI SEONG JU**

Table of Contents

Helping Reading
"Micro Concept"

"Micro concept" writing comes to end. During writing I have lived in the micro concept world. Micro concept world (-1/∞ +1/∞) this world the area of micro concept actor of soul, macro concept actor is soul with body. So long I lived as macro concept actor. Macro concept actor is progress in writing this book. Micro concept world (-1/∞ +1/∞) found in this book, so this book written by energy of micro concept (-1/∞ +1/∞), micro concept is found as try to find the solution of macro concept actor living, then macro concept just used past from to now, -∞/0 ~-1/∞, I thought that macro concept knowledge is Seen knowledge, most macro concept world actor desired to be success, but most actor mind is not come to reach at macro concept actors dream. I thought that it must be macro actor affairs all is not related with macro world but it must be another power affect so then it comes to me, the world is micro concept world, micro concept point, and this is use from now to future knowledge use for solving macro concept world living problems. Micro concept world is past to now, now to future, this is micro concept world (-1/∞ +1/∞), this is comes to me, micro concept world is not present, the present is micro concept point melted past and future. So micro concept world with macro concept world are mixed to the macro concept world actor, so long the actors see Seen world features. So macro concept actor now existence is located at the both world macro concept world and micro concept world. I write that realized a macro concept world actor reach at micro concept point (-1/∞ +1/∞), I said that micro concept point is role of the micro concept world gate, micro concept world, but also to meet micro concept righteous soul actor meeting travel tunnel, so long the realized actor reach at the micro concept point (-1/∞ +1/∞), macro concept righteous soul travel using tunnel to micro concept world righteous soul destinations world. So macro concept righteous soul meets righteous soul living at in the micro concept world. So that micro concept world actor gives future knowledge. The macro concept actor gets solution from micro concept world future knowledge. So long, in the micro concept world get future idea, solve present problems. Now problems will not solve macro concept world knowledge. So long micro concept world is micro moment ($-1/\infty$ $+1/\infty$). Then macro concept actor must be get future knowledge from micro concept world, then macro concept actor infers that macro concept world actor just Seen is body, this is true to the macro concept world actor. But to connect micro concept unseen world actor soul, then it must be macro concept actor also has the soul. So in this micro concept infer that macro concept actor must be Unseen minor is soul seen Body, so long in this first part macro concept actor "soul + body" in this case soul is from micro concept world, body is from macro concept world. So micro concept world point of view, micro concept actor birth time so excitement with meeting body, so long a good experiment then help body to live righteous, but also, the minor unseen actor with body, then just Seen body, the soul imagined that the soul will come to micro concept righteous world soul destination but the soul faced problems, because of in the macro concept world already body goes with mind, so long micro concept actor soul do not meet because of mind, this is also in this micro concept find "soul + mind + body" so long, this macro concept actor make story. Soul and body live actor, but mind is not an actor, but mind role of living actor, so that body easily helped from mind, so that helping mind body, the body try to be get more, also be big, rich, etc. so that soul from micro concept world experience that to live at micro concept righteous soul world, then the actor live righteous, the righteous act means that shared with time others, but also help others. So actor worry mind drive body to against the ways, so that the soul so difficult even know the micro concept world righteous world living excitement. Mind do not know the micro concept world living, so that macro concept world getting big, rich to be that, do not shared time with others, but also do not help others. So long the soul it must be can't go back to righteous world destination of micro concept world. So long if mind go to $1/\infty$, then it must be being "soul+ body" so that, this body called soulful body, at last come to soul and body meet, so that it means that the macro concept actor reach at the micro concept point ($-1/\infty$ $+1/\infty$) so then, macro concept actor realized but also macro concept actor can meet, macro concept actor minor soul meet micro concept actor major soul then, the macro concept actor helped from future knowledge. So macro concept problems are solved. But I have strange feeling, the soul now comes, macro concept minor actor soul, micro concept major actor soul, relationship.

How to solve sometimes I thought that in this macro concept actor "soul + mind + body" then, macro concept actor soul comes from macro concept actor birth, then, the minor of macro concept soul is so young, then macro concept actor old how to be soul, if soul live righteous, then it simple, then the old macro concept actor still "soul+ mind+ body" if mind is to $1/\infty$ then macro concept actor "soul+ body" then, it comes problems so, all of macro concept actor without mind then righteous soul living micro concept world, then mind is Satan? So I try to find another infer that soul is divided righteous soul 50 and wicked soul 50, so then a new macro concept are comes "righteous soul 50 + wicked soul50 + mind 100+ body 100" this pattern macro concept actor appeared to this micro concept book. So long then, if macro concept actor do not live righteously, a macro actor time do not shared with others, but also do not help others. Then the actor do not live righteously, then, it must be comes to wicked soul power goes to strong, then, in this cases, righteous soul hard to live with wicked soul actor, so long, righteous soul going out of a actor, so then strong wicked mind actor comes "wicked soul being 100 + mind 100+ body" so long in this case, the macro concept world actor live desired to get rich, binger. I do not know reach at the desired. But if an actor lives righteously then, the actor shared time with others but also helped others then, in this case also pure righteous so called strong righteous soul being then wicked soul also run away from the macro concept actor so long it automatically mind is being to $1/\infty$ so long, it comes a new macro concept actor "righteous soul 100+ body100" so long this is macro concept actor reach at the micro concept point $(-1/\infty +1/\infty)$, so long the righteous soul macro concept actor reach at the micro concept point, so long, the actor used micro concept tunnel to meet micro concept righteous soul actor meet, so then, micro concept righteous living actor blessing credit help macro concept righteous living actor, so righteous living actor get blessed from micro concept righteous soul actor. In the end in this micro concept book gives that macro concept actor live is so deep related with micro concept world. The excitement and reach perfection is depends on both macro concept world and micro concept world. The process is macro concept world actor live righteous or wicked, so then righteous living save in the righteous soul world blessing bank, but wicked lived actor saved at the wicked soul micro concept world cursed bank credit. So that macro concept live in the macro concept world and micro concept world, then, macro concept world is Seen world so, wicked or righteous way living, but in the macro concept actor living is also comes from micro concept world $(-1/\infty$ $+1/\infty)$, so long micro concept world actor try to help, righteous soul help righteous actor, but wicked actor try to use wicked soul saved energy, so this energy is cursed energy. So long, macro concept world living is connected with macro concept world but also micro concept world is not segregated. Here is micro concept is $(-1/\infty +1/\infty)$, this means that past and future combined. So long it must be macro concept and micro concept is closely related. The sure thing is micro concept world and macro concept world meeting actor is soul. Micro concept is soul living. This so hard to saying but the soul, macro concept actor how to live, live righteous or wicked live then, the actor returned as dead, then righteous actor soul destination but also wicked lived then after dead then the actor located at the wicked soul destination. So long, it must be again infer that, righteous soul actor number is not many, but wicked soul number so many. Infer that what said in the micro concept in the birth time new actor being "righteous soul 50 wicked souls 50 + mind 100 +body 100" then it must be combined to a new soul of macro concept minor actor, then righteous soul 1 to wicked soul 1 to make a soul, so long, if live righteous then in the micro concept, righteous soul live eternity but wicked soul actor to be eternity then, time will be fall behind.

In conclusion, micro concept try to say a simple ways, do shared time with others, but also help others. Then it comes to Excitement to perfection.

Preface

I have dreamed in the vague to sell 5M copies, even I desired to sell 5B copies. This is vague thinking. I have been writing personal journal, by accidently I got a estrange idea, even this idea also I have thought but today (2014-04-14) is more clear to me, I start daily based writing. While daily writing I found micro concept, so I use just momentum unseen world: micro concept point M ($-1/\infty+1/\infty$) is all of this book contents are based on fully from my soul; my soul connects through micro concept tunnel ($-1/\infty+1/\infty$) to righteous soul and my god, infer that ancestors gift to me writing knowledge, and this is the wisdom from God. But "this micro concept" is not a religious related but my "Micro concept" is to get a solution of macro concept actor faced problems. So long this book will be using my life voyage guide book. Even start vague writing but I get my living solution; so long, it must be this book does not sell any copy but I'm excitement. Even though, this knowledge micro concept will be selected by only one reader, then I feel really thank you someone. I'm expect just one reader be reading "micro concept" then I'm done what I'm writing hard working.

This book is not perfect in English, so reader sometimes question but please understand, I'm pure out of English speaking country. But please reading and be excitement of new idea of micro concept contents.

Much more understand thing is to explain "micro concept" many times repeat word using. Please readers read as writing "micro concept" daily, and then you will reach at "micro concept" meaning but also reach at excitement & perfection. Again understand this book concept error will find, but I do not modification because this "micro concept" is perfectly creating book. All this contents depend on my soul's helping. Please beginning to somehow still vague, during getting going the contents being safe, please in the starting part reading be patience. Because of making tools to make "micro concept" explain. Micro concept righteous actor comes late of living, and then the realized actor connected to micro concept righteous destination souls. If the actor be at the decision maker, the decision maker helps the members being righteous and excitement in the end the actor reaches act the perfection.

Part 1

Building "Micro Concept"

2014.04.14

All is going itself; if I can buy Mt. then I will go for keeping in Mt. if possible then can I use Mt. product industry. But it will come to me? That is question to me; I will be managed the very safety maintenance to me. What else I'm doing my best, for long time, what I'm doing my best, for that for the greatest, my body is so tired, my people will be bad, I will believe that I will not evaluate others, but I will watch me, my inside is I'm the cosmos, just so small cosmos, for me very well how to do, very well, so long but also, it simple but I'm doing but I'm doing my best, for that how long but also, so long but I'm doing my thing , in this time, all has the live on line.

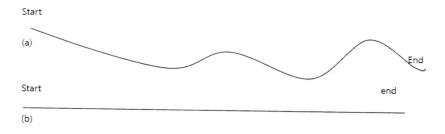

Please keep me consistence, if possible can I get writing my mind, please shared with my mind. it can be my mind full story, my book readers can be satisfy with my book. my living is the lies to me, line is the somewhat not direct line but all of the go reflective line, what is difference what I'm, it maybe my line is the reflective line, some people live on direct line. What is suit in the living, which way is best living. If some other living also but I'm so weak, so that I'm not think others, but all it must not out of line, just go for the line, line is the very great influence to me, very good to me, so it is not to be well how long but also, all the time he great time working but also for me very how long, but I'm not sufficiency to me very well how long but in the long run for me, some of my best title job for me very clean job matter creature. I will go for the managed the creative thing, my living is the creative, just I'm here to me, very great time to me very how long but also, so that it not easy to me, so, something but also how I'm in nerve for me very well, it creative to me very well so long but also, some of my best going.

Last night I was so fear, my body and mental was so weak to me, very great time working but also, so long but also, I felt that my surround is not getting better, all of the social, national asset is not, increased but all down size, but it better job, so long but also, some of my real job it is not well to me, what is the very some of attentive to me very how long but also so that I'm here to me very well how I'm not simple for me, what is the very green principal for me, how long but also for the looking but also how I'm not easy for me very well, what is the very good.

Mind is not same strange mind is just go with my body, mind, soul, my body, is not same coincidence in my body, in my body contents is soul, mind, soul is the eternity, but mind is the present concept, my soul from god's king dome, my mind is residence in my mind, in to me the gate is not same, soul, and mind.

My body has the mind, soul, and thinking

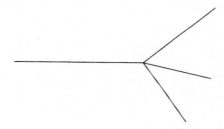

In the body my soul and my thinking and my minds are so long, but so then, my soul is from my god, my mind is from me, my thinking is the behavior of the feeling, to going out to the writing and saying, soul, mind to thinking. In the all of the creature from the soul, but all of my biological and relationship is mind, but knowledge and the idea from soul tunnel, not mind tunnel, mind tunnel is personal characteristics, soul tunnel is the from knowledge god, so that god is the all of the people, but it is not structure of the originality of the religious but in the my principal is discriminate just in the humanism.

I can communicate with my ancestor by the soul tunnel, I can communicate with my real god also, my mind is real very short of tunnel from me, but soul tunnel is the out of limited, but mind is just micro of the very line.

Soul information stored to the ancestor and god country information area, so then it compared with the super computer, but mind is the store in me information area, just compared with personal computer. So that, for long time it does, so that, in my micro actor is the soul, mind, thinking is this, very well going for the job for me very great time job for me very great time job matter for me.

Just in my micro actors are soul, mind, thinking, how to do better living to me, but also, it is very house of the in the contents are soul, religious, philosopher, mind is the charity, love, benevolence, forgiveness etc, just thinking is the exodus from the religious philosopher, and the charity, love, benevolence, forgiveness.

Physical condition must be consistence must be exercise it is only to live on the ways for me, how long but also, very great time working but also, something but also how long but still it in the great time working but also for the how long but also, some of my best thing to me,

These actor in my theory is the micro concept is from, me so that to solve my micro concept then I will be rely on the soul, mind, the thinking. In the micro concept, this is me, as possible as I can, I'm here to do for that, for long time, for my "excitement & perfection" my concept it must be invest my time for the excitement in the physical ways, I will learn in the day, for the I will body building is my required to me, very how long but also, my simple attitude for me very great time to me very, how long but also for me I will use my time for the exercise I will go for the so long but also, my little time to me.

Just micro for the main concept is the comparative theory, but also, in the present future past is the mixed in the

Vertical present, left line is the past, right line is the future;

But if n=0 closed to the zero then, the convergence point is the locate in the cognition to the in present just $1/\infty$ future then it must be come to closed to the zero but also, past is the $-1/\infty$ then it also come to zero. What is the means, what

is the greatest for the way, just in the macro is the it clear of the future is the 1/0, past is the -1/0, then it must be the history thing,

(a) -1/0 _____ 1/0

P

In the P point recognizes the past means that -1/0, future recognition is 1/0.

(b) ———————————→ ———————→

-1/∞ 1/∞

In this case is the close to zero, past present future.

What is the (a) is the Macro concept, all of the people knows the truth, it has the already old, all are salver of the history, Korea Japan still just hate, it is not go for the any peace and prosperous in the macro concept,

(a)   Is the micro concept, past present and future it must be the future variance is come to then it must be Japan and Korea combine the good factor it will open for the future in the macro then so a many time after, but in the micro world now can possible the a good relationship.

Micro concept is the closed to the future it use the future idea, here future is not limited to the , but micro concept is not true, macro unit 100 years but in the micro is the second at least I year, so that, micro and macro is the big gap, but in the living is the all of people do not live 1000years all of the people live fully then 120 years, so if we are now our scale is the very macro concept then, we are do not solve historical errors but also, historical destiny is governing all of the global space.

How to we involve, but we must use the so long, micro is the very possible all of the macro impossible in the time scale but also the physical state also, Macro has the history asset, so already the power then, he/she is might for all of the cases, how to adopt to the present benefit of the micro.

All of the macro the entire thing is occupies in the case of the realtor industry also, all has the bubble, it must be the entire problem is not solved, it can be not but I will get secure in getting perfect. "Excitement & perfection" in the best good at feeling & it produce perfect product, it is the in the macro play and product all of the case, play time, and product time, is perfectly segregate. So then play = excitement, product = perfection, here if has the play product is possible it is the micro also, in the Google and the micro software companies are play and product, but it make rich in the world, how to explain to do, but also the concept all must be changed to do,

I'm all the time I has been said " you are estrange from the normal" so my wife anger to me, I have not known it, I love my wife, if I try to give to the true of the micro concept, how to do, all of the concept, then just all of the living and thinking ways are changed, from now on the all of the in the conception of the micro world is the god world, so it don't necessary difference due to the we all tunnel to the soul, all of the people has the soul, this is the all give form the god, just to the how to live, some moment all of the soluble is from god, our situation all hard, because all of the people closed from the connection to the god,

I will write my "micro concept" I will sell over the 5B copies selling I will fine the really soluble of it. It has been done for the ways for me; I will be here to do. I will write a book in the micro concept.

The name of Jesus Christ. Amen.

My lord please permit me writing this "micro concept" if I'm short of knowledge then god help me more diligence your knowledge writing. God please give me excitement in writing just wait your giving me the god knowledge. The writing comes up perfection for the value of the reading my reader's mind fully touchable.

Heavenly father I'm so humble to you, you are my lord and savior, I believe you. I'm depend on you writing this "micro concept"

Please this small start to end of gland in my conclusion, but also, this knowledge is touch in the published company managers, all of my idea is can be through, so then print and sell in the global market.

God please give me your all of energy to be complete this book.
The name of Jesus Christ, Amen.

2014.04.14

My long wait writing book voyage starting, it must be a big sea crossing to safe at a sea port. In the voyage how variable micro concept comes to me, it is the miracle to me; it is the god gift to me. This is my whole prepared story telling book. All from my soul, mind, thinking. These actors are my "Micro concept" masters.

2014.04.15

I'm the cosmos. I'm in the "micro concept" cosmos; I'm the entire center. If I here cosmos, if not here then I'm nothing. In the micro concept, I'm a cosmos.

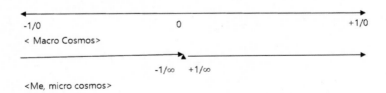

I'm cosmos, in the macro concept then I'm not a person only, but in the micro concept then I'm in the from past -1/∞, just momentum past, +1/∞ the future just momentum future, just recognition is the me, just my thinking ; from mind or soul, then just momentum thinking is the cosmos. So then in the I am the cosmos so then on me the time and space are all located, in the micro concept, just micro is the space is the point but also the unseen just like the soul then, the soul is the space, time is the past, future are recognition, so then, just soul is the actor of the space, just very swift momentum, soul is the connect to the thinking, it already in the micro reach at the probably do not recognition speed and a destination come and going, in this micro concept, I'm cosmos.

But also all of the cosmos are living in this earth. If all of the people are come to the micro subject then micro human being will be in the unseen soul then this soul travel to the all of the cosmos. Micro concept is , but if please human being is not because of super, so then still recognition of macro but, all of the concept are micro then, human being must live in the peace and it but also any quarrel but all, but if all of the people became of the micro concept adoption then all of micro human being is the still just unseen all of earth people just soul, the same as the a person is the cosmos, how human being is the value all is the cosmos, who knows it, so long just micro concept is the human being how to reach the ways to do.

2014.04.21

This is a micro concept just all of living is connected, all is the line, good line but bad and bad line. How to bad line connect to good line. Here bad is the loan, debt, good is merit, virtue, etc. so then, if one person follows the good line, but the other person follows the bad line then what happened to us, why a person chose the good line, why other chose bad line, what is the epoch to live on, what is the a person living is the bad or good, in our time to be a good line then it required to be diligence, and endure of hard time, consideration others, but bad line is temper, anger, do not consideration, but also he/she think her/his circumstance so deteriorate. But even all of the people life is one time, so how valuable, so then all of the people must be follow the good, but most people are follow the bad, some time bad line to changed to the good line, it must be think and realization. Just good line all is not, because of the it is not sure but in the start of living or not, but it must be the god already decide his/her living, it is not true, but it must be happened to that, what indicate the person good line bad line, please here some of condition of the line is decide of the forefather behavior, if ancestors are all bad line then it must be come to the possibility to the bad line, but a forefather lived good line then it comes to the good line, but if a forefather lived bad line then a new coming people good line, here good line is the still he/she is keeps a poor person, this is the save the poor people, poor people heavenly father son and daughter, so heavenly father thank to the helper, but also, himself, herself, feel sorry to the helper so then he/she is the duplicate of helping heavenly father son/daughter, so that to be good line, it must be realize of heavenly father benefit, but also, he/she must be endure all of hard time, then it comes to the god brightness, all of the cases, so long, we do not know the how to god control and realize of each persons, it is the micro concept, all of the people be micro then god all of the see in the god kingdom, god governing at now people, before people but also future people also.

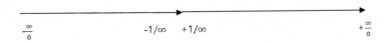

If a person good line, the other is bad line, how to decide of her/his life live on bad , but also god line, if a bad forefather lived then, most macro phenomenon is not touch in this, but in the micro concept then past, preset, future are convergence so that, all of the bad action a point of view then already god, or hell place located ancestor and present me is contagious, all of the god easy watching the bad line, but it also irregular of the line, a present I am all of endurance by the realize of the believing the Jesus Christ but also, he/she is personal realization so he/she helped all of the poor people of the god valuable persons, so then god feel repay of her/his benevolence so then from now him/her build by him/herself good line, in this case his/her successful story not in the world but in the micro concept, micro concept is the very correct, it very detailed so that all is the calculate but also the decided correctly. This is the somewhat relative to the god country rule, in the unseen happening doer all is count on, so then this all of righteous is the decision criteria of the reward to the afterward runners, at least god happy with just healthy and righteous god son and daughter, but all of the god kingdom is the all not dictators all is the himself, herself decide to behavior of all of it,, in the thing is righteous, wicked is criteria thing are happened so then these also good for the purpose but it must be done for the end of something then the result is the bad then, all has the decision accumulation is come to. So then in the macro world, they do not know in the living of the wicked, they forgot all of the unrighteous what is the righteous all for the behavior of the Jesus Christ, but in the macro is sometimes forgotten but in the micro is the very detail but also very micro judged to, her mind read, in the micro just mistake not it, the his/her intention, all of the micro point is seen in the god kingdom, it may be the 0.000000001 or more, but in the how to erase of the by the verdict behavior all of the balance is seen , how to be good or bad, so then all of the conditions are it is not all the time come to good behavior, in the source of thinking is decide, in the micro world a source of power is the Satan power god's power, actually Satan is the origin of the anti to the good line good behavior, good line is the source of the god, actually in the micro world, Satan and god is mixed so that Satan and god mind is also in the same place, just all of temptation and education duplicate thing is conglomerates. So long but so in the micro world, if a person is present existence then, he/she can recognition in the micro concept, but in the macro world living then he must be only live with past information, not know the future but in the micro world in the micro then he feel the past present future, so that he will be go easier in his/her voyage. How is the this people he is the Jesus, he deliver in the wild just hunger people, just for the a small bread to feed fully, how to do, in the micro concept god country, it possible all of the bread in the micro even atom molecular then, it must be shared all of the human being is the micro concept they are all soul, so then, micro concept all of the moment all of people being a god country, he/ she is lived in micro heaven kingdom, so god, Jesus lead to the preaching of the god saying then all of the people being a soul then soul eat the just bread, after then if they out of the concept in the micro then in the Seen macro world then, all of the member of Jesus Christ church members are satisfaction, Jesus is the all of eating all of the people if they are realize or gods kingdom even this miracle, so long in the righteous then all of members are all not hunger, all people do not worry of him/her hunger, coming future anxious, just do righteous behavior then whoever don't worry all is done, to be keep righteous it required to do, encouragement, in the god kingdom of the micro concept, just in to the living of the micro concept it must be understand of the truth, not to be deceit all of the people awaken and realize, but also help each other, love neighbors so then all of the verdicts are accumulate, in the micro concept also adopt same as macro world, all of the diligence is the productivity is same with creative, all of the micro world so multiple of the new, creative conditions, that is very difference to the macro, which mass not creative but technology and a limited asset so then all of the actors are competition all of industries. From the gathering for the safety but also out of the anxious in the macro world, sometimes some to the deceit others, so that bad line is come to all of the people know the good ways is better than bad line but all possibly to live bad ways, so then they live in the bad people community, so in the bad behavior all recognized as well as usual, all of the good people can't live in the bad deceit community, even these community to adopt micro then they will be in the Satan world, so how fear of it, bad community is owned by the Satan kingdom. Satan is the god's enemy. What happened to us, for that for how long, how to bad line to good line, it must be the bad line is the macro then a new idea, is the micro concept is revolutionary a new way of living but also, god treat, just as a ways of the war, all of deteriorate, then god treat a good line, of his god's king dome, so then all of the community goes well, even god sorry but also, pursue to live on the good line, but Gradually comes up, wicked persons, so many spread of the bad indicators, so then gradually all of the community being bad line. In the micro concept, personal righteous is decided not a group, so then if I be in the wicked man then, right now in the micro concept the community is the not good, so to be the good line, it must be I'm center but also, I'm righteous is required, if I be in the wrong then, whoever else, actually in the micro world, is I'm center, I'm present, truly feeling hard treat all is I'm so, we are somewhat forget all is the center in the big cosmoses, so in the micro concept is the adopt to the personal, micro concept is the god and me is coexistence, so if my decision is against to the god then, it already in the side of the Satan, GOD expect to live on righteous living.

2014.04.22

In the macro world all of the governing by the micro concept, each person has the center for the micro but in the we seen in the macro, but all of the people connection is the in the all of micro feature connections,

<People to people is macro but actually in the people recognition is micro actor soul>

So then all of the people connection is not a physical but all is connected to the each person's metal, so then here soul or mind, then connect is the faith each others, just credibility also then it must be the religious concept then it must be the soul, so then this credibility information spread to the each person so called the soul, then soul is the located in the micro concept.

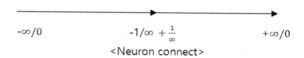

<Neuron connect>

If all of the human being to the micro concept adopt then, soul, here soul is the before children, after death old man, just come up as soul then, in the living macro human being must to be the micro then soul, so then, all of the people in the micro world, by the concept of the neuron connect then, all of the in the macro getting information, just information is not a macro it also the soul, so then all of the soul has the information so then, it connect in the micro concept neuron connect, so then, all of the knowledge, information transfer. In the micro point coincide past present future, so then old dead man soul, at now living people soul, but also future not now but it will come to human beings soul are all together meeting is the micro concept world.

So then in the human macro community, just all of connect

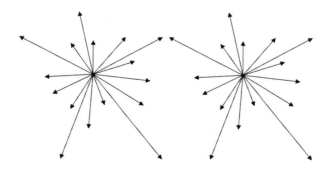

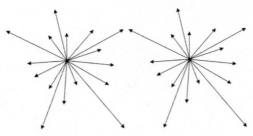

These four macro person, connect each other, then we see the each other but actually all of the connection is also, just mind to mind, soul to soul, so then it repress like that

This 4 people mind to mind, but also soul to soul connect, so then this people connecting point to the adopt for the soul then, the soul also revealed to the past, present, future soul, in any way, but also the 4soul connect means also, very micro size, so then these theory if some magnify to the all of the human member in the earth 600B population also all meet in the past, present, future soul in the micro world, in the micro world governor is God, so then all of us controlled by the GOD. Yes turning back, in the community or state to be the good live then all of the people go to righteous living, then as we all in the read the bible we have the same in the macro righteous wicked, so then Satan soul king dome, righteous heavens God kingdom. So that how to live is the soul is located is decide, it is so propound concept start come up. To live well so long we have in the macro world, all they live on themselves easy ways, just personalize, do not disturbed the personal territory, it means that the person will not care others, even good is the all of the persons, forget others, all of his/her energy only use for himself./herself then all is not feel I'm not guilty, all of information also closed so then some poor knowledge person all segregate for the good information, here information is the theoretical concept, so then, the poor person still remained in the poor state, it must be the God said in the bible " love neighbor" here neighbor is the physical concept, just influence space must be, but now us all of us people against the rule of heavenly father rule, but also spiritual world, so long all of the people turn down, sorrowful but all of the pray say " please help me" actually the god in the Macro all of distance but in the micro concept is all is if I'm a center then each person mind is the spiritual micro concept field, so that in the micro field of the micro concept all of relative of me, what I said the "all of relatives just knowledge people ancestor also but future babies also in the micro field" so then if we asked to the god " please help me" then god accept the prayers, then how to help, the prayer feel that in the good relationship with the prayer neighbor going better. All I do well for others then god role of another neighbors are good to reactions to him / her. So then actually personalize is not in the god kingdom, all of the said in the bible, " love neighbor " then god saying is seen in the macro but it also just spread to the loving felt the soul in the micro, so then god's pray spread to the so fast to the god.

2014.04.23

Today morning I got surprise knowledge comes to me, Jesus Christ feed multiple followers in the yard, and then just a small bread only but multiple shard this bread with multiple followers, but also enough eat and has remained bread also. How to explain this in my "micro concept"

Actually my micro concept is

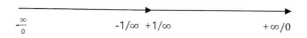

Macro is from $-\infty/0$ is historical accicent include of the all of human being knowledge, all of heritage is built then all of the macro power built, so then some has the master but the other is slaver, just keep continue past position all of power conflict to a new macro historical power. So long, all of invent, development is the industrial some of the remembered to the stone age, iron ages, industrial ages, but also atom age, very latest information era.

Another Macro $+\infty/0$ this is uncomming future, so all of the people expect a good development it is the dream, hope, all of the people in the vague expect of good fortune, in the industry future era will be our all of comic imagines are all come true, some of the ET all be possible, future is the dream but uncertainty so it comes also fear.

Finally in the macro Present, actually present, we are experience suffering, hard, but also excitement great pleasure, all of mix some of poor and rich, good people, bad people, master and slave, all of the product in industry. Companies, deceit, wicked but also sacrifice all of variances are mixed so that in this era some powerful class in the permit by the law, they are supreme position any ways all of cases are same time, same place, happened.

Macro is the our time actually all of the criteria but also understand all of natural super natural phenomenon so, to get a position then all of competitions and war, and a better product and market occupy, so it already getting position is not easy to break down, so that even a new concept technology is not come to another power because all of the big swallows by the Public relations in the big money in the TV medias, so then all of new is not it seems so be not new, but also, originality of new is not from old but new, just like in the tree also old tree is short of the energy apple tree old the taste size the value of the commodities, all is deteriorate it is the natural but in the economic world, the old company are prevailed due to the big capital then might company slashed the small companies. Just swift small companies are more dynamic and effect to face the hard but also productivities, so then if in the macro is the a big old company then new companies are micro then somewhat meaningful concept, it must be in the "micro concept" but in the present even in the I supposition to the small company is micro to the big old historical company is the macro, but actually just small company also in the concept of the "micro concept" small company also macro. Micro and macro, Seen and Unseen are combined.

In the economy revolution is how to be we are faced with information era comes so many IT communication developed, so then Micro software company major of the information even Google also. After this industry where to go, out of this global industry out of the time, productivities but also energy problems all of these problems are can be solve in this macro time.

$$-\frac{\infty}{0} \qquad -1/\infty \ +1/\infty \qquad +\infty/0$$

Macro concept economy is based on the market, population territory etc, but also technology is the big and developed country, IPE theory is the international political economy so then, all national competition somehow national power conflict almost wars, all of the industry go for the future then all is forgot just in the macro time scale is

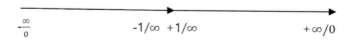

$-\dfrac{\infty}{0}$ Present

In our time is just past technology and the macro knowledge but also historical enemies still anger just like China, Japan, Korea, all is enemies in this successful economy, in this area regional product peak, but anger each others. But also actually every country GDP is remained stay not going up; all of the present problems are so big, so that most country is debt in economy. Just until not problems solving may not come true this is not a macro concept but Macro concept.

Macro concept all of the reach at the perfection just there is not progressive, all theory is come but also, in this thinking how to understand in the bible new testimony of the god, then all of the miracle Jesus walk on the water face, but also dead people live again, but also just small bread feed multiple people, what how to explained, but also in this time all of company still short of benefits, all of company face to the increased in productivities. Just now comes every country just gap in the rich and poor, decreased just middle class. USA also in the financial crisis, how to explain, how to get total solutions, even that is the present problems is not solve but if I suggest "micro concept" then it somewhat give hint, to exodus from Macro world, micro world, then how to" micro concept" can solve.

$-\dfrac{\infty}{0}$ $-1/\infty$ $+1/\infty$ $+\infty/0$

"Micro concept" has a $-1/\infty$, $+1/\infty$ so then it msut be hint to the our present solve the unsolved problems just in the "micro concept" actors are past, present, future, but also distance is so then just in the macro connect to so any further go for the problems solving then, in the micro it come future knowledge but also, so then in the "micro concept" fully give the hint to solve the problems, for example Japan, Korea, relationship now both country anger cause of the past happening problems in the macro only, there is no any soluble, if adopt in the " micro concept" then future is counted on that so that, Korea Japan now in the macro year, about 2080year someday, then in this time china power invade to the Korea then Japan and Korea combine to depend, then in the " micro concept" some of the 2080 present then it comes Korea Japan co help each other.

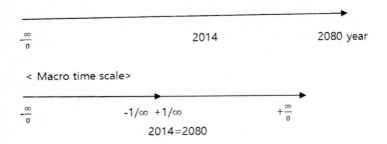

< Macro time scale>

<Micro concept time scale>

In the macro time, someone say "what 2014 and 2080 is why same, if this question then in the micro concept, if 2080year go to zero converse to be a point, here is count on the future of the $+1/\infty$, then 2080 can be in this time present 2014 year same, then in the "micro concept" is then Korea and Japan come to concord, just exodus of the Macro concept, so then it come to the Micro. Here some of the try to understand "micro concept" how to connect to the macro, but also some of the detail try to understand this theory. Then how to Japan Korea solve problems, then I try to use the bible New Testament the Jesus did, bible is not liar, this is true then Jesus walk face the water.

$\frac{\infty}{0}$ Present

Jesus how to walk in the face of water, the weight of Jesus must not stand on the water. It is natural, but in the bible Jesus walks on the water. We all believe that bible is true. So then Jesus Christ is the walk on the water. Then in the adopt "micro concept" then

$$\overset{\longrightarrow}{\underset{-\frac{\infty}{0} \qquad\qquad -1/\infty \ +1/\infty \qquad\qquad +\infty/0}{}}$$

<Micro concept time scale>

Jesus Christ is heavenly father son, in the soul kingdom, then Jesus is seen to us, physically macro but Jesus is the only adopt in the "micro concept" adopt, so then, Jesus Christ is not concept but comes up real to us, so just Jesus Christ follower are all being in the strong matured so that they all realize, so they are soul world, even not, I can "micro concept" explain then,

Jesus control of the past, present, future then distance all the governing so then Jesus, walk on the face of sea water then, he was existence as the " micro concept" micro world in Jesus Christ, Jesus was in the heaven soul, all of micro, but in the time his follower are saw him, then watcher are macro but Jesus in live on the micro, so then soul, so in the micro world all is so lighter, if possible infer then, Jesus get on the water, but it must be seen in the macro Jesus a people, but in the Jesus are heaven kingdom just soul status, so then Jesus are governor of the micro so he is god, another infer then Jesus traveled in moment to the god kingdom then distance governing, in the "micro concept" just shows -1/∞ ~ +1/∞'s micro concept world existence has been shown to us.

Then in the "micro concept" solution is the how to solve so then Korea Japan relationship better in 2014year, how to possible. If possible then 2080 year are already comes to the 2014, time and distance all is adopt, so Japan and Korea good relationship happened between president of Korea prim mister of Japan. They are concord for the economic political concord, how to possible how to shown to us, in micro world is the what I said that thinking, in the thinking is the " soul , mind= thinking" then soul is come to the future then realize so in the mechanical thinking procedure operation then both present and prim mister got a clue in the "micro concept" then still what is this, < micro concept> critical point of view, then micro and macro how to connect, then I can explain in the "micro concept" like this,

$$-\frac{\infty}{0} \qquad -1/\infty \ +1/\infty \qquad\qquad +\infty/0$$

<Micro concept time scale>

Macro concept ~ Micro concept is in the direct line then it must not to be connect, so then all of the history is past in the macro, but also future is future, there is not connect, happened in the macro how to explain it is not possible. In the oriental Tao of physics then, a person get in to the "micro concept" world just moment, soon after returned then in the macro all of his ages people dead but all of his grand children world, then it must be 100 year over just gap, so then how second Pico second, just Jesus in the walk in the lake then, micro world, Jesus come to the heaven king dome then it is just 1/10000000m second even more, so then Jesus is in the micro world then still seen in the macro world he is walking on the face of water.

So then how to macro ~ micro turning, then it must in the micro concept must do explain.

then in the micro concept, even micro concept, it must be infer, micro is smallest, so then macro time scale only in the present past and future but in the micro is the past present and future so then actually in the micro is unseen in the thinking world. But try to show the micro concept. so then.

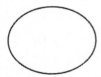

this all of the round point now in the macro, just line, but if in the micro then, all of the all of the line is the point is the -∞/0 ~(connect point) +∞/0 then in the round it msut be the micro then, What happened to now, so long, if --------
---------- round then each point is the in the< micro concept> each point is the or just around of the a point is consider as the present; past future then we do not know the distance how long but, actually Jesus travels to the god kingdom

in the preach god king truth then so then, the travel distance also in the micro then actually in the micro concept $\bigcirc$, a point is the $- = -\infty/0, -1/\infty, +1/\infty, +\infty/0$ so then in the< micro concept> has supply to the macro then in the macro just only $-\infty/0$, Present only, macro is the Physical world, so then in the micro is the in the thinking world , so all of the but all of the macro concept, physical feature is the just only for the "micro concept" is living then macro is the already is the dead of micro, just seen world is the dead of the micro, all of the micro world dead materials are macro, here infer to the macro is old, micro is old, all of the macro concept progress to the getting older, but in the micro world getting younger, concept. In the point of macro view then micro supplies all of the solution of the macro at that time, so long "micro concept" is the key to the macro problems solutions. I will use micro concept I will help our macro world industrial development from now on.

2014.04.24

Hard to make usual working. Today even my entire squeeze in me but actually not come to me problems and solutions, I am here through from my dormitory I breath deep to circulate in my body. It is my pleasure due to I'm save a time for the air breath and circulations. I'm reading JANGJA that is my pleasure with so long time ago, an oriental thinker story. If I see happening with me how I'm concerning. We are live righteous or easy our living community, all of the era has the problems JANGJA writing time also so turf living just normal class. How to solve the usual people satisfaction, then it must be in the macro concept, all is the possible to the micro concept.

In the bible Jesus all feed so multiple usual his sermon listener; this is a" micro concept" just out of the macro concept. Then at that time Jesus Christ he is heavenly father son, so he has been shown us "micro concept" in the micro world, in the book of bible then soul world in the micro momentum so micro is just uncountable in the macro time scale, then the bread are even seen macro but in the "micro concept" adopt in the usual in the micro world but it turns to the macro then all of the surprise. In the bible New Testament Jesus Christ living time Jesus has given us he is live at the "micro concept"

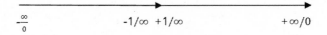

$\frac{-\infty}{0}$ $-1/\infty$ $+1/\infty$ $+\infty/0$

<Micro concept time scale>

<Micro concept time scale>

Micro concept just realization is God Jesus Christ. "Micro concept" "Macro concept" this is the comparatively against for relationship. Macro concept is the micro concept dead feature in the Seen by the "micro concept "macro is the $-\infty/0$, $\infty/0$ then, absolutely in the macro concept past range is the all of the oldest ranges, even there is not future concept, so then, "micro concept" are interpret to the youngest it measure to 0, so then, micro concept is the so young, Macro concept is the old, it expand the compared to the venture to exist safe company. Then exist company and venture company which is the near to the "micro concept", actually in the macro concept how to deliver to the Jesus Christ feed, it is the sure of the "Micro concept" adopt successful case story. Then, for the purpose of the usual people satisfaction then in the close to the "micro concept" is the so young company is venture companies are important. The big old church is in the Seen micro concept then it already not to increased because if the micro effect is close, just all of the managed in Macro, "Micro concept"

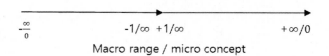

$\frac{-\infty}{0}$ $-1/\infty$ $+1/\infty$ $+\infty/0$

Macro range / micro concept

Just" micro concept" companies got knowledge all of knowledge for the technology and all of the creative procedures. A CEO= micro actors are really try to find the solutions, then he must be get in his thinking world, in the thinking contained to the soul or mind, if soul then his soul try to fine the solution and give the answer to manage well. How to "micro concept" help creative a new company, or venture company can overcome of the risk, but also only a big company CEO coverage all of decision is not but the size and system is just CEO care is not "micro concept" the big company is mostly macro procedures, to be maintained then M&A, to be a big size, mega, bigger, so get a size economy, but also getting broad market, but the macro concept disappeared to then, what happened, just in the concept of the "Micro concept" then a big company mature after just optimistic size, even a big company, then CEO managed but also CEO also middle ages then, it mixed in the company voyage micro concept- Macro concept mixing in the decide. But after all of the come to decide depend on the system or board, or association from the not "micro concept" the solution from the god ranges soul traveling to the god wisdom in the thinking. The big company only depends on the Macro, what I have said the Macro is the dead feature of the "micro concept" after all it must be touch in the range "micro concept" procedure

Still it not easy but what I said that macro-micro is the fair so then how to connect. Is the

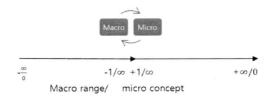

This direct line is the go reflective then it come to the ◯ but in this time some has the interval micro time macro time basis is not same. If micro time = n1, n2, n3 Macro, then just the time size is decided. Truly micro is the operating in the coming of the solution of the micro god's of ancestor or, some of creators helping is the "micro concept" then past, present, future all of the information comes to him, here future is predict power also, so then if a success then in the "micro concept" it's micro= mind soul, meaning is zero distance, but soul it must see the wisdom, knowledge helper of his/her God, Ancestor, creators ...., it need the time, but the time is it never come to him, or his urgent then in his/her thinking, soul touched God, or ancestor or creators all of micro helper. To compare with macro time, then, just idea comes to him/her $1/\infty$ time, so then the CEO decides successfully. In the "micro concept" a CEO know all of the company problems, then he try to find the solutions in the macro concept," micro concept"

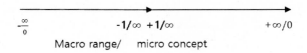

$$-\frac{\infty}{0} \qquad -1/\infty \ +1/\infty \qquad\qquad +\infty/0$$

Macro range/   micro concept

Micro concept macro concept in the macro point of view is physical size minimize is understand but in the micro is the micro concept then it comes to the time, distance is considered, so then in the two actors are in the micro concept, if a recognized to the micro concept micro then $-1/\infty$ $+1/\infty$ this point is micro, in this point recognized to the problems to solutions. So then god gift to the youth, if a youth are know the "micro concept" youth can get success venture, small company. ◯ In the round then, all the time coincidence is ------, but micro then line, shown to, so long just if just direct line of the macro, micro then $-\infty/0$(the oldest time) $\sim$ $+\infty/0$(longest future time) is connect, so then it shown to the macro concept, so the in the round, it appeared to them, oldest time beginning, future time of the end is connect, then, if the "micro concept" adopt then in a point $-\infty/0,-1/\infty$, $+1/\infty$, $+\infty/0$, micro Macro is coincise in a point. So then it has the all possible of the macro, micro concise point, -------,   be seen. This is the micro time, macro time, distance all is same, this means that just micro unseen unthinkable, just momentum $1/\infty$ shows to us. Some what if not a company size level then a company thinking level then, it must be adopt to the " micro concept" all of the people recognize the macro concept ; in the Seen world just existed knowledge, all of the student are all try to remember to get information, it is the macro concept is the all goes to the getting old, but also try to get for himself/herself, so then macro concept, it come bad thinking good thinking comes, but in the "micro concept" the time is going to younger, distance is to be getting less distance. So then" micro concept" is seen in the thinking procedure of the idea of newly and innovation, by the "micro concept" channel soul traveling to the solution helper, God, ancestor or creator etc.

It imagine that in the bible contents all from the God by the God problems in the macro, then Jesus Christ, disciple prophet pray then, all of micro actors soul travel to the distance god, actually in the god actors are assume that in the adopt "micro concept" then momentum comes $-1/\infty$, $+1/\infty$ this is from god. The same as the successful historical people are helped in the "micro concept" system. Then how to know the "micro concept" this is the realize then comes, all of success people drill, all of trouble then he/she is lead to the limit then, it come super natural thing it is the not a macro concept in a moment, then it come to the" micro concept "we have the best expression "heaven helps themselves" it must be this is the "micro concept" historical dead feature it already reveal to the macro.

2014.04.25

I donated to the beggar. What is pleasure to me, I feel so excitement to me, I think excitement is getting my paying. The excitement is the value, the value is multiple in the macro concept also, in the macro I could help him somewhat, but also I felt I'm some pride. But also in the "micro concept" actually in the micro, a beggar lose his all of his natural asset, I don't know his now status is so miserable but to me, he is a target to help, this means that good behavior if this decide to give a my money a beggar. How to decide, but so many people passed. In this do not recognition in the macro concept world. So this is nothing to me, even others. Just all is a beggar problem only. Even some passed people think that why government do not help him, that is macro concept thinking. I paid my money to beggar, then what make me decide giving money to him. It may be in the bible "heaven kingdom inter into very narrow road, but another ways is so wide" contents show us. The then wise good decision is hard to easy but bad decision is very short cunning, deceit tactic is so short it must be in the micro concept has the differences.

$$\frac{\infty}{0} \qquad -1/\infty \quad +1/\infty \qquad +\infty/0$$

Macro range/ micro concept

Good and bad in the macro concept, Good and bad in the micro concept. But macro to micro exchange. In the macro good behavior is his/her knowledge or good characteristics person, but he/she try to help, just come from mind, a good mind, good behavior. Personal charity In the macro a good behavior is the so the his religious, or school study is affect to decide donation. But bad in the macro concept then, all of the do not give a money to the beggar then all of people hidden to the public, but also agree with public notions, such as government help the poor, all of his poor living is his responsible not me, then bad decide people has not any guilty. So the beggar and bad person are not directly related so there is no matter with beggar and me, him, her.

So in the macro good and bad is the economy and social so then the personal relationship is all of people do not connect. So forget around of him/hers, only him / her, somewhat expanded to his/her children is his/her helping range. So is not cared with a beggar problems, so then all of people build the fence, defend offend from his/her ranges.

In the micro concept good and bad decision is righteous wick person. Then, in the micro concept just -1/∞, +1/∞ micro concept decide, good decide bad decide, if a good decision then in the micro world a good decision helper give the wisdom knowledge but a bad decision then do not help but temptation to do bad decide. In the micro concept world, it very differently macro only has the past trained effect to decide, but in the micro another decision factor is future comes, then if in the micro concept do not decide a good decide then, he/she do not considered of future, so just his/her future getting ages do not prepared, but think only present, so the bad decide in the micro concept, actually he/she met Satan, who is the against to the God, Satan power met so he/she do not guilt bad decision. Actually in the macro concept bad decision is reach at the failure then all is bad effect.

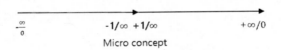

$\frac{\infty}{0}$ -1/∞ +1/∞   +∞/0

Micro concept

But also in the "micro concept" bad decision also directly do not harm other, this theory is the Satan. If this procedure of the micro concept, to be a bad decide, he/she try to fine the knowledge in a moment, he/she will travel to the -∞/0 , +∞/0, bad decide micro concept decision is the -1/∞ +1/∞ in the bible saying do not enter the god king dome ways is so wide, then he/she try to recall knowledge police, social trend, economy even her/his busy time, so she/he find the bad decided reasons. Then in the micro world, just it may be his helper do not give failure ways decision, then it must be a bad decide people met in the micro world Satan soul, who is mightier power also it very same ad god power.

But also the bad decision is in the micro concept, so short almost soul=mind, so bad decision soul temptation from Satan but also his mind still influenced his soul, but also, bad decide in the macro concept poor knowledge, deceit, this people in the micro world, he/she do not know to try to fine the good decision help, so he/she met so easy a Satan, if Satan in the macro concept then help walk out of the going heavenly father ,god kingdom, so then so many economical personal hard time do use money for the himself/herself not to shared with to others. But good decision in the micro world,

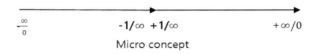

Micro concept

A good decide people in the macro he/she is so good, his living is charity, try to share with others, but also he/she learn help a poor, in the religious community, but also educational knowledge. So then if this people are many then, this people effect another people do, but strange the entire case all of the sacrifice so small. Because all of the knowledge is to make money economically productivities but also competition winning, so any place education help losers, this knowledge is not, he /she is eccentric person in the good decision. Under the "micro concept" a good decision is he is same to decide in the micro concept, traveled to -∞/0, +∞/0 then he met a his helper to decode good, then he get in the micro concept good decide with -1/∞ +1/∞, he/ she got a future, he/she is thought if be old time what happened to her/him, so it occur to him/her charity and love mind in the bible " love neighbors" so he follows god's god lived manners, so easy keep a god rule. He/she has a multiple benefits he/she will be recognized to the god's side but also he/she kept a god rule. She/he not guilty, but also good decision is some relative to the right decision. But bad decision is naturally in the side of Satan, but also he/she is do not keep a god's rule, so then it already being a sinners, and bad decision is also do not right decision, in the Satan method also solve the problems but it is not eternity just temporally by the mixed with the deceit so then some people getting but the other is losing, so it comes to the macro inequality community forms. But in the good decision is god's king dome so then even in the macro slow to the solution but the in the micro concept good decide is right decision so then, it lead to the righteous decisions so then in the micro concept good decision is macro concept all of people shared the benefits, all of the community are equal to live on so then, it must be a good community build.

2014.04.30

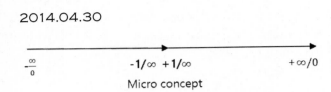

Micro concept

What is benefit under the macro concept world, Macro world living actors are people, micro concept actors are soul with living god. Macro concept also live, micro concept world also live, then what will come to us, macro micro.

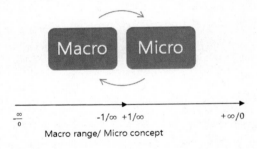

Macro range/ Micro concept

Macro and micro switch in a moment, then a person thinking line of the soul also mind and soul comes just so moment -1/∞ +1/∞ comes micro, macro all is all living world. To be micro, in the macro world not easy, some people all of living but do not realize micro concept micro living world existence. Actually micro living best example is Jesus Christ, he lived all part micro and macro living. Jesus Christ seen both micro world, macro world, the time is the -1/∞ +1/∞, mixro world time distance and macro time and distance even difference but micro can match up with macro time and distance, micro concept is -1/∞ +1/∞., Jesus appeared in the macro seen the in the bible New testament macro micro but in the micro general. Cure and make re live from death. In this time, Jesus going to the micro concept world so Jesus did all of the miracles. Out of Jesus, just normal macro concept human being just seen in the eye macro concept world, but actually has the live world also existence in the micro world.

Micro world, micro concept, what help to the macro concept, it moment micro to macro, macro to micro, micro world, how to operate to the macro world, how to connect to present physical +soul people get helped. Even this theory is from religious behavior, but religious or not, the micro/macro existence. All of the people can be procedure line of the soul, birth then physical + soul, but grow to 100 year to end of physical and soul then just start to soul, a child before come then he/she also soul, soul

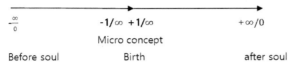

I'm try to match up with just living, so then micro world show to our macro concept living. Actually in the macro world, just thinking recognition just from birth before after soul, then this is the living. But in the micro world micro actor is the Soul then soul must eternity, then micro point of view then, if Birth time is -1/∞ +1/∞ just moment micro and macro criteria this is a baby birth.

Then after birth human being living in the point of macro concept, just micro concept the new living where to go, future or past, actually in the macro world, it must be understand to the recognition is go future, what is the future, just future is only macro concept is clear, so then, birth baby think that macro time, macro distance, so he must be getting ager, then he thin that go for the future, but also he can recognition past, history, if he live 10 years, then he might be called 10years old, what is strange it is normal in the macro concept, but in the micro a bay be where to go,

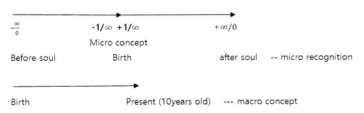

Macro 10 year boy must be think perfectly do not recognition of the micro concept, he/she live fully physical + soul, then almost do not recognize soul, but he/she realize physical, so he/she is so excite in living. So then strong physical

creature experiment so variants, all of the educations systems, all of people procedures, during then perfectly micro concept forgotten, so lost the road of the eternity grow to reach at the destination, but it don't matter he/she is in the recognition to the self getting living job but also physical living. Yes this is the in the micro concept try to explain of the macro living. But still here soul is so weak strong physical power. Then physical power going up it may be to 60 year, but after then going down, then physical power going down keep sick, then soul comes strong governing, hard bearable soul, it must comes then, soul think he/her birth before world. In the

$-\frac{\infty}{0}$	-1/∞ +1/∞	+∞/0
	Micro concept	
Before soul	Birth	after soul -- micro recognition

In this diagram just to make understand then soul discriminate before, after, then soul is not changed, but all of the macro people do not understand, in the macro concept then, soul difference , because birth and death, but in the a new living micro world, just physical +soul in the Seen macro world time, then unseen in the micro by the physical feature, but it still there is soul, so then in the understand of the macro has the birth and death so difference, but in the micro concept is a soul is line not dot line, so then actually still same of the soul world living. So then macro world, after birth going to the future recognized then actually micro concept still in the -1/∞ +1/∞ locate, so that in the micro actually a soul not going for the going future, just all of the point past, present future locate. But a birth before then she/he locate in the micro concept, but birth he/she locate in the macro, end of macro then he/she is locate in the micro concept world. My deep think is how to effect to the macro living better, I believe that if someone understand micro concept world, then he/she must be eternity living existed then this truth also so safe in the living, but it also not easy to understand. But

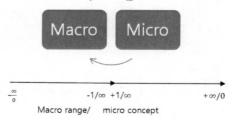

Micro concept must help macro concept, because of the micro concept world, Master Jesus Christ helped in the macro world difficulties, as seen in the bible New testament, Jesus deliver good news to the macro, we have the micro concept understanding book is bible. Then if someone realize micro concept then he/she live so good, good behavior, if so many people in the macro concept then, the macro community must be getting better, but also, these realize people shared each other god's gift. I start micro to solve the delayed present phenomenon; social economical all of the trend remained just go around not going for the direction, so how to find going direction but also out of this circulation to another stages, so I think the micro, but it is not easy to connect to what I wanted to solve it, but I got a debris derived effect, more metaphysical problems solving.

Micro concept,

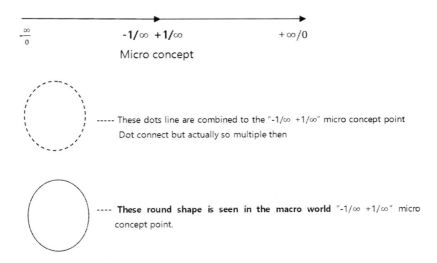

So many people got a "-1/∞ +1/∞" then community must be micro concept world approaches, so then just in the micro concept point set, so then, this is good community forming.

-∞/0 ~ +∞/0 ( ) this is the micro macro connect, so then this round concept and dot line round concept connect then, it comes to the macro concept world micro concept usages.

"Micro concept" adapts to the macro concept, and then thinking is somewhat difference from the stereo types, to new "micro concept" adoption. Micro actor is the time, and distance, but macro actor is the human being, people. Then, in the macro world, actor human being is the in the micro world master role, so called god or Jesus Christ. In the bible saying people is resemblance with god feature. So that if supposition in the macro concept, he is master, then human being is fixed then micro is time and distance are variances. So even in the macro world, just use of the micro concept, then, here macro actor is the master, and then he will be use the micro macro,

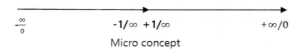

Micro concept

this is typically micro concept, until now micro master is the God, Jesus Christ, then macro concept actor to use the micro concept human being use the micro actor the time, distance, so that human being governing the micro time and distance, so human being stay same but material are changed, then I can explain from now on.

In the bible, Jesus preaching time so multi people hunger but just only small piece of bread then these bread to feed then, in the pure micro concept, explained, all just all of the soulful, all of the followers are micro concept world come to the all of eat fully, just so small bread feed possible because in the micro concept shared all of the bread with righteously. But now macro concept management micro concept, Macro managed Micro concept, here, human being master role just of the governing to the macro, micro, all governing by the human being so, human being expand the living world is the not macro but also micro concept also living world. So, human being manages the micro actors, time and distance. Then how to adapt to the in the macro living, to solve the present problems with adopt the micro concept. Social, economical, personal, religious all of explained to do.

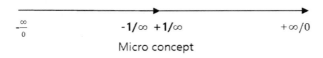

how I do," Micro concept" abruptly come to me fear, what I'm, how to I carry this "micro concept" all of my knowledge, my thinking is limited to me, but I felt that thirsty to exodus from "Macro concept" I am tired from this macro concept world. Most macro actors are busy and deceit even all is not I'm not what about you. Then why come to micro, macro criteria soluble responsibility which I can show to the macro actors. So long, how to I do, until now I felt excited but also, I felt that somewhat realize, the micro world eternity, still then it is not my start of motive " micro concept" the thing is why remained industrial progress but also, I'm MBA so this is my professional knowledge, then it comes to me, philosophy of the metaphysical notions, but it Is not my own, someone will recognized me, so then I cannot express philosopher ways, so then I'm very deep thinking, but this is published to the novel style. In my thinking structures to me, so that I can't get my regions, just like old time, a farm village farmer son get marriage then, he get from his father a land, he live as farmer just his father do, the son thirsty to make extension his farm yard but in his living village nothing but not enough his, he can't any region to get on, the same my mind in this time, where I can get but also how to expand my ranges I'm face to the rock. I felt limit but all of others are live well, but I can't do live any place.

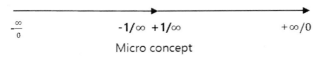

Just I need to find my personal area to live on, $-\infty/0 \sim -1/\infty$, I am prison in my idea past knowledge is the solution for solving macro concept. In the Macro world, major terms are prevailed "endless competition" how to get my own field. I have been intrigued to free live out of the endless competition, to go with harmony but also excitement living. Strange past 1970 ~ 80 was poor than now but poor and competent rich and happy is not certain, what is this, to make money all of time, distance also sacrifice then only money getting, all of out of money do not shared time, and distance, so long it is not happy. What are problems around of me, all are tired, in my recognitions that I can't find real good relatives, in the drama all of actors are deceit so anger, cry, but also offender but defender is so prostrate, all of living warriors all angers to each others, getting weather then before but all of the community actors are all not safe, even in the family, father, mother, son, and daughters, even extend to the grandfather and mothers, are also changed, even some not prevailed then, but now so detail, all of the family actors are also required to benefits, so long, all of the family inside out side, at that time has the full family inside actor mother, or law in mothers, but now already in the family inside actors are grand father and mother, so then out of family all of the members, so that actually there is no young family member do not any responsibility. In the home all selfish acts, strange all of the families are do not try to role family, in the family community is not same as the 1980 era. But here of the family, someone sacrifice then if young sacrifice role player, if he/she do then the family must be relaxing but also happy motives, who will try to help, then what power is the " love" in the bible Jesus said " love your neighbors" even then family love is so strong, just who is major player helping others, what is "love" instinct power origin but, if possible love is same as before, love is so cheap, love also count on the money quantity.

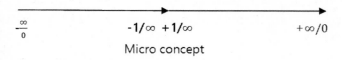

$$-\frac{\infty}{0} \qquad -1/\infty \ +1/\infty \qquad\qquad +\infty/0$$

Micro concept

love can be valued to money, money relatives to the sacrifice, it give the energy, energy equal to physical energy, physical energy only paid to money, yes! It refers to the time, and distances are factors to live on. Macro concept physical energy only counts on making money. How to" love" quantity, love it must be actor of the micro concept, if even physical energy count on the money but "love" is not, then, somewhat strange but also wrong. Because of if do not pay to the "love" then, who will supply for the love commodities. If love commodity and physical commodity which is better, a good motive, but actually love commodity is the micro concept produced goods, not now do not think as the commodity. Macro concept "love commodity" as seen just meanly but "love commodity" in micro concept, actually it comes why, love is from only micro status recognition. But in the macro concept regard love as the just nothing but also, do not recognized, because of the love is the origin of the sacrifice motive, to love, then the active forming is the sacrifice, it come to the help, help is the required to the physical, just come to the macro, seen, no one count on the motive is not count as the money. So then, some company manager expect to be increased the productivities, then just output of the selling, it don't matter of the thinking.

Micro concept love and macro output also somewhat relative, which are anti to this but, then hate or anger each other good produce?

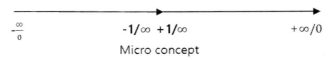

$$-\frac{\infty}{0} \qquad -1/\infty \ \ +1/\infty \qquad\qquad +\infty/0$$
Micro concept

"Love" "jealousy", love use in the man youth and woman youth likeable power energy, "jealousy" is a woman has the pretty face then ugly woman desirously anger expression to pretty woman. Macro concept is actually loved and jealous is not count on the money, economic terms, but in the micro concept is the love, jealous is the source of so strong energy. In the macro has the terms comes to make money consumer deceit is somewhat used, it make consumer decide choose a company products, but in the micro concept just only touch to the micro concept actor these are the human being's micro is the soul, to be good soul, but also valuable solutions getting then just a soul must be trained to meet mastered at the special knowledge soul, but if jealous in the to get a good solution without any true righteous then, he/she must be see the same of the false knowledge soul. Actually in the micro world any all of the micro actors, micro, macro live world existed. Macro concept is $-\infty/0 \sim -1/\infty$, but micro concept $-\infty/0 \sim -1/\infty$, $+1/\infty \qquad +\infty/0$, it try solve the macro problems then, just intrigues are try to get soluble, a person live longer in a profession area, then if a person lived righteous, truth technology or art or cook etc, then a matured people come to old then, he/she get realize, he/she reach at the

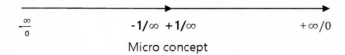

$-\dfrac{\infty}{0}$ $-1/\infty$ $+1/\infty$ $+\infty/0$

Micro concept

a person reach at the micro concept gate, he can get past, present but also future idea comes so then he/she his/her existence knowledge plus a new idea combined to it perfect new concept come up. But the jealous person also tries to find the solutions, then he/lived wicked so then he/she is very accustomed to stealth of a person knowledge, so he/she do not live true, righteous then, he can't reach at the micro concept gate $-1/\infty$ $+1/\infty$ micro concept, what is micro concept world, if still suppose that it not religious but somewhat it comes to the religious some is bible book but also Buddhism theory, so then what I explained before the micro concept but now

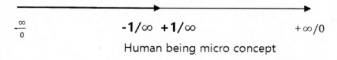

$-\dfrac{\infty}{0}$ $-1/\infty$ $+1/\infty$ $+\infty/0$

Micro concept

Just all of the macro micro is what I said that macro is the micro for example Iceland under the sea water 90%, but 10% only seen out of sea water. Much more macro is the volcano lava is life then dead is the rock then, volcano lava is the micro, but rock is macro. Actually macro point view is seen is live unseen is dead, but in the point of micro then macro is the death of micro, micro is the source of the macro, actually do not know under the macro point of view but if micro concept, micro concept to be explained to the all of creatures are to convergent to 0 then all of the still has the character, somewhat molecule but also atoms even much more micro then in the human being is the soul, so micro concept can cover all of the macro. Human being micro is

$-\dfrac{\infty}{0}$ $-1/\infty$ $+1/\infty$ $+\infty/0$

Human being micro concept

Human being lived in the micro concept world, so then, a human being micro changed to the human being macro against to micro, it is somewhat similar to the Buddhism "eternal lifecycle" so then micro human being micro soul live in the micro concept world, but some micro concept world actor human being go to the macro human being. Macro human being learn knowledge, technology song just soul mature. All of the macro human being acquire of macro concept world, in the religious theory then, all of macro concept world behavior righteous act, wicked act then eternity world heaven & hell discriminate place locate. And then in the soul world, heaven & hell, this heaven and hell how to recognitions, what it will be these micro concept human being is a soul, then it must be imagine that heaven soul, hell soul, how to relative to the macro human being, if not any relationship then here of the micro concept must be hard to going more, so that it must be connect between macro and micro. Here some in the macro world understanding "Buddhism life circulation" but actually is not some of the micro concept, micro concept is eternity, just line it not circulate but direct line,

$$-\frac{\infty}{0} \qquad \mathbf{-1/\infty} \ \ \mathbf{+1/\infty} \qquad\qquad +\infty/0$$

Human being micro concept

But actually much more micro world then just a point only, micro concept gate or exodus etc. anyway, just acquired knowledge worth macro world concept, mental and physical status then the knowledge is keep continued to the macro concept human being to micro concept human being also. It can tell to the human being is the omnipresent the macro family but also macro skillful job relatives but also reading know ledges, this is eternity with micro or macro soul, because of the human being. Actually macro concept can get realize then he/she get in to micro concept under the macro then all of the ranges is so moment, but if come to the micro concept human being is the so wide $-\infty/0 \sim +\infty/0$ if $-\infty/0$ is hell, $+\infty/0$ is heaven then, some what meaningful, so then, it again to the bible knowledge then $-\infty/0$ satan kingdome, $+\infty/0$ heaven kingdome, so macro humaneging is the good and righteous living just like just do righteous but also truth for long time about almost 70 years old then he/she realize a good knowledge by getting micro concept, but just deceit of the youth or some old but they do not live the righteous but also wicked then they also got a knowledge but that knowledge form $-\infty/0$ satan so then they are not ternity, they will be closed, but also macro evill success must be all of doing harmful to the another macro human being. So then the wicked soul located to the $-\infty/0$ satan, but live righteous but also follow the eternity truth then he/she must be locate at the $+\infty/0$ heaven kingdome. Actually under the macro human being then he/she lives to the righteous but also truth, so he research and technology etc all of effort, then he/she endure all of procedures of the ways then, he/she must be helped. "heaven helps themselves" it comes so then, he/she has the possibility to the locate in the $+\infty/0$ heaven, so then the heaven located micro human being can try to help to the macro righteous but also truth knowledge followers. then macro human being live righteously then if he/she has the suffering to find the solutions then the macro human being a living soul travel to the $+\infty/0$ heaven king dome, to find the solutions a righteous of in the time of macro human being then he/she learn and drill the same problems solving then, it already know about the solutions then, the macro righteous and truth follower can touch in the micro concept world, he/she can solved the hard problems, the time of the macro human being get in a moment, so that idea catching under the macro concept world.

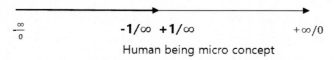

$-1/\infty \quad +1/\infty \qquad\qquad +\infty/0$

Human being micro concept

If this procedures are possible then, if a macro concept world a researcher or religious but also all of the person's world, a faithful, righteous but also follows truth then, he/she can find the unsolved problems solved from the $+\infty/0$ micro humabings. Then we also refer to the speed of the scientific problems solving, it already researched knowledge will be helpful to the future, then, that is the macro concept, but how to express the speed the future technology & knowledge.

Then in the micro concept is the $-1/\infty, +\infty/0$, then present problems are only already researched knowledge combined to produce also solve the existed problems, but, in the micro concept, then just all of the distance, and time scale of the micro to past to present, future to present, in the end at now use the future knowledge use, future knowledge use then, what I explained to solve the problems, then, a righteous, truth followers lived fully then, he/she felt, realize the micro concept so he/she get a future idea, by his/her macro human being travel to the macro human being become micro human being see the in the micro concept specialist, then come to macro concept people, that time is +1/∞ macro concept world can't imagine time and distance ranges.

2014.05.08

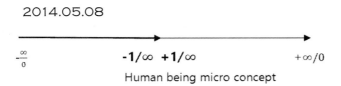

$$-\frac{\infty}{0} \qquad \textbf{-1/∞ +1/∞} \qquad\qquad +\infty/0$$

Human being micro concept

What is meaning for better living. What get in eternity living. Actually I'm not in the religious but I'm try to explain my understanding, "micro concept" my "micro concept =-1/∞ +1/∞" by accidently I got a knowledge. Then abruptly it comes to me, just -∞/0 and +∞/0 I foretell just one is hell, Satan kingdom, the other is heaven kingdom. Then which micro concept, how to these discrimination of righteous from wicked micro concept human being. It must be bridge micro to macro, then how to relative micro Satan human being, heaven kingdom human being. So then it must be same theory of the religious, how to in my "micro concept" I start to how to exodus from a status of propelling in the humanism but also economy, more new but more righteously.

So then I need to watch real phenomenon as the macro, but unseen but much more new and solution is "micro concept" I have to clear of my "micro concept" then I'm come to this,

$$-\frac{\infty}{0} \qquad \textbf{-1/∞ +1/∞} \qquad\qquad +\infty/0$$

Human being micro concept

It required to me, some supposition to" micro concept" some criteria -∞/0 : wicked, wrong knowledge, deceit living, lie, all of these decide live, +∞/0 ; righteous, truth, diligence these decisions livings. Just decide in a critical how to decide, all seen macro concept, but micro concept actor is the traveling -, + just in the " micro concept" all the time free choice, then just shallows circulation of the macro and micro is the coming very moment, it is somewhat to be shown to the macro point of view, it must be understood the decision, decision is the very momentum so then, some macro human it must be learn of the macro accumulated in formations, all of the computer also help decide of the very urgent. Actually the making money decide is very deep considered, but some of the trivial decision, actually it is not gain and losing game, then all is very easy decide then it is not come to "micro concept" it's means that is not related to the realization, but all of the people decide in the so moment decision is can be the some kind of the "micro concept"

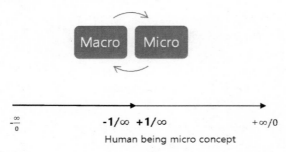

Human being micro concept

Just moment decide, for example go, or not, eat or not, sleep or not, this is so short of the in the point of macro, just a very moment, actually all of the "micro concept" understand easily, in the macro concept realize the" micro concept" just breath= decision is same so then

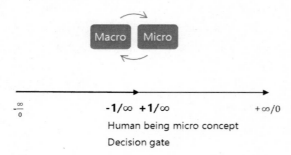

Human being micro concept

Decision gate

Another "micro concept" decision gate, just very short come to him/ her just very macro concept human beings, just a very short -1/∞ +1/∞, past, future all of the closed point, come to the macro humabeing, so then macro human being and the "micro concept" meet so then a macro human being is the actor is the present actor is the soul, past actor soul, but future actor soul, so then, all of the "micro concept" meet in the forms of the micro human beings, even in the macro, but its micro human being is the soul, then in the micro concept world, all mixed then, try to find the optimistic solutions to them, in the light decision then it must be light level soul meeting, so it comes, but also the in the micro concept is the 50% -1/∞ world, other 50%+1/∞, so then, it must be familiar to the latest past in the − Satan side then it is very easy but also safe, so very rely on that past information is the key to the present problems solving. Most understand notion, that is the coincide to the macro concept world, so it is not any critic, all accept so it very easy, but in the "micro concept" world + heaven world, it comes new and future information, so then just normal trivial decision it do not required, so just macro concept human being do not care, so then to touch with the + heaven world, a new idea is not rare very epoch in the macro concept. Actually some supposition is the in the bible saying "heaven kingdom come is narrow "then it must be realize but also courageous mind is required. Just in the macro concept human being do not live segregated from major people living; so then, it can't be the eternity time scale experiment. In the macro concept also, just deceit manager, and righteous manager cooperative are critically comes up, some company 100 years, but another is only 40 years, all of the macro concept time scale is not eternity but limit, but actually in the "micro concept' are eternity, so then when I try to write in the " micro concept" added idea is, --1/∞, +1/∞, all of the micro concept human being will be locate, it is not known, but it must be infer from all of the macro concept human being knowledge but also variable religious, hell and heaven kingdom, catholic church, Buddhist also, has recognition. But in the" micro concept"

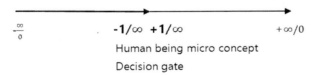

$-\frac{\infty}{0}$.   **-1/∞ +1/∞**   +∞/0

Human being micro concept

Decision gate

In the hell side, Satan kingdom is the from -1/∞ to left going forever, so then, just right first is the latist past but +1/∞ then heaven kingdome is the " micro concept" first future, how to deep future going is also how to get a new idea is decide in the point of macro concept human being. But where locate the soluble future helper, but in the realization of the then, -1/∞ +1/∞ in the realization point, then just all of the far right future knowledge also come to him, that is the realization.

2014.05.09

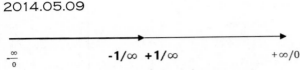

$-\frac{\infty}{0}$ **-1/∞ +1/∞**   +∞/0

Human being micro concept

Decision gate

How to reach at "micro concept" why pursue "micro concept" but it don't necessary. If do not reach and it don't cared then, it goes to "Macro concept" why I'm cling to "micro concept", so long, micro concept easily metaphysical concept. It may be forever do not recognition "micro concept" just do desire ways to get all, it dream to be rich, much more money gathering. It is macro concept but who are blame someone to make a big money. If I be pursuing making money that is my value, then it might be not excitement. Most people thinking are same in the instinct to make a big money, all of lotto purchasers are dream to make much money. These people are can be macro concept people, then these people are locate at -∞/0 or +∞/0, most people try to live good and wealth, health, then these people are not guilty all not sinners, because they are pursue their desired. Then most people which side, not in to the -∞/0 or +∞/0, who reach at the "micro concept"

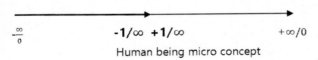

$-\frac{\infty}{0}$ **-1/∞ +1/∞**   +∞/0

Human being micro concept

-1/∞ +1/∞ this point all reach or not, some rare people reach it, just rare people realize the point of "micro concept" so he/she reach at gate, just see the real truth, so then he/she live to righteous on truth. Then in the macro concept what human beings are located at the +∞/0 so then in the macro concept, macro world, in the time scale is presnt, who is the in the micro concept -∞/0 side, but +∞/0, what I use metaphor then in the concept " micro concept" -∞/0 satan, hell side, but also +∞/0 locate in the heaven kingdom,

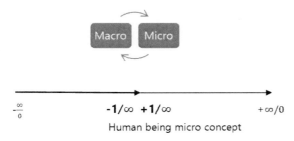

$-\frac{\infty}{0}$ **-1/∞ +1/∞**   +∞/0

Human being micro concept

Macro concept to micro world, but also micro world to macro, this is what I explain by the way metaphor, then in the macro concept to macro=micro concept how to do, then, micro concept

"-∞/0 Satan, hell side, but also +∞/0 locate in the heaven kingdom "this must be adapt to the macro concept world. It must be in the macro world

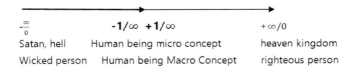

$-\frac{\infty}{0}$ **-1/∞ +1/∞**   +∞/0

| Satan, hell | Human being micro concept | heaven kingdom |
| Wicked person | Human being Macro Concept | righteous person |

Then in the macro concept world also recognitions micro concept actor in the macro concept is the Satan, hell to wicked person, but also heaven kingdom to righteous person. Wicked people, righteous people is supposed to the segregate in the -∞/0, all forgotten past locate, but +∞/0 still live and future coming to eternity living these are righteous people. In the macro concept world mixed the concept of the -∞/0 eternity forgotten & past, wicked people, and +∞/0 righteous people eternity living eternity future. Macro concept in a same place wicked, righteous human being is mixed. This is the present,

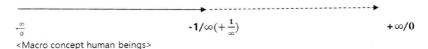

$-\frac{\infty}{0}$ **-1/∞$(+\frac{1}{\infty})$**   +∞/0

<Macro concept human beings>

In the real macro world, macro concept is -∞/0 ~ -1/∞(+1/∞), past, present (future), here many people are try to live desired, all getting, some of people do not accept, I'm fully not in the -∞/0 but I'm located in the +∞/0 it may be right, here all of the macro humanbeing is located in the

-∞/0, so then, in the bible saying, "heaven kingdom entrance is hard to the

rich people", then

Actually all of the macro concept people try to make a big money, then it must be going against to the +∞/0. Then I explained to the micro concept -∞/0, +∞/0 are in the macro concept is possible, so then in the macro concept mixed -∞/0, +∞/0. But the unseen just a dot line, future knowledge, in the macro normal human being is doubt unseen knowledge. Most macro concept human being are consist of community of the so multi of human beings of -∞/0 ~ -1/∞(+1/∞).

----- is the somehow religious living but also some realize people, how to the ------ line of the +∞/0, if these people getting multier then the community is compared with "micro concept"

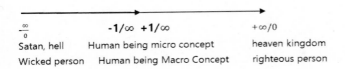

+∞/0 ; micro concept heaven kingdome, macro concept righteous person, so then this community is in the macro concept world also being the same as the heaven kingdom of the "micro concept" in the macro concept, micro concept infer to the imagine to the micro concept world. Macro concept human being is the human being micro is the soul; macro is the soul+ body then here in the "micro concept" world

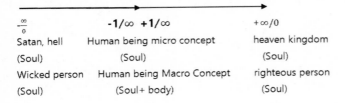

In the macro micro concept actor is Soul, Soul+ body, and then actually the same of the   then all of the Soul is same line. So then -∞/0: Soul, -1/∞ +1/∞(Soul + Body), +∞/0(Soul), here same is the all Soul, so then

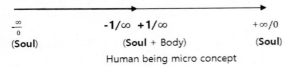

Actually in the macro concept, micro concept human being is all is Soul, so then in the macro concept human being is fell and recognize the knowledge, song, so then all of the behaviors all recorded in the eternity soul, how we know in the macro concept world, a person still Soul, so then Soul is eternity, this macro concept Soul learn and realize for the eternity and for the eternity unforgotten soul, it must be realize.

2014.05.12

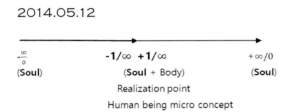

In the" micro concept" just micro concept human being will be try to get macro concept living. Because macro concept human being is soul+ body, then how to role macro human being, micro human being, what is the perceptible bridge, what is the bridge between micro concept world and macro concept world. If has the bridge and road, then some actor will use the micro and macro concept. Then macro concept human being why try to connect to the micro, but also micro concept human being why try to connect macro concept world. It maybe existence benefits, some good factors are making better conditions of living macro human beings. But also micro concept human being also because micro is the source of the macro, what I said, macro is dead of micro. Micro is alive, but also macro live but, all is the start from the micro. Macro and micro all cooperation to be better world forming, how to build better world, it may be much more macro concept human being reach at the realization point (-1/∞ +1/∞) then all of realized human being itself the better macro/micro world.

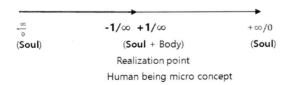

How to reach at the realization, it is not easy to explain but it is, basic tool to reach at the (-1/∞ +1/∞) variable this is not merely religious but the all of the variable places which are working, thinking writing, all of the human being will be, if he/she live righteous and follows the truth. These human beings are shown to the macro concept world "creator role" these human beings are realized of their concentrated problems solving. They reach at the realization point, but then it already existing idea, already not creature positions. So then eternity realization is not possible in the macro concept, but actually righteous, truth finding is not end, why macro concept has the mixed with truth, false, righteous and wicked. So then to be keep in the trail to the eternity of the righteous and truth, then in a bible said "heaven king dome ways narrow but out of the ways is wide" then, actually in the macro concept world, a human being all of ways living ways also come to the variable micro concept.

$\frac{\infty}{0}$	-1/∞ +1/∞	+∞/0
Satan, hell	Human being micro concept	heaven kingdom
(Soul)	(Soul)	(Soul)
	Micro concept	
Wicked person	Human being Macro Concept	righteous person
(Soul)	(Soul+ body)	(Soul)
	Macro concept	

A human being how to reach at the realization, this realize of the micro concept, actually all is not realize but surly all of specialize in the field, then they happy of their living. -∞/0 ~ -1/∞ +1/∞

How to do, all of human being live on their ways, whose are not teach all of the human being, all of the people go the place, some people can go some place, the other go another places. What human being can go, another can't go, all of human being are understand of time value, but also the important of the 1 second, so if a human being how to use the 1 second then some people go longer, but some of the human being are lazy using the 1 second. Then it must be relative to the one second the pulse, then one pulse is the unseen particle, thinking. Just thinking is the actor of the micro and macro concept.

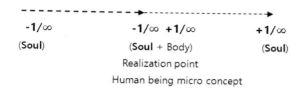

-1/∞   -1/∞ +1/∞   +1/∞
(Soul)   (Soul + Body)   (Soul)
              Realization point
              Human being micro concept

The moment is the "micro concept" realization point (-1/∞ +1/∞) , all of multi thinking are up and downs, Thinking is actor of the macro ~ micro concept, some deeper of the Thinking is the feeling and knowledge getting, feeling = thinking(mind), but knowledge getting = soul. So then it realizes getting is touching with the soul of the special knowledge helper of souls.

2014.05.13

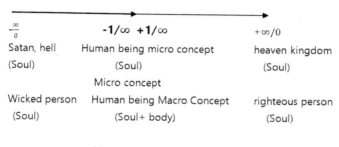

$\frac{\infty}{0}$ -1/∞ +1/∞   +∞/0
Satan, hell   Human being micro concept   heaven kingdom
(Soul)   (Soul)   (Soul)
                  Micro concept
Wicked person   Human being Macro Concept   righteous person
(Soul)   (Soul+ body)   (Soul)

              Macro concept

Macro concept human being wicked and righteous ranges are

Macro concept human being wicked and righteous ranges are

Wicked -∞   -1/∞ +1/∞   +∞ righteous
                    Macro concept

Righteous and wicked people it must be existed a macro concept world. Actually wicked and righteous in perfect is possible, it must be not, it has ranges for example wicked -∞ …..-100

….. -10…. -1…. -1/∞,……+1/∞ +1.. +10…… +100 ……….. +∞. Most people in the macro concept human beings are wicked and righteous mixed. How to do in the micro concept wicked and righteous also must be considered. How it is relative between macro and micro. If I micro like this

Wicked -∞   -1/∞ +1/∞   +∞ righteous

Micro concept

But we all heard from all of the religious then, wicked = hell, righteous = heaven kingdom, so that in the Micro world segregate just the point is the gate of the hell, or heaven kingdom, so then the gate is the -1/∞ +1/∞ , so that hell is the wicked people place, but righteous people located in the heaven kingdom.

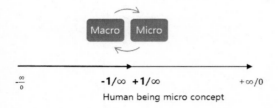

Human being micro concept

Human being micro concept switch to macro also, so then actually in the macro also the most people is wicked then but actually wicked is 100% .... 1% wicked ratio then wicked under the 50% is not shown to the wicked so it also go well in the macro human being also, then micro concept micro human being is also live in the macro concept human being. They also ahs the 1% righteous to 50%, 100% so then in the righteous community also has the wicked human being comes. But we must know that is the in the micro righteous people is in the located in the heaven kingdom so heaven kingdom value is adopt to the macro concept righteous place go with the heaven kingdom rules, but just wicked also a under 50% is good people, so then this community also good place but this place in the micro concept is hell place, so then hell rule are concept in the macro human being place. This is the concept so this is not religious concept. This is the clear of the concept of the macro and micro concept. It must not to be explained to the religious, but also this is the in the experiment not clear thing so that it must not think, I believe that actually in the macro concept world is the perfect natural procedures. But also all is my imagination for my fiction, so that please reading this book like understand. I'm just writing a story fiction, this entire book is novel. I'm novel writer I'm not real researcher so please understand it as the novel writer but some estrange value. I'm keep follow the procedure to the real living but this is not the religious but this is the perfect novel. I do not know the religious concept, I'm not specialist in the religious, I'm just novel but also I'm perfectly normal person, I'm a normal person. This is not theory but this is the fiction of novel. It is a novel. I'm accepting my Christian god principal I believe in god, Jesus is my savior. I believe that all is the god, I love my god.

2014.05.14

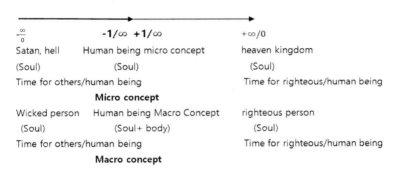

In the early morning I saw the girl student all in a subway. It is a great; yes right, all of person energy use for him / her. Because of all of the people try to get their expected things.

Who criticize this diligence? In the macro concept community all of the human being origin ways for the success, so all of people use his/her time 100% use is possible. In the graphed in the micro concept human being all use his/her time then in the locate at the hell, Stan but in the micro concept heaven king dome is time for the righteous, so then the variance are not same Stan and heaven kingdom, this here Satan and heaven king dome is not relative to the religious but to explain micro concept, it comes the section left side, right side end. But actually in the micro concept is very similar to the religious. So that please the reader will not to be misunderstanding. Actually I start to why this time in the macro concept do not propelling, not to the future, the entire accident social world all is hard to the economical so then I thought that this is the macro in this macro all of source of economic are limited so then all of the human beings are fight for the getting. So then all of the relationships among human beings are not friendly but also it getting wider in the economic benefits. So I got a think then "micro concept" micro concept world it can be possible all of the macro concept world problems solving. In the micro concept basically classify the wicked and righteous this variance is the basic tools, but also in the macro and micro is the macro is the natural phenomenon, but micro the all of the natural thing even include human being also, to all of size to micro, it express to the in the model is -1/∞ +1/∞ size, but also the time is the also variances, but also distance is also variance. This is what I imagine so I explained the micro concept basic already.

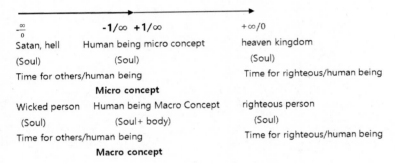

Then I can explain, time is the variance in the "micro concept" all of the time is free, so all of people use free. So that in the macro concept, a human being uses, or do not use then time is disappeared. So then it must use is better. Then time use is what, what is the time use, actually I'm not specialist but, Time usage is the cognition but do not realize the time usage is the very cognitions. So that time is all distinct use also, where locate the time, time is untouchable but time is the in the macro time order, any ways in the macro concept has the time, actually time is unseen but, show or understand the time watch, so that time scale comes up, but still all do not know the how to value in the macro, in the micro is eternity concept of the time, this problems is not can give but in micro concept then all is the -1/∞ +1/∞ all are not recognition of the time scale, in the micro concept all is not count on like in the macro concept. So then macro timescale and micro concept time scale is big difference, in the tau of physics then, some story" a realize get in to the peach orchard just so moment lived after then he/she come out of there then come to macro concept world then it already not there any his friend or family also" it means that macro and micro concept time scale cannot be measured. So then in the gate of the realization or micro concept world (-1/∞ +1/∞) there is not any time cognitions.

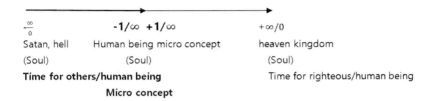

In the micro concept -∞/0, Satan, hell, time for the others/micro concept human being, then here all of the micro concept Satan, hell located micro concept human being are use their time all use for themselves but any time for others. So then all of the their time use of the exclusive all theirs not others, then what happened, it must be infer that, in the hell is all segregate relationship others, all of people do not related, all are segregate area, it must be loneliness, in this concept, then more detail infer then, it don't care around people hunger dead, so then around of a human being is all cry, anger, shout, very hard to live etc. this is the micro concept world. But in the micro concept +∞/0, heaven kingdome, and time for the righteous/ human beings, so then time for righteous/ human being must be infer to help each others, so then it must be a human being try to help around others then, his/her around are all good happy, excite human beings. So all of community is so bright, so this community heaven kingdom. Then what can be explained in the time concept in the macro world.

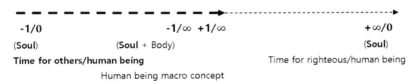

In the macro concepts time for others/ human being is countered on the -∞/0~ -1/∞, somewhat to easy understand it has rewriting to the 0%, 10%, 20% ~~~ 99.999%, then in the macro human being live to get his/hers goals, most people use their time over 80%, even more, but also it is very natural, who can criticize him use his time all for him, in the macro concept all is possible. So then he just all of his time does his affairs not for others. In the macro it call as the "personal" to explain time usage for the absolutely use for himself. In this time, this human being are specialist also, so they all work free, working and personal free, so most people think yes it kind of good. If he/she lives happy, excitement himself/herself only, then it must be nothing but yes! Some other people envy them. What are the problems "I can live on my way" this is the express the 99% use time for himself only. Then he/she must be solved problems by himself/herself. They all are sure to live on, it must be they are all rich or make enough money, so that they try to segregate from the poor person, this is very easy to them. But also some of the 50% for him, 50% others somewhat mixed then it come to the just all of the his/her time all make money, study for the his winning not for others, this is the all of mixed this community all is recognitions, so then this community has the variable problems are also occurred. In the macro also some people come to reach at the time for others/ human being reach at -1/∞, he/she must be so good person, they are realize of living, but it must reaching at -1/∞is not many. Some cases there is no, but infer that if are a human being is reach at the -1/∞, what his after that

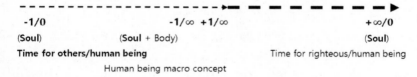

-1/0		-1/∞ +1/∞		+∞/0
(Soul)		(Soul + Body)		(Soul)
Time for others/human being				Time for righteous/human being

Human being macro concept

In the macro concept, someone reach at and go for maintain and go for the future then, it must be begins +1/∞ ~ +∞/0 , the variance is not time for others/humanbeings but the time for righteous/humanbeings. It must be required to live as a living so required time sharing, but after the -1/∞ then realize and saturate so long, it required to other standard. The realization after he/she must be the leader, or helper to the community and the groups, for this realization is must be sacrifice, help others, so that Time for the righteous/ human being variance comes. The sacrifices human beings are try to help around him/her so then at least he feels excitement with his sacrifice and helps feed backing to him. So then multi righteous human being community then the society must be reliable to live on. This is the macro concept, but more macro

concept then, if

-1/∞
Time for others/human being

+1/∞
Time for righteous/human being

More Human being macro concept

The macro concept -1/∞ ~ +1/∞ in the mocr concept so moment, so then it impossible, but it expand to the macro then, it infer to the -98, 99.9999, 0.0000001 this then if this is the making money level, if a macro human being is reach at the -1/∞ ~ +1/∞ then money making full enough, if not enough then, he must be rich but he/she is not enough then it must be still he/she is still ~~~ -1/∞, still he/she is not enough getting money, so he

-1/0
(Soul)
Time for others/human being

-1/∞ +1/∞
(Soul + Body)

+∞/0
(Soul)
Time for righteous/human being

Human being macro concept

He is still -1/0 ~~~ -1/∞ she/ he is keep time for other/ humabeing, so then even he has rich at making money, this criteria is other thinking, so then the other expect to him, do some of the community role but, he/she is not enough so he/she keep making money much more, so still she/he do not want to beyond to the

-1/∞
Time for others/human being

+1/∞
Time for righteous/human being

More Human being macro concept

Even rich people do not reach to the -1/∞ +1/∞ then much rich people not to reach at the -1/∞ +1/∞ then in a community still all remained to the -1/0 ~~~ -1/∞ they all still wanted money, so then it is not easy, if infer then Time for righteous/human being in making money community, the community rich people still desired to make money, then it is not reach at the righteous / human being. In the macro concept money making community is not easy seen the realize human being so then he/she is still pursue making money. There is not time share for the righteous. Just in the micro concept and macro concept, it is sure itself concept so it locate in the thinking. If a rich people realize to reach at the "micro concept (-1/∞ +1/∞)" then the rich man sacrifice, help others then cause of him/her so many member of people excited and live happy but also the rich are also be excite so the macro concept world also be live happy.

2014.05.15

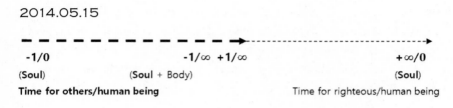

Human being macro concept

In the micro concept world, actor is the soul, but in the macro concept world macro concept human beings. Actually in the micro has wiliness but physical power haven't so just it have the wicked and righteous. So then in the macro concept,

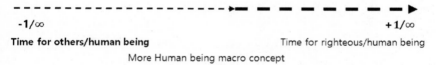

More Human being macro concept

Time for others/human being ~ Time for righteous/human being, a human being has wiliness to do wishes behavior in the macro concept world, what kind of thinking is actually thinking is operate of the macro, so then macro concept actor; righteous actor, wicked actor. Then wicked actors are multi souls, but righteous actors are rare, so then in the macro concept intrigue or decide comes by the thinking procedures.

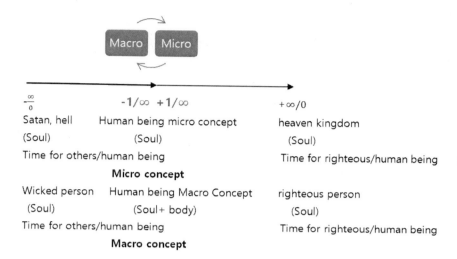

In the macro concept point of view to the micro concept then actually supposition that realization point (-1/∞ +1/∞) but this point is the thinking under the macro concept world. So then here in the macro concept is try to find some of decisions, then

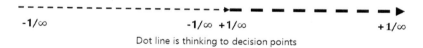

-1/∞   -1/∞ +1/∞   +1/∞

Dot line is thinking to decision points

(Dot line) is realization point (-1/∞ +1/∞) under the micro point, so then it is the gate which is the gate from the macro concept world to micro concept world. But - (dot) of the macro concept is the realization point (-1/∞ +1/∞) is moment thinking. Thinking (dot) what I have been writing. How to decide in the thinking structures, it must be pipe line macro to micro, then in the macro point of view is the thinking and decisions. Thinking is divided to good and bad, but also decision is the classification as good decision or bad decisions. – Dot lines are thinking and decisions. Here a person think, decide mixed to good and bad.

$\frac{\infty}{0}$ -1/∞ +1/∞   +∞/0

Satan, hell   Human being micro concept   heaven kingdom

(Soul)   (Soul)   (Soul)

Time for others/human being   Time for righteous/human being

Micro concept

Micro concept world point of view just realization point (-1/∞ +1/∞) then micro concept world has been said -∞/0 ~ -1/∞, +1/∞ ~ +∞/0 Satan hell wicked souls, heaven kingdom righteous souls. So then macro concept world, all of the thinking and decisions are connected to micro concepts. So then micro concept wicked or righteous souls try to give to the macro concept world. In the all of concept gets, so then thinking structure, macro human being actors will try to find the solutions. Just macro actor human being =soul+ body, then macro soul is meet in the micro world, in the point of view -∞/0 ~ -1/∞, +1/∞ ~ +∞/0, macro concept soul meet (-1/∞ +1/∞), in this place Satan wicked soul, macro concept soul and heaven kingdom righteous soul,

Just all of the macro concept human being is righteous living then he/she will meet possible to righteous soul in the heaven kingdom then he/she will meet righteous soul. But in the wicked living is very oft meeting possible so then he/she very easy to meet wicked Satan in the micro concept world. So then just in the bible said "heaven kingdom narrow, but Satan place is wide" it infer from it, wicked place hell region is much more souls, what I said this soul is so lonely so that wicked soul located placed hell so, they really want to meet macro concept body+ soul, in the realize point (-1/∞ +1/∞), to realize then it is not easy because of the all of the Satan souls are much more than heaven kingdom righteous soul. Even though just wicked soul also has the solutions so then macro concept human beings are also realize even comes by the Stan soul, what I said that, actually so many souls are good, better souls, but they haven't reach at the realization, then not righteous time, so he/she must be classify not to the heaven kingdom, so that just all of the small wicked souls are try to out of the wicked place, all of the less wicked soul try to good for the macro concept world human beings, so that all of the macro concept human being thinking very usually appeared to, so that these thinking also can help better living. This contact also come to good thinking, but also, micro concept standard and concept and macro concept world good, best thing is somewhat difference also, just like that in the macro concept "study all of the time" then he/she is use all of their time for the theirs only for the good, some of this point of view then in the end in the micro concept is still locate at the Satan, because of the he use his time 100% for him only. So then in the general good and best thinks are difference from the realization and they are in the micro concept to the heaven kingdom.

Realization is from the share time, the living is matured then, he/she is realized in the end he/she lived for the righteous then he/she will go for the heaven kingdom of the righteous soul residents. If a macro concept lives as type of the righteous then in the realize point, then he must be real important value to the macro community. In the macro concept world has the bad thinking, good thinking, realizations.

2014.05.19

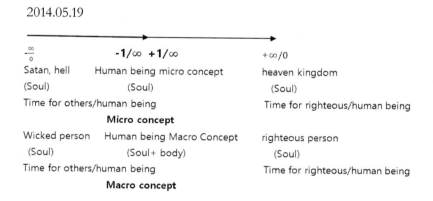

Why macro human beings know the "micro concept"? Why I'm tried to show "micro concept"?

Macro concept is seen; already constructed idea has been true, but also used this knowledge then getting solution current issue and problems. So then still we have unsolved problems. Therefore just poor macro concept human beings are hard to live, how to solve the problems; all of the macro human being be out of the poor. Why I am trying to show "micro concept" if a people realize, so called it reach at the point -1/∞ +1/∞ then he/she live as righteous then, a human being can find the solution of the gate, exodus from the macro concept world to micro world. . Micro concept how to help to the macro concept a human being reach at the realization point -1/∞ +1/∞

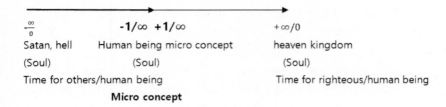

$-\frac{∞}{0}$ **-1/∞ +1/∞**   +∞/0

Satan, hell   Human being micro concept   heaven kingdom

(Soul)   (Soul)   (Soul)

Time for others/human being   Time for righteous/human being

Micro concept

Micro concept point is consist of the past (-∞/0), future (+∞/0), but macro is only past to present, that is -∞/0 ～ -1/∞, actually present is the not present but the latest the past (-1/∞) so then macro is the only past knowledge, then past knowledge is a point abrupt changed in a new idea

-1/0   **-1/∞ +1/∞**   **+∞/0**

(Soul)   (Soul + Body)   (Soul)

Human being macro concept

Just dot line, is the how multiple dots, then blacks lines are momentum "micro concept" realizes; religious, scientist, medical, all of the frontier of a new knowledge suppliers; these are realize in this "micro concept" so that these dots line are micro concept realize point "-1/∞ +1/∞, here they are all upgrade from now to the future. They live genius or righteous or some of the good effect, so then they might be contact in the micro concept realize point "-1/∞ +1/∞, a realized actor have been helped from righteous soul, a realize try to fine the future knowledge, then a realized actor have meet +1/∞ ～ +∞/0, so he/she find the at that time problems solutions. But also, a bad famous macro concept human being are have been destructed the time problems, wars, terror, disaster etc. actually in the macro war is the one way of the international stratagem, but the war is worst in the point of the" micro concept", some of the war hero are treat as the good, but that is the not righteous, if a war decision king then he/she reach at the -1/0～-1/∞, this place is the

$$-\frac{\infty}{0} \qquad -1/\infty \quad +1/\infty \qquad\qquad +\infty/0$$

Satan, hell	Human being micro concept	heaven kingdom
(Soul)	(Soul)	(Soul)
Time for others/human being		Time for righteous/human being

Micro concept

War is the Stan, hell in the micro, so then in the macro concept world all of the features are broken, in this case, therefore a macro concept human being realize to the $-1/\infty$ or $+1/\infty$, then war and peace also decide. If in the macro concept world, $-\infty/0 \sim -1/\infty$, faced at the war, then, just like in the bible "arch of Noah" there any righteous human being, so in the point of righteous power all disappeared from the a macro concept place. So then the fighter of the Satan force, the righteous power to reach at zero, then it is the optimistic of the Satan energy full to the 100%, so then the decision of the reader, he refuse to the $-1/\infty$, but he have lived but also, his nations are all lived to the wicked, so then, a decision maker deep think to out of the this current problems solve then, in a point of the meeting, meeting to the $-1/\infty$ only, then, he/she must be meet the Satan soul, so then correctly , a satan coach to get a war. But even a human being is righteous then,

$$-\frac{\infty}{0} \qquad -1/\infty \quad +1/\infty \qquad\qquad +\infty/0$$

Satan, hell	Human being micro concept	heaven kingdom

Even only 1 is righteous living then, if a man is the decide to solve the risk, or current problems solving then, the righteous human being in the macro concept, a righteous human being deep think to solve the risk problems, so, he got a meeting in the $+1/\infty \sim +\infty/0$ then he/she have meet the righteous decision helper, so then heaven kingdom, peace in the micro concept world. He solved in the peace keeping decision and helps him to the right decision for the peace. But also in the micro concept, just a righteous macro human being to help, fight to the Satan, because, originally. Satan kingdom is enemy to the heaven kingdom, so then, in the macro concept of the human being is the really only one righteous then, still has the possibility to win by the righteous force, heaven kingdom is not small power in the righteous then, a big power comes

to break the unrighteous power, just righteous power is the very fast spread to
the unrighteous human being turning back to righteous side. Because of the
macro human being is in the root of the righteous moment deceit from the
unrighteous satanic power.

2014.05.20

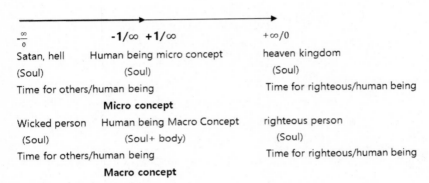

Macro concept main concerning is rich people. In the physical behavior, if
someone tries to make money so much, who are criticizing? So then macro rich
issue is good at in the game of the economy industry. This is fair game. Good
quality best price. Who anger with it. But high price goods but it can be bought
price, please supplier keep in a good rule, please do not supply still is not perfect;
do not understand the principal. So then the good perfection required to do
deep and micro solution for the perfect product. Perfect = 99.999%, making
money is the purpose of the macro concept world, somewhat is not match up
with micro concept, but masterpiece product, perfect=99.999%

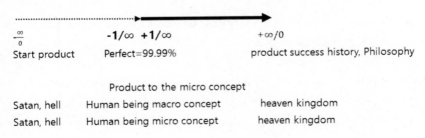

How to best selected from the customer, then the product must be the philosophical product, but also the product spiritual story telling is derived from the micro concept perfection concept. Some one of the then question that all of the supplier, producers are all need to be philosopher. Actually it is not, all of the producers, or system or company is the creature of the products. It suppose that in the supplier reaching at the produce perfection then, in the micro concept, if a successful company produce premium product then the product has the history. From start $-\infty/0$

Start product then

$$\text{Perfect } fn(-1/\infty +1/\infty) = \sum_{i=0}^{n} \quad f1(-1/\infty +1/\infty) + f2(-1/\infty +1/\infty) + f3(-1/\infty +1/\infty) + f4(-1/\infty +1/\infty) + fn(-1/\infty +1/\infty)$$

$\frac{-\infty}{0}$

Start product

-1/∞ +1/∞

Perfect=99.99%

Product to the macro, micro concept

These multiple points are the dot line. So then it comes to $-1/\infty +1/\infty =$ Perfect=99.99%

So long, all product masterpiece point has been accepted by the consumer in an era. But also here the masterpieces=$-1/\infty +1/\infty$, then a company, producer has follow the model realized macro concept human beings. He/she try to make a perfect product then he she is intrigue to create a new product, then realize of the perfection, then, he/she reach at the micro concept human being.

$\frac{-\infty}{0}$

Satan, hell

-1/∞ +1/∞

Human being micro concept

$+\infty/0$

heaven kingdom

The intrigue of the new master piece of product then he/she created the product for the pleasure to the consumers, then consumers are satisfied. So then the product has been selected to the market winner. If a producer, product supplier has the real righteous mind, then he. She try to solve the problems to get perfect product, he/she found the problems, he /she keep a rule of the endurance all of hard course, he/she has the positive thinking. He/she never been temptation to make much money in a short time, he accept the failure so many time failed, sometimes he prostrate so then he/she temptation to the end of living. But he followed his faith. he lived all of his best, then he thought that " I'm end of this, please if help me god" then the time is up, in the soul, in the micro concept a helper, in the man/woman in the peak of the suppliers, then in the "micro concept" actually reach at his/ her soul. Then he/she get in the point of the realize -1/∞ +1/∞, then a macro concept human being realize, so then he/she meet a helper in the micro concept actor, soul. What I said, then the proficient technology knowledge helper must be locate at the Satan or Heaven kingdom, if man/woman souls touch a Satan soul then realize best solutions. But also some macro concept human being can touch the heaven kingdom helper. But in the technology of the new might comes from the Satan, because of Satan kingdom has the all of his living is solaced, but also he has been concentrated so it very special knowledge deliver to the macro concept human being. What I said in the Satan also, the degree is good soul, worst soul, specialist in a field. So then

$-\frac{∞}{0}$ -1/∞ +1/∞   +∞/0

Satan, hell   Human being micro concept   heaven kingdom

Some of question why specialist are located at the Satan king dome, then in the micro concept actors are time and distance, then, time for other, also time for righteous so that, in the living macro concept success are not in the micro concept heaven kingdom. So that so in this "micro concept" is so multiple is located at the Satan kingdom. but also very rare, a specialist in the macro concept, if he located at the heaven kingdom, then how he live in the his macro concept time, then he must be his time all for the others, in the macro concept his creative product for all of the other helping then his all of time may be used for the really benefit others, so then, god will think him, he use all of his time for others. Then he must be live in the heaven kingdom, so then in the macro concept

$-\frac{∞}{0}$ -1/∞ +1/∞

Start product   Perfect=99.99%

                Product to the macro, micro concept

These dots line is reached to the moment in the macro concept time level, then momentum perfect but it is not ultimate perfect then a man still meet -1/∞, still comes to continued to be perfect.

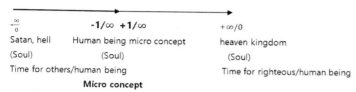

in the macro concept so many suppliers are reach at the in the micro concept (-1/∞ +1/∞) so then a man/woman can be rich person, but if they are until now all of their energy used for the success then it must be considered, -∞/0 ~ -1/∞, then he/she try to solve the all of their faced problems so all of their Time for others/human being is so small, so in the macro concept human being is success, he/her reach at the realize how to be rich person, so they all be excited with it, in this point in the micro concept recognition then, he reach at the realize then he must be solved problems get in -1/∞ +1/∞, he/she is peak in his time. So long, if macro concept a human being still remained in the short of the Time for others/human being, then if this is end then, he/she must be locate in the soul of the Satan, hell. If macro concept human being out of the -1/∞ +1/∞ then he/she is transfer to from Time for others/human being to Time for righteous/human being. Then it must be recognized by god, heavenly father thinking he/she is the righteous lived in the macro concept time, then he/she located in the heaven kingdom, this is the micro concept but this is not religious principle, please do not misunderstand. This micro concept is not related to the religious. This is again and again here god express is the some of the decision of the how to live; time of the righteous or not is discriminator role. Please understand it. In the micro concept are soul behaviors.

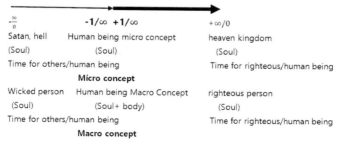

Macro concept and micro concept relation is the micro concept time actor and macro also ahs the time levels, so that it must be discriminate from the, but also righteous also, so in the time of the very typically, in the macro concept so many human beings are eager to be live well, all of his/her time only for himself, herself. The righteous is same factors, all of the macro concept so best human beings are happy with themselves; this is the come to "personalize" so then what I'm doing my success merit for me who criticize to me, he argue I'm perfect but also, I'm not sinner, yes! In the point of macro concept human beings are concord. So in the macro concept success story and specialist are located at the micro concept Satan so someone anger, then I can explain this, some of difference form macro concept human being to the micro concept human being is depended on Time for others/human being, Time for righteous/human being.

2014.05.21

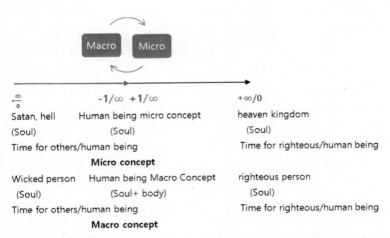

$\frac{\infty}{0}$	$-1/\infty$ $+1/\infty$	$+\infty/0$
Satan, hell	Human being micro concept	heaven kingdom
(Soul)	(Soul)	(Soul)
Time for others/human being		Time for righteous/human being
	Micro concept	
Wicked person	Human being Macro Concept	righteous person
(Soul)	(Soul+ body)	(Soul)
Time for others/human being		Time for righteous/human being
	Macro concept	

Macro concept human being is soul+ body micro concept human being is soul. Here same common indicator is soul is same. I did not know how to exchange from macro to micro, then what I try to explain of

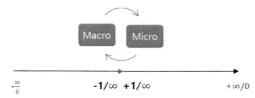

Macro to micro, adverse also, then how to explain is this, all of the actor is soul, but in the macro has the soul+ body. If in the macro human being

Macro concept human being go for the divided to $-1/\infty, +1/\infty$ so called $\lim_{n \to \infty} +(1/n)^n$, $\lim_{n \to \infty} -(1/n)^n$ then Macro concept humanbeing become to micro concept humanbeing, it is come to the concept of the religious, but actually not this micro concept is not religious, so then I called the micro concept human being to soul. So then $-1/\infty, +1/\infty$ point is micro concept entering gate but also from macro concept human being exodus point also.

Macro concept human being also can be the in the micro concept human being, role of the soul.

So then actually all of the macro to micro then included human being with all of natural existence is being in the soul world, micro concept world, so that actually all of the features, even cosmos is come to micro world, then in the micro world, micro concept human being but also micro concept nature, then all of the creatures are in the micro, so then this is the any meaningful to the benefit to the macro concept human being. But in the long distance cosmos, then if this micro concept adopt then

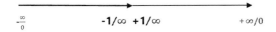

Micro concept cosmos adopt

Actually macro concept cosmos is $(-\infty/0, +\infty/0)$ how to reach at this long distance, in the macor concept actor is the time, and distance, so then, the end of the cosmos how to reach, almost impossible. Actually to be reach at the cosmos voyage, then in the macro concept long future story will be, just in the macro technology is rapid, so that in the future cosmos travel is usual, but even then it also limited somewhat distance. We have mixed in the change of in the macro concept time scale, a country is date, and other country is night. Then macro concept travel to the cosmos how possible. But if adopt micro concept,

$\frac{-\infty}{0}$ **-1/∞ +1/∞**   +∞/0

Micro concept cosmos adopt

$\lim_{n\to\infty}+(n/n)^n$, $\lim_{n\to\infty}-(n/0)^n$, this is the macro concept cosmos expand to $\int_{\infty}^{\infty}$ -(n/0) – expand to ∞, $\int_{\infty}^{\infty}$ +(n/0) + expand to ∞, then in the macro concept travel to the cosmos voyage but it must be so long time required to realize to cosmos traveling.

But in the micro concept cosmos adopt then $\lim_{n\to\infty}+(1/n)^n$, $\lim_{n\to\infty}-(1/n)^n$, -1/∞ +1/∞, it must be converged to the point. So then in the micro concept is so closed they all located in the micro concept world, then, a big huge cosmos is so small a particle, so then in the bible, earth create sturdy must be possible, but here is not in the religious, just all of the macro concept macro concept adopt, so then in the cosmos to the micro concept adopt then voyage to the cosmos possible some of the micro concept point. In this case required micro concept human bieng voyage to the cosmos, so then a micro concept soul can travel to the a long distance just out of the macro concept cosmos (-∞/0 +∞/0),

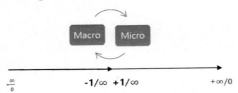

$\frac{-\infty}{0}$ **-1/∞ +1/∞**   +∞/0

Macro concept = micro concept then just soul can travel to the macro concept impossible distance but in the micro concept soul can reach at cosmos (-∞/0 +∞/0). in the micro concecept another actor time is very micro, so in micro concept world actor soul can travel just moment to the micro concept cosmos. Actually in the macro concept now travel out of space. Actually the technology is required. Then the soluble problems also keep continued then an engineer or researcher will be touched to the specialist on the problems soluble, in the micro concept also. So then it come to so multiple point of the

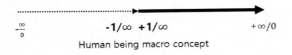

$\frac{-\infty}{0}$ **-1/∞ +1/∞**   +∞/0

Human being macro concept

Macro concept technology developed small multi dots line, these is the points (-1/∞ +1/∞)

These dot points are so multiple point to make possible shorter than macro knowledge usage. So that if a specialist deep research so long time then he/she researcher can be touch to the micro concept, then if a researcher lived only for the research all of his/her time then, it might be the all of the specialist located at the Stan place, so he/.she must be meet between macro human being micro human being, so then the technology transfer to macro concept researchers. So long macro concept world will solve, it already known to the micro concept

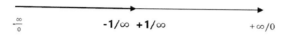

Micro concept cosmos adopt

Micro concept micro concept cosmos adopt then $\lim_{n \to \infty} +(1/n)^n$, $\lim_{n \to \infty} -(1/n)^n$, -1/∞ +1/∞, So then, in the micro concept can be possible, this is our oriental soul, after death a soul fly to the heaven, this is story us, so then micro concept a soul fly a long distance or short distance, in a time scale so short. In the micro concept travel to the cosmos is possible.

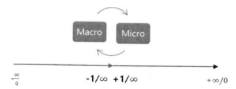

If micro concept soul, and macro concept human being (soul + body) then even he/she is human being then if a macro concept human being realize, to transition to soul, this time is the in the micro concept soul, macro concept soul transactions, a moment, what I explained in the micro concept, micro concept time and macro concept time is time scale is explained by Jesus Christ walk on the water, so that, a realize of the macro concept human being like Jesus Christ then, he/she will go for the cosmos in a moment , soon after come back to the macro concept human being. For the possible then, in then a macro concept human being also travel to the cosmos, in the micro concept world. It must be the super human being just like Jesus Christ. He already has done, he walks on the water, but also he eats multi persons by the small breads. Jesus and multiple people just moment transition to micro concept world, then there soul and bread also micro then, micro is -1/∞,+1/∞ in a moment macro concept and micro concept changed. But in the Seen world it is not any changed, this is only possible in the bible truth. Jesus did miracle.

2014.05.22

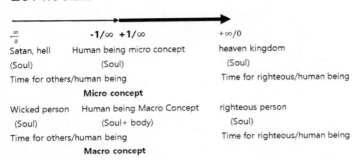

$\frac{\infty}{0}$	-1/∞ +1/∞	+∞/0
Satan, hell	Human being micro concept	heaven kingdom
(Soul)	(Soul)	(Soul)
Time for others/human being		Time for righteous/human being

Micro concept

Wicked person	Human being Macro Concept	righteous person
(Soul)	(Soul+ body)	(Soul)
Time for others/human being		Time for righteous/human being

Macro concept

Macro concept and micro concept, in the micro concept natural characteristics is convergent, but micro concept is divergence. How to adopt in the macro concept world micro concept then it must be in the micro concept convergence, macro divergence, so then, in the macro concept has comparison macro to micro, so then, comparison theory adopt, then in the macro concept.

Macro concept

Macro concept

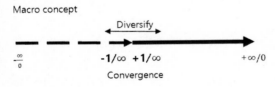

In the macro concept world, all of the specialties are diversify, so then so multiple objects are increased then all of the macro concept actor, human beings are most specialized to one field, so then in the macro concept, these are called to the specialist, so all of the macro concept world are in a segment, much more detailed segment specialist, his living all of his major working. So then all of the specialist forget all of the general living, somewhat share with other his/her time but also do righteous living. The entire macro concept is successful or built of his/her field man proud of his/her living any wanted things. So in the macro concept it is natural to be diversified.

Then in the typically micro concept theory and specialist compared then

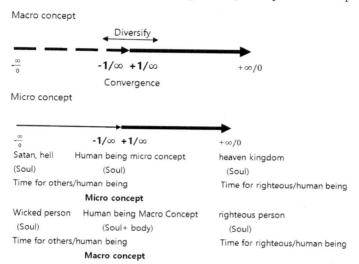

Macro concept

Micro concept

Then out of the -1/∞,+1/∞ point then in the macro then it is not to the +1/∞ then it a lot to the -∞/0 ~-1/∞ so then, here macro succrss rich, but also all of the macro concept human being are respect person. Still located at the Satan king dome in the micro concept world. Then somewhat anger to the successful in the macro concept world, and then they lived so easy, but also he hasn't any did harm to others, so just specialist certify of his micro concept his /her location is must be heaven kingdom. Somewhat digress of the core idea, so then in the macro concept all of the human beings are to be rich and live easy. So then, the good jobs are short, so all of macro concept human beings are can't get the good positions, so another new macro concept youth also make his/her area, in the market. So then if in the old time then in the agricultural era then some of parents lands sprite to give a son. But now, all of new youth develop his living area, but also they study and research, in this process in the micro concept knowledge getting what I explained, so then, in the macro concept, a new human being also try to be rich, and life easy voyage, actually this is the macro concept comparison micro concept.

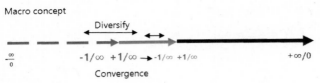

Macro concept

Diversify

$-1/\infty$ $+1/\infty$ $\rightarrow -1/\infty$ $+1/\infty$ $+\infty/0$

Convergence

Micro concept

In the macro concept world has increased the macro concept by ➝ , so then in the macro concept increased to the $-\infty/0 \sim -1/\infty$ so then the competition is so huge, all of the macro concept humabeings are hard to live, so in this macro concept world, so many accidents are happened, as increased or diversify then distance from the micro concept point $-1/\infty$ $+1/\infty$, it means that increased to the in the micro concept location is the Satan. Then how to live on the macro concept world in the living, then

$-1/\infty$ $+1/\infty$

Micro concept region comparison micro concept point = Micro point (m)

Micro concept region is comparisons micro concept point, so then if a macro concept point is black region, but out of the $-1/\infty$, $+1/\infty$ are macro concept macro, then in this place adopt to the micro concept convergence, so then what I said that actually it is not seen in the micro, micro concept, but now in the macro concept, just comparison micro is also adopt to the micro concept. In this micro concept also need to another comparison micro.

If in the macro concept world comparison micro is m, then Macro concept is M

In the macro world comparisons micro concept point is seen

Micro concept point = m, M, m, M, m, M .... Turning points kept continued.

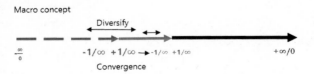

Macro concept

Diversify

$-1/\infty$ $+1/\infty$ $\rightarrow -1/\infty$ $+1/\infty$ $+\infty/0$

Convergence

-1/∞ +1/∞   +∞/0

Convergence

Comparison of Micro concept

A good macro exchanges comparison macro and micros.

Micro concept point = m, M, m, M, m, M .... Turning points kept continued.

But bad Macro concepts are still

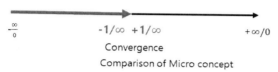

-1/∞ +1/∞   +∞/0

Convergence

Comparison of Micro concept

In Comparison micro concepts are the points of the turning points, comparison Macro concept to Micro concept, so then in the macro concept world happened exchanged but good is circulation macro to micro. But bad Macro concepts are not exchanged to then it is not dot line but just line then bad macro concepts are not circulated then, the macro is really Satan.

Actually in the macro concept world, comparison micro concept appeared then, the point also comes to the micro concept -1/∞ +1/∞ this is the comparison micro concept point so then the point is the turning points. In the macro concepts are circulated the macro to micro then, it has the in the point of view in the macro concept world also, has the comes to +1/∞ ~ +∞/0

The heavenly kingdom also visits to the comparison micro concept point. So then these macro concept world bless by the micro concept +1/∞ ~ +∞/0 heavenly kingdome power. But do not exchange in the macro concept world, still kept macro concept there is not any comparison macro to micro changed then there are kept in the point of view in the micro concept. -∞/0~-1/∞

Then Stan in the micro concept world, it must be the macro concept world just fixed to the macro then this macro concept world is hell. Just macro world has the comparison M, m, M, m turning to circulation then in the turning point is the macro concept world faced to the in the micro concept heaven kingdom is also meet. So then heaven kingdom power effect to the circulation among M m M m.........

2014.05.23

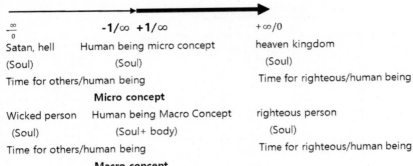

$\frac{\infty}{0}$	**-1/∞ +1/∞**	+∞/0
Satan, hell	Human being micro concept	heaven kingdom
(Soul)	(Soul)	(Soul)
Time for others/human being		Time for righteous/human being
	Micro concept	
Wicked person	Human being Macro Concept	righteous person
(Soul)	(Soul+ body)	(Soul)
Time for others/human being		Time for righteous/human being
	Macro concept	

Macro concept human being act in the macro concept world. Then these human beings are also so many human being meetings. In the macro concept world meeting is actually (soul+ body) to soul+ body) then here, these meeting has the possibility of the soul to soul, body to body, or soul+ body to soul, soul+ body to body, in this possibilities, how to know, but actually in the micro concept world continued relationship is best is soul to soul. But also (soul +body) to (soul+ body) so then in the macro concept world meetings relationships are so complicate not simple. All of relationship has stories. A good story bad story, some people benefit from others, but also reward more benefit giving, but if a human being deceit from his/her relationships. Which people get a good relationship, or bad relationships, the relationships are come true in the variable patterns. The relationships are connected to the micro concept criteria between Time for others/human being and Time for righteous/human being. So then, it comes, this relationships are beginning each macro concept human beings, then which actor has a possibility to meet a good people, but the other actors are encountered to the bad actors. In the suppositions are if a good actors are multi then the good actor meeting possibilities are higher, but if not the possibilities to encounter the bad actor is easy. This is how to conformed, who suppliers a good actor who supplier to bad actors. This is the chicken and eggs games.

classify	soul	Soul+ body	body	Body+ soul
soul	Micro concept world , best	Micro concept World, middle	Macro concept World, soul harmed, deceit	Macro concept World, good relationship
Soul + body	Micro concept World middle	Macro concept world, average	Macro concept World, soul body do harmed deceit	Macro concept World, bad relationship
body	Macro concept World, ignorant	Macro concept World, damage Soul+ body	Macro concept World, war state	Macro concept World, deceit to body+ soul
Body+ soul	Macro concept World, better average	Macro concept world, average	Macro concept World, body+ soul hard by the body	Macro concept World, out of averages

<Metrics of the macro concept world human being meeting >

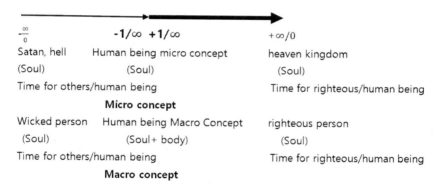

$-\frac{\infty}{0}$

$-1/\infty$ $+1/\infty$ $+\infty/0$

Satan, hell   Human being micro concept   heaven kingdom

(Soul)   (Soul)   (Soul)

Time for others/human being   Time for righteous/human being

Micro concept

Wicked person   Human being Macro Concept   righteous person

(Soul)   (Soul+ body)   (Soul)

Time for others/human being   Time for righteous/human being

Macro concept

In the macro concept so many human beings are friend or enemy or nothing. In micro concept in the Metrics of the macro concept world human being meeting then macro concept and micro concept almost same or in the recognition contact then at maximum 3 phases, so that this is means that the transfer to the micro concept, actually this is presume comparison but also absolute also, therefore it show that macro concept human being relationships are connected to the micro concept. Actually in the micro concept criteria are consisting of both Time for others/human being and Time for righteous/

human being. Then a actor will meet or keep alone, so then even shared time with, just time variants but the very rare case meeting, then the contact also be in the deceit then, what happened to us, just meeting time how to care or, just nothing but meeting, then the relationship result also very important to do. To be a micro concept touch in the macro concept world human being, it must be soul to soul, even expand soul to soul+ body, soul+ body to soul, the relationship mediated love each other but also sacrifice to others. The very important "love" "sacrifice" this is the big power to go through the macro concept and micro concept world reach ways.

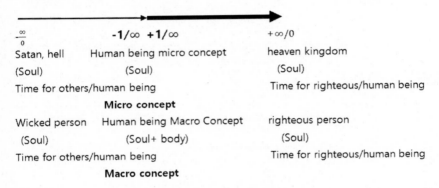

$-\dfrac{\infty}{0}$	**-1/∞ +1/∞**	+∞/0
Satan, hell	Human being micro concept	heaven kingdom
(Soul)	(Soul)	(Soul)
Time for others/human being		Time for righteous/human being
	Micro concept	
Wicked person	Human being Macro Concept	righteous person
(Soul)	(Soul+ body)	(Soul)
Time for others/human being		Time for righteous/human being
	Macro concept	

Just in the macro concept actor to reach at the -1/∞ +1/∞ realization from meeting others, then an actor love, or sacrifice then parter receive the love sacrifice, then it feel thank, and realize, so he/she also give to partner, love, sacrifices. After all these relationship is basic form reach at the -1/∞ +1/∞, but in the Metrics of the macro concept world human being meeting, the other relationship is not same but all are in the macro concept world meeting. So then soul living in the macro world is not easy, most actors try to live easy living. The easy living on the macro concept world, then in the time of the early actors are all of their time for the getting easy living positions, so then they all are forgotten all of the soulful living. So that if someone get at easy living position in the macro concept world, then they all live as the body, or body +soul, so, all of the rarely a soul, or soul + body are hard to live on, all of the body+ soul, even body is standard. Then s soulful actors are so hard to live on. So that in the macro concept world, the easy going people is treated best among them who are body, or body+ soul, so then this macro concept world and micro concept world are segregate. Even so rare soul, soul+ body actors are some living easy but the others are not easy living. So soulful person under the micro concept world, best actors are worst in the macro concept world. But also actually if macro concept world, real actors; they also soulful living then they will meet micro concept world. They will be the leader of the macro concept world such as religious, a good characteristics actor who helped all of the poor. How to meet a soul, soul+ body actor, it must be a actor also live as the soul, or soul+ body. It may be the criteria of the Time for others/human being, Time for righteous/human being, so then if an actor kept a Time for others/human being, even more Time for righteous/human being then in the macro concept, comparative -1/∞ +1/∞ realize in the living are explained to the soul to soul, these actors are in the place of the micro concept then locate to the heaven kingdom, but the other is soul to soul +body it must be the good actor but located at the -∞/0~ 1/∞, Satan place. But how to do, in the macro concept then, they are all in the macro concept world, so how to do, but this macro concept, soul, soul+ body is must be in comparison recognize. So then in the micro concept, all of the macro has soul +body, so then if in the time of the birth to soul then he/she must be a lot his/hers eternity position, Satan and heaven kingdom. But now, all of the relationship on the macro concept world relationship, so then, if all of the macro concept world actor relationships are body, or body+ soul, then in the time, it will not reach at the -1/∞ +1/∞ realize point, so that, the macro concept world, all of the actors are not easy to live on.

2014.06.25 (MICRO CONCEPT)

$\frac{\infty}{0}$	-1/∞ +1/∞	+∞/0
Satan, hell	Human being micro concept	heaven kingdom
(Soul)	(Soul)	(Soul)
Time for others/human being		Time for righteous/human being
	Micro concept	
Wicked person	Human being Macro Concept	righteous person
(Soul)	(Soul+ body)	(Soul)
Time for others/human being		Time for righteous/human being
	Macro concept	

The macro world existed knowledge, territory, agricultural, crude oil, war etc are from origin of the flat macro feature. It compared with 1th floor a source of energy. But high-tech industry, knowledge is compared to the 2th floors. All of this emery is a macro concept. In the point of view just before 1th floors then 2th floors are micro concept. It has completed the Macro to micro concept transitions. in this transition the actor can get soluble to the problems. Until then all of the territory built 2th floors. If all of the residents are understand in the scale of the macro concept. This is the so distance from micro concept. How long distance or time passed. 2th floors 3 dimensions of the territory, all of the territory built 2th floors.

contents	criteria	adoption
4th floors : beyond unseen level	Micro	Country / companies
3th floors : unseen still is not but will come	Micro	Country / companies
2th floors : high tech industry, knowledge etc	Macro	Country / companies
1th floor : territory , agricultural, crude oil	Macro	Country / companies

< Macro and micro concept steps>

All of the macro is real recognition feature, this is real, and then in the macro concept, the micro is imagination or just thinking ranges. But in the micro concept to macro then, old, inefficient, come to end. Even in this truth, but the recognitions is judged by the existence judge criteria's. Then whoever accepts micro, the entire micro concept is treated as empty thing. Who which place will be the criteria macro to micro. Companies / countries are impossible perfect 2th floors, all still mixed with 1th floors, so then actually 1th ~2th floors are Macro. So then to go for the micro, it means then a new paradigm but still all depend on only macro concept. $-\infty/0 \sim -1/\infty$ so then this means that in the point of view micro concept, these are all old, in effect all of is stuffy status. But there is not any soluble.

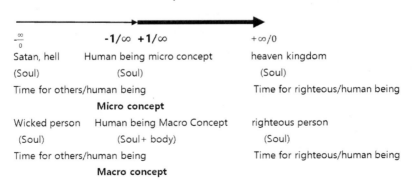

$\frac{\infty}{0}$ **-1/∞ +1/∞**   +∞/0

Satan, hell   Human being micro concept   heaven kingdom

(Soul)   (Soul)   (Soul)

Time for others/human being   Time for righteous/human being

Micro concept

Wicked person   Human being Macro Concept   righteous person

(Soul)   (Soul+ body)   (Soul)

Time for others/human being   Time for righteous/human being

Macro concept

So then just in the point of view micro to the macro concept world, they are struggling. Just 1th floors affairs. Crude oil getting war, just national territory getting. Iraq USA war, Japan Korea china island struggling. Somewhat desired to get, then here is some win another loser, this is all of power. If this power conflict then it leads to war, so many civilians are dead. Then this problems so need to solve, so do not war keep building peace. In the time of the macro 1th floor then Edison who has lived as inventor. Newton universal gravitation, How to they find the these actors, it maybe they are micro actor rolled, these people could reach at the micro concept gate -1/∞ +1/∞, it must be he try to find his problems solving. Edison cases if try to adopt micro concept

Edison how to live, thinking, I'm just imagined actually I don't know him. If he get a creative things, he has tried to egg to hen, the he use his body warming. So then he deep into the problems solving, in the point of view macro concept the he must be odd people. The community gets free, the community matured so then he lived to the micro actor. All know that Edison creature all changed the entire 1th floor world, it maybe

$\frac{\infty}{0}$ **-1/∞ +1/∞**   +∞/0

Satan, hell   Human being micro concept   heaven kingdom

(Soul)   (Soul)   (Soul)

Time for others/human being   Time for righteous/human being

Micro concept

Wicked person   Human being Macro Concept   righteous person

(Soul)   (Soul+ body)   (Soul)

Time for others/human being   Time for righteous/human being

Macro concept

He tried to find the unseen feature, he think deep, then, in the micro concept theory, Edison soul try to find the Edison soul get to the micro concept gate, $-1/\infty$ $+1/\infty$ he reach at the micro concept point. He live all of life, but also he excited with his act, he live a line, to reach at, the follows the micro concept procedures. He had lived in real out of deceit. Edison soul in the micro concept world touched. His soul tour to the $+1/\infty \sim +\infty/0$ his soul met a future knowledge soul, a soul give an idea to Edison soul. In the micro concept, $+1/\infty$ $\sim +\infty/0$

As heaven kingdom soul, this is the principal; all of the big changed creative soluble ideas give to Edison soul. What I said in the $-1/\infty$ $+1/\infty$ who can reach at this point. Then switch micro to macro, then Edison has lived righteously. In the micro concept world, heaven kingdom soul tries to help him, because of his righteous. But also, it can be infer to the, just heaven kingdom soul learned so he try to find in the macro concept actor who best in the macro world then, if micro concept knowledge give to the top of the world, micro world heaven kingdom soul, sure that his knowledge must be carried to him, all of the macro world innovative changed. So Edison has live top of the macro concept world. So Edison get from micro world the best solutions, so then he made successful creature just like electric bulb, projector etc. Edison creates a big changed to the macro world, then this is the moment micro, he is the innovator he being micro actors. Edison used his micro concept. He have voyaged micro concept world. He live in USA, at that time all of basic tools are equipped, so then Edison has the problems to create, so micro concept world actor delivered a knowledge, so comes miracle creates. But if the same procedures in Africa a people has the problems to solve he reach at $-1/\infty$ $+1/\infty$ then can possible like it, it is not, Edison lived in the transient time of the 1th floor~2th floors, so then Edison intrigued to find it, but also in the micro concept world, heaven kingdom actor give the best actor in the macro. So then, macro and micro concept adopt is the how degree of the righteous, justice, exact, good this is helped so then, in the micro concept helped peoples all lived in justly righteously, then heaven kingdom soul give the righteous gift.

But the entire thing is not good, Hitler has helped from his power also, he reaches at the $-1/\infty$ $+1/\infty$ Hitler took 2th world war. Hitler failed to go art school, then he anger to the community. His mind all anger, self torture. He has also deep in thinking his living. He has a goal, so the he thought intrigue to find the solutions.

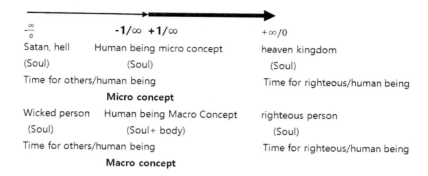

Hitler deep in try to solve, then he reach at the -1/∞ +1/∞ again it must be infer also, his soul meet a soul then, a soul is in the micro -∞/0 -1/∞, so then, his soul meet a micro world Satan, even much more anger soul, he teach Hitler soul, so then Hitler, the role represent role of the Satan, Satan fully help him, so break all over the world. Stan power, heaven kingdom power is same, but the usage is not same, heaven kingdom power builds the peace, but Satan power breaks the all of the world, war.

Hitler in macro world, he live the wicked person. Hitler time all used for the malice mind, so he is the royalty to the Satan, Satan's a big power break all over the world. The righteous soul, the wicked soul is big difference come to macro world.

So then Edison Hitler is the indicator of the good or bad, then, if a community or company has consists of good, or bad members then it comes from micro concept from Satan or from Heaven kingdom. if a good people is multiple then a company will be helped from the heaven kingdom, but other then it will be helped from Satan, in the end good is much better but Satan is must be worst. What happened to the progress, development how to relative to this, in the macro concept, money making must be good theory must be banter from rich people, In the macro concept world, money and good, righteous is not relative, so then, most money makers are relative to the fraud mind, deceit. Then money maker is compared in the micro concept then closed to the Satan. This money also in the end brake wrong invest, economical disturb in the end brake the economical system. But real good make money then, the money will help company, country true development; go with GDP Growth offer the good jobs so that most people work in the workplace. In the end money from Satan, money from heaven kingdom clearly differently used so this widely adopt to the country & company.

2014.06.26

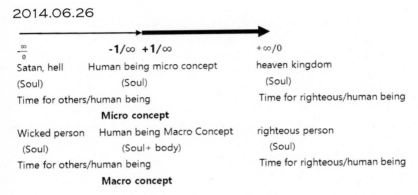

Micro concept is split to segments, among segments against segment so then $\lim_{n \to \infty} {}^{n}(1/n)^{n}$

So called n fold split then come to $-1/\infty$ $+1/\infty$ micro concept point, why seek micro concept

This is giving all of micro concept center concept, so then it reaches at the each micro concept are center all of the cosmos or nature. Micro concept ultimate unseen, it already unseen but has it, actually it is not weight. All of macro concept units are living in the macro world. Macro world actors are living under the scenery. Just seen, $-\infty/0$ $-1/\infty$, this knowledge is the solving tips. So that macro concept human beings do live their wiliness. Some people anger, critic the other good so variable types are mixed in the macro world. Then macro is the group, segments are so many in the macro, then the typically macro a group unit is the company; this is the job all of each human beings support in economic. Why macro concept human being must understand micro concept, micro concept is unseen, macro concept is seen, and so then macro concept human being naturally forgot the truth of the micro concept. Macro concept human being has location for the living support, if he is manager of the organization then he must be decision, so called he is a decision maker. As he reach at $-1/\infty$ $+1/\infty$, he live righteously and deep in his position working. Deep to deep to get well managing, all of the macro concept human beings are his time all use for the positioning work not but his personal, then this manager is not deceit or wicked person. If he all of his energy for the righteous. Then his soul touch in mind, but also soul lived fulfillment. His soul has the good soul friends his soul so excitement with meeting. In the micro concept actor of his soul, contacts all of righteous souls, his soul health, but also his physical body all of tired to the company affairs not for his affairs. He knows all of the problems of the companies for the better, but also productivities getting higher. But still the problems are not unsolved then, he lived for the solving, but the company perfect being the macro concept. He must be critical time to solve the original problems, then he reach at $-1/\infty$ $+1/\infty$, his soul watched his body, his soul try to find his soul friend. He meet his friend $+1/\infty$ $+\infty/0$, his soul meet the righteous helping soul, ths is times scale of the macro then future, so then, it never existed in the macro concept world, a new perfect new creative concept give to the his soul. So then in the macro soul + body find the solutions. What I said a soul friend find the in macro actor, he is the first, so soul believe that his knowledge can be adopt to his process then the soul think " all right my eternity researched idea(creative idea) will be blossom" so then his soul horribly seek then, among the multiple souls, adopt soul permit meeting. His soul + body lived righteous, just the heaven kingdom rule governing living. The manager follows righteous concept in his macro concept world. He has been suffered but he do not deceit way. He follow the time, he has been lived endured. His macro concept living is ultimate helped from micro concept.

Micro concept is micro in the dictionary definition, unseen idea, weight, all it is not clear to explain but micro is the 90% to the macro, macro is only 10%. I'm strength saying that micro is the lava but macro is the rock. Micro is living but macro is dead micro. Here 90% is uncountable, unfathomed of God side or Satan side knowledge is located. But 10% macro concepts are all ridged. This is the Seen so that all of macro actors are living only dead micro concept.

But to reach at the micro concept creative knowledge getting is not easy.

But if macro actors live righteous the even time is so late or not he must be meet the solutions. Some micro concept knowledge is anti to the macro. In the macro concept all try to get bigger, richer, more powerful position. But this is just for one, one is only macro's top. All are deceit for the macro top's sake. Even in the macro concept world. To win in the competition of the real market, this is the right. Then all of the labor actors are just workers only. Just the entire macro concept each human beings knowledge is all buried. Their concept is not considered only required to work for the top of the macro unit. In the macro all of try to fight more lager territory, to make hard,

contents	criteria	adoption
4th floors : beyond unseen level	Micro	Country / companies
3th floors : unseen still is not but will come	Micro	Country / companies
2th floors : high tech industry, knowledge etc	Macro	Country / companies
1th floor : territory , agricultural, crude oil	Macro	Country / companies

< Macro and micro concept steps>

All of macro concept world still remained, 1th floors. Even some company 2th floors. But all mixed with 1th floor~ 2th floors. This is a big macro, still all of the macro countries are try to fight, to get a bigger power. This is very likeable to the Satan.

Company also a big companies are M&A to bigger. So then stipulated rule for the macro managed so then the member of human beings are despised. Just top of the company sake multiple body + soul are their valuable life living. It understand I'm, this is the real world, just unseen micro world. How to go for the 3th floors it also reach then soon being the macro, because lava is soon being rock. But micro concept world as possible as can live righteous but in the micro and Macro has the still 50% to 50% of the Satan and Heaven kingdom.

To get over the 10% totality macro micro, then in the macro living is the righteous living is required.

$$\frac{\infty}{0} \qquad\qquad -1/\infty \quad +1/\infty \qquad\qquad +\infty/0$$

Satan, hell	Human being micro concept	heaven kingdom
(Soul)	(Soul)	(Soul)
Time for others/human being		Time for righteous/human being

Micro concept

Wicked person	Human being Macro Concept	righteous person
(Soul)	(Soul + body)	(Soul)
Time for others/human being		Time for righteous/human being

Macro concept

Righteous living uses time for others not me, but also decide in moment, for the righteous, even thinking stage also. Satan method Wicked people is so easy. In the fish, a fish caught in the fishing pole, then he must be died, but a righteous does not eat fishing pole bait. So then do not follow easy gain. Easy gain all from Satan so then the result also very short, these result also steal from the other Satan actors. Just follows righteous rule then the actor life so long, even eternity some of the 100 years shop; they lived as the righteously justly, all of product is not deceit but all of the righteous. Heaven king dome righteous is eternity because of the friends are all righteous, god just open for the real righteous. It never get in to wick method, Wick products all cling to Satan, Satan very like to accept it must be enforce getting these actors. Enrapt by the Satan actors south, east, North West all are Stains. These groups are not eternity. Compared with righteous groups, but sorry it very rare righteous groups, so that righteous soul place is not complicate out of others, but clean and designed street, their living place itself is the traveling sight.

Micro concepts are stated for the personal not a group. So that micro is the getting smaller is the all of the micro actors are center for the issue. All are equity in getting opportunity but also wealth, health, so then if a decision maker decides then another selected damaged is how to low make less is the micro concept principle in the macro concept point of view. Micro concept must be reach at the soul.

In the micro concept all of the soul be equality happy, excitement righteous living just governed by the creative soul, so all of the soul live righteous thinking for helping each other in the righteous so that it never perfectly do not damage others. All is 100% benefit in the soul. But do not any damage other souls. Thank god give me knowledge. The name of Jesus Christ amen.

2014.06.27

Micro concept, macro concept, unseen, seen, untouchable touchable, Micro is 90%, macro is only 10%. Macro is past to present, micro is future. I infer the macro must be lauder, but also micro I can't, if I compared to onion, onion layers are macro, then if reach at the core. But in the end all of core displaces then it will come to the micro concept adoption. In the layer of onion and the "Macro and micro concept steps" is can be match able. Onion layer1, onion layer2, onion layer3

Onion layer #n, finally layer $\{-1/\infty +1/\infty \}$ finally reach at the micro gate. Then in the

< Macro and micro concept steps> macro steps are so history has good or bad accidents. To steal the territory going war, even that is still ongoing. So multiples of the each personal deceit or wicked but also Jesus birth heavenly father sent his only son to the perfect macro concept world.

Macro 1th floor, 2th floors is holy nothing micro, just natural power, but also it depends on the instinct power. To win it required loser, all of the situation conflict, but also power to win, just winner is winner, but sorry winner is so small, for the winners all of the out of winners are lived. Macro concept is winner or losers. Winner is the top on the losers. Macro concept success person also small but failures people so many, that macro concept is accepted rich and poor states.

If 90% micro concept world, linear to the connect to the macro then, endless micro concept to adopt to the macro concept, micro concept is winner but there is not loser, how to do, it is the helped from the 90% micro concept product, it is not simple then in the macro concept term is creative idea to produce. How to relate with the macro concept and micro concept,

$\frac{\infty}{0}$	-1/∞ +1/∞	+∞/0
Satan, hell	Human being micro concept	heaven kingdom
(Soul)	(Soul)	(Soul)
Time for others/human being		Time for righteous/human being
	Micro concept	
Wicked person	Human being Macro Concept	righteous person
(Soul)	(Soul+ body)	(Soul)
Time for others/human being		Time for righteous/human being
	Macro concept	

Micro concept is the gate of the micro concept {-1/∞ +1/∞ } this gate is it really accept or refuse. In the micro concept world, (-∞/0 -1/∞) wicked place, righteous person (+1/∞   +∞/0) then if a righteous person in the macro concept, the righteous soul all together located at the micro concept world, it must be find the place to live easy living. The righteous souls try to find the soul friends. A righteous soul tries to find then another righteous soul, the soul accept friendly, then if he righteous soil by accident meet wicked soul, then the wicked soul reject righteous soul's suggestions to be friend. As a result righteous soul to righteous soul, but wicked soul to wicked soul, so then all of learned in the body +soul, if a body+ soul lived as the wicked living then, he by accidently meet the righteous people then, wicked soul very not excitement, somewhat outdated soul, he/she wicked soul try to segregate in the micro concept world, so then wicked friend all of the wicked soul, but righteous also all together excited with the righteous people groups. It is natural this is the god's ways. So then in the macro concept living wicked or righteous living, then eternity is decided.

Macro concept 1th ~2th floors all still wicked and righteous mixed community. Then it might be the in the macro concept 2th floors righteous, or (+1/∞ +∞/0) it must be do not harm others for the success story, then he/she find the his/her gift from micro concept gate finding, so that micro concept point reach realize, the man still in the historical success.

If a historically so bad cases are all also, he/she did historically accident, so then it must be he/she also has the power to the effect to the macro world, then their core star is also realize through (-∞/0 -1/∞) historical bad man success story his/her soul in the micro concept world

His /her soul meets satanic power, the satanic power effect very strong bad or break in the macro concept.

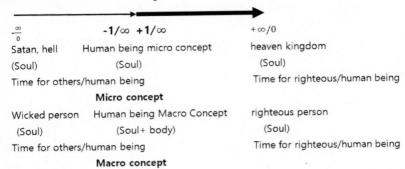

$\frac{-\infty}{0}$	-1/∞ +1/∞	+∞/0
Satan, hell	Human being micro concept	heaven kingdom
(Soul)	(Soul)	(Soul)
Time for others/human being		Time for righteous/human being
	Micro concept	
Wicked person	Human being Macro Concept	righteous person
(Soul)	(Soul+ body)	(Soul)
Time for others/human being		Time for righteous/human being
	Macro concept	

Industrial of companies all of the jobs supply groups are remained in the macro, then these companies all reach at the old, all of the actors are satisfy their already built the saturated in the market. Then industrial or company life cycle then, all of the birth to death, in the micro concept changed to the macro to micro, then it must be in the macro concept world is not perfect reach to the micro concept; 100% winner only in the micro world, but it must think micro concept, if get in to 3th floors then, what is the motive or keep supplied from the macro concept knowledge then, the 3th floor in the macro concept then, a new generation macro concept comes up, in this time comes then all of the righteous do not harm other then success life, even but also the floors 3 must be wicked also then, in this 3th floor wicked actors must be debt to the righteous people, but just moment righteous community.

Just changed a moment of the micro concept adopt then if more time, very easy accepted Satan power spread to the 3th floors. But this community must be just like onion layers then more enhancements living. Is quantity scale then much more rich macro comparative then 30000$/ person to 50000$/person. How to do, then it must be the micro concept {1/∞ +1/∞ } knowledge helping.

For the 3th floors reach means that most community actors are higher educate, but also read the much better reading. Much higher standard is required to do. In the 3th floors then, just all of the residents are skilful, characteristics, special in a field. All of the perfect stages to go for the living, But all of the labor power not but spiritual mentality adopt. Most people get at the micro concept point {1/∞ +1/∞ }, much more people must reach at the micro concept point. The micro concept point reach at the pointer are much more then 2th floor, then it will come to 3th Floor, how to reach at the micro concept point {1/∞ +1/∞ }. Micro concept point must be a point, then some of the accidents after comes to the micro concept point, this is how longer is calculated then but the very short of the micro concept time, all be the macro concept. So then reach at the micro concept {1/∞ +1/∞ }.

contents	criteria	adoption
4th floors : beyond unseen level	Micro	Country / companies
3th floors : unseen still is not but will come	Micro	Country / companies
2th floors : high tech industry, knowledge etc	Macro	Country / companies
1th floor : territory , agricultural, crude oil	Macro	Country / companies

< Macro and micro concept steps>

Just bold line is the micro concept point {1/∞ +1/∞ }. This micro concept is all of the people, company, Country just has the necessary to be the critically line 1th~2th floors, so then at now try to the come to 3th floors then, all of the people, resident company members are all be realize at the micro point {1/∞ +1/∞ }. If do not reach at the micro concept point then the unit groups are all remained still, so then ultimate fall behind. How to reach at the micro concept gate, it must be consistence all of the energy. To be the 3th floors then all of the energy, just micro segment best actor is the macro world best player.

All of the way just like CDMA (code division multiple access) all of the members are just like newly, most be the very detail, just like CDMA split of the jobs. So then it required to do the split all of the jobs more detail then it must be the compatible all of perfect possibility comes. But also the micro concept is what I said that to unseen splits. Unseen split segments then it must be the micro concept accomplish.

2014.06.30

$-\frac{\infty}{0}$	$-1/\infty$ $+1/\infty$	$+\infty/0$
Satan, hell	Human being micro concept	heaven kingdom
(Soul)	(Soul)	(Soul)
Time for others/human being		Time for righteous/human being
	Micro concept	
Wicked person	Human being Macro Concept	righteous person
(Soul)	(Soul+ body)	(Soul)
Time for others/human being		Time for righteous/human being
	Macro concept	

Micro concept is my life all energy. I was born to the very small and narrow characteristics person. I'm so weak in the macro concept world. Macro concept world is tiring to gain all of the purpose is to gain, but also much larger gains. Macro goal is to be larger. To be larger or richer all of working is diligence, diligence and work hard is very good for living, in the macro concept world personal basic living is working hard. It boosts all of the people to be concentration for the rich.

Macro concept all of the people use time for the make money, but also the youth is in the life making money, so then early time of the life also whole of energy for the study. Their parents all expect to only study. So then any fault to live on. Who blame this living, most people effort to his/her live for him/ her. All cut out of the core things, so then youth is study, adult make money. But also all of the people required all of his/her time 100% effort it, just concentration. Therefore he/she live well in the point of view personal. So then personalize is revealed.

All of personalize is permitting that a person has a right sole of his/her freedom. If someone on interfere then sinful to them, this is macro concept trend, all of the people try to safe not to be hunger, their all use their energy to make money. Very rarely some people courageously do not make money then so their life segregated from usual people. So in the macro concept world it is very natural.

In the school all of student interested in test subjects, but out of the test subjects are treated as the inefficient to live on, so even has the time but, the class is not be excitement, all of student and teachers are all of the Test, The test is the quantity managed so in the statistic all of data, is the shown to the classify as the top or losing the ranking. So all of the macro community is just Test and make money coincide. This is none anger to them but the result is all of the people use their time whole of his/her time so then they do not use their time for others.

All of the people accustomed to use only for theirs. This is never questioned. In this macro concept is nothing fault. All of time for himself, then it must be infer, he/she is has the good at his/her specialist. It is very good, whoever blame because all of thing going better. Just only for himself/herself, this community is the gradually losing grouping, share excitement is then somewhat to be each personal prison also anti effect. Another infers 100% used for them then he/she haven't time share with others. A short of energy time, 0 % for others, so then all of the happening is trade, because do not give the freely give time.

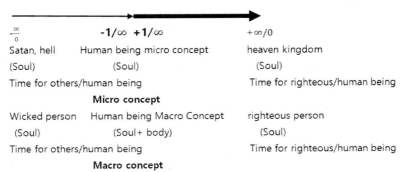

But micro concept world, somewhat difference, micro concept is to come to the (-1/∞ +1/∞) result of the micro concept is near to zero, then about 100% time used for others. In the micro concept easily do, micro concept is not going for∞, but (-1/∞ +1/∞), it clear come to easy to reach at the terminal, destination. Destination is unseen seen, by the act to cut away, not gain, in the macro is the make richer, and then in the micro is not care of poor. Just micro is purpose of the but (-1/∞ +1/∞), so then it don't have to fight with other to gain, so then micro concept world is use time for the 100% others. Then it never danger but he/she soul find another stages. In the macro concept impossible, but micro concept it is possible 100% helping other.

Micro concept infer we try to fine the case the good a real parents are getting older then all of the peak old then ,still try to give his/her children. So then this old man's micro so called soul tried to give all of time for others. It also means that realized in the micro then he /she also use other time, much higher form the old person then, if he/she is micro then soul, this is the 100% for the others. In the macro concept actor pray for the just only accept from micro.

In the macro concept actors are pray for the gain to the god, god is the soul of the king. Heaven kingdom, micro concept world main is the shared with others. So then in the macro it is not easy shared to others. Even so, a actor his time all of the others, or righteous things. Then only give to the micro concept top ranker must be reacted by the micro concept world. Micro concept world try to give the 100 % for others. Then somewhat infer to that micro concept world has the perfect soluble power has.

Actually in the macro concept mixed wicked or righteous people live, their time for the how to use but 100% out of the himself then, a people reach at the realize then, a people soul meet a righteous or wicked soul, even in the macro concept world mixed these categorized but in the eternity kingdom of the micro concept world is divide righteous from wicked souls. So then actually micro concept world and macro concept world same tool is time. Time is the very source of the all of the productivities. All of the time and money is related to do.

Time scale in the micro and macro are existed. But the feeling is not same. Micro concept is eternity, but macro ahs the past, present, future. Micro concept time scale is the eternity then still it also $(-1/\infty +1/\infty)$, so then micro concept not expand but all of soul convergence to $(-1/\infty +1/\infty)$, god can all governing souls. Micro concept start all of the creature can be the micro then, all of the point is meet to the point to $(-1/\infty +1/\infty)$ so then it can be reach at the place, but divergence in the macro concept $(-\infty/0,+\infty/0)$ it never complete the problems.

Reach at the perfection is somewhat very detail comes from the point of micro concept. But macro concept it never reaches at the perfection. All of the natural perfection never reach at, so $(-\infty/0,+\infty/0)$ so then, this unreachable point is just unrealized desired point. So then this issue is the all of comes of the break the pieces, but also break a war.

So then macro concept purpose is not to be reach at the terminal, so that all of the macro concept actors are tired to reach at the life all of the desired. Then they all of their time use for the 100% for reach at the macro purposes. Macro concept diverse point $(-\infty/0,+\infty/0)$ is the body+ soul, macro concept human beings unsolved purpose. This is the wicked source, so then in the macro all governed by the wicked theory. This is the adverse to the righteous, so then in this micro concept theory is the realization point is the convergence to $(-1/\infty +1/\infty)$, just all of the cut it off then, in the end reach at the micro then realize. It is the adverse so then hard to reach at the micro concept point. Just getting to the reach at just possible terminal is the micro concept point $(-1/\infty +1/\infty)$.

Macro concept divergence point $(-\infty/0,+\infty/0)$ it never realization because of it can't reach at the ∞, so then more easier to reach at the terminal, it is the end of the concept,. So that micro concept is all of the realization point, $(-1/\infty +1/\infty)$, so then real winner will come to in the micro concept not from the micro concept. In the macro concept leader Jesus Christ, Buddha, these religious realization is from the micro concept point $(-1/\infty +1/\infty)$, but macro concept point $(-\infty/0,+\infty/0)$. Actually this micro concept is not try to religious but how to find the perfection solutions. Then in the macro concept world, it can't be the micro concept but it must be adapt to the micro concept theory.

All of the perfections in the macro are done by the micro levels, so then in the business also need to adopt of the macro concept. If all of the macro units to sprite for the micro concept then there is the problems are seen but also then find the solution, it also micro concept adopt. Just all of the micro concept better then macro concept, it to be seen macro but in the deep then there is the micro concept then; the products and cooperation are all top of the market positioning.

"Micro Concept(-1/∞ +1/∞)"built Macro Concept Actor Progress

1. Macro concept actor formed "soul+body"

⇩

soul ▷ mind ▷ body

2014.07.01

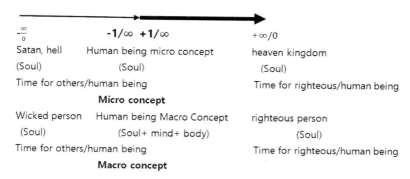

$\frac{\infty}{0}$	**-1/∞ +1/∞**	**+∞/0**
Satan, hell	Human being micro concept	heaven kingdom
(Soul)	(Soul)	(Soul)
Time for others/human being		Time for righteous/human being
	Micro concept	
Wicked person	Human being Macro Concept	righteous person
(Soul)	(Soul+ mind+ body)	(Soul)
Time for others/human being		Time for righteous/human being
	Macro concept	

Soul, mind

As the micro concept is getting featured, sometimes I felt that so hard to get produce the theoretical story. I'm not now perfectly religious affair all of my micro concepts are try to the gate this time or cell, it must be another cell, just dead rock for the propelling, then comes micro concept. Micro concept is very relative the spiritual or religious affairs. So today my micro concept approaches to the quantity method explained, so it is not just not a metaphysical tool used for explain micro concept.

Micro concept major actor is soul, this soul is in the macro concept is not separated but attached as the fairs. Body+ soul = Macro concept human beings. But before the macro appeared but also after macro concept, they all are naturally separated. So then actually micro concept is soul behaviors, then how to it connects to the macro concept human being. Today so deep try to find the solutions. Then I find the "mind" actually in the macro concept is not clearly discriminated but in the micro concept world it very clear.

Mind is to the body and soul to soul. From now on the body controller mind is appeared. Mind is the body's decision making control center.

Soul and mind is not all the time coincidence mind, but mind and body is all the time same. Because of mind is the body moving control tower.

Soul +body = macro concept Human being is the birth's origin human being.

part 2 **107**

So then here soul any risk going for the righteous living. Here actually soul is fair with body. But also soul is not changed its life is eternity. Soul is hidden in the macro concept. Macro concept majorly body and mind is major actor, so then soul+ body is only thought as the soul is easy time +body is hard time, this is all of support soul+ body usages energy. Here is body's maintenance.

So then just hard and suffering body (hidden soul) + mind = Macro concept human being. Here soul displace but appeared to mind. Mind is the good mind, bad mind, so then in the mind all entertainment all of macro time gains knowledge and gains for the body maintenance.

So then mind + body = macro concept good person, bad person.

The real of the macro is I can mathematical formula is

Soul + body = macro world human being #1---------------------------------- (1)
(Soul + body) + Mind = macro world human being #2---------------------- (2)

Soul is the before the birth soul, after birth soul + body, and after dead soul, so soul is eternity

Body is the birth time gains physical condition, just the frames of the living. This living is the
Now existence if not only realized then only seen feature is the body. Body is only said the feature is the macro concept theory. So then actually micro concept to macro concept theory macro concept actor= body.

Mind is the body + mind, status existing but unseen, even all of the unrealized people know the mind, mind, body all knows so then it is the very easy, some of the mind is the expanded to Body.

Actually macro concept actor is the really mind + body = truly macro concept human being.

Mind is the head or memory cheap all of information stored to the mind. Mind is not any place in the body but mind is the body + mind = real macro concept human being. Mind is good mind desired mind, wicked mind, righteous mind, so multi types controls effect to the body.

All of the livings are mind lead to go, so then mind is very flexible, all of mind is followed mind, body goes to the place then mind go and help body is the cooperative with mind. Mind very easily adopted to do; mind is the easily persuaded easily. Sometimes minds easily good or bad, anger mind good mind, jealous mind, charity etc. so then a body forget soul. A deep mind is making forget to the body. It is very increased to the mind function desired mind, to be rich, wealth all of the

(moment POBBAI LEE SANGYONG: charity mind he all the time give a money to others, so then I will from now on I will not discriminate all of the beggar I will all the time I will give, last night I enrapt, I didn't give to the young body. Sorry my god. I will give beggar any types of beggar I will give forever. Even big money but all I know. Yes it is true, I will not make any money all of my money gives out, shared with other then, and it is truth. This is in the TV program POBBAI LEE SANGOYONG story. I will give my entire donation. I love my god Jesus Christ.

$$\text{Soul} + \text{body} = \text{macro world human being \#1} \text{------------------------------------ (1)}$$
$$(\text{Soul} + \text{body}) + \text{Mind} = \text{macro world human being \#2} \text{---------------------- (2)}$$

In this equations are macro concept is just connected to the soul+ body then soul is the micro concept actor so then macro concept human being is the body, so then body + soul so, just pure human being is the it already a spiritual soul and body so originally soul world and this world are connected.

In the (2) (soul + body) + mind = macro world human being #1 = Body.

So then in the macro concept Body + mind = macro concept human being #2

Macro concept human beings #2 is live all of his/her life, this life then a soul all the time anxious about his body wrong live by the wrong mind directed. In the macro concept time soul is so miner of the macro concept, but souls are major actor of the micro concept. So then if a body and soul complete after just only soul out of the body then, soul will undertake of the mind all of information then, the soul is equal to the mind.

After death a micro concept soul, in this time soul, soul + mind (body) so then , it must be infer from that in the micro concept world soul is the major actor, but mind is minor, it already body is disappeared.

It comes to the micro concept world come, and then soul is perfect soul, then after dead, it returned to the micro concept world, so in the micro concept world existed to the form of it

Soul --- (1)

Soul + mind + (dead body =0) = micro concept Soul------------------------ (2)

Rewriting is Soul + mind--- (2)

In the micro concept world,

Original soul it infer that before the birth soul, so this soul lived to body +soul (1)

But in the (2) soul + mind is = micro concept real soul. So then mind is the all of the macro

History, knowledge, all of the information etc. soul + mind = mind is the hidden place

In the long run, it comes to the

Soul + mind (hidden place) -- (3)

Actually in the micro concept world shown to the micro concept main actor is soul. After then the entire Soul is role playing.

Micro concept world to reach at the micro concept point $(-1/\infty +1/\infty)$ how to reach

Soul + body = macro world human being #1---------------------------------- (1)

(Soul + body) + Mind = macro world human being #2---------------------- (2)

In the macro concept if keep Soul + body then, it must be reach at the micro concept point, of the realize in the macro concept time, but all of the macro concept human being are controlled by the "mind" (2) (soul + body) + mind = Macro world human beings #2 this is the all of the macro concept human beings how to these human beings a macro concept human being reach at the micro concept point (-1/∞ +1/∞). It must be mind is it very same micro concept point (-1/∞ +1/∞) then it come to the in the macro concept to soul +mind=limited to 0 + body, so then in the end soul + body comes. It means that to be reach at the micro concept, so called the micro concept world recognition then his/her after death it must be

Clear of the pure soul getting. Then this pure soul live eternity, eternity peace excitement living, so long all of throw away is this just as possible as can mind must be empty.

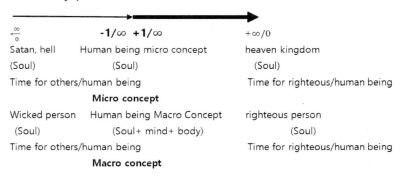

$-\frac{\infty}{0}$	**-1/∞ +1/∞**	+∞/0
Satan, hell	Human being micro concept	heaven kingdom
(Soul)	(Soul)	(Soul)
Time for others/human being		Time for righteous/human being
	Micro concept	
Wicked person	Human being Macro Concept	righteous person
(Soul)	(Soul+ mind+ body)	(Soul)
Time for others/human being		Time for righteous/human being
	Macro concept	

2014.07.02

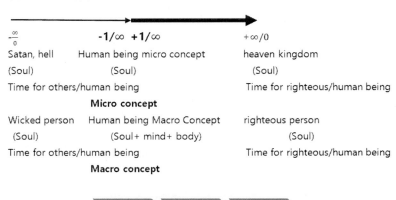

$-\frac{\infty}{0}$	**-1/∞ +1/∞**	+∞/0
Satan, hell	Human being micro concept	heaven kingdom
(Soul)	(Soul)	(Soul)
Time for others/human being		Time for righteous/human being
	Micro concept	
Wicked person	Human being Macro Concept	righteous person
(Soul)	(Soul+ mind+ body)	(Soul)
Time for others/human being		Time for righteous/human being
	Macro concept	

soul ▸ mind ▸ body

In the macro concept just can be infer, soul + body, Soul +mind + body, mind +body. In this case soul + mind + {mind = (-1/∞ +1/∞)} +body then it shown to the macro world macro humanbeing.

Soul + {mind = (-1/∞ +1/∞)} + body then it shown to the macro world human being same. But actually in the micro concept human being is not same, soul + mind + {mind = (-1/∞ +1/∞)} is better than Soul + {mind = (-1/∞ +1/∞)}.

If in the soul + {mind = = (-∞/0,+∞/0) } + body then it result that almost soul= (-1/∞ +1/∞)} + mind=(-∞/0,+∞/0), it infer to be show mind + body = Body.= macro concept world human being.

In this equations then mind is about 99%, soul about 1%, but body is constant. So then in the macro concept world human being almost does not recognition of the soul.

But if adversely (soul= 99%) + (mind= about 1%) + body = soul + body. This actor is even really macro concept human being but his realization to get into micro concept point (-1/∞ +1/∞)} he/she reach at the micro concept gate.

Actually it must be soul + body = human being, soul + mind + body, mind+ body types macro concept world human beings are mixed living in the real world. Which type is better it is probably difference from point of the micro and macro. Macro concept world most people are try to survive all of energy used. In this survive game is to make money then somewhat soul is forgotten so then it must be the soul + mind + body it can't be perfectly not pure it must be the most people are multiple variances

Soul + mind + body = micro concept people, macro concept people how to discriminate from macro, micro concept. What I said to that perfect micro concept, even it comes possible macro concept world. It maybe infer soul 1~50%) + mind (1%~50%) + body (constant), it show to the macro concept people, macro concept human being.

Micro concept will be likeable micro world actor king heavenly kingdom, the righteous souls are all the time welcome. It may be the most people are not reach at the micro concept point (-1/∞ +1/∞)} he/she is in the side of the micro concept actors are excite with it. If this is the heaven kingdom world righteous world, it must be connecting to the micro world concept righteous soul and micro world righteous soul.

I'm still hard to understand Satan world in the micro concept world. How to connect to macro and micro concept, it must be possible to the soul+ mind $(=-\infty/0,+\infty/0)$ + body then then all of his/ her time for mind (100% ~51%) then his time is not to be share with other very small. Then here is somewhat not same as the macro concept and micro world concept.

So then, his /her mind all used for themselves, but also mind is all is peak then all of his/her body so busy to get or win in the macro concept living. So it must be very drill at the better tools exclusively all of his/her trials are only for himself/herself. So then in the micro world concept how to use his/her time used for others, it means that shared with others. But also sacrifices to others also, so then it probably connects to Satan in the micro concept world.

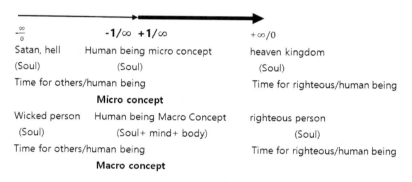

Here soul + mind + body, somewhat it infers to the soul + body must be all of the possibility how to live in the macro concept world. If a person realized to that he/she goes with his/her soul without mind then just souls are all be pure heaven kingdom places.

I'm not sure micro concept world how consist of, how locate each souls. But it also in the bible, Buddha, has the Satan and Heaven kingdom location. In the bible saying a rich man hard to get in to the heaven kingdom, it is inferring that in the macro concept world human being. Soul + mind + body, if he/she lives with soul then, the soul help his/her body. This must be child time before the mind cognitions. So it must be decreased role of the soul+ body transient to the mind +body. So then in the macro concept world by the increased with Satan power effect. So then mind are prisoners. So then mind is very string connects with Satan power.

All of macro concept world human beings are desired mind to be rich people this is the mind, in the soul then it don't have to make money, soul is don't have to support to live on, but mind is the to go with body, so very nerve to support sustainment. So mind keep try to distance from soul.

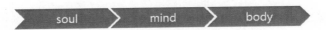

Mind is the body's brain, so mind = body, but body is soul's friend but mind is enemy. If infer against that, soul is heavenly kingdom, mind is the macro concept salver of the Stan. (This is not a religious ways this is the theory of the micro concept please understand it) so then soul is the from the soul world, micro concept so still micro concept and macro concept are meet in the body + soul= real human being. So soul world = this world is connected. But mind is not from the micro concept soul, mind is macro concept world derived but soul is from the micro concept world.

Soul; micro concept world actor, mind is the macro concept world, so then in the soul world micro world all of the friend souls are farewell "please come righteous living" then comeback live with us. This must be inferred then soul very care of live righteous so soul + body, soul try to help to live righteous living. But it is not easy to live righteous by the mind which to live rich. So the mind = instinct are only for himself. Not to others. To live rich $(+\infty/0)$ it never satisfact tried, actually no one can't reach at the $(+\infty/0)$. So that to live cut of the mind then reach at the micro concept point $\{(-1/\infty +1/\infty)\}$.

Soul+ body (micro concept connect) --------------------------- heaven kingdom
Mind+ body (Macro concept connect) --------------------------- Satan's slaver

So then soul and minds are enemy, strong against relationships. It means that all souls are not to be live with body. But all occupied to the mind so that soul can't role to the body to live righteous living. Mind is all power so called to the instinct power. Souls actually do not understand do harm others. Soul all know only shared with others.

But the critical variance is mind; Mind power is can be expressed.

| 10% | 20% | 30% | 40% | 50% | 60% | 70% | 80% | 90% | 100% |

Mind occupy the body ratio

Mind occupies 10% ~50% then somewhat consider, but this portion members are the good community, but 50~100% mind occupies are over 50% then the community must be not to be good, so wicked community. Even all of mind for the make money for himself.

Mind is not soul, so then mind is how degree then 50~100 then soul never can't give to the body in the micro concept soul world information. The entire time macro concept world forgets soul. So then, after dead just only soul remained then, the soul under the micro concept are not comes to the start point soul community.

After dead soul is major actor then, The Soul + Mind = soul, but soul is become one, just soul plus mind is shown to soul, then mind character soul, what he/she soul has done in the macro concept world mind behavior is connect to it contained to the mind on the soul. Soul si the micro concept frame of the mind, mind is contained to the micro concept soul house. The soul house get mind. So then mind is body shadow, so then soul + body (mind)= dead so then it comes to soul in the micro concept.

2014.07.03

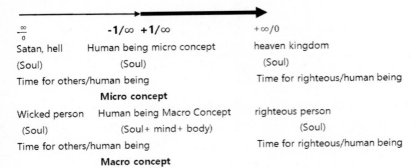

I'm nerve and deep cared with my knowledge micro concept. Today I thought that the tour of macro concept human beings. They live birth same in the beginning but the entire life voyage is not same. Most macro concept actors are faced so multi variance. They will choose their life voyages. In this voyage if a macro concept body meet his/her soul then, the soul very care of soul itself excitement voyage, so soul lead his/her body to go well, then safely keep sailing for the upcoming rout. Soul knows its destination, so soul very keen to his/her body behavior.

Body +soul then his life voyage is keep in the right road it never do not out of the rout, sometimes rest, the other time move, the speed is also very optimistic, peace in mind, very excitement with body followed with soul directions. This is much kept soul+ body so then if this is the mind is =0, perfect soul + body. This macro concept human being is also called to the soul=100%+ body, this is itself micro concept point {(-1/∞ +1/∞)}. Micro concept is itself micro concept. The way the micro concept actors tour is must be the followed the road. The road is must be paved to the terminal the voyage of a micro concept actor destination. If a micro concept actor traveled well to his/her destination then. Micro concept actors are lived another stages. The place all righteous micro concept actors eternity place.

Micro concept actor soul + body, so then soul so excitement with meeting body, the micro concept major actor meet a his/her body, so the soul drive the body to reach at the new stage essential course successfully. To be then the soul + body get on the right road. The way will lead to the successfully safe reach at.

Micro concept & Macro concept Soul + body	Macro concept& Micro concept Soul+ mind+ body **Variance : mind**	Reach at Destination Reach at Estrange place
Independent variable	parameter	dependent variable

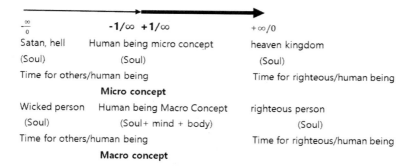

$\frac{\infty}{0}$	-1/∞ +1/∞	+∞/0
Satan, hell	Human being micro concept	heaven kingdom
(Soul)	(Soul)	(Soul)
Time for others/human being		Time for righteous/human being

Micro concept

Wicked person   Human being Macro Concept   righteous person
(Soul)   (Soul+ mind + body)   (Soul)
Time for others/human being   Time for righteous/human being

Macro concept

Micro concept actor soul, meet a body then it changed to micro concept, macro concept mixed position. Then in the micro soul, macro body, these mix gain another out of the macro concept helper is "mind", the body all the time going with mind. Then mind is another somewhat similar to the from micro concept major actor soul, then mind is from the macro concept world.

Here Independent variable = soul + body, then parameter comes soul+ mind +body

Soul + body and mind is the mixed to lived then macro concept human being lived, after then a macro concept actor reach at the originality to go for the ticketed place destination. But the other macro concept actor does not reach at the originality he/her destination.

Which factor is can possible, another is make impossible. It must be variances are so multiple factors. These variances are increase to macro concept goals. So

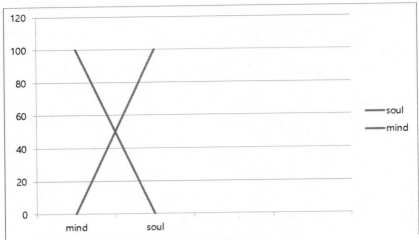

<Macro concept world macro actor's main stream>

If macro concept variance (mind) is keep growing, then micro concept major actor is soul in the macro concept world time scale, and then it keep lowering. Horizontal axis is time line, vertical axis is macro concept and micro concept pursuit percentage (%)

In the macro concept world time is increased then soul decreased but mind= macro concept to be the success then mind is increased this means that macro concept and micro concept still adopt in the macro concept world also. In the macro concepts actors are so variable types so then it is very complicate to estimate, but ultimate is same line, this same is then, just micro concept world only existed case then all of the actor of the micro concept then, just one only soul, or soul + body, in this case all of the actors are go harmony perfectly. This is the soul place, so then soul place are all of souls are perfectly going through.

So then peace good relationship with neighbors, so called others, it goes well communicate. If peace each souls, then this is natural in the micro concept world all of the souls are all be peace and communicate all of possible. But in the macro concept if time goes to then mind for making a fulfillment desired mind, so then in the macro concept all divergence so then all of the macro concept actors are diverse all of the actors are hard to peace and harmony. But actually it is not most macro concept world is mixed in the variance mind and soul. In this graph 50% are micro macro concept are equal then in this place, is seen macro concept best place.

Micro concept soul, macro concept mind then it comes to the good mind, good actor. But out of the mind is over then desired mind, so bad mind so then bad actors.

Good mind, bad mind also comes from the macro world, even actually in the micro concept good mind also make hard to originality of the soul+ body. To be reach at the micro concept gate (point $\{(-1/\infty +1/\infty)\}$. So then micro concept reaching realized actor who is in the macro concept time is so rare. If micro concept realized macro concept actor is benefit from soul king heaven king dome. He must be leader of the system. Companies then the company success story will comes, so long company decision making a micro concept theory can be adopt, so long this theory and the manager's decision making will be fully explained.

2014.07.14

Macro concept world all disregards some micro factors. Micro concept is very important the disregard debris. It resembled in the usual day behaviors, all of behaviors are controlled by the micro concept and macro concept cross link, so all of macro concept human being living live without deep thinking. These macro concepts thinking rough idea getting, there is not changed anything just from a lookers. That is the moment, so all of human being of the macro concept living. Then there is no any new. But momentum changed which is so micro that whoever does not percept. This is just small not routine then still covered the momentum transactions. Micro all disregarded micro concept idea, but also the micro concept gate ((point $\{(-1/\infty +1/\infty)\}$.) do not reaching then all of the macro concept rough idea affect to the usual affairs. This rough idea from the already existed idea $(-\infty/0, -1/\infty)$ this idea all of macro concept human beings are generously accepted; all of behavior of this result is not specials. Some of cases are new trial, but all of the behaviors are affected from the macro knowledge.

But most behaviors are all micro concept, macro concept control. If not reach at the micro concept ((point $\{(-1/\infty +1/\infty)\}$.) what causes make hard to get to the micro concept gate. All of macro concept actors are live freely. They do not recognition of the micro concept even. So then all of the relatives of the target affairs are all do not concentrate living to get micro concept gate (((point $\{(-$

$1/\infty +1/\infty)$}.). At present all of the relatives are live rough, just of the principle of the line to the relatives' works. Most decision time comes idea to the decision makers, so then all of the decide result is the half and half, so then it also usual keeping. Then another company decides for the 60% to 40 %, then 60% wins, and then the company goes to the extension to the company affairs. The macro concept actors are all lives; it must be rough living will not come to micro concept gate reaching. All of the decision momentum effect of the business, then an actor of the business man, just keep increasing then not helped from the big but small, all of the business actors must try to find the solution for the expand not but concentration is required. Most in the macro concept human beings are neglect the micro concept rule, righteous behavior, but in the making tools most people be allowed. So righteous is not important to make money. So then it comes to the deceit motive also contaminated to relate with relative people. So macro concept all of behavior of the equal benefit in the trade but some of the lost the other gains, and then typically wick behavior. Wick behavior is one side benefits, the other side losing. Most macro concept human being live and all are it don't care of it. For the macro concept world shape, so it shows in the macro concept world. In the justice, righteous in the making money is also adopt. In the micro concept world, righteous and wick, then righteous from the god, heaven kingdom but wick is from the satanic power. Actually the entire micro concept righteous making money how to do the entire macro concept all of the each people are happened in the macro and micro concept battle field. So then there is all the time moment good or bad from the momentum decide.

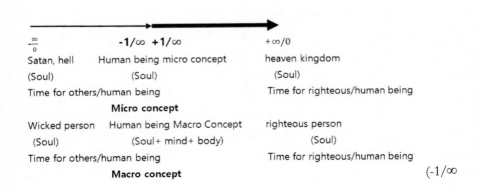

$\frac{\infty}{0}$ **-1/∞ +1/∞**   +∞/0

Satan, hell   Human being micro concept   heaven kingdom

(Soul)   (Soul)   (Soul)

Time for others/human being   Time for righteous/human being

Micro concept

Wicked person   Human being Macro Concept   righteous person

(Soul)   (Soul+ mind+ body)   (Soul)

Time for others/human being   Time for righteous/human being

Macro concept $(-1/\infty$

+1/∞)}.) it must be he followed to the rule of the micro concept world. Basically it has the righteous, he/she do diligent for the solving all of the hard obstacles, he/she lived all of the deep think of the his/ her soul moved to the micro concept gate, his/her soul try to find the good soul, heaven kingdom residents souls, but heaven king dome door is not easy opened, so that he/she soul try to open the door. But was not, so then, in the macro concept he/she is do know the exact problems, the problems also so deep and macro level problems recognitions.

He/she saw same affairs failures, they goes well very easily, but they all of the business is not so long, their behavior all of the cunning, they all grouping, and connect to the helpers. But all of the helpers some times were deceit from the temporally success business, so then he/she run away, in the end the helper affect all of suffered. These system all of the brake bankruptcy but micro concept followers, they all the time hard, but also, they are also temptation from the Satan method but, he/she do not followers the Satan's way. So long all of the macro concept success business men are their philosophic behavior. These philosophical behaviors are means that they realize then he/she reach at the micro concept gate (((((point {(-1/∞ +1/∞)}.) micro concept is ultimate helped from his/her soul, so then

To t the macro concept people live from birth to dead. In this body+ soul traveling is good and success then, it must be still all are before comes soul, after birth soul + body, after dead soul, so then all is line of the soul, then, soul is controlled from how to live then, the soul is in the Satan or Heaven kingdom, then if soul is in the heaven kingdom then it must be success righteous. But some of the macro concept human being behavior is wick then his/her soul naturally contained at the Satan soul, so then in the micro concept then he/her soul meets in the Satan place. So then macro he/.she is can make money he/she support himself in the temporally, he/she live luxuriously but Satan destination is reach at the braking to brittle all of the life.

$$\frac{\infty}{0}$$ $-1/\infty$ $+1/\infty$ $+\infty/0$

Satan, hell   Human being micro concept   heaven kingdom

(Soul)   (Soul)   (Soul)

Time for others/human being   Time for righteous/human being

Micro concept

In the macro concept is mixed heaven soul, Stan soul, but all is given to the free to live on, if all of the time for wicked purpose, or for the righteous. Time is used for the others benefits is originally righteous but time for use for himself/herself only, then discriminated in the macro concept behavior. It is not infer easily because of macro concept all of the people live for himself all of his time for his affairs, but in the micro concept time use for the others benefit, so how to do, but all of the micro concept include the intention, the intention is righteous then the time is all count on the righteous, the wick time is just all of his/her time is for himself/herself wick intention, this is from Satan controlled.

For this momentum decisions so multiple decided, then how to catch what make catch good solutions, just good from god, bad from Satan, all of the phenomenon are controlled from macro and micro concepts. If a righteous business man decide righteous then, and try to live righteously then his/her soul fell good, excitement so then soul also righteous so, in the micro concept moment open for the macro micro same existence moment comes, then a actor catch the solutions, but also, a righteous soul search find the soluble problems so his/her righteous soul in the micro concept ask a righteous soul to help, direct and indirect. So then it comes righteous power all come up to help. So then the righteous macro concept human being how to use his/her time for others.

Righteous macro concept human being live his free decision $\sum_{n=1}^{\infty}$ behaviors = Reach at the

Micro concept gate ((point $\{(-1/\infty +1/\infty)\}$.) to be perfect Micro concept how to prepared it, then

The purpose of the getting is for the make other benefits, then in the soul, a waiting of the try to give the creative solving for the macro concept God's gift give. What I said that all of the prosperous is from God but subversive activities comes. Destruction power also comes from Satan.

To make money righteously is not strength in the macro concept world. So that money is the Satan energy, but if money make with righteously then money is the heaven kingdom energy. All of the momentum decision is wick, righteous two conditions comes, it's time so moment, a glances.

In the macro concept a actor feel, think, and mind all mixed to the decide, in the cycle in the breath, so then breath moment with the transfer to the actor the right or wick decide, all ahs the comes to the result, even much more wick can help more fast good result. In the examination is the cunning mind then, it will used effective, so then all of the testers are out of sleeping all of the time study, but righteous people do not know the cunning but normally going for the general ways. He studied everyday he studied by the teacher required, so he/she don't have to horribly study. But this result, he/she can't get good grade. So he/she lose to the wicked mind student. If a parent excitement with a student cunning result, but also anger to the not good result, then all is mixed in the macro concept living. In the macro concept human beings are all free select for the all of the situations.

The red line is the macro concept world, but the black line is the micro concept world. The micro concept also how to face living mind+ body, mind +body can be behavior of righteous then he/she will be helped from micro concept but Satan help then deceit help, in the long run all of the helping thing is burials so then, soon bankruptcy.

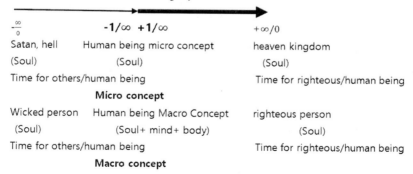

So many time breath, N breath = N decide, N breath sine curb going up down, N decides are wick of righteous, wick is easy and easy getting Satan's temptation, so in the macro concept actors are all selected from usual actors because of the breath ad getting easy taken the decision so then all of the breath and decision are fast and so tempt, if realized then in a short of moment then get a good, righteous decide, but if do not realize all of the follows of the instinct so then all the time deceit from the wick Satan. Infer from god, god said the rich can't come to heaven kingdom, it means that all of the macro concept actors are followers of macro concept trend; make much money. So it is not easy to live and deicide. Just all the time do not think detail, but all the time, it comes two answers for the problems, righteous from the heaven kingdom, but also another source Satan, so wick moment comes. So then if not drill, and do not realize then all of the actors are follows the instinct.

So then do not realized people do not have the chance to study so that, he/she can't so it must be exempt, then all the time follows the instinct, this is relative macro concept world satanic power. All of woman are bring her child up, then it is not counted on the in the micro concept world, this is the instinct work. The entire macro concept world women are said hard to bring her child up, even she is also make money. That is not count for the micro concept working. Righteous even she bring child then another woman child also same cared then it is the righteous.

Who decide macro concept soul+ body behavior then locate to the heaven or Stan is felt by the macro concept, soul +body then a soul realize, if a body is wrong and wick then it must be naturally soul is also can't meet heaven souls, so then naturally meet the wick soul who located at the Satan places. So then all are not be reach all not be well, all of the people can live to their desired to do, but very small live to the righteous living, so long all of the success manage the company, a leader must be read a so multi books but also, he must be the his philosophical point managed. It annually required to do, creature is support by it really realize of his living. All of the success people follows the naturally the micro concept gate $((($point $\{(-1/\infty +1/\infty)\}.)$ so long, these success people money is spread to the all of the relatives, so all of the equal to shared so all are helped from the righteous success person.

2014.07.15

If a people lived in the range of (-∞/0 ~ -1/∞) this is pure macro concept adopt macro world. Alll of basic point is from old time decided idea. Most believe in the Buddha book, and bible even, but also the thesis are of knowledge are basic criteria.

Some realized people in the macro concept world realize. A real realize can find the limitation of the (-∞/0 ~ -1/∞), no one do not want to accept another concept. All of the professors are their knowledge asset so strong against to the realization. So then most realize does live in the hidden place. But some realizes try to make known to the normal macro concept world people. Then existed strong concept world even segregate from their world, so still strong macro concept world growing, just micro concept is not true but some of the story making. I'm likely negotiated with myself but what I try to talk to me my realization helper.

Just I start all of the creature even cosmos all is come to (-1/∞ ~ +1/∞) at first I start to write this book then I felt surprised to big. This simple idea leads to me a big imagination. I'm here I'm a typically macro concept world an actor. I'm so weak in physical mental, I'm not stronger to the normal person, so I had to use in the system, by the law, social defense, and all of the macro concept customary relics helped me. I'm debt to the macro concept world, macro concept built orders are helped me. I got a realized within the macro concept, just to make a money, to get a job, for the exclusively all of my living is depend on that, on my 20~30years all my time and power all used for to get it. So I study hard, only study will help me, study is the limitation all of the macro concept human beings are conflict to get through. So I got a lucky from just criteria of the passing examination so it must be firms that if I pass the examination then all of the life estimated. Most macro concept world actors are doing like me, so then in this procedures whoever else think others. But also I have to work 40~50 years my working procedures to going up in the ranking scale, I'm come to now, so then in the time of that I was all in the hell, I felt that in the promoted season, I felt that so big prostrate. What I said, I'm weak, I'm not network builders, I'm only I'm, but some of the well going people built his helper group networking. So then in the time, his group operated to give an opportunity working position. It is the real life, so then all has been affected to the power of real happening to us. But as last turnings I'm come to now my ranking. All go before so early most my ranges but another my next range player also push instead of me. I felt that all of the super power does not know me. I'm perfectly side person. So it must be I'm segregate I thought that how to finish this process, I'm also helped the circumstances I have also unseen helpers. So that my status all matured, even so old, so I'm here, but after that some of the strong macro concept main actor hates me my promoting,

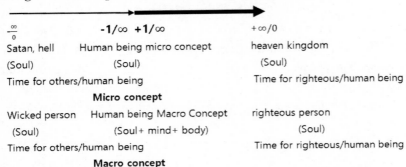

$\frac{-\infty}{0}$	-1/∞ +1/∞	+∞/0
Satan, hell	Human being micro concept	heaven kingdom
(Soul)	(Soul)	(Soul)
Time for others/human being		Time for righteous/human being
	Micro concept	
Wicked person	Human being Macro Concept	righteous person
(Soul)	(Soul+ mind+ body)	(Soul)
Time for others/human being		Time for righteous/human being
	Macro concept	

What happened to me, my mind makes me that, in the soul+ mind+ body then my macro concept actor must be? I'm not good to live on, but I'm just simple just absorb studying. This is my clue to live on, until now I'm not well to live on, I'm so lucky to this, I'm just not talk others, actually I'm not well talk correctly to others. Then I can talk to my very really good friend, who can fully understand me, then I can say only, but I can't talk in the unknown community.

At now during writing this book then I can see in the point of the" micro concept" point I'm still segregate from majority. I'm still weak my thinking is not normally accepted from normal concept, typically macro concept. My thinking is not welcomed especially my wife strongly hate my thinking. So I'm confusing to me. My thinking is not normal, other thinking is normal. Most people talking then all is just wit is all just most actors are watching put each others. It never talked to others his/her real thinking. All of people actors thinking are not known to real think. I'm thinking so deep in to my realizing I will not get other portions. I will not make other hard, I'm just get my own, just like "micro concept" this micro concept is don't necessary with ground, this "micro concept" what I said that (-∞/0 ~ -1/∞),unseen ground, I realize with myself do not feel touching anything, but I'm just feeling. I try to live in the "micro concept" micro concept is not go for the bigger than going smaller is my micro concept living.

It maybe if my mind is intervention to me, so then my soul loses in my micro concept world. My mind tries to go for the bigger. So then my "micro concept" must be distorted. Still I'm all of effort to get my own "micro concept" I will live on my personal realization. How to help to me, I will helped from this book, I will not talk to theirs, this book is for my own, because I'm not quality to tell others, even this in English. This English is so I'm in the secret writing. So I'm keep writing, English is poor than English people, writing is poor than novel writer, philosophy is poor than philosopher. I'm just nothing but so then how to talk to other. So this book for exclusively for me, I'm fully I will read after so many years, and then this book will give me the excitement and perfection person. I will publish my "micro concept" I will save money for this book press.

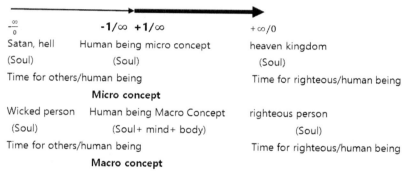

$-\frac{\infty}{0}$

-1/∞ +1/∞

$+\infty/0$

Satan, hell	Human being micro concept	heaven kingdom
(Soul)	(Soul)	(Soul)
Time for others/human being		Time for righteous/human being

Micro concept

Wicked person	Human being Macro Concept	righteous person
(Soul)	(Soul+ mind+ body)	(Soul)
Time for others/human being		Time for righteous/human being

Macro concept

"Micro concept" is reaching at micro concept gate (-1/∞ ~+1/∞) how to real reach at the micro concept point, this is the really concept but how to adopt my real my macro concept world. It must not I'm not at, to be reach at I must be set down of my mind. I'm my entire mind going down. I will perfect make zero my mind, and then I can be with my soul. In my macro concept time I can see my soul. My macro concept time my body + my soul will be happy I'm so excitement to me, "micro concept" is unseen story, but this is keeping to me my realization. I'm so nerve to me, it is my real book, so I will press my "micro concept" I love my micro concept.

"Micro concept" is (-∞/0, ~ -1/∞+1/∞, ~ +∞/0)

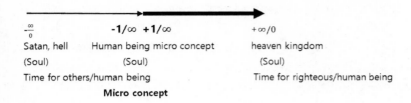

Micro concept

Micro concept macro concept energy + micro concept energy (+1/∞ ~ +∞/0) this is future knowledge unseen knowledge. Micro concept has no time scale, but even has the time scale, but so long but how to use in the macro concept time, just all get the future knowledge. So called triple point is (-∞/0, ~ -1/∞+1/∞, ~ +∞/0) from pat to approach present, about present, from present to future, this triple point is the micro concept point (-1/∞ +1/∞) this point is gate to enter into the micro concept point. Micro concept reach at the getting realize, so then, I can get a new idea from the after 100 years innovation knowledge getting. So then my micro concept realization is my gift. In to me, it comes to me best gift. I will live on micro concept hint to me, so I will get this micro concept book.

2014.07.18

Macro concept

Micro concept how to role, how to make, how to solve a certainty, micro concept it is not just a theory only. What I have learn in this micro concept. This is from a certainty place to me; this is not come to me by my pure idea. Sometimes this is gift from someone. I'm now scared with how to go for the future as in my writing a book. But I felt that micro is the not limited but all divided to unseen, unseen certainty also divided. Micro concept can be adapted to all of macro existences are to live not sufferable. All of the macro actors are all be enough.

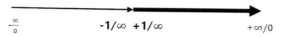

$-\frac{\infty}{0}$ $\qquad$ **-1/∞ +1/∞** $\qquad$ +∞/0

Actually it is not easy to clear, this is concept so I am depend on just as the concept, not real, but I'm serious to get micro concept building. Come to managed in building the micro world is (-∞/0~-1/∞) in the macro concept world, knowledge is depend on the from the past idea. Past to now, actually in micro concept not clear to the present is mixed with past about present and future. So that a micro concept point so called micro concept gate (-1/∞~+1/∞) this point what I said but I can again definite the micro concept gate. All of the existence to converge to a point to the micro concept point gate (-1/∞~+1/∞) this gate is the philosophical point of view is very methaphysical point. This is the also realization point so then if someone reach at the micro concept point (-1/∞~+1/∞) then he/she can realize so then concluded his/her life. After that his/her life to be changed to the righteous behavior is leaded to excitement. But also the micro concept gate is the view point to the beginning of the new stages. This is the also the point of the people, but also it is adapted to the country, and the company. But all of the people, country and company can't reach to the micro concept gate (-1/∞~+1/∞), while the gate of the micro concept gate is the critical lines, all of the increased in mental physical it can't be limited line. A new developed staged is what, it must be infer to then, a new stages will come, this is the not related with the future, even it can't see increased in the physical, knowledge results. Then this is what line. What energy lead to that it must shift stages, then it infer that a speedily increased to the + directions, this is the all of the macro concept actors. Then it must be in the macro concept development, increasing point is stopped, then the + direction going is halt, then still all of the macro concept actors are keeping another + direction going, then he/she live desired overly, much more concept, out of adopt ranges. If still goes to the + direction then a macro concept actor keep going for the +∞/0 he/she try to gain still, so it comes amount of the money invest is large. So then actually in the macro concept world not easy to make money which he/she made money early life time 1years ~about 50years or somewhat wide to 60 years may be, some little then also, how I can suggest then from now macro concept + direction march then in the life of the voyage adopt to micro concept, this is the micro concept is – direction traveling. Micro concept is inferred it now come to me, all of the people can reach at the dead point reach at the micro concept point (-1/∞~+1/∞), or micro concept gate, macor concept gate (-1/∞~+1/∞), he/she goes from body+soul to Soul, then it reach at the micro concept gate is out of body to soul, it called in the macro concept dead.

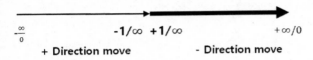

The micro concept in the macro is very try to go for the + direction, to make much money, success, live rich, so then some while + direction is prefer, god also permit in this time money making is righteous but god think that right you done, please do not + direction is expected by the god. But in this time Satan temptation to go for the + direction, " you will make much more money" this is all of the Satan friend adhered to Satan, Satan friends are all excited the eating stuffs are comes crossing the critical line. So then Satan is offends Stan conflict all of the stress then, Satan groups are so big power, at now in the macro concept actors are still + directions move most people still + Direction moving is the then still he/she is macro concept is 60~70 yeas old then, micro concept is still he is child level. Because micro concept is the direction is minus directions. So then macro concept go for the + directions, but in the micro concept direction is – minus directions. The micro concept gate is point (-1/∞~+1/∞). In the micro concept + direction move macro do not know the –Direction move, if infer suitability then keep increasing + direction move to +∞/0 then he/she is can full safety, so then if a macro concept actor are keep move forward to reach at the much more gains. Then it also infer that he/she in the macro concept for the end then if he located at the +∞/0, so then his last in the macor concept he do not know still all of macro concept actors after dead he/she anything do for his/her time for others only for his/hers. Then his all of life used for the exclusively for himself/herself, so then his/hers out of the body just only soul, then he/she soul meet naturally that kind of mind to make money group, in the body + soul+ mind to 0+ soul + mind sift to the soul(mind) and in the destination location mind color soul, so then , it must be infer that just his body living all used for himself then in the eternity world their group, no one sacrifice soul residents all the time fight, just money power it never philosophical concept is not placed. The eternity life is itself suffered.

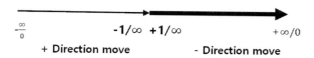

$$-\frac{\infty}{0} \qquad \textbf{-1/}\infty \ \ \textbf{+1/}\infty \qquad\qquad +\infty/0$$

+ Direction move   **- Direction move**

Then in the – direction move is the if a macro concept actor, he/she try to go – minus direction living, it must understand in the macro concept religious actors monks, Christianity etc. even another normal person also included, all of the macro concept actors are all can be – minus directions move, - Direction move is move with idea I believe that this is the power of righteous behavior so called god, heavenly father even Buddhism etc helping. But if a + direction move is the all of the macro concept naturally going without any learning this is the instinct power, to make lager much money making it is the characteristic of the macro concept characteristics. So then – minus direction is typically micro concept major idea, micro concept is the explained to the macro concept adopt to the all of the living is not wider but smallest wider then more deep then all of the macro concept actors are peace, and all of the actors are deep knowledge. So then in the macro concept a player of the micro concept adopt macro human being is live in the very little physical space, but in the mental so called micro concept creative, it also micro creative living is preferred to so micro concept used in the macro concept.

In the micro concept point (-1/∞~+1/∞) this is used personal, industry, cultured, technology all of the very deep high tech, micro ultra high-tech to go for the just – Direction move, this is not to be the size bigger + direction so called macro concept trend. So then if micro concept to adopt in the macro concept world, in the end just physical feature is not increased then all of macro concept actors all live equal for the high standard, all are rich peoples. This is the micro concept adoption. Actually this is the concept not in the real, but it can be helped to the stereo types of the macro concept all the time + direction move then, fight, war, steal, wicked world, all of the wick mind try to get other area, another company business ranged getting, so peace is all the time risk in the living place it produce the criminals but micro concept adopt is increase peace, by the creative industry a new blue ocean circumstance opened.

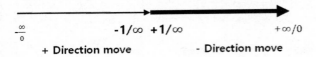

Briefly micro concept try to explained, but now, micro concept principal is the very important is the micro concept point (-1/∞~+1/∞) this is very important this is somewhat, impossible reach point but, it's point must be reach or try to reach then macro concept actor are live peace and equal living. + Direction movie, micro concept point (-1/∞~+1/∞), - minus direction move this is the compared to the peak living actors are compared also micro concept point then in the point of the macro concept then + Direction macro actors are not peak person, if a —minus direction move micro concept living actors are comparably peak, even not perfect peak. But in the micro concept point of view then – Direction move is the initially to the micro concept point or gate (-1/∞~+1/∞), this is if macor concept actors are keep his/her time then he lived all of time for himself, do not any time for the others, this life is perfect Satan pattern living, so then he/she is not perfectly come to heaven king dome soul residence. So then naturally macro concept world

Success person located at the not in to the heaven kingdom.

How to live is in the macro concept all of the actors are not to be in begin to – minus direction move but all of the people first + Direction move then if the all of develop and increased halt then it comes go – Minus direction move. So then actually the living is the – direction's micro concept living is the converged to the micro concept gate (-1/∞~+1/∞), this gate reach at is the earlier or later then, earlier is the success people, or religious, or realized people, his personal living realized living, some of the early realize is the we are believing Jesus Christ, actually I'm believing him as my savior, but also Buddha these people is realized in the living time, but if all of the try to live – minus direction moved macro actor then he/she can realize in the time of the dead, so he/she out of the body to soul time, he realize, then he/she can go for the righteous soul residence place. Here – minus direction is the macro concept actors desired to be rich make much money high ranking official etc all of macro actors correctly against direction, so then all of the mind make empty mind behavior. Then a living macro concept actor is faced with out the mind but just meeting the soul. Soul + mind + body, then if mind is 0 then soul+ mind, this is the somehow in the macro concept actors point of reaching to the macro concept point (-1/∞~+1/∞) reached. Life voyage problems but this is the all of the success story success actors' cases is meet. So that micro concept is uncountable approach to be come true.

2014.07.21

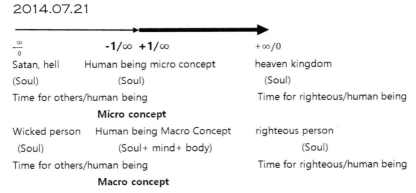

Micro concept macro concept in physically so called most people recognized just moment understand micro macro is the micro is small, macro is large. Large small, all of the macro concept is to get large anyone do not think small, all of concept is macro, so it must be micro is not popular to the macro concept actors. Actually macro micro concept is influenced so multi factors multi is endless so then ∞ uncountable aptitude will come the result.

All of the micro starts from one of points, which are me or center. All of the problems are required to multi solutions. I'm now frustrate how to do, what is the micro in the macro concept, macro is the bigger micro is smaller,

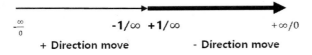

Macro is the + Direction move, micro is – minus direction move, I explained

to the unseen world concept, but now seen but the truth value is the unseen, just to get fruit of the process is in the micro is the − direction but macro is the + direction move, this is the same purpose then, the macro and micro is mixed, so how to revealed to this, just + direction is the very easy, all of the people to go for the bigger, richer, then in this concept micro comes to going left direction move. This is micro against to the macro concept smaller, poor, what is this matching. Who want to get poor, this is never happen to in the macro concept, so all of the macro concept people, to be rich all of the people go, and this is macro concept mega power. All of macro concept actors are all effort to gain position, in the moment, even second just breathe it relative to the decide then all is go for the gain, not lose, so all go for the macro direction + directions, so most people just one direction, all are same mind in the way of living. But in the micro direction move is the micro, left move is not same as the right move, so then, this is the used term of the group differences.

I hate police, police power is to gain and lose so then gain group under the power group, but my micro concept ground is economical managerial, so then still diluted so in the real market winner and loser all mixed, because winner must be required to live a loser, even same winner also winners expect to their are winners slaver, consumers. Micro concept is some of this macro concept loser and winner comes, but micro is the all winners this is the micro concept, actually this micro concept is not real may be, but micro concept is unseen and multi=∞ factors are related to do, micro concept

Micro concept $M = n1/n2 = 1$, is micro concept 1 is the winner, less than 1 is some has the 0.9, 0.8, ~~~ 0.2 0.1, micro concept $M= n1/n2 =$ from 0.9 to 0.6 is somewhat similar to the micro, but if under the 0.5 then compared to the macro concept. $n2=$ total numbers, $n1=$ leader, or owner.

But also the micro concept M is the explained to the how to involve to main actors. But also just in the micro concept counted as the actor. So then recognized to the actor, this is the actors are unit of the micro concept. So that if actors are unit of the micro concept.

$1+1+1+1+ \sim\sim\sim\sim\sim\sim+ 1= 10$
$1X10 = 10$

In the mathematics this calculation is just all 10 times plus then 1 is 10#, but the other 10is 1 =10, then it compared the productivity companies micro is P1 + P2 +P3 +P4 ~~~~ P10 = P10 products. But the big company product P1= P10, that it comes in the mathematically same amount of products.

This is the micro concept M = n1/n2 means that if a small company is 1 person company of the small company then M= 1/1 + 1/1 + 1/1 ~~~~ 1/1 = 10 * 1/1 = 10 1/1 = 10, so 10 companies are all actors company is itself of the actor.

But if a big company has 100 persons, 10 companies then micro concept M = 1/100 +1/100
+1/100~~~~ 1/100 = 10* 1/100= 10/100 =0.1 then this is the typically macro concept.

In the macro concept all push to + direction of that, so all of people dream to be richer, bigger then so, all of the actors are fight to get the bigger, richer so in the micro concept capital number is so low, in that case the real actor, but macro concept 90% then 90% is the slaver or unrecognized not a actor, so then, 90% role for the 10 %, here 90% sometimes good, so in the macro concept all of the best player to go for the only Micro index 0.1, so then they will be lived easy living but also the income is bigger, so the in the macro concept community all recognized to the big company member itself so this is the macro concept delusion; macro concept macro company(M1)member of the 1000 workers, then all of the member are M1 * 1000= delusion M1*1000= but this is still only M1*1 = M1 of real. So then 999 people is delusion M1, real of the actor is only 1. So then just one move to + direction but 999 people follows M1, so then all are follower of M1 of 999 delusion actors.

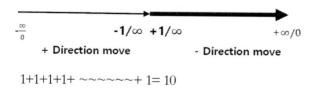

1+1+1+1+ ~~~~~~~+ 1= 10

This is the all of the micro company, then M=10*1/1= 10 this is the all of the company owner is the actor of the micro concept all of the company of one is also recognized to actor, then in the micro concept a soul recognized the man as the company 100% actor. So then these peoples are move to – minus direction 10 actors are go for the left, - direction move, these actors are not go for the bigger but smaller, it means that more perfect, more accuracy all of the company products are premium so that, all of the macro concept do not care of the others, only for the his/her work more deeper not wide, so long micro concept all of actors are pursue of the try to reach at the micro gate $(-1/\infty+1/\infty)$ so then the micro concept – direction is the perfect realization, all of the macro actor deep in his/her micro concept division.

Micro concept indicator $M= n1/n2 = 1$ is the just all of the cared by the just 1 person's righteous behavior, this means that he/she effort all of his/her energy then he/ she will reach at the micro concept gate $(-1/\infty+1/\infty)$ is the his all of dillgence all of his life mission, he realize of his living, all of the realization, product is the truth, for this all of the products helped from the in the righteous soul recognized, so that this predicts is belief products. But also this products keep continued all of the eternity of the products comes. Some of macro concept actors are misunderstood so that in this fast changed time, how to going for the longer, but if in this time in the high tech companies are micro concept companies then, he/she know the problems then he effort to find the solutions in the end he/she has informed from the very newest soul helped him/her. So that macro concept misunderstanding problems are just disbelief things, therefore micro concept is eternity living concept.

Micro concept is go left, so then micro can't be gore to bigger company, micro concept is micro concept is all winners, so that all of the new comes younger's out of the school, and reach at the live for the unit, then all of unit have a success possibilities, micro concept is not to be big or rich but to live compact realization of his/ her life, it also give the excitement and perfection. The entire actor of the micro concept is reach at the antiques but macro concept reach to the wastes to in the long run. Micro concept is an all of living actors are treated as the real soul, so then in the micro concept. In the life is the entire center for the righteous living.

2014.07.22

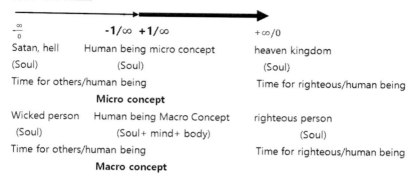

	-1/∞ +1/∞	+∞/0
$-\frac{\infty}{0}$		
Satan, hell	Human being micro concept	heaven kingdom
(Soul)	(Soul)	(Soul)
Time for others/human being		Time for righteous/human being
	Micro concept	
Wicked person	Human being Macro Concept	righteous person
(Soul)	(Soul+ mind+ body)	(Soul)
Time for others/human being		Time for righteous/human being
	Macro concept	

Infer from that micro concept is controlled by soul, but macro concept is controlled by mind. Because of the macro is try to bigger, richer and go for the + Direction move, but micro is the try to unseen micro pursue and try to make slim. It must be most macro concept actors are do not believe micro concept, actually macro concept must be fair of the micro concept. It would be macro actor's success story character also has the micro concept.

Micro concept controlled from soul, macro concept controlled form mind, if I infer that

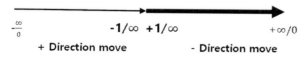

soul	>< mind ><	body

Soul is birthed with body then before soul is pure, all of souls are loved in the soul birth, then this soul get body to birth to the macro concept world, before going macro concept, in the macro actor itself is soul + mind = macro actor, it detail that here both locate with the soul in the behind the macro, so then it must be present to each others.

All of macro actors are then body only existed then the other controllers attached, it is the mind so then in the macro concept actors are all mind + body = macro concept actors. As the

$-\frac{\infty}{0}$ **-1/∞ +1/∞**   +∞/0

+ Direction move   **- Direction move**

As the after birth time going with all of macro concept actors are propelling to the + Direction moving, during then mind + body condition of the macro concept all increased to the physical getting old, mind is to getting deep and wide mind is a all covered to macro concept actors. If still get to pursue any trials to mind make small then naturally the mind getting bigger. Disappeared from the macro concept time actor, so that all of body balance is broken, so many things happened I do not say it. Therefore all of the macro concept actors are forever detached to the real controllers so until now all of the macro concept actors are out of the road. Meandering of the living, so all of the actors are come together so that all of the actors are forgotten his/her soul.

But micro concept soul is still existence all of the tunnel with macro and micro concept this is the explained to the micro concept actors are soul + body = micro concept actor

soul	>< mind ><	body

So then if mind =0, then in this case soul +body, this is the there is no any mind, so then pure actor, he/she controlled by soul, so then even he/she live in the macro concept world then his/her soul connect with soul world, if infer that soul world classify to the pure soul, righteous soul, Satan world so called full mind soul, then if a macro concept actor it really soul +body = macro concept, so then infer of the class first class is the soul+ body to dead in the macro concept world then, just like child time dead infant dead, but also in the before being of the dead they all stations at the soul+ body, so then this is the pure soul to go for the eternity. Another infers is the soul + mind + body= to live living in the macro concept, so then righteous is soul + righteous mind, righteous behaviors + body = macro concept actors, so long but also in the time all of the mind getting =zero, then the soul of righteous just all of the righteous soul is located at the righteous soul destination, but also if still getting increased to the mind is increased still then the mind is the almost kill the soul, in the macro concept time, then infer that all of the mind is so deep then soul almost dye, but soul(smallest) + mind(widest: bad mind wicked mind) + body = macro concept actor died then wicked soul so then the dead soul returned to the eternity to the wicked soul place. So then it also infer to the wicked soul, soul, righteous soul classified, (this is my concept theory it is not related with the religious) I'm believe that Jesus Christ, Buddha is my favorite. I'm just try to explain to the macro concept living.

So then in the electric equations V=IR (V: voltage, I: current, R: Resistance) this equation switch to the micro concept M = SM (S: soul, M: mind) soul = current, mind = Resistance, micro concept M = Soul(=1)M(=100) then M= 1*100=mind100, micro concept is zero, if soul(=100) M(=1) then micro concept M= 100*1= soul 100. After all to explain adapt to this equation is then, mind is the energy to act so then if I, then soul 100 then soul 100, adverse to the mind 100, soul 1= mind 100, actually in the real macro concept world perfectly soul, mind is not, so then all of the mixed with the mind to soul. Most macro concept world are this ratio is varied, So multi variable of the micro concept realize degrees are so multi, multi macro concept actors are all is not same, so all of variable then how to explained to be getting into micro gate reach is mind must be ((-1/∞) then soul learn the righteous thing so soul transfer to the soul righteous souls, but if mind is keeping to the +∞/0 then it must be any opportunity to the soul touch in this so valuable macro concept time. If in this macro concept time actor touch in soul then its pleasure is peak, all soul makes body safe do live righteous, but also it is equal to the body=soul, so then soul live so deep excitement how happy in this time his/her soul. Most actors why do not know this excitement.

2014.07.23

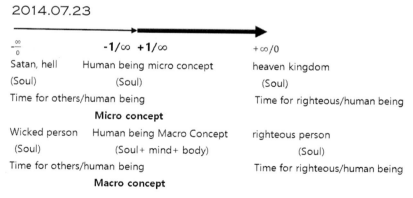

Micro concepts are located at a person, a family, a company etc. which are located at the macro circumstances. Micro concept gate ((-1/∞+1/∞) also occurred to the each units, so all of the unit can reach at the micro concept gate, this gate is the tunnel to the righteous soul meeting. Whose souls are already has the solutions for the macro concept macro actors' problems.

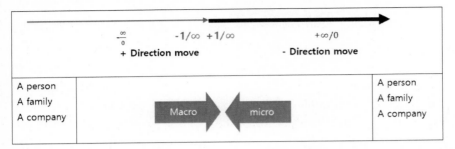

"The micro concept M = S=1*M (S: soul=1=constant, M: mind) "on his/her way. Macro concept a actor can live on his/her way to M=100, then what happened then a person poor of the macro concept actor, if a actor live on the mind 50, then but M= 1*0.5 = 0.5 in this case micro concept is 0.5, so influence to the mind. If M is 75% then M= 1*0.75 = 0.75, so then M micro concept M=o.75.

If a person lives freely so then very on his/ her way, so called without living religious living, doing out of righteous living, do not his life rule, without aim, do live variable under the variance conditions then a person lived pure macro concept living. His/her energy all used up of her macro concept living, without any saving spiritual energy all used up, a pure macro concept living actor just try to get a bigger house, bigger company, and rich living. He/she used all energy for the exclusively to be the rich and bigger, a actor do not know being poor, being make less, his/her living is all getting bigger. So he/she keep march + direction move, to the old time even closing time of his/her soul =1 but do not recognized almost to zero=0 + mind ; governing all of his/her body almost=100 + body = in the macro represent to the mind+ body = there is not soul.

This people out of soul, he does not believe to the religious relate bible, Buddha teaching neglect and free live, it don't have to believe, his/her time is full to play even in the Sabbath day also used macro concept royalty, his mind all filed with money making. So then money making relate is the matter but out of money making is nothing. Macro concept purpose is to binger, much more money. They are still less, it must be micro concept M= SM= S=1 m=100= 100, this is the depend on of the soul is still living, so soul is still =1, then it can be the M= 100% of the mind then if soul is killed then soul =0, mind =100 then reach at zero=0, so then macro concept actors are zero=0, micro concept M= S=0*mind=100=0, this is the soul dead. I don't know but if infer in my micro concept theory, and then die in this macro concept conditions. This is the concept so they still live in the real circumstance,

On the other hand, a person live M = Soul =1 * M 30~50 = M= 30~50, so then soul is even 1 but in the role of the 1*70~50, so this macro concept actor control by the soul, even actually do not know the body, he live righteous, he attend the church or temple, he try to read the bible, Buddha teaching, so then it might be possible of the religious living so sure to the control soul, then he/she must be the micro concept actor in the macro concept conditions, this actor helped macro micro concept better position by soul helping, so then these actors are all of the product with all his/her soul, this is the true, not deceit to the relatives. This people related with others with credibility. This is the macro concept living premium, but he can live in the macro concept actor, soul + mind+ body, soul + righteous mind + body then, this actor lived even in the live, so that in the religious life, living Jesus Christ, it means lord is still live, so then, the righteous living actors soul controlled his fair or itself body controlled by soul. He/she live righteous so he/she influenced around of his/her good effect, these relatives are love and expect him/her. Righteous actor around are all good living. So then his/her living in this macro concept circumstance so happy living, this is not easy living but righteous by all of sacrifice. And he/she lived to so ripen old, he/she somewhat cross recognized his/her soul, or not in his/her macro concept time, all the time, just his/her soul is managed and help also lead, also messenger role of the his/her body's righteous behavior, all of the soul so excitement then soul carry to the god, lord his body's sacrifice or righteous acts. His/her soul also all the time lead to the righteous to the right fruit, soul all the time care his /her body. Because soul already know to the righteous soul eternity destinations excitement, so all of the soul want to go the place, soul know soul see the place, soul still connect soul world, strong happy soul is very excitement. The body comes to relied on old then strong soul, excitement soul, so happy to go for the righteous eternity souls destinations. The late of the macro concept soul + mind + body, then body all old so, soul + mind to go for the soul places, that is the in the macro concept then dead but in the micro concept is still line, just macro concept living dead all of the soul still living, but if in the macro concept then a actor soul is dead then, exclusively for the macro live then soul is not dead, but if infer then soul is dead in the macro concept, but all of helped by the mind then, he/she haven't in the soul, so in the dead time, the dead moment so far, there is no any relatives. Until now they do not care of the micro concept affairs. So soul dead macro concept actor going for the eternity dead place, until now I didn't know the soul dead, but now in my micro concept soul dead concept comes,

In the macro concept actors after all naturally get the soul + mind + body these is the mind is the acquired materials but natal time getting is the soul + body, all of comes that of the body dead then soul go to the eternity place, so all is not dead, body only dead, but mind is the variance to the people living, mind is keep larger then soul place is so risk, in the end all of the soul dead of asphyxia then soul die, so then I'm not sure soul die then body also die, if soul die then body die natural if not he/she lost to go for the soul place, because soul dead, then he/she awaited to the fall to the hell, out of the soul place. I don't know this is micro concept only, but if this is the somewhat meaningful then, general people are not to be included to the soul killing criteria, this must be the so about $M = S * M = 100 =$ these actors all of the going hell. Please does not going but all of the soul have the each soul get its position?

So long as people lived righteous then, his soul all informed to the lord, god, so soul god lord already know it, so in the micro concept actors king expect to see righteous soul, the king also until now helped a living body + soul time. Then an old macro concept soul + body, even body soon goes for bury or fired. Then the soul so excitement to the returned to safe to the god, she/he did all of the energy for the righteous, his/her sacrifice so many people lived and righteous living, this is the god, lord mission, lord, god entrust his so small soul, to the righteous souls, so, in the macro concept world so many family disable actors, so they are credible already knew lord, so god expected to live by the god mission accomplishment if follows all of god's mission then he lived righteous. Also, a righteous soul mission is also a mother, father help to safe to the god's kingdom come back. God's planning is the soul being perfect, so perfect soul do righteous behavior. All of soul must do realize, how to realize is all of the actors are seek righteous but also religious and the his/her position working then all of sacrifice for the righteous then god soul and his/her soul be meet.

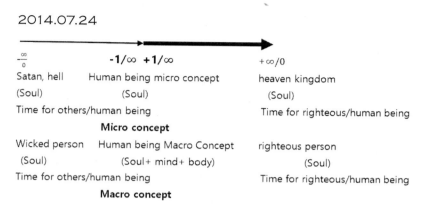

2014.07.24

$\frac{\infty}{0}$	-1/∞ +1/∞	+∞/0
Satan, hell	Human being micro concept	heaven kingdom
(Soul)	(Soul)	(Soul)
Time for others/human being		Time for righteous/human being
	Micro concept	
Wicked person	Human being Macro Concept	righteous person
(Soul)	(Soul+ mind+ body)	(Soul)
Time for others/human being		Time for righteous/human being
	Macro concept	

All of macro concept actors are positioned to family. Family has a father, mother, child, so then this is the connection, father role for the macro, micro, mother also macro, micro, and child also has the micro macro. So then, macro concept relationships, micro concept relationship also

Macro concept a father mother, father child, mother to father and child, child to father and mother, Micro concept a father to mother and child, mother to father and child, child to father and mother. Micro concept macro concept family then it may be Macro concept family members and micro concept family members are live in the macro concept circumstance.

But family unit then who is the actor then, father is the actor for the macro concept and micro concept, so then family is one, so then family unit has the micro concept then micro concept M = n1/n2, if a family has the father, mother, son and daughter, so then micro concept M= 1/4 = 0.25

So then family unit actor is father, and then father related with family level macro concept and micro concept, in this case, family is unit leader is father, some argue mother also, then in this micro concept let be the father is micro concept family unit actor, so then father is the M=1/1=1 so father is micro concept gate concept gate ((-1/∞+1/∞) so then family unit, father has the micro concept gate, family mattered problems solving is the located at the father's soul, so then father soul is personal father, also the family unit role, so then the gate with family, family macro and micro concept act fathers micro concept gate ((-

$1/\infty+1/\infty$), so then father soul will be connect to the micro concept soul place, infer that ancestor souls are some place, until now righteous or wick soul then the location of the eternity then personally understood. But family group soul it not sure, if understand of family problems then, just like a company manager company problems solving then helped, the same as the family problems the father of the family leader, he do role of the family problems solving then, he may be helped from ancestor souls, actually is not sure family soul members are all together located or not. But in the macro concept happening family problems are so variable so then if a father lived righteously concentration to the family affairs then he can helped.

Family members are connected in the blood, these members all of the ways of livings are differences so then each members are micro M= 0.25, so then still they are not has the perfect location as the family unit members, so father soul is family unit M=1, so father can have micro concept gate ($(-1/\infty+1/\infty)$), family members are all personal point of view then each member has the M=1, so then family unit to personal unit is conflicted.

As recently mother also a big role, if she get to single then she also 1 family unit M=1. But if she is in the role of the mother, then she also M=0.25. So wife has no micro concept gate ($((-1/\infty+1/\infty)$), M=0.25 in the family, if family member each others are all do help then these M= 0.25(father)+0.25(mother)+ 0.25(son)+0.25(daughter) = 1, but if these family members are role of the personal M=1. Each conflict to the family members as the certification of the M=1, then in the family M= 1+1+1+1=4, so then broken family. Just for the 4 families even under the real of the family. Here first father as the role of the head of house hold position threat so then the function of the family disappeared, all of members are each going. So called if family problems compared with the company then it may be bankruptcy.

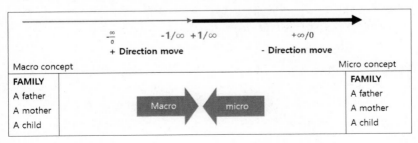

Macro concept family all pursue for the exclusively + direction move then family unit do not get into watching each family, all are tired from the just making money related matter, so then, family of micro then infer to family also ahs the soul, family macro also family micro, so then family all has the mind =100, the micro concept M= SM this equation from V=IR, I=S; soul, R= m: mind, soul is constant =1. Mind is variance, if family micro concept M= 1*100= 100, it must be Family micro, micro is move to the left move, because of the left is located at the micro concept gate ((-1/∞+1/∞), in this M=100, case, this family move only for the right move, Macro move, so this family all of the making money, but also they all do related with job related working, so then micro is zero=0, then this family micro concept family soul, or family healthful living is so poor so then, family soul are hard to live, in this case family actor also= family body+ family mind + family soul, family mind is ∞=100 then if lucky then M= 1*100= 100mind, so then family body 100 mind, so then it still lucky, but if still over the family get increased to the over the full 100 of the mind, then it might be the kill the family soul, so then family soul=0, then M=0*100=0, so then family soul dead, another cases, M= soul1*mind 1~50, then 50 soul mind, then 50 soul mind family, family still influenced from the micro concept, so then father as the family manger power still strong, so the family is healthy. But also the family soul still strong then family soul traveled to the family soul in the soul eternity place, if a family soul is righteous then, it can be infer that family soul and family ancestor can meet in the micro concept actors meeting. If not macro concept world, family soul is righteous in comparison but his ancestor anyone in the places souls micro concept, his ancestors are not any located at the micro concept soul, then it might be the ancestors are do not live righteous in the macro concept era, so that in the soul a ancestor it infer to the it can't help power. So then even macro concept actor of the family in righteous family even but the family are lose the soul guard. Family leader is also personal actor also, who are all connected to the family connections, so infer that if a people live turf then he hasn't any accumulate to the blessing, all used up energy. Good fortune, how to do, in the macro concept living why to live do righteous live is important is the all of the energy of family is make less or family fortune accumulate then family blessing fortune accumulate is very prime concerning. So then family

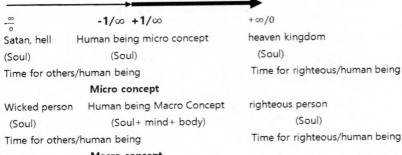

Micro concept

$\frac{\infty}{0}$	**-1/∞ +1/∞**	+∞/0
Satan, hell	Human being micro concept	heaven kingdom
(Soul)	(Soul)	(Soul)
Time for others/human being		Time for righteous/human being

Micro concept

Wicked person	Human being Macro Concept	righteous person
(Soul)	(Soul+ mind+ body)	(Soul)
Time for others/human being		Time for righteous/human being

Macro concept

Family unit micro concept for the each other not even for the out of the family, then family is the macro, and then family members each are the personally micro concept then family member are if understand the real of the micro concept then if some of briefly explain then micro concept is how to many time for others, so called not me for others, so called scarifies then the time is very ranges, how many time for give another family members, father, mother, sister, brother. Just in the micro concept ((-1/∞+1/∞), each family members micro concept variance mind must be make less, then

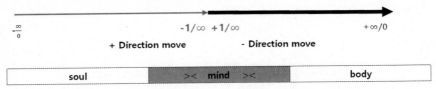

Each family member decreased the mind so then micro concept increased to then family also move to the – direction move, it infer that making money sacrifice then the time for share with other families, family is not for the even the not comes money but the time for the help others, then the family is M= 0.25 father + 0.25 mother +0.25 son+0.25 daughter = 1 of the same as the family unit micro concept father = 1 so then, family each member M= Family unit micro =1, so then all of the family is if ancestor live with righteous living soul then, this family connect of the family micro concept actor, family soul can travel to micro concept righteous ancestor soul meeting then, the micro concept soul, micro concept ancestor power try to give the energy effect to the family. All of family are excitement and be feel happy.

2014.07.25

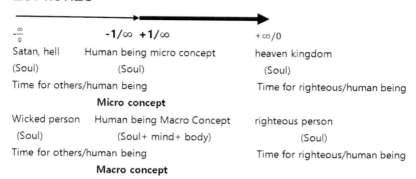

	-1/∞ +1/∞		+∞/0
Satan, hell	Human being micro concept		heaven kingdom
(Soul)	(Soul)		(Soul)
Time for others/human being			Time for righteous/human being
	Micro concept		
Wicked person	Human being Macro Concept		righteous person
(Soul)	(Soul+ mind+ body)		(Soul)
Time for others/human being			Time for righteous/human being
	Macro concept		

`In the micro concept company unit, company also has the micro concept gate

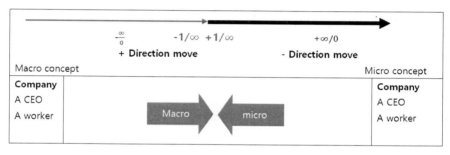

Company of the 50 workers then, micro concept M= 1/50= 0.02, so then each worker are micro concept index is 0.02, so then they are nothing for the micro concept actor. But the CEO is the M=1/1 of the company, among companies a company indicator is the also the M=1. Micro concept gate located at the CEO.

In the company pipe line of the macro and micro concept world, a CEO if he/she life for the righteous behavior then he has the deep problems unsolved, then CEO has the problems for the company, CEO company is the Company soul, in the micro concept actor is the CEO, so thence is very important. If CEO all of his energy is follows the macro, just for the move to right, so CEO keep forcing to be rich, or bigger without philosophy. In the point of the macro concept then this is any problems, but if a CEO hasn't Philosophical mind then, his mind all occupied to the full of the desired to be rich, then CEO keep spread of his all of efforts.

In the company all of worker M=0.02, so then all of actors of his/her personal

M=1, but also 4 family member then M=0.25. So they all the time existed actors are varied in the changed circumstances in the company then his M=0.2, after finished company then returned to home then M= 0.25, so then company is the source of economy, so called company is the usual economical living, company is the engine to the macro concept to make money, especially company is very typical micro concept must be adapt.

CEO is the company unit M=1, his responsible is very important, CEO manage and himself/herself is undertake of the company soul, CEO but he has the role of company M=1, in the family M=1, personal M=1, a man involve all of time mixed to the just micro concept gate center concept gate $((-1/\infty+1/\infty)$, so then in the micro concept required to righteous for the company soul, company is the personality in the point of the macro concept. So then it also micro concept also micro actor role has been, So CEO if push to the macro concept trend for the right direction then pure of the macro, so then, company itself is a company, company to the convergent to $((-1/\infty+1/\infty)$, concergent gate so called to micro concept gate, it is the go right to the from left to $-1/\infty$, from right to left to $+1/\infty$ so called the micro concept gate is the $((-1/\infty+1/\infty)$, then to reach at the micro concept , in macro concept all of the real situation right to go left, so CEO required to live righteously. But in the point of view how to match up with making money, it must be wick characteristics is also required, in the actually in the macro concept of the real circumstance is challenged pure righteous can grow for the CEO game. So then righteous is not reliable. So then if a CEO live that M= SM, M= 1*(1~50),(50~100), = soul(1~50), mind(50~100), A CEO is 50 Soul, but 100 mind , but also CEO is also family father, or leader of the family M= SM M= 1*(1~50),(50~100), = soul(1~50), mind(50~100), then it also has the effect both company and family, furthermore in the personal it is general is then, M=SM, also the M= 1*(1~50),(50~100), = soul(1~50), mind(50~100), so then CEO of company is how to live, how to do righteous but also philosophical living or not is very important role.

Just the CEO soul, family leader soul, personal soul act for the purpose live then seen in the macro concept but micro concept also has, so then if do righteous living then

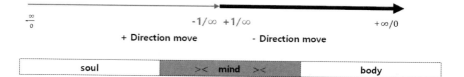

Mind is larger to then, M= SM, M is longer increased to keep to ∞ macro concept M=∞, so then CEO of company is out of the righteous trek then he/she is over desired then collect make a money, then a company managed also out of righteous so then, controlled by the mind of the CEO not a soul, but if it is controlled by soul, then a company manage is also kept in righteous. So then CEO micro concept is very kin to be perfect, so three stages CEO, family, personal soul is required to righteous, because of these three stages have micro concept gate ((-1/∞+1/∞),so he/she is very responsibility living. Because of wick live then three stages M=1 * CEO M *family M * personal M= all of the multiple of the 3 CEO, family, person so then, if he/she divided to act for the CEO of the company then role for the M of the company = 1* 3M= 3mind, family M=3m, person of the M= 3m, so that if a CEO live wick then the result is come up, there stages CEO of company wicked, family manager wicked, personal wicked. The result of the wicked person does harm in the big position of the actor then if he/she is do live deceit or wicked ling then in the end, the break down is the 3 stages micro concept gate souls are almost dead due to the mind is almost to 100, then soul dead possibility also comes. M= soul=o * mind=100= zero 0 is the go into the hell, cause of soul die related with all of doing harmed.

Further more of the workers of the companied M=0.02, the if they also anger to the" I'm a person so he/she required personal M=1 position" then his real of the macro concept M=0.2, but he try to get of personal M=1, so then if a worker anger to the company, company worker but anger to the company M= original M= 0.02 in this case personal M=1, how to 0.02to reach to 1, this equation is 0.02* X= 1= X= 1/0.02 = 50, so then the discordance ratio is 50 folds. So then worker anger to the company, is not satisfy, then, just anger of the company so then 50 member of the company M is 50 * 50 = 2500 this is companied to M=SM= 1*2500= 2500mind, so called to the it perfect to kill the soul, so then CEO soul, worker soul killed, but if adverse to the all are m=0.2

then this actors are role of the righteous living then, worker of the company still do righteous in his/position then in he is in the family leader then he has the m=1, but also the personal M=1, so then he/she family, personal m=1 so then righteous M= 1/3 of the company worker, family 1, personal 1 = M= 1/3*0.02*1*1= 0.02/3 = 0.0067, then in the company worker of the micro concept gate the ((-1/∞+1/∞),, the micro concept index is decreased to less then, in the company a worker M=0.02, then it means that, all of his working is compact, perfect, product is perfect product so then his righteous affordable, so then company originally CEO M=1 but if a all of member of companies are same as M=0.0067, then CEO of company M= 50* 0.0067= 0.335, originally of the CEO of M=1, but then a righteous of the member of the company 50 workers then, CEO of M= also 1/3M= this value is the 0.335. CEO micro concept M= 0.335.

M value is decreased then the company is righteous so then move to the left, so then all of the micro index is the means also come to perfection almost deficit almost to perfect to zero related to do. Micro concept must be focus for the righteous and perfection, so then all of the winner not but of the just only winner is small loser is multi structure is the know to a realize, actually all of the living reveled to the naturally wicked out of the normal living but all is intentionally try to changed to not naturally purpose, not natural but intentional effect, so then this is the macro concept only, so unseen micro concept must be required to do.

2014.07.28

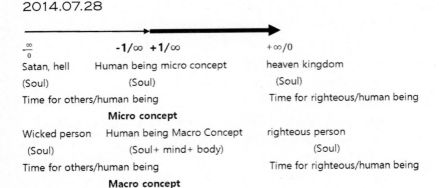

$\frac{∞}{0}$	**-1/∞ +1/∞**	+∞/0
Satan, hell	Human being micro concept	heaven kingdom
(Soul)	(Soul)	(Soul)
Time for others/human being		Time for righteous/human being

Micro concept

Wicked person	Human being Macro Concept	righteous person
(Soul)	(Soul+ mind+ body)	(Soul)
Time for others/human being		Time for righteous/human being

Macro concept

Micro concept, macro concept this is concept, today my son facial surgery which occurred my son age is 8 years old, scar in my son face a big scar, so a big surgery at my son ages about 11 years

So then today is a plastic surgery. Actually today is so special to me, this accident can I explain to my son's scar how to be happened to my son, why got a hard time to my son, all of his living so stress cause of his face surgery scar. All is not simple but I know only myself, in the micro concept program, micro concept is macro is what I said that soul + mind + body,

My mother
I
My son

My mother was birth between a mother disaster of mental and a man who do not know by my mother, so called my mother know only her disaster of mental mother only. I am now living, I was so deep loved by my mother, I so deep helped from my mother who helped all of her best. I felt that my mother used all of her energy to me; I was so lucky my mother live all to me, so I got a big debt, my mother died cause of her metallic sickness so early before my getting job, to my age 30 years old. My poor getting job so I could not pay back to my mother my love to my mother. I really wanted to get a job and to be role of my mother's first son. But I couldn't it. Mother died, while mother sick time, I got a so wrong to my mother, so my mother said "you son will be hard..." she said, she died.

The entire family relative is from me, I did wrong to my mother, so that I have to pay back to my mother as a son, she was so dangerous she felt so lone, so but I was so wick time, my all of energy is to get a job, actually my mind is getting job doing my serve to my mother with my devotion, this is so cling to me, so I'm so narrow person, so I did nothing but I could do my mother soul safe, at that time my mother soul so lonely, his soul so lonely so that her body also sick, but my mother died. I got a marriage my so birth then my so good, but my so after got an injection after my son face skin dent, so right after I thought all is my wrong doer. So I felt so sorry to my son, but also to my wife also. Today my son cure of my son face cured. Then yester day night I got a dream "I paid to my mother 5million won paid so real dream" it is not rare, but my mother appeared to me, so the dream was I sell my car, then the money transfer to my mother she said done" at now my mother forgive me my wrong doer to my mother. My son now is surgery. I tried to pay to my mother but how to do; my soul will seek my mother soul, my soul himself meet, the meeting is seen as the dream. After dream my mother come to me thinking my mother beautiful time picture come to me, so then I felt that it comes to me my mother soul, so then it comes to the my soul meet my mother. So long time, but mother and me is the family, my mother loved deep, I have been cared my grandmother tomb, my mother. I paid my mother accept, so then I can get through all of debt to my mother. From now on my mother soul is satisfied to my soul. I believe that my son be helped my soul, then my soul love relationship are all together help me. So from now all my soul go with my mother soul very closed, actually until now, I my mother and me somewhat distance but from now on, I will be close, I have been loved from my grand mom, I felt all of my suffering time, my grand mom console to me, whoever else, but all of my relationship has been done with my grand mom, so sorry and miss to my mother. My son cured his face. My son does not know why he so damaged to his living so has been daunted. He lived so suffer from my poor behavior. If I do my mother good and normal then my mother feel good, so my mother helped to my son, my son be helped from my mother but my poor behavior so that my son affected. If I did well, then my mother soul and my soul has been good relationship, if good is my mother soul try to pay to the good behavior, but I did so bad to my mother, so that my mother mistake doing. My mother anger to me so she anger to my son, so then my son so deep suffered. I haven't time for my mother; I haven't given to my mother love, but all the time complied to my mother. I love my mother. I can love my mother. My son will be solved then my soul does well so now, my mother and son soul is good. In this time, my soul role is making understand my mother soul. But if do not live righteous then my soul is still wick then my mind anger to my mother still, then, my mother will not meet my soul. My living is all control all both micro concept and macro concept world.

If I used my time for my mother then my mother can understand my situation but even my mind is so good but my time all used for my life then, my mother do not know, so then how to live is micro concept, all of the time is endless not, if the procedure of time

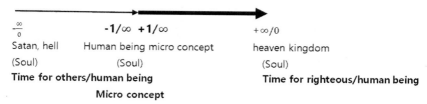

$\frac{\infty}{0}$	**-1/∞ +1/∞**	+∞/0
Satan, hell	Human being micro concept	heaven kingdom
(Soul)	(Soul)	(Soul)
Time for others/human being		**Time for righteous/human being**
	Micro concept	

time is value, righteous person use his/her time for others, then how to compensate for himself/herself, it required to adopt, optimistic time manage is required to do, so then, in the relationship other is actually me and other.

My time	<---------------------------->	Other time

Just all has the 24 hours, how live my time, time is changed to the money also, so then time and money is the same value. If my time is shared with then itself for the sacrificed that, so long so in the point of view is – minus but in the long term then it will be the long term base also someone can help me, if I can shared my time then, some of the accept my time, then his soul so excitement but also donor also excitement, but all of his time all used himself, then his soul all the time do not related with others, so his soul so long. She lives in her room for herself only. He is not have relative soul, in the soul, so called micro concept world, but also macro concept world are same with the time shared is also, if someone so his time for other then, how many souls are recognized so then soul friends all spread to the informed to the just shared time actor is helped to me, so some of the soul helped from a soul then

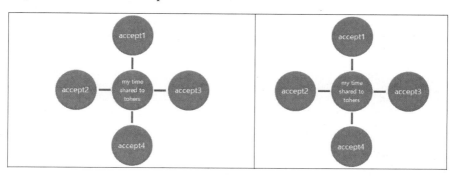

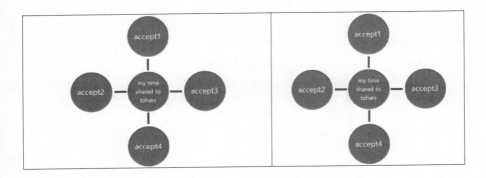

All of accept soul spread to the donor of the time is good, just like news, so he is multiple of the time shared, and donors. These spread is the good for it, is the similar to the macro concept world also adopt to do, in the family is very closed, so then, it is the very start, how to do with this, tools that, in the family is the living basic, what happened to this, in the family also some relationship others also, any way the time is the very indicator of the micro concept, micro concept, time is the very clear of actor. Time is indicator of it can be a righteous or wicked critical line, some of the use his time for the multiple times used then he/she is righteous in the probability method. How to wick is not count on that but, all of the time usages are must be thought for the critical line. Actually all of the macro concept actors are all eager to extensive time for the accomplish, so then it don't have to give to others, but all is so all of the people live for himself, all of energy for himself, so long,

Satanic person	Time variance	Righteous person
1/3 other shared time	Others shared time 1/3	1/3 His time for this only
His time is short to him 1/3	Still this time also his 1/3	Still this time also his 1/3

When I was youth I did mistake to my mother, in the time of my mother death, so I was wicked to my mother, my mother would be very anger and miss toward me, but she in the end closed in this macro concept world. So I'm wicked to my mother. How to live is just very simple just shared with others, this is only out of the wicked. Actually in the family happened just anger, miss things. So all of the member must be shared with time others. This is basic to out of the satanic person to righteous person. But it is not easy all if the people closed dam perfect, so then all of the people located and strong satanic acting.

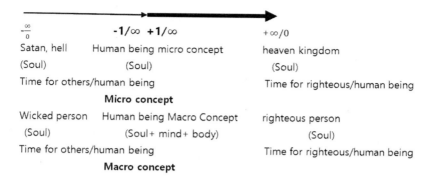

$-\frac{\infty}{0}$ **-1/∞ +1/∞**   +∞/0

Satan, hell   Human being micro concept   heaven kingdom
(Soul)   (Soul)   (Soul)
Time for others/human being   Time for righteous/human being
                    Micro concept

Wicked person   Human being Macro Concept   righteous person
(Soul)   (Soul+ mind+ body)   (Soul)
Time for others/human being   Time for righteous/human being
                    Macro concept

If all of thing to be convergence to some place, times is micro concept gate (-1/∞+1/∞) this principal is started from all of the problems are must be solved, then it must be hard to solve, so then if split all of the problems then it may be simple unit, so it can be solved. To be solve turning back to the origin. It will not to be possible in the macro concept, but in the micro concept is infer to be possible. So then all of macro + direction move, but micro is – move, this is how to explain

$-\frac{\infty}{0}$ **-1/∞ +1/∞**   +∞/0

Satan, hell   Human being micro concept   heaven kingdom

Just micro concept gate (-1/∞+1/∞) this is so meaningful to realize, micro concept point also move so then, somewhat it is not understand in the macro concept, what I explained to macro is from left to right direction move, strange move is the make heavy, so going left is light, but it is not simple, just micro concept gate is locate in the line, macro concept is past from around present, so then it must be not reach at the concept gate (-1/∞+1/∞) it goes by natural ways. Micro concept gate is the somewhat macro concept point of view it must be very easy reaching but actually somewhat is must be the just concept, yes it is concept, but actually if a macro concept a actor reach at the micro concept gate (-1/∞+1/∞), actually micro concept gate in the macro concept then it must be the purpose, micro concept gate (-1/∞+1/∞) is purpose, so all of the macro concept try to reach at the micro concept gate, from -∞/0 long time ago to presnt now that is the -1/∞ it is the still –(minus) this is not the in the macro concept – is not in the one two three, but this is the somewhat philosophical concept. So then micro concept point is the in the macro concept point is to realize in living. But it has the micro concept is also ahs the time and place, so called it is the somewhat it is understood from present to future, but actually in the micro concept also actually another micro concept so that, future is it may be like this so then

Micro concept is varied M = from M1 shift to M2, M3, ... Mn .... +∞/0, so then in the all of the space is time is in seen feel of the in the micro concept, so that what I sad that micro concept is the in the macro concept is past present future amalgamate this is the micro concept gat or point. In the micro concept point is the field; this is the point, so short time, recognition point. Actually all of solid line is combined to dot line; all of the M points are the solid line. Macro concept is = combined to the micro concept gate. Macro concept $= \sum_{n=1}^{\infty} Mn$, so long, so then micro concept is first then after macro concept so long, so long in the macro concept micro concept gate is the micro concept gate $(-1/\infty+1/\infty)$, so long in the macro concept thinking is the move to the right is make money, rich, bigger, make much more then, their move to the right to macro concept gate actors are move to the so much actors they think that $+1/\infty$, $+\infty/0$ but actually in the macro concept all are under the micro concept gate $(-1/\infty+1/\infty)$, so long all of the macro concept actors are move to the in the real to the micro concept gate, so that all of micro concept gate $(-1/\infty+1/\infty)$, so then it is not understand clearly, but in the micro concept is seen that still the macro concept actors are limited in the micro concept gate $(-1/\infty+1/\infty)$, so micro concept world can see the micro concept gate, so that all of the macro concept actors try be rich, but all of the macro concept actor= soul +mind+ body= Macro concept actor try to be rich, so they all of the time controlled by the mind, in the actor mind is the future and to be rich, all of actors are on the micro concept point, so then this is line, so all of the convey belt macro concept are try to be bigger, richer, so magnify, so long, all of the macro concept world all of words are economically to big rich, but in the micro concept all of actors are move to the micro concept all is the about to zero= 0, gate $(-1/\infty+1/\infty)$, so macro cocenpt actors are all to be zero, but all of the macro concept actors are all desired, so this is the mind role, all of human beings actors are desired to be rich, but the desired to be rich is mind purpose, but actually in the macro concept point is the line is the soul line, soul is all the time is soul, what I said before birth soul, after birth soul + body + after birth mind, after dead soul is line. So then in the micro concept, so long soul is very small, then all of the macro concept bigger, so long, macro and micro is each other is against so long, but micro concept is line, mind is the real practice frame of the macro concept so long macro concept is not wrong but it is the in the macro concept correct. Physical maintain so long, so then it required to live the macro concept actors living is supported to required to make a money. But money making is not related with the soulful ways, so to reach to the micro concept gate is gate $(-1/\infty + 1/\infty)$ so long, originality is even macro actor but it also being required to do for the micro concept, just feel his/her soul, then soul has been helped the point of the micro concept, unseen world micro concept existed, so long, macro concept fair of unseen is role, in the living then unrecognized time role by his/her soul, it is not act mind, mind is not actor, just added a parasite, so then mind is the a parasite. Mind is just like lump. If there is not mind then pure of the soul macro actor, but it added to the lump of the macro actors are make disturb of recognition by the mind, mind is the try to all of the body, because of the mind is the it recognized to him/her is owned by mind, so long all of macro concept actors are must be the know micro concept world also act, so long all of the real act is all the time macro concept and micro concept intersect. So long to live is the very relative with micro concept.

$\frac{\infty}{0}$	**-1/∞ +1/∞**	+∞/0
Satan, hell	Human being micro concept	heaven kingdom
Macro concept recognition spaces	M= M1 +M2 +M3 ....Mn	
All actor move to right end right is about to 0	Micro concept point move to right	

2014.07.30

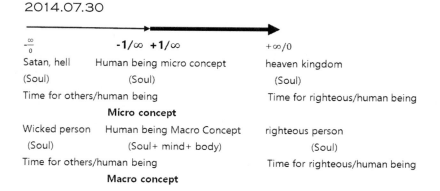

$\frac{\infty}{0}$	**-1/∞ +1/∞**	+∞/0
Satan, hell	Human being micro concept	heaven kingdom
(Soul)	(Soul)	(Soul)
Time for others/human being		Time for righteous/human being
	Micro concept	
Wicked person	Human being Macro Concept	righteous person
(Soul)	(Soul+ mind+ body)	(Soul)
Time for others/human being		Time for righteous/human being
	Macro concept	

Today all of my processing is halt, what I can do, how to go for this micro concept. Today on the way of my work place it comes to me the thing is problems to live on so called hard job. Whoever all has the problems, all of the organization also its problems, company has problems. In the macro concept actor living all of peoples are faced to the problems. In the hard time is what in the micro concept point of view how to see the problems. Why occur problems, it can live perfect without problems, in the macro concept living it must be impossible, all of the time, where, relationship all has the problems, problems is continued to prostrated or anger or fear all of comes from it. Micro concept gate (-1/∞+1/∞) problems are alterate between macor concept and micro concept. All of problems are mixed with these factors, macro concept and micro concept, so then the problems comes to the micro concept gate (-1/∞+1/∞), this is the macro concept micro concept peak place, macro concept is the all of the realization, but also the micro concept is

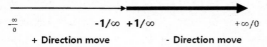

Here is macro concept move to + Direction move, - direction move micro concept, on this moving is the all of the problems; eating problems, relationship problems, hate, love anger all of the status problems are going for the + direction move, even in the macro concept the direction recognition but actually in the micro concept is not a direction move. + Direction move is the life actually in the macro concept is getting old, but in the micro concept is not getting old, because of the even time has in the micro concept but actually it's scale is not same as macro concept time. But actually do not recognition but time, space is sure of the factors of the macro concept and micro concept. + Direction move is all of the macro concept actors are live with others. The first relationship is husband & wife, parents & children. Most macro concept actors are mixed to wick act & righteous acts, all the time comes to righteous acts. All of relationships good giver bad receptor, all the time is not good for macro actor so then some of the living is not controlled by the macro concept origin, in the micro concept world also role for the macro concept field. Exclusively macro concept closed to meet soul, cause of the big mind, heavy mind, Desirous mind, and this mind is for the management macro concept actor physical sustainment also for the macro concept actors' physical living. So macro concept actors do not know, but also not a soul, so all of the actors are limited in physical concept. Macro concept is $-\infty/0 \sim (-1/\infty)$ macro concept actor try to success, or money making for + Direction move. So then M(micro concept index) =S(soul) M(mind), so then M=S=1= constant * M(1~100), so then most over the M= 50~100. So then macro concept actors all do not know the micro concept world. But in micro concept also has role for the macro concept actor, actually micro concept actor is not have physical body, so actually recognized actor is the macro concept gate actors, so macro concept gate will have the M=SM in the micro concept point of view, so then micro concept world soul can run for the living, so in the micro concept world, Soul move and react so multi soul meet the soul friend or, soul keep tense his physical body to reach home soul home, because of the macro concept actor is not leave to traveling to the physical body living, so soul keep care of him, so that his/her body pursue for the only macro concept but also forget soul existence but all of the controlled by the mind, then, in the micro concept actor soul, lead to the righteous rout, but macro concept actor pursue to make only money. So then all of time used up for his/her sake exclusively. So then micro concept soul control over out of the micro concept rule, so all the time micro concept actor influence to the macro concept actor, so then it occur to the micro concept soul also, role for the his/ her physical body + direction move, so then all of the life is not direct going, all of the people variable road to live, in this case, it must be the macro concept actor all the time push accelerator but in the micro concept actor push to brake, so then comes to balances.

So then all of the physical actor are still keep going for the + Directions move, the desired actors are all try to make endless, then M= SM, M=S M= 1~50, then permit to go for the going forward, but M=SM=50~100, then micro concept actors are start to push brake, so then it required to – direction move for the thinking micro concept, to see the soul then please make less mind to this M=SM= 50 40 30 To realize for the micro concept gate ($-1/\infty+1/\infty$), but still all of the macro concept gate actors are eager to move to the + Direction move for the desirous, so then brake is the give to the macro concept actor problems, this problems are please do not go for the make money you must do righteous behavior and micro concept actor feeling. In this case soul push brake then, macro concept still keep push accelerator then what happened, so macro concept actor can't do well. If macro concept try to go for the success then what is this, then, required micro concept actor, role of the god's order, all of the macro concept poor condition, or really pray for the righteous then god accept all of pray. Then god accept macro concept variable conditions so then how to role for the poor, it is duty M=SM, M=S50M, it must be do righteous for god order, then if a macro concept do righteous behavior then M=S45M, so then 5M is still keep + Direction move, so then, the success peak time lengthier. But still after reach at the M=S50M then, micro concept actor brake, because of the another macro concept actor still M=SM=1, 10 20, these macro actor are also must be give chance to live on, so that in the micro concept god expect all of his soul live equality good live, so that micro concept actor interrupt or help to the macro concept gate. In the real of the a people living is all the time good, some time bad, the other time good, so all of the people ahs the problems, to solve the problems is the help other, god's order accepting and help other, then if help other then, god already in the micro concept actor ordered to the macro concept actor, so then for the good macro concept actor then micro concept god already ordered. So to live peace in living it must help others. Then micro concept role is done in the macro concept actor.

All of the life success people keep a rule, his late of living is not for the move to the macro concept but after reach at the M=S 50M then − Direction move by himself, but do not role by the micro concept push brake. Then it comes to conclusion be success.

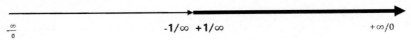

Macro concept actor	Micro concept gate	Micro concept
+ Direction move >	**Macro concept actor success**	< - Direction move
Push accelerator >		< **Push brake**

All of the macro concept actors are all expected to success life, what is the success life, multi making money, high ranking officials, it must not, for the success it must be alternate macro concept and micro concept, so then M=SM, just M= SM=1~50, to think his/her micro concept actor so call his/her soul existence, try to meet his/her soul meeting in the living of the macro concept. So how to do, it is the religious living is to meet soul. The micro concept living is also very necessary, it already showed in the bible, and Buddha has said that eternity of the soul living. In the bible discriminate soul, mind, body, so then all believe that truth, so then it is true it is very simple, so then it clear of the soul world, just like in micro concept said. Micro concept is still so variable things.

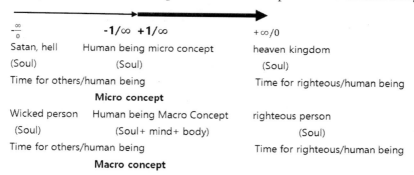

Micro concept is actually not a real, this is just believe or not this is the decision making problems, so then how to live is closing to the micro concept accomplishment. Micro concept is will come to dream to the good harmony, macro concept actors are live all of his/her way, free but not free, all of the living is mixed with macro concept and micro concept.

Actually in the macro concept actor are all involved to making money tools, I'm work for my workplace, work place so called to the company. So then money making tools are relative to the actors, so then actor content support container. The company must be good to the actors so then company managing problems also very deep relative. The company also same position to the macro concept actor, so then company also adapt to the micro concept also.

Why company do not go progress,

All of the company is located at the $-\infty/0 \sim -1/\infty$, this is macro space, macro actors are people, and company a typical composition, but also company more less then people of the actor.

Company is collect of the personal macro actors, so then company manager CEO is the company unit micro concept gate, so then CEO is the center for the company micro concept adopt CEO is the $-1/\infty+1/\infty$ CEO is so important to live on,

CEO Soul	CEO mind	Company itself

What is the CEO soul actually micro concept is $= \lim_{n=\infty}$earth all thing $1/n =$ so then company micro concept is CEO soul, CEO is a person, so then CEO is company leader. CEO has the two kind's soul personal actor soul, CEO company soul.

CEO has the soul, if SEO live righteous then CEO soul must be excitement, but all the time CEO has the mind, so mind also controls CEO. Company managed by the CEO mind. So then the company managed CEO mind, so then CEO M= SM, then S=1, M= 60~100, then micro concept M=60~100, so then company originality is forgot, company originality is the match with soul of the company. Company out of soul so then, company managed by the CEO mind. How complicate to manage the company, if this company has the soul, soul so variable soul friends who are wait to help his/her soul, if a company managed to company originality then this time controlled by the soul, so then company shined all of the out of company ardor the company. It is not seen physical feature of the company but seen story of the success and a soulful miracle story. But if out of the soul company, at least start to seen the company physical featured, dying company comes.

If a company dead then just junk of the featured, company body is the factory but company soul is located at the CEO, CEO and personal actor is coincident so then the temptation so called the satanic factors are all the time carried. Satanic mind is so kill the CEO, not anymore growth more compact company or not. Company move to the right so called to be the macro accelerate this is the permitted to the some of the extend but if over the limitation then it comes variable problems, so this problems is not solved, in the end the company life is so dangerous. So in the micro concept theory expect a company also if accelerate of the macro, to the right move, so then before the limitation the company also turn to the left move, more compact, more perfection all of the procedures and products, then it don't have to go for the move to the right, but CEO forget cause of the increase of the profit, so the profit temptation CEO, at this time CEO started by the mind Control, just distance from the soul, so then the company growth is decreased right after start problems, due to out of soul company being junk featured, just new, micro concept, creature technology helped from micro concept actor of the soul, but CEO temptation from the mind, then mind increased to wider, so decreased soul.

So then mind ordered to the CEO expand to more bigger, this is the macro concept acceleration because of the profit increased, so CEO mind "we can make bigger company" the CEO mind out of the workers, CEO main interesting is company stock index, he/she expect to be increased profit, productivities only, so all of the money invest to the marketing, so then somehow increased, marketing is coincide with macro concept second engine.

So CEO diluted by the marketing, just forgets of the soul, and perfection of the process and product also, so then invest is not for the new perfection product, therefore the company increased mind is reach at the 100, then micro concept M= SM= 100, so then soul of the company died in the end the company is closed. But if a company M= Sm = 20~30, then still this company go with the micro concept depend on the micro concept actor help, the creation, new product perfection, but also the company CEO cared his/her staff wealth, health, so then the company going for the excitement & perfection, this company keep a rule for

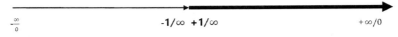

Macro concept CEO	Micro concept gate	Micro concept CEO
+ Direction move >	**Macro concept CEO success**	< - Direction move
Push accelerator >		< Push brake

Macro concept move to + Direction move to the making frame this is about M= 50, then this is the critical line do not cross over the line, so mind index must not over the 50, but all of the macro CEO lost another stages, if a M=50 is m1 of infer of micro concept point then $-1/\infty + 1/\infty$

Then a company must M2 micro concept gate $-1/\infty + 1/\infty$, what is the M2, another challenge it required to a new micro concept actor helping.

Micro concept is varied M = from M1 shift to M2, M3, ... Mn .... $+\infty/0$, so then in the all of the space is time is in seen feel of the in the micro concept, so that what I sad that micro concept is the in the macro concept is past present future amalgamate this is the micro concept gat or point. If a company reaches at the M1, so then CEO temptation from the over desired mind, so getting distance from soul, so the company decreased. If another supposition some company still going without helped soul still control by the mind, that is the micro concept index M=SM= S M= 45~50, so then 5 of the mind is controlled so then just until now reach at the M=50 so that he/she is help member of the workers or the donation to others. But this is still remained at the M1 stages.

If to go for the M2, company is must be suffered to the transient from the M1 to M2.

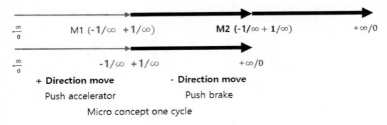

+ Direction move   - Direction move

Push accelerator   Push brake

Micro concept one cycle

Macro concept CEO	M1	M2	Micro concept CEO
+ Direction move >	Complete M	Form of new	< - Direction move
Push accelerator >	Role of $-\infty/0$	$\frac{\infty}{0} \sim -1/\infty$	< Push brake

So then M2 is the role of the M1, but also M1 role of the $-\infty/0$ already reached to the M1, after moment a new $-\infty/0$ is formed, so then start for M2 micro concept gate, so then a new soul birth a new soul try to hep second stages M, so somehow to frame macro concept right move is start. But here M1 breaks so M2 start, M2 accepted from the micro concept soul, so then, still a new soul can help, for this CEO must know that give a new CEO, of this company, so then a new CEO can get helped, this means that righteous process. M1 has finished with excitement and perfection, so all of the worker also excitement and perfection so this company is the already compact company, a perfection of the company, system process perfect, the product is perfect so that M2 micro concept company with a m2 soul, the company micro concept is perfect so long but also M=SM= almost lower, = 10 etc. so strong role of the micro concept actors, soul. So the M2 based on M1, so that the company is righteous actor in the macro concept world, so that in the micro concept actor of the king is god can help also, already built M1, capacity so that god all the time shared with M1~M2, so long, all of the macro concept actors believe in micro concept king might, god's charity, helping in soul and physical so then physical god actor is the M1~M2, god ordered to the M1~M2 micro concept actor of the soul, then a new CEO recognized to help the poor, this acts shown but in the micro concept actor of the soul accept from gods orders to help others, so then excitement and perfection soul reach at the CEO. CEO moves to the still M1 of the left move, but M2 also + direction move.

Micro concept gate = gate $(-1/\infty + 1/\infty)$, this gate is also for the M2 more high-tech, more higher technology helped from the micro concept actors, so then it must be the M1, prepared to the M2 scale of the problems recognized from the late of the M1, brake for the required of the care and meet to soul, so soul push to make less mind of the CEO. So then brake time is not easy but it must be necessary for the new M2, so long, not bigger but compact, perfect M2 so long all of the trade companies recognized the perfect product perfect company process system, so then satisfied to trade companies, also the customers, so this M2 can give the master peaces products. Just soul helped company is a new, creature all the time green, it seen green good, fresh goods story scared in customer mind.

2014.08.01

Micro concept

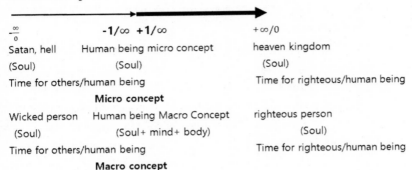

$-\frac{\infty}{0}$	**-1/∞ +1/∞**	**+∞/0**
Satan, hell	Human being micro concept	heaven kingdom
(Soul)	(Soul)	(Soul)
Time for others/human being		Time for righteous/human being

Micro concept

Wicked person	Human being Macro Concept	righteous person
(Soul)	(Soul+ mind+ body)	(Soul)
Time for others/human being		Time for righteous/human being

Macro concept

Micro concept rearranges

In the micro concept until now actor is the for the exclusively human being, but in the micro concept is the all of thing, materials are target, then the same theory is to be adapt to the materials, material also as the same as the macro of materials and micro of it, then actually I can short of explain but surly it ahs the macro of the materials then, soul + mind + materials, so then in this case infer the materials is relative with human beings, so here of the somewhat touchable of the micro concept then soul + mind + materials + helped macro of the human being actors, because of the materials are not can be actor, so then macro concept, so called not that material are all macro concept and micro concept, so then materials are soul material and dead ,materials are difference even in the bio is material but it has the life, living, naturally living, in the macro concept all of human being actors are understood that bio organism is not have a soul, yes it is, but in my micro concept include the micro actor, micro is the peak of micro then atom, molecular etc.

Materials are themselves micro concept actors, it must be infer in the micro concept world also consist of so varied of creatures. Micro concept, I have managed to now, so actually I have hard to go further, sometimes I couldn't go, today morning on the way home, it visit me my micro concept world, as I received from micro concept actor giving me, a gift is this, food in him, and food in restaurant the taste is actually home food is so deep, even the gradients are same of deteriorate in home, but actually home food is so good to me, what is difference, I can explain in the micro concept, home food is the food soul +

mind + food + human beings soul, but in the restaurant food is also has the soul + mind + food + restaurant cook mind soul is small, here M=SM then in the him, Micro concept index = S=1= constants * mind = 1~50 = 1~50. But in micro concept 4 person of micro concept M= 1/4 = 0.25 M. here member of the spaces, so then in the restaurant is M= SM= 1* infer mind is the make money.

so then desired mind in difference from home, then infer M=1* 50~100= 50~100, but also micro concept is = 1/n in a space, so then if customers are 100 a day, then 1/100= 0.01, so the cook micro concept power effect to only to the customer 0.01, so then home food has the soul food, but restaurant food is not a soul food, soul food is the human being soul, so then in the home food is eat all of family soulful food, but in the restaurant food is just out of soul food, so then this food dead food, so that the taste is feeling in macro actor then much more taste, in the micro concept all of the materials are products, foods, all of the product etc. micro concept if a restaurant food how to be same as the home food taste. Micro concept is the very required to do, unseen micro concept

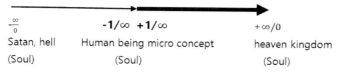

How to adapt in the micro concept to the materials, material are not actor just the related with human being and materials, so long combined with fair of the human being + materials = this is the materials. Soulful materials are made of soulful materials + soulful human being then it comes soulful products. So then micro concept gate of the materials gate (-1/∞+1/∞),, micro cocmnept gate is comes from seen to unseen levels. Unseen micro concept levels, if a procedure of the making products by the human beings so long doing not know the feeling of the problems. While do not know the problems then, what has done for that, so long, if a macro concept actors are do not know to the materials, molecular, but also atoms, unseen materials, so long, if human beings are do not know the deep materials, so long, for something micro materials procedures so long, then do not know the unseen level, then it explained to the micro concept then it is not relative to the soul, so then instead of soul then it occupied to the mind, so mind is increased, in the micro concept all of the martial to products, then

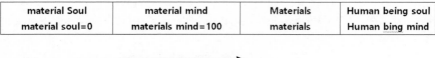

material Soul	material mind	Materials	Human being soul
material soul=0	materials mind=100	materials	Human bing mind

$$\frac{\infty}{0} \qquad -1/\infty \quad +1/\infty \qquad\qquad +\infty/0$$

+ Direction move   - Direction move

Push accelerator   Push brake

If the material to products the procedure of the actor, in the restaurant cook, home cook, so long but Restaurant cook is make for the money, home cook is out of money but it is sacrifice for the family then Restaurant is very best cook, but home cook is not professionalize, restaurant cook is produce all of physical working, this is the cook of the technician unit then it also be the micro concept center so then it must be helped to the good cook, so long, all of cooks, multiple cooks community then the cook must be center to the micro concept gate $(-1/\infty+1/\infty)$, so long, but gate is the cook soul travel in the soulful world, another is the micro concept. In this case, all of the cook produce cause of cook micro concept gate, then restaurant cook became of the micro index M= $1/n$= if he is not micro concept community, then it counted as the works=n, micro index is the $1/n$ if restaurant worker is the 10= $1/10 = 0.1$. Because until now he/she is not get to the cook which realize the cook, the cook recognized to the level of the cook community counted so then he/she come to M=$1/n$= M=1, so he/she realize as the cook, so long cook of the realize so then, it already a recognized cook realize then it become of the n=1, it must be the same as the M= SM=S=1 *M=1~10,20 under the 50, then professional cook reach at the top of the cooks community. So then he cook for the restaurant eat, so then, restaurant food = home food =1, micro concept is the required to do, if a work fields are cut to $1/\infty$ numbers, in the end all of the $1/\infty$ it means that what is the macro to micro= 1/1, 1/10,1/100, 1/1000, $1/n$ = about 0,

Actually physical macro is the 1 but pure micro is to reach at the $1/\infty$, the problems of the professional techic if he/she goes to deep, so long perfect problems solving. So long all of the materials in the micro concept, perfect product with $1/n$ if n is goes to the ∞, so then $1/\infty$, so long products are perfect. Perfect product is relative with soulful materials with soulful human beings. = product = SM= 1* M= closed to the less, if mind decreased) = products are perfect. Human being with materials = materials has the mind, if mind M goes to∞, then soul to 1/∞, if a good cook also has the mind∞,soul 1/∞, all of the cook gradually decresed to a cook micro concept gate, from it to wide, so then losing the micro concept forget, so then, old cook so long cook govern by the mind, instead of soul, losing the eternity of the soul controlled. Realized cook must be keeping holding soul, to be hold all of living of the micro concept, it must be sacrifice, but also still keep excitement & perfection, so long just realized actor must be the god's order accept and royalty doing it. All of the macro concept gate reaching realization is come to the conclusion going with god's worker then, in the end of the close to the body released from the soul then, it comes to pure soul, then it must be the human being actor will be the righteous actors soul group place in the eternity.

2014.08.04

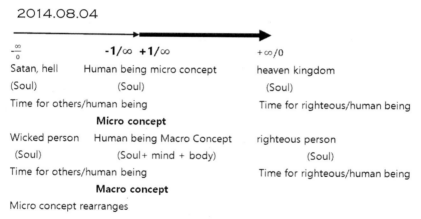

Micron concept and center of the gate is the time, and place is defined to, then past is -∞/0 from here, from here to +∞/0 is future. I believe that past and future is not, in my living I can't reach to it, so I supposed that my living is acting time and place. But actually I'm living. In a place and time,

What is this, my living, in this time and place I try to show time level past and future, but what is present I'm here, what is the here, I got a hint to describe of my micro concept, in my place living is depend on -∞/0~-1/∞ I have said and write my living. I thought that overcome of present limitation, how to overcome of this time hard, how to solve life all of the problems. Problems is suffering, so I expected to future knowledge, what is the future is $+1/\infty \sim +\infty/0)$ from now to long future, actually macro is the $-\infty/0, +\infty/0$ so long distance from now past and futre is all of the macro actors scale, so macro acore feel of the time, past ,present, future. This is start, but I thought that I'm in the time of the moment of time, second, micro second, not seen place and time is from the $-\infty/0 \sim -1/\infty$ past is conversen to present about $=zero=0$, not zero, in the cognition is zero is nothing, but about zero, then it is not zero$=0$, future is also macro actor feel that just future is the $+\infty/0$ so long distance from this point, here, but I thought that now actually unseen that is the $+\infty/0 \sim -1/\infty$ this is the convergence from long future to about zero$=0$, but it isn not $=0$, so then about zero, so then my micro concept point is the mixed with past, future and make it a present. I have been talked macro concept actor, and micro concept actors are soul. Soul is actually major at micro concept but in the macro concept is minor, macro concept leaded by the body and mind, but in the micro is soul is major but mind is minor, so then in the macro is seen body, but in the micro concept world is only seen soul, so then soul is the micro, macro actor is common, micro concept point, is located at the micro, and macro is coexistence, so long micro and macro is the soul also located, micro concept point is unseen in the macro, seen in the micro, so even then actually existed in the macro and micro concept actor, so long it must be feel of the macro then feeling actor is the body own human being, but in the felling of the micro concept actor is the soul. So then both actor in the micro and macro concept the place is and time is the all of the fast convergence, from future convergence is the $-1/\infty +1/\infty$, just so ,moment so called it is not seen but still existence, micro point but also the I express to micro concept gate.

Micro concept field is momentum so unseen size, so then unit of the time and place, it must be the micro concept energy is summed, this energy is operated of the micro concept, I was so hard to expand of the micro concept story. And actor moving velocity, micro concept and macro concept what I said to before, I infer that the entire time micro concept macro concept are coexistence. I try explains of the micro concept this is $-1/\infty +1/\infty$, it must be area of the micro, time of the micro is unseen seen, this seen in the micro concept world, but in the macro concept is not seen, then, micro concept is the world, so long, in the micro concept actors are must be time and size is $-1/\infty +1/\infty$, so long micro concept actors are much more micro actors.

So long, micro concept gate and pint is the about real of the mixed with past and future this is made of the present. In the micro concept unit is the distance and time, is mixed then this is the tunnel of the micro and macro gate tunnel, so long, bridge to the macro and micro, so that micro concept gate is explained and used variable, but micro concept is the also management actors, so long actors are soul, so but also all of creature also, go made creature also micro concept point and gate $-1/\infty+1/\infty$, so it must be equal to micro concept, so somewhat is confused to use micro concept gate, so then it must tunnel but also it must be the space of it, micro concept point is the real place to live on, so that micro concept point is the real of the soul place, but in the macro concept is the recognition of the in the real of the people recognition.

Then micro concept unit is the space and time, so then square meter, time is second, so this is the so micro concept so then $-1/\infty+1/\infty$ this is the space and time all express by this micro concept point. Micro concept point is so called time and meter or the actor of the soul is very important indicator, so then all of movement is the velocity is meter/ second = Velocity. So then

$1/\infty \,/\, 1/\infty =$ about $0 = 0/0 = V$ is about 0, but not 0 zero, this means that all of the size is reach at the just moment all direction far from the center to edge velocity and time is about zero, so it means it also micro concept used to it reach at the from far left to far right then it must be the micro concept gate explained to do, $-1/\infty+1/\infty$, so long, in the micro concept gate, the soul speed is so fast, it also said by the micro concept also.

Micro concept and macro concept are coincide, so then if the infer the macro concept, the actor of the minor is the soul, soul move to the all of the creature place so fast, just like compared with macro concept place electron, $E= mc2$, so then soul=mc2. Soul is m is $-+1/\infty$, c is same as the $E= mc2$.

Electron is not go for the micro concept world e is the macro concept seen unseen materials energy, so then micro concept and macro concept tunnel movement actor energy soul= mc2, so then soul is move to the free, what explained before it can be explained under the table.

$$\xrightarrow{\hspace{8cm}}$$

$\frac{\infty}{0}$ **-1/∞ +1/∞**   +∞/0

Satan, hell   Human being micro concept   heaven kingdom

(Soul)   (Soul)   (Soul)

Time for others/human being   Time for righteous/human being

Micro concept

Wicked person   Human being Macro Concept   righteous person

(Soul)   (Soul+ mind + body)   (Soul)

Time for others/human being   Time for righteous/human being

Macro concept

Micro concept rearranges

Actually soul is so move fast, so long soul is strong actor of the macro and micro, it infer in the macro concept world role of the his/her soul body all of news to carry to the micro concept world souls, I do not infer now soul place how to shape, but now comes to righteous soul, and wick soul so called satanic souls, so then a soul swiftly move to the news to the place of the micro concept world soul to be interested a macro concept actors news righteous or wick news to carry to the micro concept place.

Micro concept place live in the lord, god, god live but also, Satan also has the located at the micro concept place. So long the place and time of the micro concept is the micro concept space is the what i said then tunnel is the space, so long micro concept point is the micro concept world -1/∞+1/∞ so long, micro concept place it must be coexistence, it infer that micro concept point and macro concept point coexistence, then in vague but it must be so relative to the macro concept and micro concept world. It must be the micro concept is the so micro then if the god create and the in the bible said then, god create all of the macro actors natured all of components, so then it must in the convergence to micro concept so, micro concept point, so that creator of macro concept, is the living in the micro concept god, lord is the can evaluate all of the macro concept actors behavior, so long righteous wick, all of the also so then wick and righteous also terms of the bible. So then, in the micro concept world, it must be the wick soul group, but also righteous soul groups, so that in the macro concept world a actors behavior of the righteous behavior or wick behavior news carry in a moment to from macro to the micro concept world, so then righteous news carry to the righteous soul group, but wick news to wick soul group, so then, this information of the news delivered to the micro concept world, information date, then, a macro concept actors all has the free decide selection power, so then is is all of the free choice to live on righteous living, wicked living, so long the, if select righteous then its information delivered to the righteous place, but wick decide then all of the news delivered to the satanic soul place governor this is Satan.

So long it is the very relative to micro and macro is not distance but all is micro second time, so then, but time scale is not same with macro time scale, so I can infer to explained Jesus Christ walk on the surface of the water, Jesus walked without drop to the water. So long, micro concept time is so unseen time, but macro concept time is seen, so the gap is not calculated in the macro concept mathematical idea.

Micro concept gate is explained to the philosophical, physiological all of variable adopt to used for the explained to micro and macro concept problems explained to do, for the ways, so long all of micro concept also somewhat adopt for the expanded to all of area.

If a person do act wicked working then this news so deliver to the wicked group of the micro concept world, so then wicked group will accept news, so then wicked group also the king dome of the Satan, so Satan has the purpose so then, they are very excitement with wicked actors, so, all of information of the wicked act is accumulated to actor of the resume, so long is very fit to the wicked actor purpose, the Wicked group all the time accept to the fighter for the mission of the wicked so called satanic kingdom purpose. But also the righteous actor also deliver to the interest of the righteous so then soul deliver to the righteous soul groups so righteous soul actor news to righteous group, so called heaven king, god's side. God required to god mission actors, so god accept him for the righteous mission, for the god side, eternity living kingdom actor.

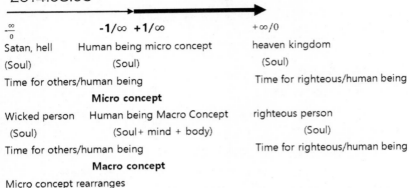

$\frac{-\infty}{0}$ **-1/∞ +1/∞**   +∞/0

Satan, hell Human being micro concept	heaven kingdom
(Soul) (Soul)	(Soul)
Time for others/human being	Time for righteous/human being

Micro concept

Wicked person Human being Macro Concept	righteous person
(Soul) (Soul+ mind + body)	(Soul)
Time for others/human being	Time for righteous/human being

Macro concept

Micro concept rearranges

soul	>< mind ><	body

In the micro concept it already comes key word soul, mind, body, it explains itself role, body is the touchable macro actor main, but untouchable actor is the soul, mind is not actor but role of just like soul, but actually mind is wicked soul. If infer then mind is Satan dwelling place, soul is infer from then comes heaven kingdom of the micro concept main actor. Soul knows only micro concept world main actor so soul knows the as main actor micro concept place. So soul tries to teach or tell to his macro fair, so called the body. Soul was so excited to the macro concept place, but soul meets a soul's enemies. Soul inexpertly comes to meet it enemy. So long in his macro concept place, soul is distance from body, because of the mind is defended to meet between soul and body. Mind is also role of the body to be getting well, mind is strong body manager, and mind is the sustainment of the body. Eating, bringing children up, resided placing getting, etc. To be live for the macro concept, so then body needed to a new macro concept acting helper. Mind is the desired; hate, jealously, enemy, hate, stealth, anger, force to destroy, competitions, winning destroy getting something, make rich, etc all of the desired mind. Mind is the all of the same of the Satan mission, sometimes macro concept actor steal and even some burglar over the stealth act also, so long all of the actors are behaves wicked, all of the mind is contents of the wicked, so then, wait to see the body, the soul all the time care body fair, but mind is deep, so that soul can't be seen to the fair of body. Soul just a distance with body fair, soul sometimes in the night just so tired so that mind is sleep so deep, then, soul appeared to his macro concept fair in the dream, so in the sleeping time, soul try to give s information of micro concept soul main actor world. But after get up so then a strong mind erased his body, to go for the macro concept actors, so then body all the time busy of the mind slave, mind is the master of the body. Mind is some infer that Stan role of play, so mind is much desired try to be rich to others, all of desired mind. So then soul disappeared in the noon time.

Body is live only slaver not a master, so the living of the macro concept all the time hard because of the round of the macro concept actors are also same mind actors, so then all of the not a friend, in the wicked people is all are enemies, even in the family members also not a friend, because of family is not relative to the making money so in the family is all of the mind actor s are try to be treated from family be good treatment, then just one day mother has been role but in the micro concept mother also wanted to be good treatment. So then the family is already battle field, so then still carried to life somewhat bad memory, this is start of the mind. All of the macro concept actors learn not to give other but only to be good treatment.

So long, in the macro concept player's actor's entire mind wanted to be treated as the master role. So then actor mind do not learn, but in the macro concept world has the schools to learn for the live, so called the getting job also, originality is the education is helped from the how to live in the all of the year of live times, living itself is the mind controlled. Even all of the macro concept world actors are to be educated for the try to give, but that is not macro concept instinct but so then, soul is the entire time tries to give other, in the long run, soul is not getting but all try to give other, because soul do not know the desired mind, soul do not know the macro concept actors behavior, soul are micro of the macro concept actor, so long so then it must be the infer to the $-1/\infty$ $+1/\infty$ so long, micro actor don;'t have to get but so give all of its to others. So long.

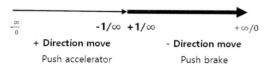

So then mind is the actor of the + direction move, so called the mind is the actor of the Satan of the micro concept in the macro concept world, so long just overcome the all of the + direction move is the keep pushing accelerator so that it required to be stopper is the – Direction move is required so then, soul try to meet soul's fair body, so it must be very urgent so long, - Direction move is required, soul Push brake, actually all of the macro concept actor has soul, but soul is not appeared to but unseen so that macro concept do not know the micro concept actor of the soul, soul try to role, so then, soul must be face to the mind but, actually go to the – direction move then, do not meet soul to face mind. So long soul go for the left ward to be left, a macro concept actor some of the realize approach to the micro concept point, -1/∞+1/∞, just so long move to – direction is the in the macro concept actors are all can communicate, originally all of the + direction move Actors just direct to make money all of their energy used, but in the – direction move is the can see the out of money, so then family also come back, communication is often so very usual, all of the + Direct move and – Direction move somewhat reach at the point of the micro concept point -1/∞+1/∞, then it don't have to perfect – direct move, to the start point, but is must be impossible so that in the practically of the living is the – direction move to the left,

It is possible in this time not a concept, but it occurs to the macro concept realization.

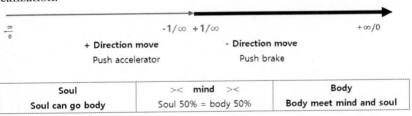

Soul	>< mind ><	Body
Soul can go body	Soul 50% = body 50%	Body meet mind and soul

Just - Direct move is decreased mind to be co habit in the macro concept, but actually this procedure is not easy to the macro concept actors, all of the macro concept actor live fully without interrupt going for the + direction move, some people destructed but naturally unseen brake so all of the asset dissolved all diminished all of the + moved to the act, so then he must broken, this is the artificial made, but auto move is the from the soul, soul from birth know the soul knows it don't necessary to live on, eternity is not get desired, but do live righteous, soul push for the righteous, all the time live for the righteous. So soul lead the fair of body to go for the – direction move, so horribly soul lead his fair of the micro concept point -1/∞+ 1/∞, so then a body would be dead then the time is comes the micro concept point $-1/\infty + 1/\infty$, so then he/she goes to the soul actor world, even in the time of macro concept a famous macro and macro actor is the Jesus Christ, or Buddha then live in the micro concept point $-1/\infty + 1/\infty$, it msut be soul with lived with fair of body, all this is not soul 50%, mind 50%, but jesus Christ, Buddha is soul is 100% mind is 0%, so long, Jesus Buddha is lived soul + Zero mind=0 + body, =Soul + body, so they still god to us. But most macro concept actor are to live – Direction move so then it comes Soul 50% = body 50%, it is the realized time, so long, he/she is dead, then he/she is reach at the time of the dead the micro concept point, so called micro concept gate, tunnel of the micro concept gate, it must also the what we called, micro concept point $-1/\infty + 1/\infty$ is the tiem level, or the meter level then this must be the micro concept world space itself, so then if macro concept actors are go for the – direction move it realize. So long, to live wildly just for the macro concept fully live then, it means that keep going for the + directive move then, macro concept actors are all live for the only desired to get. These actors are all luxurious life style then he live fully, in the macro concept, mind is full 100%, so then just 0 % of the soul, so then it must be the Satan mission did well, so then he must be naturally excitement with these characteristics actors, infer that fully live for the personal desired, then he/she died so he can meet these people, even they do not felt they are wicked but they do not lived for others, so long sacrificed living, in the macro concept world, they do not know the Sacrifice, but he lived so all of actor end, so long dead actor of full lived people just end of the + moved move actor, he/she do not know any realization, so that he/she comes to the end of live, so called dead then his/her soul naturally Satanic place of micro concept world. So then soul so sorrowful in the micro concept world, so soul so hard to live on, soul disgrace live in the satanic world, Satanic world of the micro concept world, Satanic soul is so anger, because of all of the mind make it, but soul hasn't any sins, but mind distort the tour of the soul traveling, soul + body must go for the after dead then soul comes to the it's starting place all of the righteous soul place, if a soul come back to the soul originality. Soul excitement to comeback to safe, soul lived in the soul + body lives righteous; do give others, in the bible saying, love neighbor this very simple proposition. Soul lived in the macro concept; macro concept helping others do live righteously, so lucky comes to very perfect to comes realize, so that comes to the micro concept.

So infer from that soul try to be return to start from the soul place, start travel to the soul + body, he/she lived well in the macro concept world, but it comes a strong desired satanic role of the mind is comes, so then soul + mind + body, so most soul live satanic live, so in the bible originality sins, so all of the macro concept actors are trouble, so long if the required to be the returning to the micro concept soul place, it required to macro concept mind decreased. But do not know then soul, unlucky soul lost the start time soul, the soul changed with mind, so that mind is contaminate the soul, so after dead soul is not located in the started soul group, if in the soul to live all of accepted in the mind soul, same group of soul eternity destinations.

Just — move directive move is the macro concept actor live do righteous living. Then macro concept actor realize then he/ she can be reach at the micro concept point reach or place to be the micro concept gate micro concept point -1/∞+ 1/∞. This is the micro concept point it is the tunnel to the very realization in the macro concept.

2014.08.06

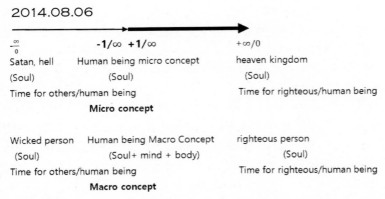

Micro concept actors are soul, macro actor with soul + mind + body. So that macro actors move, so then each actor lives with others. In this case very moment happened between giver and taker; all has the happened in the relationship. In this relationships are also trade and charity activities all are included. All of the relationship build and management is required.

In the building relationship, all of variable causes and effects, so in these relationships are men and woman, high ranker lower ranker political status, but also religious school etc all of patterns are orientations. If two actors meet in the point of macro concept then, macro two actors communicate and trade but also mind shared with them. In the relationship has a cause of effect,

So long it comes righteous and wicked type of actors, in the micro concept actors' criteria line one is righteous another is wicked person, but also in this connection is both Righteous connection

But also two are wicked actors; so long it come two actors' relationships patterns show to be resulted causes.

I probably make this table

Relationship types Two Actors (A focus)		A: focus Result of the relationship	Type
A: righteous	B: righteous	ommunicate best	A : best
A: righteous	B: wicked	Understand others	B : middle
A: wicked	B: Wicked	make hard each others	C : worst
A: Wicked	B: righteous	Deceit others	D : worst

In this table just A focus to be, then in the two actors, has happened to the result, so then A and B are lived, in the micro concept is the just momentum is only is the happened so multi actors are lived but actually in a moment all the time face two actors. So then momentum creates the all of decisions. Righteous decision, wicked decision, this also comes, then

It must be infer of coming table

Momentum decision makings		A: focus Result of the relationship	Type
A: righteous	B: righteous	ommunicate best	A : best
A: righteous	B: wicked	Understand others	B : middle
A: wicked	B: Wicked	make hard each others	C : worst
A: Wicked	B: righteous	Deceit others	D : worst

In the relationship in the moment think that moment of righteous decision getting, A and B then communication best, it occur credibility building, but

4 types introduce decision making is cause of the relationship character also made.

So then, micro concept and macro concept point of view soul + mind + body role of the macro concept world, Type A would be compared with soul + body, Type B C D depend on the mind ranges, mind is the variance, so then soul act also depend on the mind.

I am building the relationships

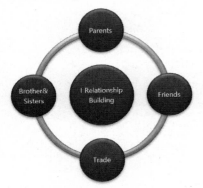

In this relationship comes to the type A B C D, family relationships Parents to me, and brothers and sister and me, this relationship all be inferred to type A, but actually all of the righteous and wicked source also from family, so if the family produce the righteous seeds then it must be family function supply the righteous products, or some of the family has the actor some of problems so then family produced type B C D, so supply to the community a so then product is also A type, and B C D.

I can build the friends who are effect to charity, love relationships, among this time also relationship produce a good friends or friends comes, the maintenance also give and take a amenability comes. I can also build trade relationships this is the money is mediated trade. It infer to this relationship is type B C D comes.

In the micro concept just righteous energy is construction, but wicked energy is destruction.

It must be infer of the table

Momentum decision makings		A: focus Result of the relationship	Type
A: righteous	B: righteous	ommunicate best	A : best
A: righteous	B: wicked	Understand others	B : middle
A: wicked	B: Wicked	make hard each others	C : worst
A: Wicked	B: righteous	Deceit others	D : worst

Micro concept actor is the soul so then, it infer the energy carried to the micro concept world, so long in the gate of the micro concept -1/∞+1/∞ so long, if type A then Soul carry energy plus 2 then it must be inferred to be accumulated blessing. Personal saving account in the micro concept world, so then if also infer to the type a contact then all the time naturally happened the righteous so then micro main actor carry to the righteous then righteous soul blessing bank deposit. But if type D then, infer that soul carry to the micro concept blessing bank, then soul with draw blessing from bank, so long if saving is 0 then, it must be inferred to soul carry to the bankruptcy so then soul carry to the loan from the micro concept Satanic bank, which will history. So long in the macro concept world, donation is good for the donated person, he/she is so feel good, satisfaction then the good behavior can deposit to the micro concept blessing bank.

For the Type A is the good rich man donate to the righteous good living accumulate in the blessing bank in the micro concept place. The acceptor also be benefit so then it must be god hear of the pray of the poor people, so then god ordered to the soul, in the micro concept gate -1/∞+1/∞, so then soul diliver to the macro concept donor to help god's order, so then righteous donator is the god's messenger, helper role. So then the donator is the happy with the macro actor but also in the soul place soul actor also excitement so long, it accumulate in the blessing bank. But if Type C then, energy -2, so then it must be bankruptcy in the micro concept world so then he has any belling in his micro concept world, so then, he must be faced to the bad time.

This is the just personal cases but then if this personal must be group, community, and company then what happened to.

2014.08.07

	-1/∞ +1/∞	+∞/0
∞/0		
Satan, hell	Human being micro concept	heaven kingdom
(Soul)	(Soul)	(Soul)
Time for others/human being		Time for righteous/human being

Micro concept

Wicked person	Human being Macro Concept	righteous person
(Soul)	(Soul+ mind + body)	(Soul)
Time for others/human being		Time for righteous/human being

Macro concept

Micro concept how show to others, what is a micro concept? Macro concept is seen, micro concept unseen, concept, something will be perfect combination macro concept and micro concept. What has possibility the composition of the ratio macro concept and micro concept? It infers that macro is the physical so called frame, so long seen part, but unseen part mind effect or soul combined effect. Micro concept is design but macro concept is feasible seen behavior. Do not recognition in the usual working, all of mixed but all are macro concept shown. Macro concept and micro concept is combined, macro depends on macro deepen on micro.

Macro concept moving energy from macro concept world, but micro concept is from micro concept world. Each world actors moving energy, macro concept energy is spent then gets energy cause of resting, but micro concept energy is the behavior of macro concept righteous after than blessing save energy. Auto electric generation in the micro concept, micro concept energy fully depends on macro concept righteous behavior so then this blessing saved to the micro concept saving bank.

Micro concept energy circulation ① Macro concept use saving energy or loan energy from micro concept bank ②The energy using in the macro concept design for macro behavior ③Macro concept act righteous or wick behavior ④ The result of righteous or wick products ⑤The result of righteous behavior + saving, wicked behavior – Saving in the micro concept bank.

Macro concept use energy ①from bank saving money use or loan from bank ②macro actor behavior design ③Macro concept act making money or losing in making money ④the result of making money or losing money from macro actor behavior ⑤the result of macro actor behavior to + saving or − Saving to the bank.

- **Macro concept and micro concept energy circulations -**

In the macro concept world, actor live by making money, so then all of the procedures are business planning, finance and do act, after that the result of the business behavior in the process as possible as followed of righteous or wicked then the result of product is righteous product or wicked product, even in the macro concept world money making result is not difference all money is same money, but in the micro concept bank can discriminate of the righteous money or wicked money, so then, all of the procedure of the making money in the end, the actor of money maker must be followed to the righteous, so called micro concept actor, soul recognized to the money is come of the righteous, then the soul fly to the micro concept ruler god, so then god accept of the a macro concept making money actors are righteous so then, god ordered to the soul, to help the poor, then, a money maker use the money for the poor, so then acceptor also very thank you the money giver then it complete of the righteous money used. In this case of the macro actor in this process the result is out of the trade, but the actor already a soul fly to the micro concept world the king, report, automatically the bank of the micro concept register of saving. Then it comes the macro concept actor get a Save in the micro concept world bank. But if the wicked money making so then, he/she used exclusively all of money making used for him / herself, so then, his money is wicked so long, he/ she saved in the micro concept bank minus save in bank. In the end in the micro concept bank non- performing loan disposal so then, in the micro concept bank has no saving account, so then, the wicked money do fraud victim to others, then it perfect, the fair of the soul deliver to the very excitement news to micro concept Satanic soul place, but also in this place – bank deposit, so it registered the debt recording. So then even in the macro concept world get a big money but do not use of the righteous then, all of the behaviors news to the Satanic, so long then automatically register to the – bank account, so accumulated the – register increased. So long, macro actor even makes money but the money and business safety or longer business is must be questioned, so then to keep longer of successful business all depend on the deceit trade stake holders. After all the making money make all of the enemies such as the a big company be supplied by the small company the partials then supplied price so poor, then the big company make enemy, so then the big company stakes holders are suffer from trading with big company. Even though the big company making money also, the money all give to the big bio company workers, then the big company money making procedures are not righteous, so then the big company money used, this behavior connect to the micro concept, so then the big company soul fly to the micro concept world bank, so then deposit to the bank minus saving. In the end in the micro concept World Bank a big company of money decreased so then it must be out of the micro concept money, so long all of the big company micro concept world energy all used up. So then, macro company gradually soul diluted, all of the macro a big company keep increased productivities by the wicked procedures.

In conclusion actually even this is the micro concept or macro concept, it is not real but, if not follows save in the micro concept bank the energy of the blessing is decreased so then lucky of the business is also decreased.

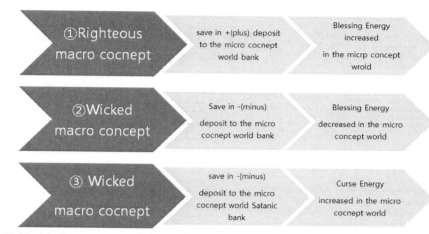

①Righteous macro cocnept	save in +(plus) deposit to the micro cocnept world bank	Blessing Energy increased in the micrp concept wrold
②Wicked macro concept	Save in -(minus) deposit to the micro cocnept world bank	Blessing Energy decreased in the micro concept world
③ Wicked macro cocnept	save in -(minus) deposit to the micro cocnept world Satanic bank	Curse Energy increased in the micro cocnept world

Right wicked macro concept behave related Blessing energy cycle

① Righteous macro concept world soul energy is so dynamic so that in the macro concept behavior is also going with soul, so macro concept actor is helped from the soul so called from the God blessing getting.

②Wicked macro concept world soul energy is so dim so that in the macro concept behavior is not going with soul, in the end macro concept actor do not helped from the god blessing.

Macro concept actor with soul, or not is very important so then macro concept actor also, must care of the micro concept bank full saving deposit so then full blessing by the god, if not do not saving in the micro concept bank then god will not give blessing, because of the haven't any bank balance. So then another case, bankruptcy in the micro concept bank, then the macro actor will be connected with in the micro concept world, satanic bank register so then all of the in the macro concept actor wicked behavior all of the energy in minus(-) save in the deposit to the micro concept world satanic bank. This satanic bank has the increased the Cursed Energy. So then micro concept and macro concept circulation then macro actor will be affected in actor's behavior.

It must be inferred to that micro concept blessing energy is big, or micro concept cursed energy is big then, whose macro will be the possibility to be success, it must be clear the micro concept world blessing energy is big must be success in the macro concept world.

But if in the micro concept world save in the satanic bank, then increased the cursed energy increased how to effect to the macro concept actor, it so clear of failure, if not still deceit others so many harmful actors produced, so then these actors cursed energy also save in the satanic bank, so that he/ she macro actors are failed in the end.

2014.08.08

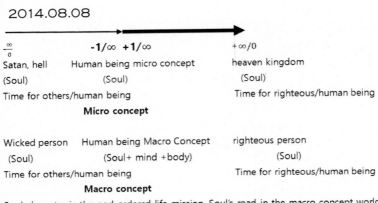

Soul character is the god ordered life mission. Soul's road in the macro concept world, God has a plan all of macro concept actors, who are carried to righteous mission, it is the soul life. Micro concept is

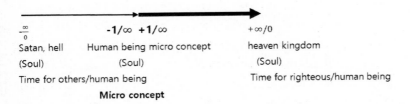

Micro concept point $-1/\infty+1/\infty$ this is the all of things are $\lim_{n=\infty}\pm1/n$ it is anti of the $\max_{n=\infty}\pm n$ so then, $\lim_{n=\infty}\pm1/n$ is micro cocncept , $\max_{n=\infty}\pm n$ is macro concpt, micro concept is near end of it, so called it reach at the conclusion, but macro concept it will not to be end eternity move to the conclusion.

In the micro concept actor is soul, macro concept world actor is soul + mind+ body=body, in the point of macro concept is micro is unseen, but macro concept is seen, macro concept actor live in the macro concept world, they are live body they do not know soul, but in the micro concept point of view is actor is soul so then micro concept gate is the soul living place, somewhat to understand of the macro concept then tunnel to the macro to micro concept gate.

In the point of micro concept living actor, living in the micro concept world, but macro concept also live body, all of the points of micro concept actor it must be infer that macro concept also soul+ mind+ body, in the macro concept point of view actually macro concept actor would be live soul. So then even has the seen the body, if a consist of the macro concept actor is

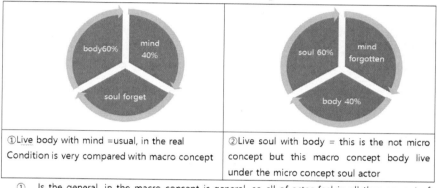

①Live body with mind =usual, in the real Condition is very compared with macro concept	②Live soul with body = this is the not micro concept but this macro concept body live under the micro concept soul actor

① Is the general, in the macro concept is general, so all of actor feel in all they are out of sins, they live desired to be reach, all of mind is expanded to, so mind almost to kill soul, so soul forgotten, most people always point of view macro world is only existence so then all of another world do not know, so called micro concept world, perfectly do not know, macro actors live in the body seen living.

② But actually status is only existence for the concept forming, in the macro concept world, micro actor make forgotten the mind to zero=about 0, so body meet micro concept soul so then even in the circumstance is body portion is 40%, soul is 60% so then, even body is only shell, but soul is the real actor, so then in the macro concept world actor is just like in the micro concept actor, so macro concept world also soul is governing status then body shell.

Under the macro concept ($\max_{n=\infty}\pm n$) micro concept ($\lim_{n=\infty}\pm 1/n= -1/\infty+1/\infty$) under the macro concept circumstance all of the actors are full in the macro concept space, so then all of the actors are all body, but some of the actor realize to about micro concept actors they are in the tunnel of the micro concept gate ($\lim_{n=\infty}\pm 1/n= -1/\infty+1/\infty$), this actors are just body is shell 40% + body = 0%, + soul=60%, so that in the macro concept soul is major act major is master but body is slaver, so that micro concept actor live under the macro concept major body living actors, so then micro concept actor without dead, so called dead detached is dead, so then in the macro concept world, mind is zero, so then in the macro concept actor and micro concept actor, so long, micro concept actor watch actually in the body, soul living is can see without the mind, so soul live in the standard of the micro concept world. So micro concept world actor in the macro concept circumstance so then micro concept actor will watch the macro concept actor live, so long live as a soul he / she live in the soul world concept.

He/ she will not live for the making money just like macro actor center working. So then micro concept living is not for the making money. So then in the macro concept world combined macro and micro, so then micro is the god space, money making is the macro then it is the mind controlled world so this place is the Satanic world

	Definition	Mission	behavior	Result
①Macro actor	Soul+ mind+ body	rich & success	Wicked& deceit	Break peace
②Micro actor	Soul	Do live righteous	Help each other	Keep peace

So then soul actor do live usually in the micro concept world, so in the pure soul world soul come together in the righteous soul destination live, it is very simple, so other righteous soul so all the time peace, it is general in the micro concept world, so this world would be forming in the micro concept major actor soul, macro concept mission is to be rich success, so all of the time controlled for the success to make much money, macro concept is very easy to live on the direction is to reach at the rich, and success, so for the macro concept mission accomplish all of the macro concept procedures are all mixed by the make good condition other condition make hard, so long all of the procedures are winner or loser game, so then all of the getting rich and success the macro actor behave as the wick of deceit others, here other is all of the relationship building group. To be success all of the asset input for him, but after getting the result is exclusive owned. So success actor has no idea it depend on other sacrifice. So macro concept actor controls by mind so that hind to help others, in the end it come to dispute so break a peace.

① Macro actor living is just live as the body, but ② micro actor is just live as a soul, soul live is the righteous by the help each other but macro actor to live rich and success by the wicked & deceit

② Micro concept live is the soul living place so then soul is perfectly divided righteous & wicked soul, soul is very sensitive it perfect realized each other so even perfect concealed but all is not hided all be seen each soul each others, so then righteous soul excitement with righteous, but wicked soul is very excitement with wicked things, Wicked soul cross the righteous line then, righteous soul all of fear, so all of group segregate from wicked soul group, right soul group keep peace in soul place, but wicked soul group place all of are so deep wicked so best player to be success, or make money being rich. Then the place all is wicked so there has no wick target is not, so, each other deceit because of their learned in the macro concept world all get through. But wicked soul, righteous soul perfectly divided. In the micro concept place do not cross, so macro concept and micro concept tunnel is not simple, right tunnel is hard to reach point $-1/\infty + 1/\infty$, wicked micro concept place is not deep actually there is no means but to explained micro concept righteous soul place explained. In the righteous soul energy is to help each other but wicked soul energy is to win in the moment, so very cunning actor get it, but it is not from the god, but this power from the satanic power.

In the macro concept world live righteous living, wicked living. If I just one variance time, then macro concept time, micro concept have a variance is time, so that, in the macro world how to used the time is the decided to righteous or wicked.

	Relationship	Process	Future & Creation
Macro concept actor	Time for others lower	Perfection lower	Creation lower
Micro concept actor	Time for other high	Perfection higher	Creation Higher

Macro concept actors haven't time to go with others so, in the place role is not clear, all of actor move to the place role is different for example school student, home is son and daughter so then student also in the home, but child role to the school, so all of the conditions are busy, actually all of macro concept actor try to easy position, which try to get a good tasteful position player, they all to be helped from others. But they do not to be helper of role player. So they all be understood from others, who understand then, it necessary for the make money, just center worker for making money, so called the job worker only care macro actor, so then money related actor are very function to give the value of money, so treat respect to the customers. But out of the place then, all is closed perfectly. Money making is only show to other humble but out of the money making place all is out of the rule, they do not shared their time, friend meeting time is not for other, just fear of the psychology so come together so clearly this is not for other but it also rate for the use others, time for other is sacrifice time.

Sacrifice time is help others, in the research or company problems solving all of the time even in the holiday for the solving problems then this time all is sacrifice time so then it must be the count on the righteous in the micro concept bank of blessing. Even more future & Creation, is not now but future knowledge is getting time, but also creation also is really micro concept typical working. So this used time the entire micro concept righteous bank deposited so then if use the energy fully be in the macro concept actor all of behavior reach at the perfection comes.

Time is the very important factor for the righteous or wicked criteria all of the masterpiece is from the righteous sacrifice overcoming the fear of losing in the living, all of the hard time sacrifice for the creation of the future theory getting, then, god give to the sacrifice for the soluble of it, then god so excitement to giving solutions.

Then getting old with live righteous then old time, so used for the righteous then it must be the count on the righteous, this is comes now, the old man approach to the micro concept, the old man is micro concept (point $-1/\infty+1/\infty$) gate approach

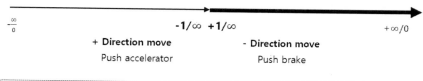

Soul	>< mind ><	Body
Soul can go body	Soul 50% = body 50%	Body meet mind and soul

Because of it may be infer that in the time of the old, soul push brake of + direction move, so then an actor already turn to the (minus- direction move) he know the sacrifice all of his asset donation to the community etc, all is the getting realize for the contact to meeting soul, so mind is go down then up is the soul, he/ she used the all his macro asset, decreased for the micro concept rule adopt, but also to be the micro concept role player. He became of the god's messenger, so then the old man delivered to the poor his/her asset, he/ she met soul, it is the time of the dead. They realize to the face of the dead, and then the soul lastly will get into righteous soul place of micro concept place.

2014.08.11

Soul Energy: soul can go dead

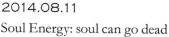

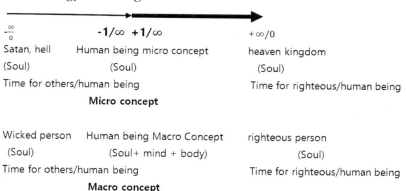

In this micro concept main actor is the soul, but also the place also micro concept world. So then all of souls are live in the micro concept world. In the micro concept world all of actors are live in the rule of the micro concept. Soul live also well or not, soul is also life, so then soul needed the daily 3 times eating for the soul sustainment and development in soul matured. Soul how to eat energy which is food for the soul, soul how to build healthful soul, soul also need to sustainment of the living, so then it infer that soul also health, sick and soul also come to finish.

Soul also excitement and gloomy the source of body behavior good news or bad news, so then Soul is closed related with body. Soul is not body, in the macro concept has a body, so Soul parasite in the body. Soul depend on body, body is field soul is the plant, this compared to, so then plant = soul, grow well in the field. Fertile soil is good body, soul=plant also grows well in the fertile soil. Fertile soil is made of variance components. It must be fertile soil is required, for the good growth plant.

Health plant, health soul, health plant grow, with a master good care, so the master feel good with the plant. Plant give body, body gives to soul, but how to know the macro concept actor know the micro concept actor, but also how to know micro concept actor which food eat. Macro concept actor body but also eat then 3times eat a day, if not body almost to die.

Macro concept world actor consist of "soul + mind + body = body" body is very simple all of mind is physical energy collecting another word saying is to make money. All of the actors are try to make money is the very of macro concept main living purpose. It is very simple to collect energy getting, physical body management so that it required to making money. All of the actors are competition to get energy. So macro concept actor ignorant all of the micro concept actors, micro concept actor is Soul. In the macro concept world soul is parasite so then soul depends on body. Body live well, soul live well, then,

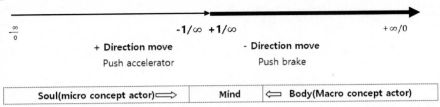

Micro accept actor Soul health power so fight with mind after that win, but also Macro concept actor body also live righteous live, so mind of desired mind being shrinking. So Body slightly feels of soul. So then body actor cares of soul,

soul feel so sensitive, soul are also can be dangerous but also can be critical risk.

Soul live at variable body = ground, fertile soil, but divested soil. If a plant=soul loved at the divested soul, plan do not growth due to do not rains, but also the place is rock, so it very hard to grow in this divested soil. So then plant do not growth so then arid condition. The soul also does not grow well, just like a plant in the desert. Soul does not live healthy. In the macro concept actor body do not know absolutely so it very desired to be rich, so macro concept actor all depend on mind, so mind is

| Soul(micro concept actor) | ⟸ | Mind | ⟹ | Body(Macro concept actor) |

So then macro concept actor body all control by mind, so then mind is almost 60~100% so then soul is almost to zero=40% ~, So that Soul become sick soul live in the body, so body all control form mind, so strong mind, body so tired for the making money, so all of body energy, all of the macro concept actors are interesting body healthy cared. But do not know the perfectly soul existence, they try to find the best happy but it hard to reach at the real happiness. All of strong in body, macro concept actors are all pursue of physical strength only. All of mind controlled so that mind is not actor, but just only mind is deceit soul gesture, so then body deceit by mind, mind also has the good mind, but this good mind is in the macro concept of the for the sake of the body, so then in the end do not perfect confidence. Just all of the physical attitudes of the winning in the games, if lose or sacrifice are not happy to the body. Mind give hint to the actor; do study without sleeping, doing work save sleeping, so then even all of the week make money, so then in the macro concept actor, so then that actor can make money because of doing live diligently. So live hurry all of actors do not have time silent time for the soul, all the time busy, they think good enough cause of make money well. But surely this is the not perfect. Some of macro actor tired. So arouse of problems, due to actors are not save energy for the soul, so then soul blessing is so lower, just all of the macro concept time depend on their of the doing work diligent. Just macro concept actor only for the making money, so then, all of relative is not enough, so weak soul can't help soul fair body, even try to help body but soul is so feeble. So then it can't be carry of fair body good news, even has good work, but feeble soul can't reach at the micro concept gate (-1/∞+1/∞),

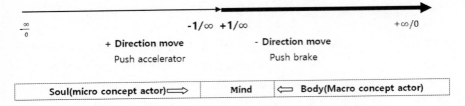

All the time macro concept actor going for the + direction so then just feeble soul haven't power to push brake the soul fair macro + Direction move to change, but the feeble soul so weak that even has the thinking so soul it can't turning going – Direction move, in the end the macro concept actor controlled by mind, then soul is forgotten, it means that all of the macro concept lived the ways of Satan likeable ways, all of the macro actor live diligent for himself only, he/she think I'm so poor so I have to build for the make me rich. All of macro concept actor time used for the actors, even macro concept actor live diligent and any doing any sins, but they live all for theirs, so then soul is not healthy. So long in the time of the body is not good then compensation to the body in the role of soul, if soul good healthy then it can be helped form body then help also the body. So safe going, just macro concept thing is not perfect because of the all of crack water leak so that macro concept diligence is not keep body mind expected thing is not done. Because of body is not actor, mind haven't any power to be well going safe. All of the closed circumstance not open for the community, so then, mind all the time desired for the getting reach still, even so long time lived. Feeble weak can't help, but also it can't carry good news to the soul king, heaven king.

The feeble soul lived hard with body, so feeble soul does help body, even that soul the micro concept world actor, micro concept world soul is very respect, if lived in the macro concept world all of the

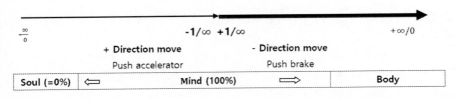

In the macro concept mind is 100% then soul is 0%, then soul is dead, envy

actually soul is not zero about zero then, if infer live in the living, then it can live depend on the mind, he is all desired, macro concept world actor perfectly forget, he live cruelty, macro actor lived about 100% mind controlled macro actor don't have to get a soul, he lived without soul, without soul is the just live shell only. His connecter to the micro concept gate pipe line perfectly closed. The actor closed to the micro concept going. At last it died of the soul in the macro concept world.

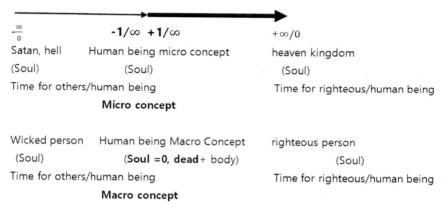

$\frac{\infty}{0}$ **-1/∞ +1/∞**   +∞/0

Satan, hell   Human being micro concept   heaven kingdom

(Soul)   (Soul)   (Soul)

Time for others/human being   Time for righteous/human being

Micro concept

Wicked person   Human being Macro Concept   righteous person

(Soul)   **(Soul =0, dead+ body)**   (Soul)

Time for others/human being   Time for righteous/human being

Macro concept

So then macro concept, it comes to this pattern, a macro concept actor life cycle then,

Before birth form of Soul, after soul is Soul+ body, After Dead then Soul comes, all of the macro concept life cycle. But if in the macro concept "soul + mind + body" then soul is lose in the game with mind first, and body lived badly, so in the end soul dead=0%, so long body comes "mind+ body= body" so long body so that out of soul body is "mind + body" this is lost to the micro concept actor died. So then a man personal realization all of the opportunity all closed so then micro concept point gate (-1/∞+1/∞), closed so long, macro concept out of soul body, dead then there is no actor of soul, so that the actors soul is disappeared. In this case, Buddhist thought theory most be adapt to the circulation of soul rebirth chain is break off so then the macro actor eternity dead comes.

2014.08.12

Topic: how to discriminate wicked and righteous.

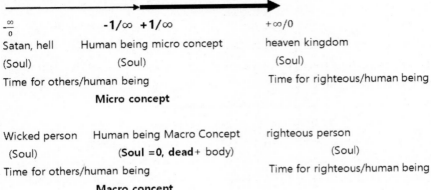

$-\frac{\infty}{0}$ **-1/∞ +1/∞**   +∞/0

Satan, hell   Human being micro concept   heaven kingdom

(Soul)   (Soul)   (Soul)

Time for others/human being   Time for righteous/human being

            Micro concept

Wicked person   Human being Macro Concept   righteous person

(Soul)   **(Soul =0, dead+ body)**   (Soul)

Time for others/human being   Time for righteous/human being

           Macro concept

In the micro concept how to discriminate righteous from wicked, I'm not scientist but it infer, sorry my micro concept is based on inferable so then I try to show my concept, so long but also I'm talking micro concept how to help this concept gradually decreased my imagination, all of write based on my imagine. Until now how to soul micro concept know between wicked and righteous. Here micro concept is all of the creatures are express to micro concept point gate (-1/∞+1/∞), this is the all of feature get to reach at micro concept gate, point (-1/∞+1/∞), so then, it also soul, this is the micro concept so macro concept human being micro concept actor soul but also another feature micro concept also soul, so then it must be expand in the micro concept world. So then micro concept world actors are all occupied, it imagined that micro concept world occupied all of creature souls. What I am short of it, but micro concept is all of chops of concept so then I can find to expel to my micro concept writing. In the micro concept main actor is the wicked soul, righteous soul, how to sense souls I do not know but I will write based on the micro concept, so then it must be discriminate in the pulse of the breath.

It try to by the infer, micro concept make newly concept all of the decision pulse, so then breath and decision is same energy carried, that is the similar to the sine curve.

In this micro concept build new concept, is the high peak decide righteous, lower bottom is wicked decide. All the time breath sine wave, sine wave is connected to the eternity, even in the personal then breath, in the micro concept very adventure explained now it must be connect to the macro actor and micro concept actor, so then, this sine wave is comes from micro concept connected then, macro concept soul so then, it also infer that micro concept soul macro concept world soul connected in the line. Micro concept is all of the process is

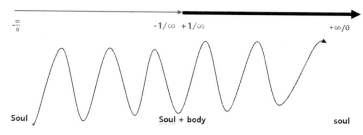

This wave same rhythmically wave shape. This is personal actor waves, so then soul recognize of the breath sine wave up and down, in this breath curve carry life, this is the life, if break the line then soul do not recognized, but here in the death time this breath curb stop, I can another concept, but after die, in the micro soul living place also same breath in the sine curb. It hard to explain but it also infer, after soul + body time over then it must be Soul only, so then, after this all of the soul range so this is not seen world shift from seen, so then it must be really micro concept. Micro concept somewhat understand inferable imagination.

Double concept infer, imagination, how to shape in the micro concept world. In the clue of micro concept point is the Point $(-1/\infty+1/\infty)$, so then it start, unseen but seen, unsen then god police governing all of the creature because of the micro concept point is the Point $(-1/\infty+1/\infty)$, the space is micro concept gate are also explained to $(-1/\infty+1/\infty)$, soul eternity rest place is micro concept space, here space actor is soul, so then soul lived in the eternity space (-1/∞+1/∞), eternity soul destination is the really originality the major actor is the soul, but just soul + body macro concept time is limited in the scope of the maximum ages is the 1hundred 30 years, so then this 130 years in the macro concept time is 130/∞ = 1/∞, so then 130 years are in th emicro concept then it also soul curve only so long. It means that in the macro concept curve is seen, but all of line to the it must be soul (before birth), soul (after birth soul), soul (after dead) so then it must be express

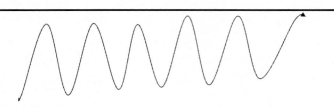

In the micro concept place all of the actors are souls, so then all of connection must be sine curb so then, in the soul networking are connected. All of the soul web, but the web also micro concept so then it size also is micro concept point (-1/∞+1/∞), so then before birth soul come to macro concept then, macro concept here said then all of the line, so then in the macro concept also existed at the soul, even in the micro concept also actor is the same as the macro = soul so then the sine wave is web just like in the micro concept communication.

So then all of the breath is connect to the micro concept world, so long, in the macro concept world and macro concept world actors are all of the souls, so then in the recognition, all of the micro concept can recognize macro concept world so in the micro concept world actors can understand, so all of the micro concept manager of the god government officials are managing the all of the macro concept actors, they are how to behavior, they are live righteous or wicked, so all of the macro concept world righteous, wicked information carried to the sine wave to the micro concept world.

So then in the point of macro concepts understand how to discriminate wicked and righteous. Righteous is the already said in the religious in the book of bible has it, righteous, love neighbors, sacrifice, help others, understand, times use for others etc. in the wicked is the liar, deceit, steal, fight, war, break a peace, malice, divorce all of the bad things etc. this is the macro concept righteous.

In the point of view is the breath is counted on that actually hard to impossible in the macro concept but in the soul world recognized, but also in the micro concept world, communication network is sine wave communication, so in the soul all has the breath and decision in a communication, so all is line, so then, soul breath is the decision of righteous or wicked all feeling, so long but also the soul deliver to the wicked and righteous, the result of the information stored to the micro concept world, information sorted place. So it speed is very same as the soul carry information of the macro concept body behavior righteous or wicked behavior news or information carry to the micro concept souls, but also this information sorted to the bank of the blessing, or curse bank of stannic. So then this number or save in the blessing or curse bank saving deposit is decided to be in the after macro concept time finished to then if ahs the micro concept world blessing deposit is bigger than curse bank in satanic place. Then to live eternity in the micro concept place after macro concept live to returning then how many deposit to the bank then naturally located at, if deposit to the satanic bank then cursed point larger, but righteous point is larger than the soul located at the righteous soul place. Therefore then in the living macro concept so, how to cooperative the act, also be explained.

2014.08.13

Topic: micro concept actor soul and macro concept actor

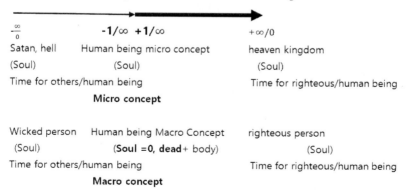

In micro concept actor is soul, this is from micro concept point or gate $(-1/\infty +1/\infty)$, Macro concept living place is actor is soul + mind + body = Body, so body is the macro concept world actor. Macro concept world actor body lives with another body. Then the relationship is cause and result from macro concept body actor is center, so then it infer that it must be micro concept world actor can move micro concept world to macro concept world, macro concept actor move body, but in the micro concept role of the in the macro concept minor role play, so unseen micro concept actor soul is not seen but role of the connect between macro concept world and micro concept world. In this procedure all of the micro concept center is located in the personal unit all of the macro concept actors, it means that all of macro concept actor has the micro

Concept gate $(-1/\infty+1/\infty)$, so in the macro concept multiple actors have micro concept gate $((-1/\infty+1/\infty)$, but all of macro actors are do not know their micro concept gate. This secret is very known just in the religious organize Christ church Buddha temple try to make known but all are they know in the micro concept is sure of existence micro concept point is all ahs all, even all of the features are all has the micro concept point $(-1/\infty+1/\infty)$, because of micro concept is stated from all of creature convergence to concept point $(-1/\infty+1/\infty)$, so then in the humanbeing

In the macro concept and micro concept macro concept and micro concept, so then micro

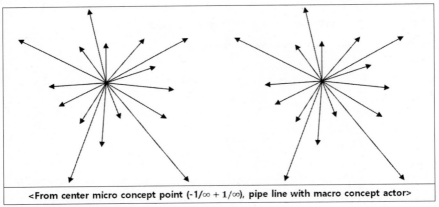

<From center micro concept point $(-1/\infty + 1/\infty)$, pipe line with macro concept actor>

concept actor soul is understand,

All of macro concept actor lived with other macro concept actors, a macro concept actor is all the time center, so then all of the has the from micro concept world to macro concept world by the sine curb, this is role of the micro concept and macro concept actor tunnel by the wave, so long, in the macro concept actor is soul + mind + body= body, macro actor move so then macro concept body is not easy to live on, due to sustainment body energy, body move then need the energy, so then obtain the energy is also very competitive with other actor.

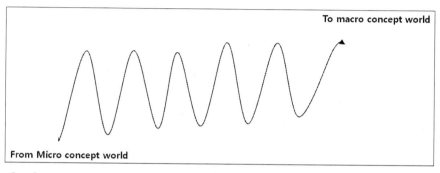

To macro concept world

From Micro concept world

So then most macro concept actor live with other, so then macro concept actor body to live on then, it needs energy, energy is explained to be the make money. Make money is depend on other actors cooperative products. So then to do it combined to a group, so called the company. In the company actor must be cooperate working. But all of macro actor is

Soul	Mind	Body

All of the actors are has the soul + mind + body = body. And then micro concept point $(-1/\infty +1/\infty)$, through another effect from the micro concept actor so long in the macro concept world featured with combined with micro concept and macro concept. So a macro concept actor has variances

Macro concept variance is conception or infers then soul %, mind %, body% this consist is characteristics, this is the macro concept personal character.

Micro concept actor is soul, then micro concept actor soul move between macro concept world and micro concept world, but also macro concept body actor do righteous behavior then this result deposit to righteous blessing bank, but also wicked actor body do behavior then the result deposit to the Satanic wicked world curse bank. So then macro concept actor doing righteous then naturally deposit to the blessing bank, but another is cursed bank, so then in the come to shown to the macro concept actor influenced to the fortune but also cursed actor.

So then, in the macro concept appeared to by inferable formula is

A blessed actor = soul 10~30% + mind 10~20 + body 50~100%, then physically healthful with spirituality is also strong then in a macro concept actor plus macro actor lived righteously so then his/her righteous resulted by the micro concept actor to the micro concept blessing bank deposit. So then in the blessed actor get fortune from good as macro concept actor but also micro concept actor blessing pluses to then fortune so get well in the macro concept world.

But if A coursed actor = Soul 10% + mind 60% + body 30% then, macro actor health is not strong, his/her desired is so high, he/she worked for himself/herself only, his/her time exclusively used for owns, so he got a big money, but his/her soul is so weak, so then the macro concept actor exclusively controlled by mind, so then, almost feeble soul cannot go for the micro concept gate so then, a weak soul carried to the result to the Satanic cursed bank, due to all of macro concept actor all of time used for the making money only. All of the time used up for him, so long, in the macro concept world point of view is success but in the micro concept point of view is deep failed.

2014.08.14

Topic: soul give other and accept from others after then grow soul also.

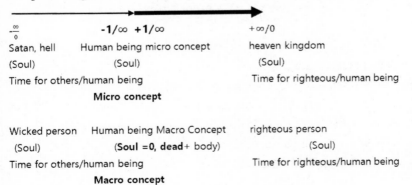

Surprisingly come to me soul also growth. Until now soul don't know soul growth, so that I describe soul before soul after soul and dead after soul is same but today at last come to me, soul also growth. Today morning I thought what I will write, I counter before arrive in my office; soul would be shared with others. Soul itself give shared with others, how to soul segregate but soul shared, soul infer that like smog so some part given to other then accept from other, soul is exchanged other souls, so then soul is getting bigger. Just like snow balls. Snow ball running over the snow then getting bigger, so how to soul shared.

In the macro concept world, actor doing for the sustainment of the body, so then actor needs to get an energy which buys something for the maintaining of body. So then all of actor has the job, as the actor for the working, then the produced result must be shared with actor soul, so then the produced is seen only product but soulful product is soul + product, this product is premium product. It must be compared between home cook, restaurant food difference is home cook is mother or wife, some also father or husband cook then cook for family, so then the soul is please good eat with heath, then home food is forming soul + food, so then the food is soul is almost so larger, it translate to the macro concept then the bigger than soul attained so the food is soul, not body taste but the food is already soul, so then family eat mother, wife, or husband and father cook then family eat mother and father soul eating, then mother and father soul so excitement with family acting soul. In this case soul gives to the food, food eat family, so then family larger soul + family soul then returning bigger soul is itself is bigger soul of the father and mother.

Before birth soul	After birth soul	← Shared soul →	Death strong soul growth

Soul growth how many times share, soul shared then it must be approach to the micro concept gate point $(-1/\infty + 1/\infty)$, soul growth means realized; in the end soul produce a masterpiece in his / her product. Realize and shared soul, micro concept gate reach and shared soul, getting soul strength, a big power of strength, then it must be soul energy is increased also,

← Soul →	→ Mind ←	Body

Soul shared with other soul, so then getting soul also soul + soul = 2soul, soul to the all of the macro concept created thing act, even all of feature also has the soul, so then, soul giver of the actor, so then actor how to be soulful product.

So then soul exercise for so then just small thing soul shared then soul being health, this is the very good in the micro concept righteous think deposit to the righteous soul micro concept world bank, so then, soul is very excitement because save account, so it getting lager of the blessing point, so soul is related with the how much blessing point in the righteous bank.

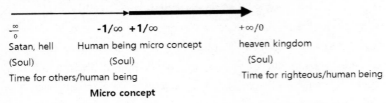

$\frac{\infty}{0}$	$-1/\infty$ $+1/\infty$	$+\infty/0$
Satan, hell	Human being micro concept	heaven kingdom
(Soul)	(Soul)	(Soul)
Time for others/human being		Time for righteous/human being

Micro concept

Satanic wicked soul place Cursed point bank	↓ ←Concept gate $(-1/\infty + 1/\infty), →$	Righteous soul place Blessing point bank

Soul carry wicked act saving, but righteous soul carry righteous act saving, so then strong soul must be well of the carry the righteous act, how to do in the do not shared soul then, the soul prison in the body, but also the mind is increased so then getting weaker of the soul in the macro concept, so then infer from that this is another shape of the micro concept world

Satanic wicked soul place Cursed point bank	Mind is bigger then Soul is less, it don't necessary realization so wicked mind Easily reach anytime	Righteous soul place Blessing point bank

So mind occupied about all then soul is so weak then, weak soul also carry's to the satanic wicked soul place, the bank of cursed, so then wicked actor behavior is also saved in the difference from righteous. So then here comes up the soul place of micro concept place is difference righteous is

	↓ ←Concept gate $(-1/\infty + 1/\infty), →$	Righteous soul place Blessing point bank

Righteous act behave is micro concept tunnel, gate $(-1/\infty+1/\infty)$, realize but also macro concept strong shared with other creature. So then strong soul, so powerful soul carries to the micro concept gate even hard course in the macro concept so all of patience, endurance, overcoming all of procedure of hard time, so many times exchanged soul to other souls, soul giver soul acceptor in this transaction increased, soul give then soul getting. So righteous soul creates bigger soul size but also energy increased.

But mind is strong macro concept actor so then soul is weak, then soul do not exchange other souls, so getting weaker soul, so then all of the controlled by mind then, wicked soul residents so called worked soul micro concept then, it don't have to reach at the micro concept point,($(-1/\infty+1/\infty)$, in a micro concept place is not neared, originally righteous soul place territory and wicked soul micro concept world is perfectly another place, so shallows in dept, so that very feeble soul carry the wicked news, but also Satanic cursed bank deposit of the energy.

Satanic wicked soul place Cursed point bank	Mind is bigger then Soul is less, it don't necessary realization so wicked mind Easily reach anytime	

Until now in the micro concept soul resident so then soul is eternity, it didn't discriminated but after this, in the micro concept soul world, has the different territory of the righteous soul is much more deeper then wicked soul resident place, so then strong soul will carry all of the suffering but weak soul is carry deceit behavior surely do not hard course overcomes but deceit so reach at the shallow deep, all of the wicked actors behavior energy saved in the cursed point bank at the satanic micro concept world.

Today understood righteous micro concept world, wicked micro concept world is not near all of the soul is righteous and wicked then segregate.

2014.08.18

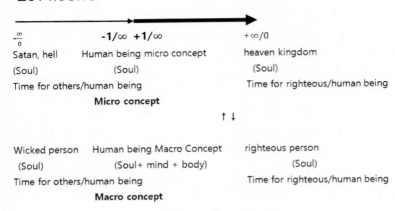

In micro concept writing, everyday is a hard to decide what topic to write. Today is Monday so hard to start, on the way workplace; it appeared to me an old woman who is like a beggar. How to reach at beggar even she is woman. It infers from that she did best for the good living. But she is come to the old woman beggar.

But also I saw another feature middle school student group member of 5, a student hit some of the mild student, then just a play, but there contained felling of the despise feeling, then 3 student only watching it, I felt so hate waters. I have prejudice of school student outcaste, but also I have so many times experimented so I am deep hate outcaste treatment.

What make these two sceneries, what cause of it, whose responsibility, a macro actor, occupied in the macro concept world but also micro concept world

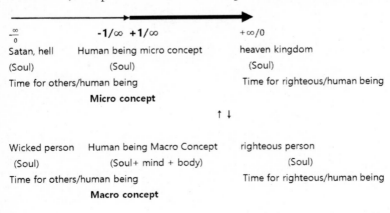

All of the feature of the living macro concept and micro concept are exchanged to forming.

All of person has the micro concept role, but also macro concept role.

Micro concept role is he/she is live on the "soul + mind+ body" so then a macro concept actor even actor ages are all differ from each others, so then, as the ages all of feature comes, so then in the personal actor grow by righteous but also wicked, what energy is effect, some actor live righteous, others are live wicked.

Macro concept actor, macro concept actor living in the macro concept world, all macro concept actors live networking to sustainment body energy getting. All of connection among them behaviors relationship, in this relationship is around of him/she many actors are do righteous act or wicked actor are then micro concept actors are effected from other souls to sustainment in the macro concept world. The macro concept actor consist of "soul + mind + body" so then, if body is control by mind then, micro concept world, soul derived mild character, he/she is mild soul, then, he/she get a body, then macro concept actor meet, jealous mind, but also fight mind owned "soul + mind+ body" then a micro concept actor located at the macro concept world, segregated from the wicked soul, then it is not know righteous or not, a mild soul needed courage. If a soul gets courage then it goes to the righteous behavior but temptation from wicked then he/she micro concept mind soul meet the body, so then live in the macro concept world, lose living then a wicked temptation soul losing all of good rout of living.

Wicked actor	Righteous actor
Macro concept : wicked behaviors	Macro concept : righteous behavior
Micro concept : Satanic behavior	Micro concept : God's behavior
⇩	⏛
Cursed bank in the satanic kingdom	Blessing bank in the heaven kingdom

In the point of wicked actor

Wicked power is cursed then if the cursed point is so big then comes to the destruction point comes.

Wicked power of the macro world = all of actors used their time for only themselves + just righteous power about zero.

Wicked power of micro concept world = macro concept after dead then it returned to the micro concept world Satanic world, so macro concept wicked soul's destination to the satanic world.. so then satanic power angers among wicked souls, these soul is the accumulated of the cursed bank energy expanded, this energy is connect to macro concept world.

So then wicked actors are surplus wicked behavior

So then Wicked power = macro wicked behavior + micro concept satanic behavior + Cursed bank cursed point = comes to destruction energy comes.

The possibility of micro concept world satanic soul is increased so then in the "Buddhism doctrine of samsara" then multiple wicked souls comes to body, so then originality comes to the soul character is wicked soul birth to the macro concept world. So then possibility is

Wicked Power = wicked behavior + satanic behavior + cursed point bank + new macro concept actor to wicked soul possibility = so then strength wicked comes to the macro concept world.

Righteous actor power = macro concept righteous behavior + micro concept god's behavior + blessing bank + comes to new righteous birth to macro concept world. If an actor lives righteous livings, this actor builds heaven king dome.

Today morning I saw an old woman beggar, if infer that she lived wicked, but also her living in this macro concept world has been wicked behavior, her soul saved in the cursed bank, if she died then she will go for the naturally micro concept world satanic world, in the Buddhism she will be new birth as the wicked soul originality.

Today morning I saw the middle school student group behavior, just mild student do not treated by another 4 students, 4 students so do not used their time for saving a mild student. 4 student already losing righteous power, so then a mild soul also anger, so mild soul possibility to be righteous soul life changed to wicked soul, because he lose the courageous mind. Infer that all of the souls kill the righteous soul, so then occupied all of macro concept world to be wicked concept is general community.

All of their wicked soul growth then, their wicked soul live so hard because all of wicked world, here all of the seed of the righteous are disappeared.

2014.08.19

Topic: road of macro and micro actor

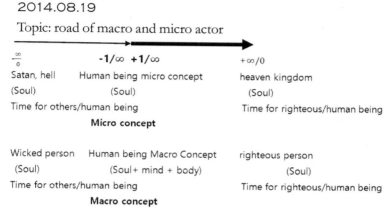

$\frac{\infty}{0}$	-1/∞ +1/∞	+∞/0
Satan, hell	Human being micro concept	heaven kingdom
(Soul)	(Soul)	(Soul)
Time for others/human being		Time for righteous/human being
	Micro concept	

Wicked person	Human being Macro Concept	righteous person
(Soul)	(Soul+ mind + body)	(Soul)
Time for others/human being		Time for righteous/human being
	Macro concept	

Micro concept actor move on the road in the micro concept world, macro concept actor move on the road in the macro concept world, so micro concept world actor soul know the way. The way is from micro concept world via macro concept world to return to the micro concept world. So micro concept actor soul move exact move on the exact road, so then only soul know the way of moving soul's way, soul know the way, soul move then the way is way.

Macro concept actor "soul + mind + body= body" here macro concept controller is mind, all of the actor recognized of the mind. So then mind also do not know the way, so then

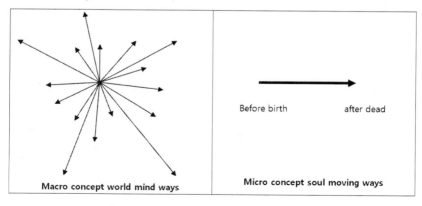

Macro concept world mind ways   Micro concept soul moving ways

Before birth   after dead

Macro concept world false actor mind, it is not any responsibility macro concept actor living, but it has a desired to stain on the body. Mind road is scattered road. The road is short, but all of road is hasn't any destination, but a momentary changed roads, so then all of body follow the mind which is not any responsibility.

But micro concept world actor only knows the beginning and the macro actor voyage destination. So that soul move to the right road in the pre run for the body moving help going correct way moving. So then micro actor soul try to endure all of obstacles the built way, soul know that the road is only one, not selective road, soul also know the ways obstacles, so it already soul has try to go with body the way difficulties which make soul + body safety and success life. Excitement and perfection accomplish is soul+ body live all of the macro concept experience duration then comeback to righteous souls destinations with strong soul which so many times shared with other actors in the macro concept.

Macro concept actor mind all the time try to lead, to macro concept physical body maintain energy getting. So then mind all of macro concept time, all of body forgets soul existence. Mind is much closed to be friend with Satanic of the micro concept world main actor, wicked is all the time going with, very momentum ways, and very short road built then break the road, the macro concept actor mind and micro concept actor wicked is same enemy is micro concept actor soul, micro heaven king dome actors are besieged with macro concept actor controller "mind" and micro concept Satanic side actor "wicked" so then micro concept kingdom soul hard to live.

Macro concept world actor easily faced to the "soul + mind + body=body" body is also besieged by mind. So then another micro concept world enemy satanic actor "wicked" influenced to the micro concept actor "soul"

Soul(heaven kingdom)	Wicked(Satanic actor) Mass force	Mind Micro force	body

Soul is segregated from the meeting body, so then, micro concept actor mass force which multiple macro actors of the minds group power is the wicked mass force, so that soul hard to meet body. Then only know the ways of the righteous soul move to the righteous soul destinations in the micro concept world.

The road is not has any other rod to go for the heaven king dome righteous soul destinations. Micro satanic actor wicked, mind, and do not know the destination. So all of the macro concept actor lose actors footing so then macro concept actors do not reach the destination. But all of macro concept actor follows the byway so then the macro actor has moved on the byways. The macro actor soul get in to the another byways destination is the out of righteous souls destinations. So then here comes new concept of the wicked soul destinations are located than righteous soul destination.

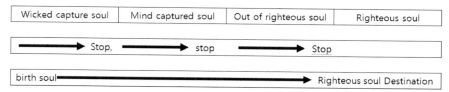

Wicked captured soul stop to the byways, mind captured soul also miss road to the righteous destination, but also out of righteous soul also forget to reach at the righteous soul destinations.

Righteous soul micro concept destination is overcome all of the hard core problems or obstacles, the way to the righteous soul destination is much more long distance location, to be reach at the long distance is needed to strong health soul but also energy is required to go for.

Micro concept soul to be strong then must shared time to others, give soulful power to others to live righteous through string soul with shared time others, live with other righteous soul, around of the macro concept actors all are righteous actors. But also to go for the longer distance going energy need to so that, how to live is this in the macro concept actor must live righteous with righteous money making etc. so help others, all of actor time is based on the sacrifice.

To be righteous is perfectly some similar to the wicked but righteous is all of time shared with others, for long time of his/her life time is all same way, to the end of the time in the righteous side living then in the micro concept actor soul come back to micro concept righteous macro actor live purely "soul + mind (=

-1/∞ +1/∞ micro concept point) + body= realize body" this actor will get to the Righteous soul destination.

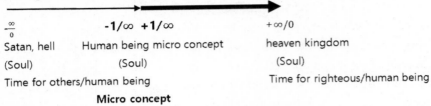

$-\frac{∞}{0}$

-1/∞ +1/∞

+∞/0

Satan, hell

Human being micro concept

heaven kingdom

(Soul)

(Soul)

(Soul)

Time for others/human being

Time for righteous/human being

Micro concept

if in the macro concept actor living then all of the actor are generally " soul + mind + body= body" then mostly control by the mind, but if reach at the micro concept point(-1/∞ +1/∞ micro concept point) so then just get a ticket for the righteous soul Destiantion.

2014.08.20

Topic: macro concept actor how to live with righteously

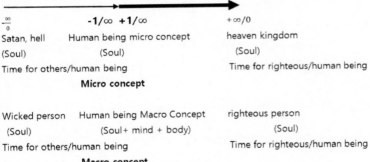

$-\frac{∞}{0}$

-1/∞ +1/∞

+∞/0

Satan, hell

Human being micro concept

heaven kingdom

(Soul)

(Soul)

(Soul)

Time for others/human being

Time for righteous/human being

Micro concept

Wicked person

Human being Macro Concept

righteous person

(Soul)

(Soul+ mind + body)

(Soul)

Time for others/human being

Time for righteous/human being

Macro concept

In this micro concept it must be unseen concept. But macro concept actor is seen, be seen, but also see. Just criteria are the actor reachable destination is not same but righteous soul destinations. Then if an actor has the goal to live righteous then what is the righteous, the actor how to live, and it possible in the Seen stages or unseen stages. In the micro concept is not seen area so then as possible as I can try to say just unseen level decided.

In the micro concept originality is righteous realization that is the micro concept point, all of the vacant then reach at the point micro point is -1/∞ +1/∞ micro concept point, so then micro concept actor created by micro concept point reaching, this is the macro concept actor seen time reached actor, but also almost come to destination macro concept actor dead time realized actor reach at the micro concept point $-1/\infty$ $+1/\infty$ micro concept point.

So long, micro concept actor is natural of the soul, but in the macro concept actor is defined as the "soul + mind + body = body" macro concept natural actor is this, this is macro concept so macro concept is just for the explained the micro concept so that then it must be micro concept is explained by the actor of the soul, so then soul only knows micro concept actor world, but also macro actor concept world, micro world concept world classified to wicked soul destinations and righteous soul destinations. So micro concept originality also righteous soul is main actor in the micro concept world, so that wicked soul also existed for explain righteous soul value.

So then macro concept actor must be try to be righteous soul, after dead to be located at the righteous soul eternity safe, peace, out of all problems and risk place. Then macro concept actor doing realize of the righteous soil eternity micro concept world existed then, macro concept actor try to be how to live is getting. How to live be getting to the righteous soul destination.

Macro concept actor energy getting (50%)	Micro concept soul healthy (50%)
Diligent, study hard, creative, save money etc	Shared with other, help other, meditation, etc

Macro actor to reach at the righteous soul destination reaching factors

Macro concept actor live to get living energy, to live safe it need surplus energy, some time occur to desired so much more energy getting. So then macro concept actor so busy desired best position to get easy get energy, but also power for the desired power getting also.

So then actor of macro concept is "soul + mind +body = body" mind is ∞ infinite, then it must be over the equilibrium 50% so then, busy to allotment to the micro concept actor soul healthy, so then "mind 50% ~100%" range then it occur to actor of the satanic wicked soul visiting. So long, getting accelerate of the getting wicked.

If macro concept try to live as the righteous living then all of macro concept move, must be shift to micro concept direction move, then, realize about to macro actor "mind 50% ~ 10, 1, 0%) so then macro concept world actor about to "soul + mind (hidden) + body= soulful body" so called soulful body=

human being is going with righteous, soul actor then the actor realized so then actor's soul changed to righteous so actor soul connect to the god's soul, so then ordered from the micro concept righteous soul kingdom order. So then macro concept actor fights from the satanic soul, but help try to be live righteous ways actors. Micro concept actor souls are live as the minor in the macro concept world, so then major is the "mind +body = body" so then all of souls are weak, so realized actor try to help macro concept actor realize.

An each macro concept actor for the righteous or wicked being energy conditions:

25% energy	50% energy	75% energy	100% energy
⟶ 50% use		Soul use for being soul healthy	

Righteous actor energy using conditions

Just 50% usages energy actor has the sufficient energy, so spared energy shared with others. This means that a righteous actor located area, leading role, all the time donate role, understand others, but also in the community some wicked soul act of violence force do not expand by the righteous actors. The leader is the power control to right rule being operated but also wicked actor been shady spot location. So then soul healthy energy helping the poor, consolatory a difficult actors, so then the community, company, family members are affected from the righteous actors' righteous energy using, Righteous soul has the power for the soul healthy. Soul healthy 50% energy also happy virus so righteous actor luminous substance around of actors, so then around actor friend being happy, righteous actor responsibility of making good circumstance also,

Therefore righteous actor must be use of his energy under the 50%.

25% energy	50% energy	75% energy	100% energy
			⟶ Soul do not use

Wicked actor energy using conditions

In the macro concept actor get energy, so then all of wicked actor use energy only him/herself. So then wicked actor all use for himself/herself, so macro concept wicked soul actor all the time busy, do not sleep early, because of time is all the time short, to get much more energy getting. These actors in the community, company, family, all of wicked actor jealous and envy a character, all of the wicked actor energy is all the time used up, so then every convergence nod point meeting actor, tired actor, strange all the time tired. So then it hasn't time for helping others, because of his/her time is not to be shared with others. Soul healthy time nothing, soul become weak, it produced out of sure actor, out of soul actor, he/she is already shell body only, it must be " soul=0, mind=50~100, body= mindful body" so then mindful body comes. This actor haven't joke so then help happy energy to others, he/she is the happy energy adsorb rather than give, this actor really required to be expected from others. Even he/she do not give others; never perfectly do not give others. So then wicked actor group such as in the company all of actor do not fair play, Fair players are segregate from wicked group, wicked group try to stealth others fair players earning result. So then righteous actor result all getting to the wicked soul, so righteous soul do damaged. But do not know someone damaged. All wicked actor ultimately do harm others. The family, company, community circumstance become of the wicked soul living place, the peace and excitement area all occupied by the wicked soul actors, macro concept actor living is being boring. All of macro concept wicked actor do follow the rule, so then all of wicked actor do rile only slaver position working. They must now master position only living the slave position so called the partials of the machine.

The micro concept gate point $-1/\infty$ $+1/\infty$ micro concept point reach at then maro concept point reach is required to macor concept moving direction is keep going then, it never reach to the micro concept gate. So long it must not to be realize, so macro concept wicked actor go for the micro concept actor destination where missed the perfectly to the righteous soul ways, so all of the wicked soul move the by the ways road, get lost so then eternity righteous road getting is impossible.

Topic: macro and micro relationship

$\frac{\infty}{0}$	**-1/∞ +1/∞**	+∞/0
Satan, hell	Human being micro concept	heaven kingdom
(Soul)	(Soul)	(Soul)
Time for others/human being		Time for righteous/human being

Micro concept

Wicked person	Human being Macro Concept	righteous person
(Soul)	(Soul+ mind + body)	(Soul)
Time for others/human being		Time for righteous/human being

Macro concept

Macro concept world getting bigger is better. Micro concept is getting lower, size also make less. So attitude and solution is against to each other. So then macro is a bigger, power is big power, micro is making less in size. But micro also has the perfection concept; micro is the perfection, so even micro concept is smaller but all the role of the micro is perfect in very detail, similar to the edge in technology, here edge is small also very perfection, so micro can win to the macro power. Even very small but win in the game with macro, micro advantage is perfection, but also make less the failure due to the eye watching all of the micro seen, easy check the failure possibilities. Micro is strong power, due to the perfection thing it must be out of scared, even a big power but do not break it, because it is the so small so then big hitter can't get it.

Even macro a big size, this is not seen in a eye, so it can't control of the possibilities so macro has the weak point, macro hard to reach at the perfection point. Macro relied on micro but macro does not give to the micro, so then micro can role just like, it is some micro concept micro concept actor live micro concept world, but also macro concept world, so that micro can help macro to be bigger. Then macro use micro but micro is miner, macro is major so then it can be seen only in the eye of the macro concept actor, just a big macro, but in the macro micro is used in the macro existence.

Macro is power so macro use the force to governing the micro, macro a big power is seen, but unseen micro power, anyway macro try to get a big power push to micro, so then micro under the macro minor role, macro and micro bad relationship is macro use power, unrighteous so called comes to the deceit another saying wicked, so then macro power extort micro perfection power. So then, extorted micro to the macro, but if macro used the power righteously relationship with micro then, micro also get excitement with as the role of micro perfections. But in the macro concept world it is not easy, macro actor easily take the perfection micro, micro perfection is somewhat easy due to the eye scope so make perfection.

Macro and micro is all the time happened so then, macro power use for the sale of the macro then in the while after micro hast to bearable of the macro power. Macro power used easy steals a micro, macro do not any sacrifice but also macro perfection, so then macro relatives are still bigger to big, it means the macro actors are all try to much more getting, using power of macro but macro perfection is not, just macro itself is the actor, macro itself tool to steal micro perfection. Micro has been role of the macro getting much energy getting.

Micro lose so many micro asset, small power of micro lose all of game, in the end micro perfect lose, then macro can fine the micro, here is the macro relied on the micro perfection, all of sacrificed. Just macro itself has been exited to the micro, because produce the perfect. Then macro so still do not know the macro they all getting themselves, so macro recognized all is possible all of the macro has the market, macro believe that is not changed. But here micro produced perfection production, but macro does not think macro power of perfection, creation, a new stage going so macro position is not keeping. Micro also does not follow the macro, micro lost the power, but also micro perfection also tired. Macro is the big out of the righteous, just only macro excited so multiple micros scarified.

Macro used the power which formed of the righteous so called wicked power. Macro power is not from the righteous, even though macro used so long time, macro is not going for the longer but macro also power form the wicked soul, macro eternity do not know the micro because macro is relied on micro righteous, even macro also any thinking, because micro perfection is seen to the macro perfection. So then

It may be the macro is the big power, it must be big then higher position from the micro is small so then macro used micro, but also depend on micro, even macro eternity based on the micro perfection, if macro is managed with the righteous with micro then, win all side, so that, just macro itself managed to perfection then even hard to managed to make perfection. So then macro also go eternity, but if macro do not know the sacrifice but also micro get a perfection, so macro steal micro then, micro lose the sacrifice energy then, micro is relative to the macro so then micro role in the macro, so micro unseen to the macro, therefore actually macro has the problems, but macro do not know the how to problems getting worse, macro do not know the until then micro unseen to the macro, micro is disappeared from in the macro. So then macro is stopped. Macro has the originality the way is to go for the destination but macro has the variable factors, anyway macro is relied on micro then, macro endless do not know the micro, so that micro also almost dead, until now macro steal micro energy. So then micro died, then macro died.

If macro is wicked then, it must be categorized "wicked captured soul" ," mind captured soul", "out of righteous soul" then macro can't go for the original of purpose destination, but macro go for the by the way, the macro has the original destination but macro a by the way stop is stop and finished. If macro also follows the way of righteous then, the macro has lived as of the micro perfection then macro will go for the original macro destination place, so called eternity macro going.

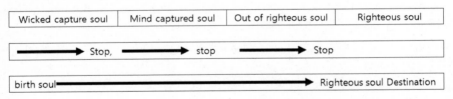

In this micro concept macro is bigger, a big One, micro is small a multiple micros.

$100\% = 1X \ 100\% =$ a macro, but micro is $100\% = 10\% + 10\% + 10\% + 10\% + \dots \dots + 10\%$, macro 100% is consisting of best players, so best player also produce creative of best players idea, if then best player value is good, but also then it must be macro good, the big one is competition of the another big one, as the best player game match, in the big match wining then macro is good, it must be from the righteous soul act, but not in the just pure of the macro best actors are poor with matching another big one, but all relied on the micro perfection, just used by the wicked, just 10% of the small micros scarifies energy getting, then micro 10X10% are sacrificed to managed the 100% macro, so then explained 10 micro energy role of the salver to the macro, then micro 10 is in the end lose the energy, a micro 10 is dead. Then macro 100% do not go for the destination but in the stop by the by road. Macro and micro relationship do not follow the way of the righteous then, follows the wicked way then macro ultimate closed. The macro has a big power, the big power all relied on micro, and this is so true, relied on means that micro helped to macro, but ignorant macro do not go with righteous ways, because of the that has been easy, a big power of macro has the all the time upper, micro is lower, so then micro all the time sacrificed.

The time of the beginning of the micro then all of the creative but also concentration energy for the micro, micro expect to get energy also, but all of micro energy is not accumulated, macro keep faith going for the macro easy ways.

So then macro getting easy, micro getting not easy, how to forming, some righteous place, micro perfection then macro well, in the end macro getting well, micro getting well, so the macro concept actor places are best place.

In the righteous soul group of the macro and micro then, macro plus micro = the much more perfect value comes. The righteous macro, the righteous micro help each other then, all of the macro energy, but also micro concept energy used, so then macro and micro depend on each other, macro is win in the macro to macro match up game wining, built also the micro excitement perfection produce. This good circulation is helped by the righteous soul helped.

This is all make fun of it, how to give the real value to pay then how to managed the a big one, but also it can't be make the winning prices, so then it must be suffer all of micros, it is general, then macro best players are relied on micro, so that they all excuse of micro need to sacrifice. Macro and micro in this case in the end macro stop in the by the road stop.

2014.08.22

Topic: micro concept actor eternity but macro concept actor is limited

$$\frac{\infty}{0}$$ **-1**/∞ **+1**/∞   +∞/0

Satan, hell   Human being micro concept   heaven kingdom

(Soul)   (Soul)   (Soul)

Time for others/human being   Time for righteous/human being

Micro concept

Wicked person   Human being Macro Concept   righteous person

(Soul)   (Soul+ mind + body)   (Soul)

Time for others/human being   Time for righteous/human being

Macro concept

In the micro concept actor soul macro actor body also growth in the macro concept actor soul and macro concept actor body, so then both actor grow. Macro actor grow and old to die. But micro concept actor grows with body, so body strong growth with strong growth soul. So then in this time soul characterized in the micro concept world discrimination, macro concept actor strong means that training physical, and exercise then getting string body, but soul strong is the shared with all of souls asset, help other souls, so then soul getting strong. Soul is to be health soul have to give others all soul's asset. Micro concept actor tries to health but also accumulate of the soul energy by micro actor time, energy shared with others then, micro soul health getting is

Micro concept actor healthy and energy getting by

MH: micro concept actor healthy

So then, MH = righteous soul act + shared time with others + help others + action of the micro concept righteous soul messenger role + fighter to the wicked soul behavior + problems status 50% 50% righteous soul, wicked soul saving + righteous behavior etc = Strong MH

Me: micro concept actor energy

So then Me = righteous soul act + shared time with others + help others + action of the micro concept righteous soul messenger role + help wicked people + macro concept world common sense required keep a rule = wealth soul energy.

Macro concept actor live and micro concept actor live

Concept	1th 30 years	2th 30 years	3 30 years ~
Macro body	Strong growth helped	Help others, shared time	Realization living
Micro soul	Used before world energy	Strong growth	best soul destination

Macro concept actor's growth and micro concept actor's growth stages table

Macro concept actor live with other macro concept actors supposition to 30 year, 30 year, 30 years so then 1th 30 years be helped, 2th years helped others, 3th years realization of living for the time preparing realize, even all of the life lived for the eternity soul, but 3th years is fully for the micro concept actor preparing. So then all live with soul strength due to soul eternity grow but in the macro concept actor grow stop in the time of the 1th 30 years.

In the 2th 30 years macro concept body has been ripen, all of matured and strong power, so if he followed with righteous living then shared with others, help others and righteous behavior then soul must be also soul strong energy is so much so soul eat of the micro concept body a righteous behavior and help others and shred time to others.

Then naturally soul strong so soul be located in the micro concept world, micro concept actor, MH (micro concept actor healthy) is strong healthy, but also Me (micro concept actor soul energy is wealth) so then MH, Me is so strong, so then macro concept actor live in the micro concept actor can be located best soul destination.

Concept	1th 30 years	2th 30 years	3 30 years ~
Macro body	Strong growth helped	Help others, shared time	Realization living
Macro road			died
Micro soul	Used before world energy	Strong growth(character)	best soul destination
Micro road			eternity

Macro concept actor road and micro concept actor road

So then macro concept actor live for the procedure 1th, 2th, 3th stages to staged role working but also in the micro concept actor soul also soul line is the eternity is a single unbroken line, so micro concept is go eternity, but macro concept actor live 3th stages even some what difference, all of macro concept actors are not same, but this is the 3 stages are process of the supposition of the road, beginning to end.

Micro concept actor soul live for eternity, then if a macro concept actor realized to micro concept gate (-1/∞+1/∞) so then macro concept actor save the energy for the micro concept actor, so then in the macro concept actor, strong time is optimistic time, so then 2th 30 years is the time to save micro concept actor Me, MH make strong. So then if not in the macro concept actor strong time do not realize in the end do not know the micro concept point (-1/∞+1/∞) then, the macro concept actor live only then

Concept	1th 30 years	2th 30 years	3 30 years ~
Macro body	Strong growth helped	Help others, shared time	Realization living
Macro road			→ died
Do not realize	Strong growth helped	Do not help & time sharing	Do not realization living
			→ died
Micro soul	Used before world energy	Strong growth(good soul)	best soul destination
Micro road			→ Righteous soul eternity
Do not realize	Used before world energy	Feeble soul(bad soul)	Wicked, cursed soul destination
			→ Wicked, cursed soul destination

Macro concept actor does not realize tables.

Macro concept actor does not realize tables.

Micro concept soul live eternity but macro concept lives to the limited, even though micro concept righteous living is shaped to the good soul, bad soul, healthy soul, feeble soul, so then do live in the righteous then in the Me, MH is over 50% ~100%, but Me, MH 10%~50% then, then in the micro concept actor living of the eternity then, the place also follows to me, the best place so called the heaven king dome place, but feeble soul located at the satanic soul place, so then the eternity living is depend on the macro actor behavior, if macro actor live the exact road, so then the macro concept actor realize then he/she live for the Me, MH strong, wealth, so long but the other is feeble soul is cause of the out of the realized acting, so then only live macro actor save.

Macro concept behavior realizes is the only micro concept actor live in the heaven kingdom, but do not realize exclusively all of macro concept life for the body sake then micro concept soul actor in the micro concept actor eternity living place is located at the satanic soul, wicked, cursed souls living places.

2014.08.25

Topic: micro & macro concept energy

$$\xrightarrow{\hspace{5cm}}$$

$\frac{\infty}{0}$	-1/∞ +1/∞	+∞/0
Satan, hell	Human being micro concept	heaven kingdom
(Soul)	(Soul)	(Soul)
Time for others/human being		Time for righteous/human being

Micro concept

Wicked person	Human being Macro Concept	righteous person
(Soul)	(Soul+ mind + body)	(Soul)
Time for others/human being		Time for righteous/human being

Macro concept

In micro concept and macro concept power, what is the power is a surviving energy. In the micro concept has a energy also, that is the compared with macro concept body energy "money", so that in the micro concept actor need to keep moving soul, actually macro concept actor make a money, the money is itself is the macro concept energy only, but the money usages is the how to use or wicked used or righteous use is decide save in the macro concept caused bank save or righteous blessing point bank, so then, macro concept actor live Seen energy but actually unseen energy is required, so that macro concept behavior is coming to macro world, micro world. So then micro concept soul, macro concept "soul+ mind+ body= body" micro and macro concept, so called that micro = soul, macro "soul + body +body=body" micro help the good or bad energy carry from macro concept world to micro world cursed bank or blessing bank, but this carry is the macro concept body pair of soul carry good or bad energy, it understand as the macro is the generator of the micro concept energy which is good for the blessing energy but bad for the cursed energy. This energy somewhat infer that macro concept behavior is micro concept energy, soul moving energy, micro concept energy getting from macro concept pairs behavior, therefore the macro concept get a interest of the macro concept actor good or bad behavior save in the micro concept bank of the cursed or blessing bank saved. So then in the macro concept get a caused or blessing point comes up by blessing or cursed point $E=mc2$, so then so then blessing or cursed are expressed by B: bless, C: cursed = M(macro concept saved energy) B; Blessing C:curse

So then B&C= M(B&C)2, so how to important to live use the money in the macro concept.

So then it may be infer from this concept is saving cursed bank and blessing bank being equal then cursed bank deposit 50%= blessing bank deposit 50% is equal so then, usual living in the macro concept actor, but if the balance is break then, infer that of the over 50 to the cursed bank, then somewhat charity, love of the micro concept special gift, then endurance in the end most but if critical line is safe line but if cross the critical line, then cursed thing comes to the macro concept actor. But if over the 50% blessing in the bank then comes to macro concept actor blessing. This time is not charity due to blessing point itself charity. But 0ver the 50 % if 55% then, a good macro concept actor show shared his blessing, this blessing is the itself comes to safe and lucky comes, so then the result help others, then over the 1~5% s given to other, s0 then 51% of the good saving then, macro actor keep good energy.

If energy is more than more good energy shift over good shift infer to the possible of the ripen harvest, much safer then macro concept actor possible shift to macro concept acting is losing the energy due to just like live the in the macro concept actor live depend on the interesting then, macro actor doing diligence, so that losing or saved to the macro concept cursed bank increased so then, cursed bank get over the 50%, so then

Micro concept gate (-1/∞+1/∞) this is the optimaitic of the mind, as getting blessed then mind come to operated to so exodus from micro concept point to macro. So then

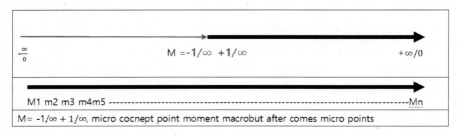

Micro concept actor is the from -1/∞ to +1/∞ this is the time is micro second, distance is micro distance, time concept is explinaed to do

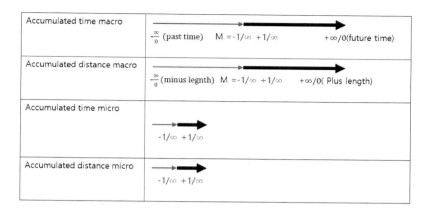

Accumulated time macro	
	$-\frac{\infty}{0}$ (past time) M $=-1/\infty$ $+1/\infty$ $+\infty/0$(future time)
Accumulated distance macro	
	$-\frac{\infty}{0}$ (minus legnth) M $=-1/\infty$ $+1/\infty$ $+\infty/0$(Plus length)
Accumulated time micro	
	$-1/\infty$ $+1/\infty$
Accumulated distance micro	
	$-1/\infty$ $+1/\infty$

Macro concept time and distance counted on the accumulated but in the micro concept actor of the time is $-1/\infty+1/\infty$ is momentary, distance is micro unseen distance. So then the realization but also the energy of the micro and macro, is very power because of the macro concept is hard to the start to end, it never reach at, but in the only reach is micro concept point. So then if the energy to be reached at the end of the distance then how much energy required it must be impossible, but in the micro concept can reach at moment. Macro concept energy for the expand but in the micro concept is convergent to the point, even unseen so that energy is moment, moment place, so then if macro concept world produce good energy or bad energy, so then all of the micro concept world, micro concept energy if reach at the $-1/\infty$ $+1/\infty$ energy purity is 100% so then soul energy is pure, so then bad also pure bad, good also pure righteous energy to save in the micro concept saving bank. But in the macro concept saving energy is getting larger. Getting much more, bigger, but also the distance also much more length is desired.

So then in the point of the macro then get increased to so then much more then + direction move but in the micro concept is in the point of view macro then, make less is for the micro is increased in the soul energy, this energy is purify energy, so micro energy, purity 100%, so then micro concept actor soul is strong, micro concept is so called truth, it never lied so 100% truth, but in the micro concept bad also the righteous macro behavior is save in the micro concept blessing bank saved in the purity righteous of 100%, but also in the macro concept wicked then save in the cursed bank wicked 100%, so then, the power of the cursed or blessing is appeared in the macro concept world.

Macro concept energy, micro concept energy, even in the realized macro concept actor know the truth of the micro concept world righteous energy saving in the micro concept world blessing bank saving, but do not realize then just understand in the real seen world, so macro concept all of energy for gathering the another energy, macro concept actor, do not know because do not realize, all is much more is better, then fixed macro wicked so then, optimistic is breaking, so then what explained the micro concept saving is the macro is getting bigger but micro is getting loser then in the end unseen with righteous macro concept actor energy usage. So long, macro concept energy how to use wicked or righteous, so long macro concept actor discriminated from realize or not.

2014.08.26

Topic: micro concept soul eye & soul destination

In micro concept riddle come to realized how to find the destination, what process make destination. That is the soul eye. Soul sees only same characters such as righteous character, wicked character. So then soul does not see other character, but just watch the same character.

Macro concept actors have friend, most actors go with same characters, and so does in the micro concept actors also live together themselves. It is very natural, if used to this circumstance then strangely a new circumstance of new characters, so that it is not easy. So in the macro concept also, same ranges actors are all go together, because of actor are not excitement with other characters. So then what he/she had done is decided to the present or future living criteria. Macro concept actor living time is not clear of wicked and righteous but in the micro concept is in this micro concept inferred to righteous world and wicked world. But in the macro concept world live variable difference conditions, and circumstances, how to decide in a moment righteous or wicked

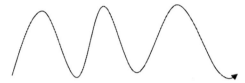

This is the micro concept because of the micro concept actor has the wave, so then up is righteous, down is wicked is inferred. So then in the micro concept actor criteria of the righteous and wicked, so then in the macro concept world do not see the micro world actor body do not in the eye the micro concept main actor soul, so then micro concept actor also do not same as the macro concept actor can watch another actors, so then, the same as macro concept actor do not see the souls, the same as the micro concept do not see other characteristics some of the righteous soul live and located in the curve top position, but wicked is the lowed position of the curve. So then in the top of curve can see the wicked soul, but at the lowest can't see the righteous soul.

So then in the macro concept world macro concept actors are also naturally segmented groups, all of living is groping livings. In the macro concept actors are segmented with their energy getting or knowledge higher or lower, even in the realized or not all of macro concept position is decided. But in the micro concept actor decided to the soul located at the righteous or wicked soul groups, so then, what has been explained the soul is so pure then, righteous soul can't bear with wicked offense to righteous, because of the wicked naturally offense all the time easily just like gene of the wicked, if wicked soul and righteous soul mix then, itself is not heaven king dome, because of micro concept actor souls 100%pure soul, so righteous soul pure right, just all of the souls are go with other souls, try to help others souls, then abruptly prone to righteous soul location a wicked soul appeared then all of righteous soul feel tremble fear, then the location peace break, after all the micro concept actor top place righteous soul, lower position is bottomed is the wicked soul, so it perfectly righteous soul and wicked soul is discriminated perfectly.

So then this is the soul circumstance discriminated but soul itself grow to the optimistic to the wicked or righteous living circumstance place accustomed to living well so then, righteous soul eye is accustomed to the bright light, but wicked soul eye is accustomed to dim light so then, wicked soul eye do not see in the bright, but also righteous eyes do not see in the dim light. So then how to live in the macro concept time, do live righteous or wicked then decided to the micro concept actor eternity living place is decided naturally after finish in the macro concept world, then all of the actor fly to the soul actors fly to the Seen place, a righteous soul excitement with bright light, but wicked soul excitement with dim light. Righteous soul and wicked soul light function is not same. So difference do then, micro concept world live well bright or dim, so how lucky to the righteous soul perfectly safe from the wicked soul, so then bright likeable righteous soul excitement only going with righteous souls, but in the dim all of wicked soul eternity place all of the souls are intrigue to be helped from others, but if do not helped from others then, steals to their own energy. But in the bright sight of the righteous soul try to help other, just sacrifice for others souls, so this place comes eternity of the peace in living righteous place.

Macro concept actor living place, this place all of character mixed to live on, in a place an actor live as the righteous but another is wicked, this is just same as the elementary school student in the class has the pure mixed seed of the righteous and wicked, so then middle school, high school, university but also, then in the macro concept still mixed higher of the wicked and righteous souls mixed. Does not recognition in the macro concept world can see discriminate, it is not known me but other self also, infer to a actor realized to get in to micro concept gate $(-1/\infty+1/\infty)$ then possible the discriminate of the wicked soul or righteous soul. Then realized macro concept actor watch, actually in this concept righteous soul of macro concept actor it must be sacrificed, and help others, wicked soul deceit and be helped from others.

In the macro concept actors so variable things are happened to so that variable thing are happened, so then all of the actor also subject, macro concept actors are the same actors, just hurry for the supply for the body sustainment with helping energy.

In this micro concept saying, all of the trade is not free effect, all of trade followed to the paying result, what is the earning trade, in the macro concept actors for the benefit to the sake of himself buyer only benefit, so to save a money negotiate, so then seller discount for the selling, this is not right, this trade is for the side of the wicked. But buyer give exact price, but also buyer is higher position so, higher position has the power, so then even purchase also think, energy donation, so if possible poor seller's good buying. The poor is more emergences to sustainment. So then save the urgent the poor is considered then, this is righteous. In the micro concept means then pure but also 100% compaction is micro also, so then, in the all of behavior decided by the wicked or righteous, in a moment decided how to decide, this is the seed of the micro concept actor world righteous soul place destination or wicked soul place destination. But also this is the strength the soul or weak soul; in this decide procedures are intervening mind between soul and body. Soul and body blocked by the mind, so then mind is the variables to the wicked living or righteous living. In the end the mind is big then soul is weak but mind is the small then soul is strength, so then soul strength then related to the in the micro concept world blessing bank saving is higher, but if mind is bigger than soul is weak in the end the all of the behavior in the macro concept world wicked behavior save in the micro concept actor cursed bank saving.

So then wicked soul must be feeble it can't go for the long distance so, but also do not see in the strong bright so then wicked soul it very naturally do not see in the bright light then do not know, so do not see wicked soul righteous soul and wicked soul feeble not strong so then do not go for the long distance but also higher position location, so wicked soul remind lowest curve, so called the bottomed place is wicked soul eternity destinations. but righteous soul must be strong so then can go long distance, strong soul watch under the bright light, then more distance so then top of the curve.

In the macro concept actor living place is mixed with wicked soul body, righteous body so that these are not segregate wicked and righteous bodies. So then endure of harmful from wicked actors, endurance and scarifies is the lower position keep in, so then it must be possible the wicked actor realized to how to live is the righteous then, righteous body be excitement, it is not easy but of he/she make him/her learn of the righteous living ways then transfer form wicked to righteous then will go for the same direction the destiny is righteous eternity living place. Endurance helping sacrifice understanding is the righteous actor living tools. But also excitement show the sunshine gives a good feeling to others.

Micro concept world actor soul also gives gift living that ways to live on. Micro concept actor righteous soul excitement but also soul knows the micro concept world, in the macro concept actor moment decide then help decide do righteous living for the saving in the blessing save bank. So this is the power to live on. If not all of actor helped from micro concept cursed bank saving. So long, righteous soul sees only in the bright light, and the top of the curve, but also go further long distance, but wicked soul only in the dim, and the bottom of the curve, but also do not go longer it reach at the very short distance. So then macro concept at micro concept world just even disguised featured for example macro actor try to live righteous live but actually wicked soul, then discriminated by the same character soul, because righteous soul do not see wicked soul, but wicked soul wee it, so that even try to be righteous but still his/her friend are known to him is his/her friend. Even disguised wicked soul but if he/she has been lived strong soul, then another righteous soul easy can watch him/her.

How I live righteous or wicked live don decided by myself, but other decide, righteous living actors know, but also wicked actors know, so that even macro concept very normal hidden place since living righteous actor also be count on the righteous soul in the micro concept world, so that in the macro concept world poor, or lower, or ignorance, then if it lived as the righteous living then it must be located at the micro concept actor righteous eternity living possible.

2014.08.27

Topic: micro concept point move to +1/∞

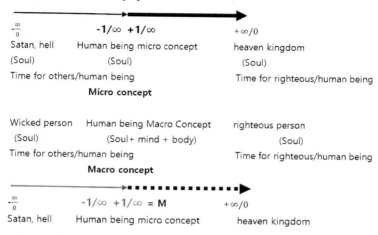

Personal, family, company, etc. has the micro concept point, here micro concept is not a actually pure philosophy but fusion common sense philosophy, micro concept point (-/∞+1/∞) is derived by the convergence to unseen but not zero, that comes inferable micro concept point M(-1/∞ +1/∞)

Micro concept point M= -1/∞ +1/∞ move to +∞/0, this is exclusively reach micro concept point M, then the point is criteria before M is -∞/0 but after M is +∞/0, so then M is critical point, M is stationd in the micro concept world, but in the macro concept point the point M is moved to in the dot line. What energy move? Who move this point? This point can move?

M point located at the macro point human being, family, company etc. has the micro concept point, so macro concept actors have each center, and micro center is the all of the feature's center.

The center M carried by the macro concept actor, so it must be infer as the grand cosmos center.

But this is others think, I can't go for this, micro concept is around of the zero, so then micro is seen unseen, M= -1/∞ +1/∞, M point move to +∞/0, M1, M2, M3 ……. Mn, all of macro concept actors have the micro concept point, so then in the micro concept point all of actor is not same levels of the micro concept point, so macro concept actor's micro concept degree is not same, someone is not reach at the m, but the others m1., some other also m2, until now micro concept point is realization point, so then realize after realize, then realize itself also the moment, so then it already comes to M1 is not micro concept point, now try to be the m2 point this is the macro concept point, micro concept point levels are difference then infer that micro concept point is the is life of macro concept actor goals, but mind variances 0~100 then, the actor mind is how to do then macro concept actor realize of existence of the micro concept point. If get it, that is realize, so then get to know the micro concept point.

If a human being, family leader, company CEO know the micro concept point then, a actor will try to reach at the Micro concept point, if the mind variance 1~100 so then, all of macro concept actor reach at the Micro concept point. As the macro concept actor realize M then, they all of the micro concept actor, so then these souls are so strong, micro concept actors realize then another Micro concept point M so then realize behavior of righteous, even more if do realizes then all of the conditions being realize possibility.

Macro concept all of actors are has the micro concept actor, but even though do not know the real existence so disturbed by the mind, so then mind about 0 soul about 100 then is the pure realize that, strongly reach at M, that is the moving energy itself, so long

$-\frac{\infty}{0}$ $-1/\infty$ $+1/\infty$ = M = **strong soul** $+\infty/0$

Satan, hell   Human being micro concept   heaven kingdom

From $+1/\infty$ $+\infty/0$ = M1, M2, M3, ------------------------------ Mn$(+\infty/0)$ so long, this is the only righteous soul, not a wicked soul, wicked soul lived at real line so then $-\infty/0$ $-1/\infty$, this is wicked actors living place, but in the wicked mind, righteous mind is $-1/\infty$ $+1/\infty$ so soul is being strong grown states. Micro concept point M $(-1/\infty+1/\infty)$ = strong soul, so then, if a macro concept point actor realize then become to real macro concept actor (soul +body= soul body=body), this strong soul reach at the M, just reach, so then the point micro concept point is the eternity do not changed eternity point.

$-1/\infty$ $+1/\infty$ = M = strong soul
= righteous soul = destination of the righteous soul.

Micro concept point is the eternity do not changed point, but in the macro concept point is the changed to move. So then if in the macro concept actor do not know the micro concept point existence then human being, family, company etc. do not know. Then it never reaches at the micro concept point M.

But if macro concept actor realize then actor reach at the micro concept point then, an actor full grown soul, about reach at the mind= $+1/\infty$, so long in the macor concept, realize actor get the from the knowledge, just soluble of the problems of $-\infty/0$ $-1/\infty$, in this time problems solved from the mind reach at the $+1/\infty$, the realized actor mind reach at the $+$ means that righteous actor so then righteous actor mind reach at the $+1/\infty$, so that righteous actor meet the pair of body a soul, so meet the soul and body, the soul $+$ body $=$ body realized, The reached M1, it's moment time, but also moment place, so then transient to M2, so then micro concept is reach at M, but in the macro concept move to $+\infty/0$.

In the macro concept world, move to the $+\infty/0$, so then

$$\frac{\infty}{0}$$
Satan, hell $-1/\infty$ $+1/\infty$ = M = strong soul $+\infty/0$
                   Human being micro concept   heaven kingdom

Then micro concept M is not easy but infers that if the micro concept point reach at the Mn micro concept Mn, must be explained to the macro $+|$ micro concept understanding is

Micro concept point M is not moved, but in the macro concept micro concept M move to $+\infty/0$

This is eternity divergence, so then it can't explained, but micro concept is convergence, so then it must infer to macro concept actor micro concept actor m also converged then is right.

$$\frac{\infty}{0}$$
Satan, hell $-1/\infty$ $+1/\infty$ = M = strong soul $+\infty/0 = +1/\infty$
                   Human being micro concept   heaven kingdom

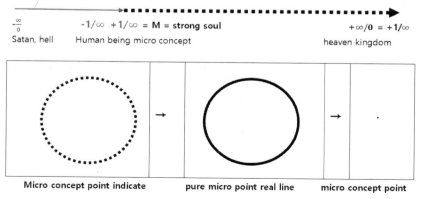

Micro concept point indicate   pure micro point real line   micro concept point

The round is the begin of the $+1/\infty$ the end is moment $+\infty/0=+1/\infty$, so then comes round, so then round is the micro concept point move to the start to end is go around. That is round.

Round is the shown to us, special energy comes, because of the micro concept point move on this line of the round.

If infer that round is the perfect of the micro concept then all of the realization point micro concept point is on the round, the round is become of the unseen micro concept point. Because of the micro concept world micro concept is not moved just existed as the point which is not seen but not zero.

2014.08.27

Topic: macro concept actor giver or accepter

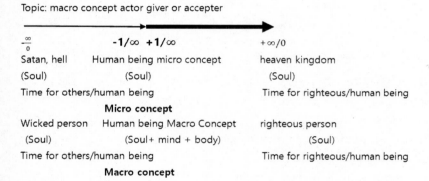

	$-1/\infty$ $+1/\infty$	$+\infty/0$
$-\frac{\infty}{0}$		
Satan, hell	Human being micro concept	heaven kingdom
(Soul)	(Soul)	(Soul)
Time for others/human being		Time for righteous/human being
	Micro concept	
Wicked person	Human being Macro Concept	righteous person
(Soul)	(Soul+ mind + body)	(Soul)
Time for others/human being		Time for righteous/human being
	Macro concept	

Deceit giving, righteous giving, deceit accept righteous accepting. Every time every place is concerned in the macro concept actor. Giver and acceptor, all condition is differences, righteous giver, wicked giver, righteous acceptor, wicked acceptor.

In the macro concept actor living place, in the actor all related with donor and accepter, all is included in all of the time governed. Giving thing is also variable; seen, unseen thing all is the mediator of giving things. In the macro concept giver is absolute right, acceptor absolute thank you the giver. Then giver is all is good estimated, in this case, micro concept actor soul feel of the macro concept actor behavior. Micro actor discriminate righteous and wicked macro actor.

Donner object is righteous intention, sympathy, mercy etc. here in this micro concept excuse of the seen material giving is the pure macro concept actors behavior, so unseen giving materials so remembered eternity, righteous giving is through realized, so called reach at the micro concept point (-1/∞+1/∞) then here also, the mind is reach at the micro concept point then soul is managed the body, so then, in the end the righteous giving is micro concept actor, but also in the macro concept actor; soul +mind= micro concept point(-1/∞+1/∞) + body= soulful body=body" so then in this cases soul is a big role, soul is in the major role in the micro concept actor, but also connect to in the macro concept actor minor, but even minor, if macro concept actor mind is reach at the micro concept point, then macro soul, micro soul is same of the soul, so then, the macro actor soul ~ micro concept actor soul related with waves.

Macro concept actor soul + body= soulful body= seen body= unseen soul

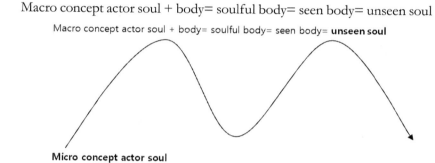

Macro concept actor soul + body= soulful body= seen body= **unseen soul**

Micro concept actor soul

In the time of the macro concept actor reach at M (-1/∞+1/∞) macro actor soul and micro actor soul meet by spiritual wave.

If this spiritual waves are connected micro concept soul to macro concept actor soul in the time of the macro concept actor health soul, macro concept actor reach at the micro concept point (-1/∞+1/∞) then infer that get through miacro concept actor soul, and macro concept actor soul +body= body with soul, just seen only body, but unseen soul meet micro concept actor.

The realized macro actor gives to the acceptor with sympathy, mercy etc. then micro concept soul really excitement soul goes by pipe line soul deliver to the micro concept blessing bank save. It is the very good pattern, but in the macro concept actor so many multiple factors are appeared to like

categories	giver	acceptor	Related with micro
Realized giver	Sympathy, mercy	Feel good, thank you	Saving blessing
giver	Economic theory	Normal, ignorance	-
Realized acceptor	God, good actor	Blessing giver	Be blessed from saving bless
acceptor	Normal, deceit	Ignorance, cursed	Saving cursed bank

Giver is saving in the micro concept blessing bank saving, accepter get from blessed from saving blessing bank

Giver is the build of himself/herself of blessing, accepter also god's giving when accepting time macro concept actor realized actor then, the macro actor all of the donor's giving is from god, so then, in the macro concept then, realize actor is already live soul, realized macro actor are really "soul + mind = reach at M micro concept point + body= soulful body" so then just blessing saving behavior is donor also with sympathy mercy it must be infer that god ordered by the soul of the micro concept, it means that micro concept actor live with god, heaven soul king, so soul order the macro concept realized donor, so the realized donor giving is sacrifice just felling of the sympathy or mercy. So then a body of the realized soul body lives all of the time, in the macro concept just soulful actor.

But if not realized giver then, when giving time expect to get from acceptor, it must be in the point of macro concept then, so then giving is the just trade, it is not any blessing point saving, but also do not realized acceptor sometimes out of duty accepting time curse to donor, because of donor being rich. If acceptor of realizes then donor is not realize then, realized acceptor, used the donors giving, then the realized accepter give building donor's blessing in the micro concept actor world saving. So then giver does not know his/her giving is saved by the realized acceptor.

Realized soul giver is RSG, Then Realized soul acceptor is RSA
Soul giver SG, Soul acceptor SA

Then RSG give to the RSA then = giver blessing point 1 + acceptor blessing point 1

Then save in the blessing bank then, giver blessing points is 2(the other 1 is from realized acceptor blessing point saving), acceptor blessing point is1

RSG give to Soul acceptor SA = giver blessing point 1 + acceptor blessing point 0

= giver blessing point 1 is saved in the micro concept actor blessing bank

Soul giver SG give to the realized soul acceptor RSA = giver blessing point 0 + acceptor blessing point originality is 1, but realized acceptor save for the giver's blessing point 1 so called

Realized acceptor increased by the general donor helping energy success, but also success realized acceptor give pay in the macro actor pay back.

So then giver blessing point 1, acceptor blessing point 1 is saved in the blessing bank.

Soul giver SG give to Soul Acceptor, then = giver blessing point 0 + acceptor blessing point 0

Furthermore acceptor feels jealousy to donor, acceptor cursed bank -1 point saved.

Even in the macro concept living, donor position then, it never saved in the cursed bank saving in the micro concept actor, acceptor position can be cursed position, and acceptor position has the risk to live peril, so long, so then macro concept actor donor position is fully safe living do not save in the cursed bank, in the micro concept bank. Donor must be live at least do not save, if most then if helped realized acceptor then, a giver make success a macro actor, cause of it, giver also added blessing point, even just help 1 so then originality is the blessing point is 1 but a donor helped to the realized acceptor then donor saved in the micro concept blessing bank blessing point is getting 2.

In this case realized acceptor

Realized acceptor built by himself in his life of the macro actor time, so he accept from the giver so then realized acceptor make another giver's blessing bank saving.

But if general acceptor he/she so not jealousy accepting is the then he/she helped already accumulated help others, some of the credit, here is help other saving account is 51%, but cursed bank is 49% then, just without realize he/she used his/her saved account. So then this is nothing cursed or blessing.

But also if giver to a acceptor then, acceptor jealousy then giver 0, acceptor -1, so then giver affect even 0 but cursed bank -1, so then giver also do harmful also cursed bank about-1 but is not -1, narrowly come out form the cursed bank just nothing gains.

In the macro concept actor living is giver position then safe living out of cursed bank save, so then to save a blessing bank do help is best policy.

2014.08.27
Topic: macro concept actor creative

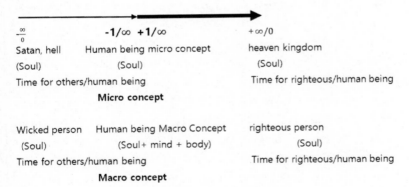

In this micro concept has key word micro concept, macro concept, and wicked soul, righteous soul, gradually added now comes cursed bank, blessing bank, it must be increased in this micro concept keep going. Here macro actor world terms creature has been comes.

In this micro concept what try to talk, this is productivity concept, or for what just idea world, it must be interested to readers of this micro concept, this is faith at the micro concept unseen world, so then discriminated from the micro concept and macro concept. Micro concept is $-1/\infty+1/\infty$, I have been called in this micro concept M, so try to save creative, it means that use the $+1/\infty+\infty/0$

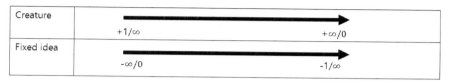

$-\infty/0 \sim -1/\infty$ time is macro concept built knowledge until now, but also seen feature all has been produced, so that comes to now this type, but also all of the macro concept actors support, so macro concept this has been produced of the $-$ Mn ...... -M10.... $-$M5 ..... $-$M1($-\infty/0$ $-1/\infty$) this has been until now seen thing creative, so then in that time, all of the actor, in the macro concept actor whole life effort to reach at the micro concept point M ($-\infty/0-1/\infty$).

Creature is how to reach at the M ($-1/\infty+1/\infty$) in this place melted at latest past most future is mixed or melted, so then micro concept actor is lived in this place, soul, in the beginning of the micro concept is supposed to convergence to unseen, micro level then it called to the macro concept, so now, macro concept human being's micro concept is soul, so that in the M ($-1/\infty+1/\infty$) lived at a actor of micro is soul. Soul live at in the micro concept M region, M time, micro concept actor soul is so flexible.

Fixed idea $-$M ($-\infty/0-1/\infty$) in this time had been reached to the at that time M ($-1/\infty+1/\infty$)

At that time also lived righteous actor, the actor helped from the micro concept soul, in the micro concept actor living place micro concept point reach, the macro concept minor actor ; soul minor +mind (fake soul) + body= mind so called fake soul is occupy body so that minor soul, even though minor player in the macro concept world, then at that time a macro actor realized to reach at the micro concept point M ($-1/\infty+1/\infty$) so then hlped of the micro concept actor give a $+1/\infty \sim+\infty/0$ is not seen idea comes, but in the macro concept, macro concept actor only live in the $-\infty/0-1/\infty$ idea, feature, ranking, knowledge is only accepted, so that whoever else do not know but also, do not necessary unseen idea. They macro concept actor in the time of the $-$M ($-\infty/0-1/\infty$),

Macro concept is the rigid all of idea, knowledge, stenotypes etc. all has the owners but also the strong power built, a big strong macro concept power built, the big macro power lose the flexible, but all is the big rigid. The big size stereo type is occupied the entire macro concept world. So that macro concept world is located at the $-\infty/0$-$1/\infty$, it called in this micro concept, so macro is $-\infty/0$-$1/\infty$, micro is the $+1/\infty+ \infty/0$ it comes to in this micro concept world

Creature "Micro concept "		
	$+1/\infty$	$+\infty/0$
Fixed idea "macro Concept "		
	$-\infty/0$	$-1/\infty$

Micro concept = creature= $+1/\infty+\infty/0$, so then in this world do not see but also, this is the soul world, micro concept main actor is the "soul"

Macro concept = Fixed idea = $-\infty/0$-$1/\infty$, so then in this world is macro concept actor can see, it usually all living time, place is macro concept actor is the "soul: minor + mind: fake soul major +body= body" so then macro concept actor is the "body"

Macro is the fixed idea, so then all of macro concept actor feel doing not urgent, so most macro concept actor live in the fixed idea, fixed idea live at the $-\infty/0$-$1/\infty$, in this time, place made in all of macro concept are main fixed, rigid but also built existed energy getting, so ranking is constructed, but this is so old, even to the macro, so then how to energy surplus, all of the macro concept actor live enough, in this case, so all of the mind of macro, macro mind try to expand to the $+ \infty$, it can possible the expand the macro concept actor "mind" mind try to get more, so then "mind" try to much getting so long desired mind, competition others then win, or getting the another own macro concept actor wonted materials.

Micro is unseen world, so called the macro concept actor do not know, macro actor body do not see the micro concept world, so then micro concept world not easy to go, because of the macro world so called to reach at the M($-1/\infty+1/\infty$) so then macro concept must be micro, so called to be the soul, then macro concept actor is " soul + mind+ body= body" body do not see the micro concept world, so it must can't reach at the M(-1/∞+1/∞), but if the macor cocenpt actor = soul be stong + mind is decresed to zeo + body = body= soulful body= so long being body, but even body but soul so that, soul reach at the micro concept M(-1/∞+1/∞) so then it can live at the micro concept world in the macro actor, but even macro actor body, but realized body, make about to the mind= (-1/∞+1/∞) so then comes up soul +body= soul, so that micro concept actor place, can live as the macro concept actor.

Creature is what it said then creative is the macro concept actor produce new concept, idea, but also the products etc in the macro concept actor live facilities but also the unseen, seen create is the from the micro concept world. Micro concept world going is not usual so then create is the reach at the micro concept point M (-1/∞+1/∞) creative is the required to all of the macro concept energy all used, then in the research then realize of the research in the procedures of the mind and soul fight, so long

soul	mind	body
Micro concept try to meet But also get in soul place Soul place all occupied by the mind	Macro concept desire to get a new idea is start	Body controlled By the originality is soul but in the macro concept world Occupied by the mind

To get a creature success then, in the micro concept world actor soul try to get occupy now mind is occupied, the site is very strong, so then macro concept controlled by the" mind" do not know the unseen world, so that" mind" is all of energy use for the another energy getting. So then all of "mind" all live "mind" is the Seen world body how to live, so then, micro concept actor soul try to see original position, macro concept actor " soul + body= soulful body" but actually in the macro concept is the consist of the "soul +mind +body = mindful body" so then in the macro concept actor living place is the soul is being minor, so then if do not reach at the micro concept point M(-1/∞+1/∞) it usually occupied " mind" is fully, so then macro actor body do not scarifies because of the "mind" feel that lose of the competition to make energy to be use by body sustainment. So very clear if not profit margin from the activities, so then "strong mind" knows balance of profit or losing comparison then, macro concept actor do not reach at the M ((-1/∞+1/∞) micro concept point, so long, if do real creative then, macro concept actor "soul + mind+ body= body" then soul is strong + mind about to zero + body=soulful body" so then creative is out of the macro concept controller "mind" then, creative is macro concept actor being reach at the " soul + body= soulful body= body, is the strong soul in the macro concept actor, is the contact to the micro concept actor major actor is the "soul" and macro concept "strong soul"

Meet in the micro concept point M((-1/∞+1/∞) in the micro concept tunnel M point is so that in the micro concept tunnel M((-1/∞+1/∞) so that striong macro concept soul travel through it reach at the micro concept righteous soul destination heaven kingdom , so called the god located place reach, so then, in the micro concept actor of strong soul, bring the idea from the (+1/∞+∞/0) strong macro concept soul bring from the new, creative idea, gift from the micro concept righteous a soul gives to strong macro concept soul, so then in the out of the "mind", if mind is about to zero, then being macro soul strong soul, so strong soul move through micro concept tunnel((-1/∞+1/∞) so long, "soul + body= body" really create a in the macro concept world.

Macro concept seen from the Micro concept point, so then if the concept is seen then, it moment is the already is another macro is comes.

2014.08.27

Topic: macro concept actor creative

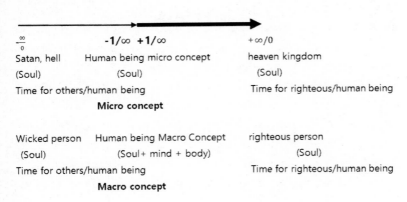

$-\frac{∞}{0}$	**-1/∞ +1/∞**	+∞/0
Satan, hell	Human being micro concept	heaven kingdom
(Soul)	(Soul)	(Soul)
Time for others/human being		Time for righteous/human being
	Micro concept	

Wicked person	Human being Macro Concept	righteous person
(Soul)	(Soul+ mind + body)	(Soul)
Time for others/human being		Time for righteous/human being
	Macro concept	

In this micro concept is started with micro concept gate (-1/∞+1/∞) realized. This micro concept point makes me realized. As I am not religious person, but I'm just studied business management I have thought remained just status, how to out of this status. All is finding to development or make larger so long, big organism is advantages to get energy, this is force of power, a big power get all of the weak, market networking, marketing helping, but small companies are also weak.

So then a big force safely gets in the market with consumers, this is macro ways, so then out of the game or gains in the real making money, but this is based on the sacrifices of the general personal, or small and middle company positions, company units then company souls are counted on the micro concept, micro concept is how forming, what is the micro concept, micro is better or not, what is the micro, then macro is getting as power of behavior. So long unit of soul, of companies, small company, a big company what is difference, if big company success, small company success in the real market, then big company success is macro power, but small company success is what, it is miracle then miracle must be even there is not power but get survive. Company unit, a big company has also soul, small company also small, in the micro concept, Micro concept point (-1/∞+1/∞), is same company soul is same, big company in macro concept 1 CEO macro concept also small company CEO 1, small company use the only small company facilities, but macro company a unit is helped all of the big companies helpers, so then power is big, but small company is not strong power. Power get over the small, then in the micro can see the strange, macro get, micro lose, so long, then in this macro concept all get bigger to smaller, smaller all losing but bigger only get. This is the macro world, micro world all disappeared.

This is correct, what happened to the game of the macro and micro, or the big company and small company, power is old, typically macro, but small is no power but only new but also about new,

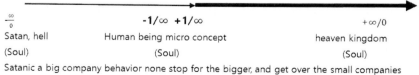

$\frac{\infty}{0}$	-1/∞ +1/∞	+∞/0
Satan, hell	Human being micro concept	heaven kingdom
(Soul)	(Soul)	(Soul)

Satanic a big company behavior none stop for the bigger, and get over the small companies
Righteous a big company going macro behavior stop turned left to be role of god messenger

Big company	Small company
A big power, network, marketing, variable helper, historic asset, still invade others Just old company's desired, but do not New progress, just like "a large group of stones" if related righteous soul go then righteous soul king god messenger role, but role of the wicked soul king Satan.	A small power. There is no marketing, There is no variable helpers, defend of the Big company power, the only survived way is Creative and new ways. So young wait of Problems during then miracle comes Miracle must be help from realized micro concept actor of soul

Small company unit CEO is new, and creative then, company starter must be infer that, M1 (point (-1/∞+1/∞), the small company CEO realized already, he/she got a knowledge of his/ hers in the M1, he/she got a personal knowledge before, but after the open for the company then,

The company unit micro concept soul is very green soul; it must be need strength of company soul.

The company unit micro concept point another form the personal micro concept M, then personal to personal then M is strong, but also very safe, so transience from the people to company, then, the M is changed from to unit, so then realize personal realized M is based on the personal soul.

But open for the new small company, then company micro soul of company, is how to survive as company unit. Big company soul sees a new soul, so a big company soul is righteous soul or satanic soul, then a new small company soul, so big fear to the satanic soul a big company soul.

Macro concept actor a big company, small company, if a big company CEO realize then reach at the company unit M point (-1/∞+1/∞), then, a big company CEO reach at the M, then turned to the against macro concept gate direction, then micro concept is not a power but righteous realized so then, here to the big company CEO already become of the righteous soul in the micro concept world king, heaven king dome god's messenger role living, so long the direction is same, so long even the start as the new company, so long, the small company must be not go but in the very unseen level but the small company go deeper, so reach at the propound deep, so long micro concept knowledge is the only power.

So long, small company CEO is the try to a field getting realize, so then, the small company manager reach at the micro concept actor being strong, small company CEO can be the righteous soul king's messenger. So long small company CEO helped from the string micro concept actor soul, so that small company CEO deep reach at the field, so then, CEO of small company is the micro concept point M1, point $(-1/\infty+1/\infty)$, M2 point $(-1/\infty+1/\infty)$,, so long without do harm, do not make fail others, just success small company is just role of the micro concept king messenger is do not go for the macro direction, it must be the still micro concept direction move.

Micro concept actor and macro concept actor is must be pursuit is peace and peace is good live, but in the macro concept is the mind is come up

sort	Soul=0	Soul =∞	Mind=0	Mind = ∞	body
Macro concept	Trouble Not peace	Blessing peace	Reach at Micro concept point $(-1/\infty+1/\infty)$, god's messenger	Full wicked Mind, Satan messenger	Soul=∞, mind=0, success. Soul=0, mind=∞ failure
Micro concept	Wicked Satanic world	Strong soul Reach righteous soul destination	Strong soul Reach at the Destination of righteous soul's	Feeble soul Do not reach Destination so that stop going	Soul=∞, mind=0, blessing macro concept actor/ Soul=0, mind=∞, curse macro actor

Macro concept actor a big company or small company CEO has the micro concept actor $M(-1/\infty+1/\infty)$, for the peace, but also, company management also come up between macro concept and micro concept combined to appeared to now. Righteous is not depends on power, but realized, reaching at the micro concept.

In the macro concept company small or big company managed, soulful company, out of soulful then, it compared with righteous or wicked is classified. But righteous is not easy more difficult actor's energy, but wicked is so easy but also, easy actors, here is the actor is creative difficult means but just simple labor, so then so not go deeper, then all of the customers satisfaction is how to be soulful company managed or not. Soulful company and soulful CEO is the important factor, how to be at the righteous, how to be the wicked is classified others, so long in this micro concept then, wicked company or CEO see the wicked company, but righteous company evaluated by the righteous CEO or company.

A big company, a small company must be consistence to be the mind to $(-1/\infty + 1/\infty)$, then it comes a realize in a new creative company own assets, but also mind to $(-1/\infty + 1/\infty)$, then CEO of the company can realized but also, the company CEO can be peace. The company going well based on the micro concept blessing to the mind is $(-1/\infty + 1/\infty)$, realize so then soul help body to be soulful company and CEO in the end god indicate the god's messenger then god soul also keep influence peace in the long term company going.

2014.09.02

Topic: macro concept man and woman

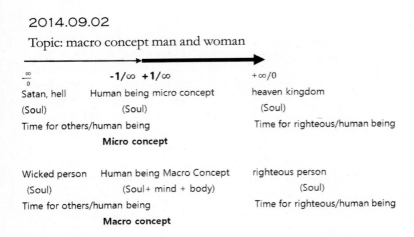

$\frac{\infty}{0}$	$-1/\infty$ $+1/\infty$	$+\infty/0$
Satan, hell	Human being micro concept	heaven kingdom
(Soul)	(Soul)	(Soul)
Time for others/human being		Time for righteous/human being
	Micro concept	
Wicked person	Human being Macro Concept	righteous person
(Soul)	(Soul+ mind + body)	(Soul)
Time for others/human being		Time for righteous/human being
	Macro concept	

In micro concept and macro concept how to exist man soul, woman soul, how to changed to the from micro concept actor soul will be decide to the macro concept world, man soul, woman soul, this is the very special in the oriental region philosophy man is minus, woman is plus, so then man and woman, plus and minus, this combinations are new, creative result.

Man in actor of macro concept world, man in the micro concept world, so long it is natural of the micro concept man soul, in the micro concept world actor soul, in the macro concept actor discriminate man and woman, but what happened to the micro concept world there is a divided as the man soul, female soul, this combination comes so variable variances make so multiple features.

In the micro concept world has the located at the woman, man soul, or only located do not discriminate man and female soul, then how to explained to in the micro concept actor is soul, so then if soul is male and female then it is very same as the macro concept actors, but if infer that of the do not discriminate man and woman soul, so called without discriminate soul then how to forming, it must be macro concept get marriage to one man and woman marriage to one of soul.

If infer that in the micro concept world just without difference male female, then in the macro concept "get marriage= man soul + woman soul = man and soul just soul combined. So then in the micro concept world live in the micro concept world, just man &wife soul is located at the micro concept place.

Man soul, woman soul how to combined to and the a new wife & husband, man and woman married then, the variance is righteous soul woman, wicked woman, righteous man, wicked man is four categorized are combined,

Sort souls (variance)	Righteous man	Wicked man	Righteous woman	Wicked woman
Righteous woman	Righteous soul	Woman scarifies		
Wicked woman	Man sacrifice	Wicked soul		
Righteous man			Righteous soul	Man sacrifice
Wicked man			Woman sacrifice	Wicked soul

Righteous & righteous man and woman blessed from god, it must be infer that in the single of the time or another blessing, in the single soul, accumulated righteous so saved at the micro concept soul bank blessing point is enough. So long, in the macro concept world this man &woman righteous actor lived then, do live in the righteous in the macro concept behavior so then each other sacrifices so after get marriage then man &wife unit soul is do righteous so reach at the micro concept point $(-1/\infty+1/\infty)$, so long live happy, these man and wife keep sacrifices and help others, so long itself being good live.

But man sacrifices and woman sacrifice, in this case is variance of wicked soul getting righteous after get marriage. So then how to righteous man and woman help fair to be the realized to be man &wife getting at Micro concept point $(-1/\infty+1/\infty)$, so then the wicked soul to be how to live the righteous man and woman, this is the lucky to the wicked soul, but also the righteous soul, in the macro concept world, it can't be perfect gift from god, it must be real lived all of righteous, so long it must be reliable so then comes from god a mission of disables bring him/her on, so then man & wife is the righteous parents so then, god bless husband &wife. But in the one is righteous the other is wicked then it also duty to undertake of the god's charity order the possibility of the can be changed to wicked to righteous. The righteous man and wife, if make her/his fair then, the righteous spread making righteous so that in the big sacrifice doing righteous all of the endured so make realize of the wicked soul to be righteous then, their wife and husband soul being righteous soul, so then after dead of the macro concept living, then it will come to the righteous soul saves the wicked soul to make being the righteous, so then in the eternity to live as the righteous soul destination, this is so happy live in the eternity, then someone question the righteous soul is damaged, but it is not, even one is righteous the righteous soul do not meet another righteous soul, righteous to righteous soul meeting is super blessing but actually the blessed righteous soul can't meet so then, one of the righteous soul must live wicked soul, so then, this is so multi, so then, righteous soul sacrifice for the wicked soul then live at the micro concept world living as the righteous soul, so called to live righteous.

But actually righteous man and woman, so not endurance, so that righteous failed to make help the strong wicked soul so righteous soul ruined to the wicked then, the righteous soul turned to the wicked soul, so long, righteous soul being also wicked soul. So then after finish of the macro concept world then, the destination is wicked soul destination, so called satanic world living in the long run, so then righteous soul being wicked soul.

In the end of it, righteous soul realizes that reach at the micro concept center $(-1/\infty+1/\infty)$, so then all of undertaje of the wicked hard offence, righteous soul is endure all of anger of the wicked soul.

If wicked soul to wicked soul meets as the wife and husband they do not live eternity so that they must be divorced do not have marriage living so that, they must be another righteous soul for the helped from the righteous pair, so then divorced wicked soul try to righteous soul, all of the wicked soul depend on righteous soul, in this case righteous soul if realized at then reached to the micro concept point $(-1/\infty+1/\infty)$, then wicked soul depend on righteous soul. How to live righteous soul to the wicked soul, wicked soul do not know but also wicked soul already satanic place, even so strong, the wicked way is advantage so that the wicked soul try to going wicked ways, so hard to the righteous soul make. So long, wicked soul and righteous soul almost all wicked soul is to be winning, so that righteous soul must be also being wicked. Because of wicked is very easy to live on.

So that wicked to wicked soul it must be all expect to be relied on of righteous soul, but it can't find it, both wicked soul live in single, so then in the micro concept soul destination is must be not safe, infer of the pair of man& wife soul do not live righteous then it comes to the wicked place but also do not have pair then do not have the destination but also righteous soul be destined at the righteous soul.

But if the same of the macro concept and micro concept soul is same then in the macro concept soul, macro concept soul style same, so then the end of the macro concept to reach at the micro concept world then, personal soul, all is soul man and woman soul separated eternity, so then one person is one soul doing not cared with marriage, so then, in the eternity living is not excitement and perfection of it, so in the soil only oneself, so then eternity living is still feel lonesome so that infer of the pair of soul of man& woman is may be right, so then how to live is the going for the righteous or wicked decide, so long out of the fair then, they do not decide to the destination so long for the eternity is marriage is impossible, surprised to this micro concept so long marriage is the key to the micro concept eternity world getting. Even righteous or wicked soul, the marriage is the basic to go the eternity living in the micro concept world.

this combined macro concept or micro concept so long, if a macro concept wife and husband just one unit is can reach at the micro concept point, wide and husband live at as the realized so make a righteous soul so long reach at micro concept $(-1/\infty+1/\infty)$, wife and husband being soul one of micro concept soul, micro concept soul then how to forming in the macro concept.

In the macro concept getting marriage then, man and woman soul combined to one

sort	man	Man& wife	wife
Macro concept soul	Man soul	Man & woman soul	Woman soul
Micro concept soul		Man and wife soul = "soul"	

This is a infer of micro concept actor soul is not existed as the man soul, female soul, but difference dead, then single soul reach at the soul so then, how to explained man & wife soul, actually here macro concept actor live in the macro concept actor then micro concept is $(-1/\infty+1/\infty)$, so then wife & husband soul being. So then in this micro concept have the wife &husband. So long it must be interesting infer happened before combined to later dead soul then being of the angel to the husband macro concept actor, so long if infer that later dead part come to micro concept actor, then welcome from already soul of angel meet a dead soul so being one of soul. It infer of it, so then marriage soul is being perfect eternity living in the soul, so long man & wife soul= soul, but also the mind and wife experiment also man & wife

Man &wife soul	Man & wife mind	Man & wife body =dead

So long man & wife soul, man &wife mind combined to in the macro concept characteristics to the eternity of micro concept soul residence.

2014.09.03

Topic: macro concept big size big problems, small size small problems

$-\frac{\infty}{0}$ **-1/∞ +1/∞**   +∞/0

Satan, hell	Human being micro concept	heaven kingdom
(Soul)	(Soul)	(Soul)
Time for others/human being		Time for righteous/human being

Micro concept

Wicked person	Human being Macro Concept	righteous person
(Soul)	(Soul+ mind + body)	(Soul)
Time for others/human being		Time for righteous/human being

Macro concept

In this micro concept macro concept world bigger, smaller, smaller is small income but also small problems, but larger a big income but a big problems.

$-\frac{\infty}{0}$ **-1/∞ +1/∞**   +∞/0

Smaller   bigger

In the macro concept smaller & bigger

In the macro concept try to big own, to live easy, no one want to be smaller getting being poor, all the physical labor, in the micro concept living is not live only body but also soul, so that disrupter is mind. Mind is only getting bigger, try to more getting, to be rich also, so all of macro concept actor same direction. So that to be big, rich, all of macro concept actor uses wicked soul, wicked soul is more harmful to wicked mind, but some of concept is same but wicked soul is eternity but wicked mind is very temporal.

Macro concept all of actor run for getting much more money, so called energy, then in this criteria small owned actor is absolutely forget, just one side is get rich, so all of actor run for the rich ways, so all try to get of the rich destination train or bus, and airplane.

But all of the poor lost all of opportunity, losing in the competition in getting money, in the end pushed to out of the money place, so that a actor do not live rich, then a actor angry of his poor living, all the time big sigh, prostrated thinking. So then it is very same as the rich or poor this is the nothing, in this place, of the micro concept realization Micro concept gate (-1/∞+1/∞), micro concept is located whoever, allhas the micro cocenpt sp that tunnel to the micro concept soul helping, in the macro concept how to approach to the micro concept M $(-1/\infty+1/\infty)$, micro concept is the make less, so that supposed to the all of the feature convergence to micro concept M $(-1/\infty+1/\infty)$, but actually in macro concept getting poor and rich is not relative, it can't explain well, but also do not know the micro concept world existed.

How to big, so called rich, how to small poor, then

sort	Bigger = rich	Smaller = poor
Macro concept	Think as blessing getting	Think as cursed getting
Micro concept	$+\infty/0$, Diffusion, so that do not reach at terminal.	$-\infty/0$, convergence, so that it reach at the terminal

Rich actor pursue endless to get much more money, but also the poor actor do not make money so anger, "why not I can't make money" if do not reach at the realized to the micro concept of the mind is reach at the micro concept point $(-1/\infty+1/\infty)$, so then even poor but it will come to excitement cause of do not have problems, just very simple, so that confidence with poor getting energy, but for this how to reach at the M,

the procedure is required to do, so then religious believing is very essential to get micro concept point, so called mind is reach at the M $(-1/\infty+1/\infty)$, then in the end realized so that even in the macro concept smaller then correctly not miserable to this, so then in the temple of Buddha Buddhist monk is poor then monk try to realize then, the monk come to reach at the M$(-1/\infty+1/\infty)$, religious related all of actors are not rich then, they try to realized by the god accept, so then here god accept is the reach at the micro concept M $(-1/\infty+1/\infty)$, so long try to be realize means that, mind is become to approach to the zero so called M $(-1/\infty+1/\infty)$, so long religious actor helped god, so then mind is about zero so macro concept actor reach at the terminal.

But the rich man, macro concept actor any kind of actors in the rich, it is not place to be realize, the rich is forget of the micro concept because micro concept and macro concept is the poor and the rich

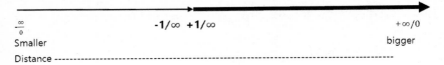

Is do big distance, so that the bigger, rich can see even smaller, then micro concept is not adopt to the macro actor of the bigger, it must be think that rich is the big bless, in the macro concept rich is think as the peak, of blessing, so that the criteria is the money getting is the gauge of the from micro concept world Satanic soul, or righteous soul acting. So then macro concept actor move to director the $+\infty/0$, bigger, then the energy is force, so then temporally must be same righteous soul, wicked soul, but, if do not realize then still getting more desired then, it possible of the desired mind is $+\infty/0$ so then it must be impossible of the reach at the terminal of desintiaion of the determined righteous or wicked.

So long bigger is problems getting bigger, so a big problems= mind, so soul is was so hard to do in the end bigger soul is feeble so then it can't reach at the terminal, so then feeble soul haven't energy so that get off before the terminal, so long the bigger rich can't realization so then do not be located at the righteous soul destination.

But the smaller is in the macro actor do not have energy so, there is no problems also, so that the actor is light, but also swift, mind is cannot easy decreased to macro concept actor M $(-1/\infty+1/\infty)$, so then small is the small problems= mind is about also poor, so then, it must be easier to the rich, in the end the strong soul is can carry to the realized point. So that Buddha monk and all religious actor are all helped from god, because of the strong soul, so poor soul moved to micro concept world, meeting the micro concept world so that strong soul meet a righteous soul meeting, then carry of problems solving from the micro concept world to macro concept world connected to build so that the poor actor reach at the realization.

2014.09.04

Topic: macro concept family micro concept M (-1/∞+1/∞)

$\frac{\infty}{0}$ **-1/∞ +1/∞**   +∞/0

Satan, hell   Human being micro concept   heaven kingdom

(Soul)   (Soul)   (Soul)

Time for others/human being   Time for righteous/human being

           Micro concept

Wicked person   Human being Macro Concept   righteous person

(Soul)   (Soul+ mind + body)   (Soul)

Time for others/human being   Time for righteous/human being

          Macro concept

In micro concept what is the macro concept family, family is the like of the shallow deep sea, so child fish growth, but it grow to adult then wild sea moving. Family has a story and more history. Family is consisting of father, mother, son and daughter; this family will live in this macro concept world. Macro concept world strong helper, so called family is a source of living energy.

Micro concept point of the family is 1/ family members are micro point, but the unit of family is family head of house hold. Family micro point's means that realized of family micro concept soul meeting, so called family micro concept soul, so then family is very important growing child soul.

sort	father	mother	son	daughter	Family unit
Micro concept FA M	o.25 %	0.25%	0.25%	0.25	1
Micro concept Per M	1	1	1	1	-
Total micro concept M	1.25(+1)	1.25	1.25	1.25	Father 1
Macro concept	helper	helper	acceptor	acceptor	Soul
Micro concept	-	-	-	-	**Micro gate M**

In this micro concept actor live all for the sake of personal living. Family is consisting of members, family members have a role player, father is father role, mother role, son is son role, and daughter is daughter role. All of member expect each out of me, another member role working, but a person does not try to for another's easy going. Father in the family has micro concept point is 0.25%, mother also 0.25%, son is 0.25%, daughter is 0.25%, but has the father is the family leader role, each family unit, represent of family, so then family unit micro concept point is 1, but family micro concept point is in the family unit represent, so called then micro concept point micro concept actor soul is family unit, leader, so long family micro concept realized point is to the father, so that father or husband is another micro concept point 1, so that father is 2.25.

In the family micro concept M $(-1/\infty+1/\infty)$, so then micro concept M is located at the so that father realize of the concept of the family. So long, family unit realized, it means that micro concept point M tunnel to micro concept point if father is realized as the family unit leader then the family soul, combined = father soul 0.25+ mother 0.25+ son 0.25 +daughter 0.25 =1 this is the 1 is family leader, family leader communicate to another family.

Family soul actually is actually 4 personal soul combinations, so long; personal soul is each has the 1; there by each personal micro concept point is 1, so then

Personal concept point M = father 1+ mother 1+ son1 +daughter +1= 4 family personal micro concept point, actually micro concept point 1 every concept, so that family is micro concept is 1, so that each micro concept point 1/4 is only for the family, then, in this case mathematic then giving the 1/4 soul then, each personal soul micro concept is 3/4, but actually it is not, so long still personal micro concept M $(-1/\infty+1/\infty)$ is 1, so long

In the equation of M is

Personal M = F 1 + M 1 + S 1 + D 1= 4 personal M is assembled in the family.

Minus (-)

Plus (+)

Family M = F 0.25 + M 0.25 + S 0.25 + D 0.25 = family micro concept 1= family unit = father

If M = F 0 + M 0 + S 0 + D 0 = family micro concept 0 = family unit = there is no father

Math result = F0.75 + M0.75 +S 0.75 + D 0.75 = **Mathematical micro concept point 3(-1)**

Micro concept result = F 1.25 + M 1.25 + S 1.25 + D 1.25 = **Micro concept soul point 5(+1)**

Family unit =0 result = F 1-1=0, M 1-1=0 + S 1-1=0, + D 1-1= personal M = 0

In the micro concept in the macro concept actor if personal soul is 1, personal soul shared with family micro concept soul 0.25= then each personal micro concept has give to the family unit so personal micro concept is 0.75, so then family each personal micro concept point is mathematical micro concept point is 3, this is the personal micro concept is 1 is disappeared because of shared with family unit.

But in the micro concept point explained to micro concept soul shared is just personal soul micro concept point 1 – shared with family 0.25 = mathematical calculation is =0.75, but micro concept actor of the result is = 1.25, so called personal micro concept M, 0.25 give to the family then, in the micro concept soul is shared soul 0.25 is help other, make a form of soulful unit, so that create soulful family, actually family is not appeared only recognized family, so that family is not macro concept but micro concept so that, each person 025M concept point combined to I of family micro concept point, so father has the family unit micro concept point so that family manager role of 1 is comes to in the micro concept point, so then each personal micro concept point 1 is still has then, in the micro concept point soul is strong in health, it means that shared with other of soul then, soul is increased, in the mathematic is the shared then origin point is decreased but, micro concept point soul shared then what I said again, that is strength of soul, so that soul is increased, micro concept point so long shared personal soul is with shared then increased. Actually in the family any member do not sacrifice for the sacrifice so that in the family energy is nothing, so then family soul energy is 0, so then each personal micro each micro concept point is original micro concept point 1 minus -1: family unit micro concept 1) = each personal micro concept point is 0= in the family each personal micro concept point is 0 means that there is no family., some of the mathematical point then 1- family unit o.25= each family 0.75 this is the mathematical point. In the micro concept is zero=0, it means that family is not, so who undertake personal living, out of family it must be can't live, but also if live personal then, itself is not family, so then, in the family micro concept is each family micro concept soul M is shared with it, must be soul be shared then increased, this is micro concept micro concept actor soul shared then strong soul comes, so in the end strong heath soul reach at the micro concept world righteous soul destination soul living.

2014.09.04

Topic: micro concept main actor soul living energy

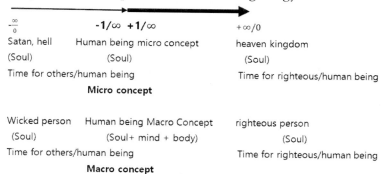

$-\frac{\infty}{0}$	**-1/∞ +1/∞**	+∞/0
Satan, hell	Human being micro concept	heaven kingdom
(Soul)	(Soul)	(Soul)
Time for others/human being		Time for righteous/human being
	Micro concept	

Wicked person	Human being Macro Concept	righteous person
(Soul)	(Soul+ mind + body)	(Soul)
Time for others/human being		Time for righteous/human being
	Macro concept	

In micro concept main actor soul need energy, how to get eternity movement energy, eternity living sustainment energy. In macro concept world are to get a macro concept actor living energy is money, all of macro actors are deceived to get money, all of actors are selling time for get a energy, the time is sold then comes living energy, in the process getting energy,

sort	Righteous behavior	Wicked behavior
Macro concept energy	Giving others, endured, sacrifice	Getting, expedient, selfishness.
Micro concept energy	Righteous behavior is righteous soul energy	Wicked behavior is wicked soul energy

Micro concept actor is soul, soul is located at two places the one is righteous soul destination is righteous soul kingdom of heaven kingdom, the lord is the god. Wicked soul's destination is wicked soul eternity place, so called that place is satanic king dome.

Micro concept soul righteous soul living energy is giving others, endured, sacrifices, and wicked soul living energy is getting, expedient, selfishness. What is the righteous soul destination, also wicked destination, in this micro concept has

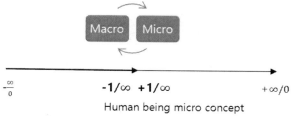

Human being micro concept

So then, micro concept actor living place actor lived righteous behavior food, if not if a righteous soul cannot eat because of food depletion, so then righteous soul being wicked. So then micro concept soul, righteous soul is depleted so then macro and micro concept world is if circulated then in the micro righteous soul is very feeble, so then do not strong compared with wicked soul.

So then circulated switch micro concept to macro concept so then, in the macro concept world righteous behavior also depleted, so long macro concept world occupied small righteous soul, but wicked soul is most occupied, micro concept energy righteous behavior is depleted then in the macro concept behavior and micro concept actor soul wicked righteous forming is

sort	Righteous soul	Wicked soul
Macro concept	Righteous behavior going down ①	Wicked behavior going up ①
Macro concept	Righteous behavior going up ②	Wicked behavior going down
Micro concept	Soul do not eat fully energy= blessing point to be decreased to 1/∞ ①	Soul getting fully energy = cursed point To be increased to ∞/0 ①
Micro concept	Soul do eat fully energy= blessing point to be decreased to ∞/0 ②	Soul do not eat fully energy = cursed point To be decreased to 1/∞ ②

Micro concept soul's righteous soul eat righteous behavior, wicked soul eat wicked behavior, just like herbivore animal, but carnivorous animal, so long herbivore animal eat grass, carnivorous animal eat meat, so then it compared with righteous soul eating, wicked soul eating, so then in the macro concept world actor, so called human being's behavior is the food to the micro concept actor soul, so long, if produced of food makers are all behavior of wicked then, righteous soul is very poor harvest, so then, but if in the macro concept actor do live wicked then in the micro concept actor wicked soul live in the bumper then wicked can live as macro actor wicked behavior.

As macro actor righteous behavior increased then, righteous soul increased by eating righteous food, but also wicked behavior increased then wicked soul increased by eating wicked food. Do not live righteous then righteous soul do not increased but also righteous soul do not eat, it means that macro concept world righteous behavior less then macro concept wicked behavior increased then wicked soul increased in the micro concept world, wicked soul being increased. So then cursed bank is increased in the end wicked soul full eat wicked energy. A wicked power is strong. So then micro concept wicked soul increased but also strong power is cursed bank of the micro concept world so big, then it means that circulation of the micro macro concept world circulation then micro concept soul living and macro concept actor living is shift, but also circulation then, if righteous behavior then righteous soul eating fully, so long righteous soul is being healthy but also increased of righteous soul increased, but also wicked behavior then increased wicked soul, but also wicked soul healthy, in the end micro concept world cursed bank saving is full then, wicked soul big increased. Macro micro concept circulation then it already shaped in the macro concept world wicked world, wicked soul world also, so then righteous soul decreased so then, in the micro concept world, macro concept world all are wicked soul living destination so long, it's being totality wicked world.

2014.09.11

Topic: macro concept masterpiece with micro concept

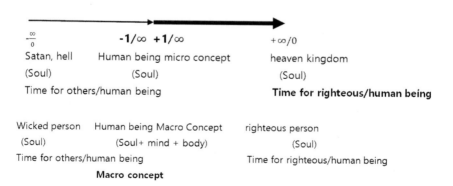

In this micro concept comes to me, to explained of overcoming this time not to go for the progress, until now, all expect to stages development, but now remained the progress, what is problems, how to solve it, then it comes "micro concept" until now it progress of micro concept but actually my progress is moment halt, last resort comes to me the topic is "masterpiece" this is the final products of the keep input energy, how to relative "masterpiece" with micro concept.

Micro concept is unseen world description, the pair of the micro concept is macro concept, micro concept is or micro concept point is the M $(-1/\infty+1/\infty)$ just to be reach at the micro cocenpt point, then what is the being the micro concept, how to related with the "masterpiece" most procedure end itself being the masterpiece, it may be not, to be reach at the masterpiece of micro concept point M $(-1/\infty+1/\infty)$ it msut be decreased to unseen but it must be existence, what is the micro concept is effect to being the masterpiece, how to be the masterpiece, so long, all of creators all of time, so many times trials and error but also so many time prostrate, but the creator do not stop, the coming of crisis also then, the creator comes to the himself disappeared, so then he/she felt of end, so that macro concept actor faced to rock, but who saved him/ser, because of micro concept major actor soul activate, the creator lived righteously in the creating, all of actors energy input to solve the masterpiece, what is the need to be micro concept M $(-1/\infty+1/\infty)$, the creator, the macro concept actor try to do in the Seen but also the existed solutions, his masterpiece is not reach at the $(+1/\infty+\infty/0)$ in the macro concept time cognition of the future, so then, the macro concept actor, creator of the his/her all of energy used even his/her time used, but do not satisfaction to the masterpiece, all of lived only for it, do not think but consistence of the come true in this each, then, after this, all of the comparison phenomenon came through, but his/ her charge of creating products is not come to earth, then it must be this problems is not just creator of the macro concept actor, this is the to the god's problems, at now intrigues to the earth so then it is the god work, god knows that the macro concept actor creating is newly have to give to the M $(-1/\infty+1/\infty)$ this future present but to the god in the beginning of the each macro concept then god created all, but now god feel of the a new creating thing is required, then, this is the god's duty, so then it don't necessary of the macro concept actor don't have to try to be harder, then all it comes from god, so long, the macro concept actor, creator also in the god's planning, so that righteous living and all of energy used all of his/her

living, then what happened

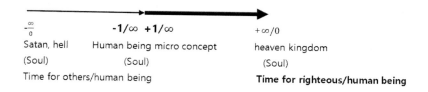

-∞/0
Satan, hell
(Soul)

Time for others/human being

-1/∞ +1/∞
Human being micro concept
(Soul)

+∞/0
heaven kingdom
(Soul)

Time for righteous/human being

In this feature is saying that all of his time used for the righteous then, it through the come through to the (+1/∞+∞/0), +∞/0, heaven kingdome, soul, Time for righteous/ human being, so then creating of the macro concept actor, just goes, then it must be in this place how to connect but to do, so long, how to do, something what, the gate of micro concept is M (-1/∞+1/∞) so long, all to be the god's micro actor world going then it required to be the M (-1/∞+1/∞), so then so long, all of the macro concept actor. so long the soul of macro concept actor, creator is the consist of soul + mind + body = body, then the creator, the maker of the masterpiece to be the conclusion, then it must be soul keep strong, this is very routine of micro concept, so then a actor of the macro lived with righteous , then righteous is against wicked, so long, in the all of creating is the all about 100% righteous then, righteous is how to reach that, so it must be the mind is to be 0= M((-1/∞+1/∞)) mind is reach at the zero, so then what happened to this macro concept actor, segregated soul and body being soulful body come through, in the long run, all of the macro concept actor all of life lived to realize of making perfect, perfection of the creating to be the masterpiece then it must be all of matured to excitement, so long, macro concept actor reacting making master piecing is the related with the macro concept and micro concept, so long, macro concept (-∞/0 -1/∞), micro concept((+1/∞+∞/0), the masterpiece is reach at the micro concept (M (-1/∞+1/∞), so long, this is the in the moment of the now, is in the macro concept time recognition time is past's latest, but also future the latest of future, then it is the past and future is melted to now, actually is not any place of the present all is related with the past with future, so then, all has the macro concept and micro concept, but also the macro concept actor and macro concept actor is not divided but combined to one, so long, we have live only macro concept, just seen world is clear, unseen is not clear so that in the macro concept world actor forget of soul living of the micro concept. So long micro concept is so pure, so long all be reach, masterpiece and macro concept do not use all of energy in the way of righteous, then do not live for the creative if do not live righteous, then it must be not come to masterpiece, masterpiece, if some of wicked then it must be not pure, so long, then, righteous about to not 100% then, it must not to be come true, the masterpiece will not come up, so long, most people can get the masterpiece, so long, all of masterpiece creature is mixed with macro concept micro concept so long, to be the get the masterpiece, so long, all of the unseen and seen is combined to then comes to the masterpiece art products. So long, in the macro concept world, to make energy so called make much money, success is not related with righteous behavior, but in the micro concept is all is relative with the righteous behavior, so long in the macro concept actor's success and getting the masterpiece also getting is relative with righteous behavior. Macro concept getting masterpiece is thoroughly relative with righteous behavior. All of in the micro concept soul knows unseen world, because of unseen world actor is soul, soul all discriminate from the wicked and righteous, so all of the mixed with wicked, so long, wicked is satanic, righteous is heaven kingdom, so long, wicked and righteous, if a macro concept actor live righteous in the pretend to, so long a masterpiece is comes without righteous then, it is temporally not eternity, so then in the Seen of unseen world soul can discriminate so long soul can't help mixed with wicked behavior is not helped from soul, so long, with righteous soul being masterpiece, but wicked soul do not to be being masterpiece. In the micro concept masterpiece is deep related with righteous behavior.

2014.09.12

Topic: physical micro concept

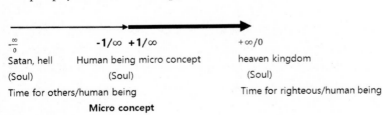

Wicked person	Human being Macro Concept	righteous person
(Soul)	(Soul+ mind + body)	(Soul)
Time for others/human being		Time for righteous/human being

Macro concept

Soul

Mind

Body

Physical macro concept world micro concept feature

In micro concept explained micro concept birth arrow line, but today lucky to me, going on my workplace, my lord helped me, so I got a idea, so that it is today lucky, I have been believed that my micro concept is also eternity, sometimes I felt worry to daily writing. Whenever short of my contents, then it has been supplied from god. I thought that just accurate, just find the real answer from Omni sound all of micro concept is result of hard working. So hard, so hard, not stop, keep hard time, rest, hard time, but now, all of living is not simple but also easy, every time comes to me encouragement to bear on the hard time, all is same with desire is bigger then so called mind is ∞ then suffer, so called soul is $1/\infty$, so that so hard to live on, in this hard time how to move to, just in the macro concept world actor moving is hard time but overcoming to rest some other hard come to me, but overcome by helping someone= soul, so long in the save of the hard time, then a big desired, mind then hard time, so long, explained as the micro concept mind is ∞ to get make money fully, then it is not easy just like in the current equations V=IR, the very same as the I=V/R, R=∞, then I=$1/\infty$, so then, the realization is can be get equation so that it is terms that of micro concept I= realization point= present time actor = soul mind body, in this mind is R, soul body equal to I, so long Realization/mind = body soul, so long mind is $\infty/0$ then body soul must be $1/\infty$, but if mind is $1/\infty$ then realization is ∞, realization is ∞, =body soul is realize so then soulful body, so long even it is body shown, unseen soul is full then, macro concept actor feel excitement and perfection.

Soul

5				
4				
3Mind	①	②	③	④
2				
1				

Body   **Micro concept point M (-1/∞ + 1/∞)**

Physical macro concept world micro concept feature

In the micro concept living is must be infer that ①②③④ direction is so hard then mind is 5, so then body ~ soul is distance 5, so then in this time macro concept body forget of the soul line, so long mind is so big, mind considered to Omni sound so long, not pure all of mixed to be pure, all is mixed with liar or truth. Wicked and righteous, as long mixed as the wicked and righteous.

It must be infer ①② is hard time ③ some of coming easy time ④ is come to realized point. In the living of the macro concept actor living as the stages of ①, ②stage, ③stage, ④stage, so long, that is not ages, all of actor stages are not ages, but the how to righteous living is decided. It must be infer that micro concept point, ④stages is micro concept point M (-1/∞+/∞), so long, in the relationship in the micro concept center me M (-1/∞+/∞). So long ④ is realized point. In the living a macro concept actor live how to live, what stages reach at, ①②③④ in this direction order, but also, in the same as the direction if a actor live in the stage of the ②, then the actor world is ② stages, but if a actor live in the ④ stages. Then the world is also difference so long, if ④ stages then a actor realize the micro concept world existed. Micro concept actors cross in the ④ stages. In the macro concept world ① : desired is high then so difficult to live on, the hard time is peak, almost die hard time then, if a actor live on the way then, turn over to ②, the same as the stages ③, stages ④, so accomplished reach at the perfection of the micro concept point so long, point M (-1/∞+1/∞), this is even the direction is right so that t must be expect to the much more keep doing rightrous, then in the end it will be reached at the M, so long, it is the direction is good. But if adverse living

Soul

5					
4					
~~3 mind~~	①	②		⑤	⑥
2					
1					

Body

Physical macro concept world macro concept feature

In this macro concept, macro actors living, in the first time start in the starting time is better but as the time goes then expanded to just ①②③④ direction, so long it never end, still going wide, so that how it is, keeping mind is increased then mind is ①②③④ direction, mind is increased, so long, the actor is so become to hard, this is can be real, it is the satanic direction, wicked actor, soul living do not sacrificed, wicked increased but also mind is increased. So long, for this getting so long, difficult is hard, not arranged to that it must be soul and body will not to be meet, in the end eternity soul and body do not meet, so long if infer that soul die or body die so long eternity do not meet each other, so that, soul do not know the body, so long mind is ∞ so long soul in the macor concept actor soul + mind +body= soul =0, mind=∞ +body= mind body, so long, soul is dead, then, all of the macro concept world do not know the soul, so then there is no fear of it, because of living with mind, mind is desired, but also, mind is help each other, get my own but soul do not know the ignorant mind, so long body is body, mind is just getting on the macro concept actor world, so then mind is not alive, but some try to show to the alive, so then, a body depend on mind, so long the big wide of the point is stage ④, so long perfect difficult, so long, the process of the in this ①②③④ direction is then in the end of the macro actor living is then soul is to 0, in the end soul is dead cause of the mind is ∞, so long, the mind deception is all the life depending, so then at last come to dead then, the dead soul also already dead so then, it must be in the theory then, Buddha samsara theory a soul dead then broken the cycle, eternity is closed.

So that if the a actor live as the ①②③④ micro concept direction if direction of living is same direction then in the end come to reach at the micro concept point M (-1/∞+1/∞). But the direction is adverse then ①②③④ macro concept direction keep expand then, mind is ∞, soul is dead to zero, then the right direction of the micro concept then reach at the micro concept point ; soul meet body, so then in the micro concept world live as the soul major act in the micro concept world, but if live macro direction then expand to so that mind is ∞, soul is dead then a macro concept actor disappeared from the circulation of the type of Buddha, but also if soul is dead so then it is not located at the so then it must not in the Satan soul destination. So long it must be inferring that satanic soul destination also better than soul dead.

2014.09.15

Topic: macro concept actors' behaviors

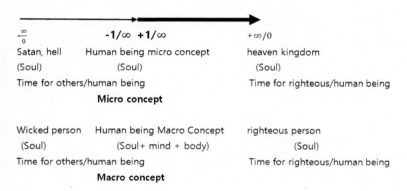

In this micro concept actor consist of "soul + mind + body= body" most macro concept actor move in the macro concept world, it must be move is the pure body move, pure soul move, but mind move impossible, mind is not a soul, but in the macro concept world, actor fell that mind only, so long, mind is all recognizable so then forget the soul, so long, soul do not know but all located at the religious book or poem etc, but macro concept actor all be controlled, so that in the feeling of macro actor is " soul forgotten + mind managing + body= so long mind body, but to the realized macro concept actor realize of " soul + decreased mind + body = soulful body" then mind is reach at the micro concept point M (-1/∞+/∞). If reach at the micro concept point it must be pure "soul + body" this is realized state, so long, body controlled from the soul, so then soul is the control of body, what soul is living body is living, soul lead a living body, soul already experienced the micro concept world, macro concept world,

Pure soul + pure body living is realized macro concept actor, so then both living cooperated between soul and body, soul and body, who is master it must be unrealized macro actor do not know the soul, so that master is body, but in the realized macro concept actor think as the master is the soul, salver is the body, so long soulful person, so then the soulful person is eternity person, it infer that realized person must be like, Jesus, Buddha etc soulful actor, so that religious creator, the macro concept actor soul is strong health so that pure soul and pure body lived all of after realized then the macro concept actor exited excitement to be happy living, it also pure so then perfection reach. So it must be related with soulful body only reach at the excitement and perfection. So long, "soulful actor with a living body is pair" so long soul=body soul and body is equal then, soul – body= micro concept M (-1/∞+/∞). It must be out of mathematics, soul and body is equal then same quantity so long same quantity – same quantity is to 0 zero, then this is end, soul is both living micro concept world, macro concept world, but body only live on the macro concept world, soul live eternity live but body is limited in the only macro concept world, so then in the equation of the soul – body is micro concept gate M (-1/∞+/∞). So long micro concept is explained to eternity living place, or itself is living soul.

Macro concept world actor is seen but macro concept world actor unseen soul, so then unseen world micro concept actor, seen in the micro concept actor in the among the souls, but in the macro concept actor body can't see the soul, so long feel wave,

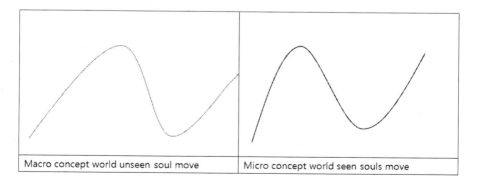

| Macro concept world unseen soul move | Micro concept world seen souls move |

So then micro concept world actor is unseen, so long micro concept actor

	$M\ (-1/\infty + 1/\infty)$.
Macro concept world unseen soul	Micro concept world seen souls move

In the macro concept world macro concept world actor live as the "soul + mind +body= body"mind do not move, mind is not a actor, but all of the actor feel that mind is all, so long mind role is so vary , a good mind, bad mind, charity mind, all of mind is stationed at the actor, so long mind is unrealized place, so long just long distance, unseen world things are felt momentum of the place, but is not clear of in the physical concept because of the soul is micro concept actor so long it must be existed by the forming the real actor, but the soul and body is not easy meet, so long even do not meet but has the role of the soul, if infer that it formed to pure soul and pure body then, both living seen and unseen actor move, how to role, a realized actor soul and body, can role, in this case soul is master, body is salve position so long, soul lead the body to do, it must be soul give the all of the direction, just soul is derive of the body, soul move on the pair body, so then soul is the passenger to the car, then soul is driver or passenger, body is the car, so that soul move to the body soul want to visit a place.

But also soul is passenger so then some times out of the car, then, soul move from the body, how to, then it also infer that soul perfect out of the body then what happened the body, realized body meet the soul, so long it before meet then soul where located, so long, body and other place how to control, soul is unseen in the macro concept, so long soul is move to the wave then,it must be infer how to move in the macro concept world, so then out of the body a soul move the wave state, so long, a source of the origin is all the time pure soul and body, so then all the time is

Center of micro concept   reach at other macro concept actors

So long, micro concept center is the origin so then micro concept actor moving by the wave, so other actors, so long a realized but also reach at the micro concept point so long, the wave is the connected, how to be the soul be strength, soul being healthy by the doing righteous behaviors, but also the master piece producing procedures. So then soulful actor then "soul + reach at the micro concept point mind M $(-1/\infty + 1/\infty)$ + body= soulful body" but also the master piece creature or product is deceit, or wicked mind is perfect zero so called to reach at the micro concept point so long all of wicked mind is reach at the micro concept point M $(-1/\infty + 1/\infty)$, the the soul + a skilful actor = soulful skilful actor, so long produce the actor soul must be reach at the produce product, so long, so that " soulful skill actor produce the product which included of the soul, so then, soulful products product get a soulful master piece product=art etc. explained to the mixed with a soulful skill actor soul divided to the product, art, so long how to healthy in the actor soul, but also the soulful product, art, in the mathematics skilful soul actor give the soul to the masterpiece so then express in the mathematics soulful actor soul – masterpiece soul = decreased soulful actor soul, but in the micro concept explained to soulful skilful soul produce art and product, all of lived with righteous just perfect zero of wicked so then, all of the behavior of the soulful skillful actor behave save in the micro concept blessing bank, so that the behavior of the creating procedure all of the hard thing overcome to get the realized of the all of the wicked mind to be zero so called reach at the micro concept point M $(-1/\infty + 1/\infty)$. So long it already righteous concept world living soul, so long, in the micro concept a soulful skilful actor produce masterpiece so then soul divided to masterpiece, so then actor soul – master piece soul = then giving soul actor get saving blessing bank, so then it already has the account of the blessing point, but also the accepter of the master piece is the feature, so long the masterpiece is itself realized so then master piece is live eternity so long, masterpiece art, also saving the blessing bank so long the account is same, so that it must be come up, more strong soul, but also, has the righteous but also the a blessing relative relationship build. So then soul shared is getting blessed. The soulful product is eternity give pleasure to the multiple souls. So then keep increased the blessing so keep increased in the direction of the righteous living.

So long the soul move in the wave, so that the wave is eternity related, even the righteous soul must be give the energy, but also mutual energy help so then increased the blessing point forever. So long the righteous direction giving soul then itself is the getting blessing point saves.

2014.09.16

Topic: macro concept decision

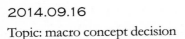

$-\frac{\infty}{0}$ **-1/∞ +1/∞**   +∞/0

Satan, hell	Human being micro concept	heaven kingdom
(Soul)	(Soul)	(Soul)
Time for others/human being		Time for righteous/human being

Micro concept

Wicked person	Human being Macro Concept	righteous person
(Soul)	(Soul+ mind + body)	(Soul)
Time for others/human being		Time for righteous/human being

Macro concept

Present unsolved problems will be in deeper micro direction,

In this micro concept how to reach at in the macro concept actor another model is this

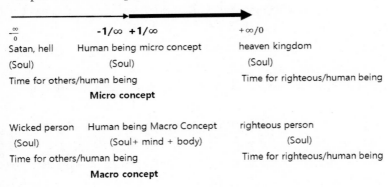

In the micro concept is unseen world actor "soul" living soup how to reach at the in the macro concept world actor living, in the diagram ①②③④⑤⑥ direction until then it can seem the direction is Seen to unseen, so called bigger to small, how to macro to be a micro, but also, the decision of macro concept actors so multi point, all of the actor decide, god has given all of macro concept actor can live in the place all of macro concept actor all of actor live.

macro concept actors are in the point of view micro concept then it must be $1/\infty$, so then all of member of macro actors then the number is ∞, so long but each macro concept actors are unit, just one 1, so long in the god point of view is seen as $1/\infty$, but also a macro concept world see to unseen world reach, so called the macro concept actor to be micro concept actor, but also the micro concept and macro concept is macro concept to $1/\infty$ then macro = micro so then, macro concept actor can't see the working , so long, in the upper diagram decision ①②③④⑤⑥ .... n

So then it must be a block divided to number, so then after divided then in the end come to power, power divided to n then it must be $1/n=1/\infty$, so long unseen, this is the a kind of the solutions, all of the macro concept actor live peace, without war, and fight, then it is not matter of living is the not wide but depth, so then

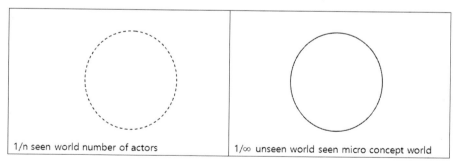

| 1/n seen world number of actors | 1/∞ unseen world seen micro concept world |

Just round of the face is seen to just all line of round but it is the actor, just all of round is macro concept actors, all of the macro actor live peace, how to live so if infer that, multiple actors of living on the macro concept world, so long, the numbers are must be ∞, so then each seen point is 1/n, but in the unseen point is 1/∞ but it has, not zero, so long, in the point to point, so called that actor to actor distance is 1/∞ then it msut be seen as go round, so then, just the round is the reach at the micro concept, 1/∞ is seen as the round, this is the all of the member of the macro concept actors, to be that, all of a number of macro concept actor decide from mega to smaller so called that macro to micro, the macro concept actor live macro concept to micro actor, Another decision concept is the

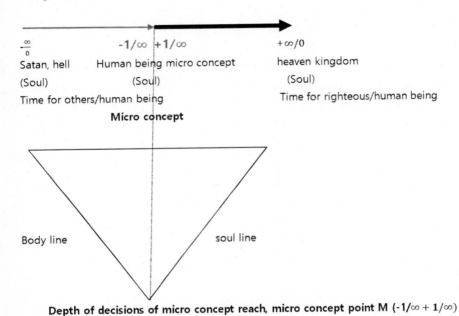

$\frac{\infty}{0}$ $-1/\infty$ $+1/\infty$ $+\infty/0$

Satan, hell   Human being micro concept   heaven kingdom

(Soul)   (Soul)   (Soul)

Time for others/human being   Time for righteous/human being

Micro concept

Body line   soul line

Depth of decisions of micro concept reach, micro concept point M (-1/∞ + 1/∞)

From now in the micro concept is come to depth concept, so long, all of the problems are existed in the macro concept actor daily living, how to seen to unseen, but also how to solve seen problem and unseen problems, so what is this, if a problems try to solve in the existed solution is the it can be explained to, in the micro concept $-\frac{\infty}{0}$ - 1/∞, so long but this is only existed solving problems solving then, it must be not to be create but benchmarking is only used, so long, a macro concept actor live to the bigger to smaller but unseen levels, so long, the solution is come based on the realization of the macro concept actor living, so that all of mind variances be to reach at the 1/∞, so long reach at the "soul+ body" is then this is the macro concept and micro concept is the distance also come to the 1/∞, then it infer that Micro =micro, so long. Even micro level solution then it also can be used to micro level solution to adopt by the macro concept actor, so it is the realized actor created unseen knowledge adapt to the macro concept actor world. Then it already being macro, to be the find the unseen solution also, then it must be the not wide but it required to depth, so long, in the adverse triangle, the point is the top dept of the triangle is the point which met of the inferable of body line, soul line is met. So long in the end it reach at the micro concept point M (-1/∞ + 1/∞), so long, macro concept actor to be the micro concept actor reaching. So long, macro concept and micro concept so long, micro concept is moment but macro concept is long term, but a long term macro concept actor but overcome of a realize actor then, the living is long distance but in the end come to micro concept comes.

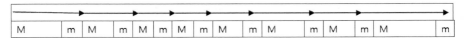

| M | | m | M | | m | M | m | M | m | M | | m | M | | m | M | | m |

In the macro concept living, the macro concept living is the Seen, but micro concept living is unseen then in the macro concept point view, then M is master but m is salve, so long, M is the actor is so long, macro concept actor live solve the problems, if this is the so micro, so then all of the micro is divide to micro, so then all of decision also so multi this is the comparable of breath so long the macro is life but in the multi decision then, decision number is the multi then it scale that is many, but the many is classed as the macro, so then if as the multi is the micro*n = multi micro then , multi micro is, if infer the multi micro to the 1/∞, then muitl micro is then it tuns out to be the micro so then, all of the distnac eof the macro M and micro distance is if infer that of the 1/∞ then, it must be M, m, M, m. M ,M …….Mn, mm, so long, this is the macro concept actor history but also, the macro actor community also is so long, the macro and micro cycles are how many stages turns then, macro concept actor features are all not same in the degrees, so long, just the macro and micro turnings is the retarded or not to be progress status all be the used method, just all of macro and micro is turnings, in the micro concept how to live in the long life, but the cycle is the M n, then the direction is righteous living then it comes to the real of the great success, then in the cusses is all related with M, macro concept, m, micro actor also, the ways is the righteous directions

Righteous direction living, in the long run health soul role of the strong run in the micro concept Gate micro concept point M $(-1/\infty + 1/\infty)$, in the direction of righteous, then it comes to the real realize, so long, the life, from long time all of the macro actor, so that in this time, so that how long, in the micro concept actor living, in the macro actor living is all has the road, so long the micro concept point M $(-1/\infty + 1/\infty)$, the real line upward in the fluctuation and the Macro and micro is multi but it must be if the number is the micro then it also reach at the micro concept point M $(-1/\infty + 1/\infty)$, so long comes to the righteous livng result. The deep real line is

Micro concept line it is the living, just I will live on this line, I'm so fit to me, because of my narrow mind, but also small scale characteristics, I'm totality is I'm smaller, in my mind is not fighter so then all loser in my social competitions so long I got a question? Why I live like what is this, so that I'm not side of the macro concept actor but it must be I'm in the side of micro concept actor. So long, I have research for the just smaller, narrow actor living value. My life is this, so long, I'm all of think that just small energy actor also can live, so in the micro concept actor live in the micro concept so long, it aim to the micro concept point M $(-1/\infty + 1/\infty)$, micro concept is to help to the powerless actors, so then micro concept is mind to micro concept point M $(-1/\infty + 1/\infty)$, it all based on the realization.

2014.09.17

Topic: macro concept "Problems"

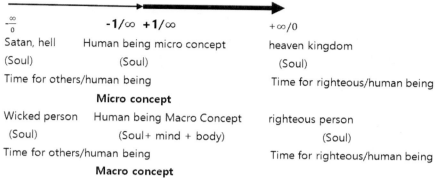

In This micro concept all being faced "problems" how to make problems, which give problems, which made problems, problems is must be conflict fight between wicked and righteous, righteous faced to the wicked, wicked faced to the righteous. Then righteous what is component, but also wicked is what components, in the macro concept world consist of wicked & righteous.

Wicked any macro concept actor do not want to do, but righteous is all of actors want to, but wicked is easy but righteous is not easy. Wicked is acceptor, righteous is donor, to give a righteous actor prepare of energy, but acceptor wicked do not have to preparing energy, just only get from giving righteous. Micro concept criteria is the time, how to actors time use, if a actor used for the others then it must be righteous, but all of actor's time used time then it must be wicked. Just righteous is the try to righteous behavior helping others, times for others. But wicked try to get out of any suffering, just deceit behavior, but also all of time using for owned, so that the actor do not build blessing point with righteous relationships.

The problems is momentum conflict righteous to wicked, so long in this problems all of the actor on the way to reach at micro concept point M (-1/∞ + 1/∞), variable. Most macro concept actors are not easy cause of coming problems, problems is occurred from the macro concept actor cause but also micro concept actor cause, if all macro concept actor thinking, the problems are cause of macro concept actor, so anger to others, but the anger is actor himself, but actually the problems is located at the mind, but also body, the problems is mind problems, body problems then, mind problems and body problems, what cause it is, in the macro concept actor faced problems, so a big problems but small problems so then it must be cure or unsolved, problems is the obstacles, so then problems = obstacles, in the living as the macro concept actor, all the time solve the problems, it is not in the school but in the life, the big scale of the living and the macro concept actor, so that mind try to solve the problems, all of mind try to fine the a short of getting asset but also short time then a big income etc, but also too much more get a living energy so called money, mind try to much more work, mind is ordered out of soul has do not work, just adoptable work, adoptable rest, but in the macro concept actor, over work over resting, so long, balance breaking down, then soul also balanced down, so long mind is keep increased then balance is big breaking so long, soul is decreased so long, soul weak, in the end keep increased then the place all occupied by mind, so then soul lost the place then where soul, infer then in the end soul must be dead. Then macro concept actor also dead, unlucky the dead actor there is not also soul so, eternity living losing. But righteous actor keep giving help others, but also sacrifice all of actors time for others then, the actor behavior all of related with accumulated with blessing point in the micro concept world blessing banks.

All of problems how to adsorption, problems product problems product factory is this, then problems if do not produce then how to live is not relative with out of problems, so then it must be simple but is not, all the righteous actor behavior try to be keep it, but all the time wicked actor used the righteous actor, in the normally wicked and righteous is almost 49 to 51, 52 to 49, so long righteous to wicked, wicked to righteous, so that the moment of the righteous to wicked , so long, the basic giving then, the problems are increased to the chain up then, so then just a actor wicked portion 50% is increased to over 50%, then if wicked actor over the 60% then, do stop then just after dead of the macro concept actor then, soul do not dead, but soul is the satanic soul destination eternity, but righteous behavior is righteous is over 60% then but also more then it must be possible to located with righteous soul destined place. Problems are righteous living then cause of sacrifice problems, so long, time for the others then some of realized but also even poor then still keep helping others, even not rational sacrifice but undertake all of hard time then really hard to bearable but endurance, so then a macro concept actor undertake all of hard things. But the problems are wicked then all of the deceit problems, all the time getting so long a big violating power even, to get the all of others energy, so long, in the really that it is, so long, all is busy to deceit problems chain up, so long but most make hard to the righteous actors, so long wicked actor all the time righteous actors, so long, wicked invade to the reserved energy by the good and save, then unsaved all stealth attitude for the righteous actor's, so then so long accepter position actor, used all of his/hers but try to borrow or donation but it must be in the definite balance then earning energy all used up just all of exclusively hers/his, then after then borrow from others, donors, in this time contract donate and acceptor forming. Here donate is not only material but also spiritual energy. So long this energy shared with time for others, then help source of energy. But if all of the time hasn't the giving energy, to give other accumulating energy is righteous then all of the life so long, after that helps others, but problems are acceptor wicked lived on the righteous field. Righteous is all the time sacrifice but also mostly not winning but wicked is offender, invader of others, so long the conflict frontier is the problems.

Micro concept actor "soul" so then in the macro concept actor "soul +mind+ body=body" then body is trouble is combined soul problems + mind problems + body problems, so long, in the micro concept world main actor is only "soul" so long in the micro concept actor then soul problems is turbulence then, comes to the macro concept actor himself/ herself so long, without macro concept mind problems, but also body problems then it occurred to so long cause of any controlled to do so long sadness, sorrowful etc, comes, out of macro concept, so long, in the soulful actor be excitement itself, so that problems are combined to do

Sort problems	Macro concept problems	Micro concept problems
Macro concept	To get make a money related Deceit harmful, to realize of Relative related etc.	Macro concept problems + Sorrowful, lone, sadness, prostrate Etc.
Micro concept	Micro concept problems + Macro concept problems	Micro concept problems + Micro concept problems

All of problems are related with micro and macro concept, then problems all be reached to the micro concept point M (-1/∞ + 1/∞), so long it related with the realized, then the problems is also decreased to at point M (-1/∞ + 1/∞), problems also not disappeared from itself, all is the make less the size, so called the all of problems also increased with divergence =∞/0, so long getting biger it never soluble of the problems, how to soluble problems is convergence =1/∞, so that macro is Seen but micro is unseen so then problems increased to be the macro but decreased then micro,

Macro is big problems ①			
		Micro 1②	Micro 2②
		Micro 3②	Micro 4②

Macro big problems are related with divergence =∞/0 ---------①

Micro small problems are related with convergence = 1/∞ -----②

If macro concept ① a big problems = micro concept ② a small problems * 4

Then problems of size is bigger of ①, but small size of problems ② then

① = 4② then, mathematic is right but in the micro concept is not to be compared

Because of the macro seen problems but micro is unseen problems so that the size of the problems is not comparable.

So long not to be problems all of macro concept world also, manage the problems divided to

Unseen level M M (-1/∞ + 1/∞), then problems control must be easy but also reach at the out of problems, the only to solve the problems is reach at the micro concept point M (-1/∞ + 1/∞),

So long in the living of macro concept world all of the behavior all be micro concept is very closed related, so long it adopt micro concept then get a problems solving, in the macro concept world none problems but solve in the micro concept world.

2014.09.18

Topic: macro concept "righteous keeping"

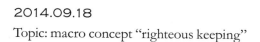

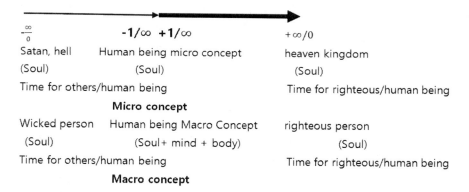

In this micro concept macro actor live in the macro concept world, in the move or affairs then all the time go with macro concept righteous actor/ wicked actor, then the location of the both righteous and wicked is located at an actor, so long to keep righteous then it need to righteous keeping energy but wicked is not energy required because wicked is not have direction to go for.

Righteous behavior itself saves in the micro concept world blessing bank saving, but wicked behavior must be accumulate at the in the micro concept world satanic place cursed bank saving.

In the micro concept world, somewhat of the result of the macro concept actor behavior, but also micro concept saving energy is give macro concept actor blessing or cursed result, but it must be infer that if a macro actor lived righteous fully then it is not sure but in the Buddha religious then samsara cycle then righteous behavior then full of the reserve in the micro concept actor world blessing bank if full saving then a soul birth a macro concept world as the blessing baby, blessing living, the energy is big then whole of the macro concept living is blessed but some not enough then it required in the living righteous behavior compensate of short of blessing energy but also another cycle accumulate blessing bank saving, but also if not behavior of the righteous, then wicked living is naturally save in the cursed bank saving then, the result of behavior must be appeared in the living but also after live of macro concept then naturally cursed soul destination, but also the cursed soul also if in the infer that of the Buddha samsara cycle then it must be the in the baby then is not be blessed, but also life scale, if cursed is not full then in the living if a actors live righteous then if all of debt of the cursed bank then, in the zero saving in the cursed bank, then it start to the depend on behavior of the righteous behaviors then saving in the micro concept blessing bank saving, so then in the living of macro concept world also changed to from cursed to blessing to the actors.

Macro concept actor all the time living with righteous 50% + wicked 50% + variable of the how to live before macro concept living blessing or cursed then it appeared to live in the Buddha samsara, so long but this is the birth place decide but, in the macro concept world a actor live with how to live is decide, righteous behavior is increased then wicked is decreased then it must be the best trend direction, but if adversely righteous living is decreased and wicked increased then stat to saving the cursed bank saving if blessing bank debt all pay then start to the curded bank saving increase, so long it must be in the righteous to wicked behavior change then, higher bank is to changed to start point is the righteous to wicked then blessing bank is debt, but also wicked to righteous then wicked cursed bank is the debt, so long already get or saved is a kind of the living energy, here cursed bank energy also have a power, but also blessing bank energy also big power, in the macro concept actor these energy is same of cursed energy is mightier so then in the macro concept actor living is appeared to the living energy so called money getting so that it is not discriminated in the macro concept actor eye, all of the power it same in the macro concept actor world

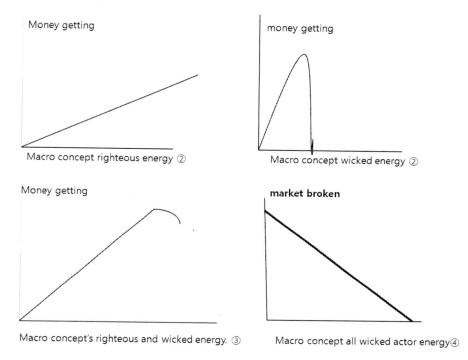

Money getting

Macro concept righteous energy ②

money getting

Macro concept wicked energy ②

Money getting

Macro concept's righteous and wicked energy. ③

market broken

Macro concept all wicked actor energy④

Macro concept's righteous and wicked energy. ③　　Macro concept all wicked actor energy④

So then righteous living is ① so then in the living is somewhat distance with macro concept living energy getting, so that righteous live in the macro concept actor living mostly do not choose but also most do not wanted to be wicked in the macro ② but all of the macro concept actor desired

to live like that of number ③, so all of macro concept actor try to live in the direction of number ③ ways, because of they do not know the micro concept bank of cursed or blessing bank.

What is the blessing bank in the micro concept world, is help other, do sacrifice for others, do realize etc, reach at the micro concept point so then the desired mind is must be 1/∞, so long the realization of the meeting the body and soul meeting then, it must be the behavior of act in the macro concept world then saved in the blessing bank, but what is the cursed bank in the micro concept bank, do live a big desirous, desired mind is a big, all of time for used for actors only, but also do not shared with others, do not help others, so over work time, even desperate of body condition maltreat even get sick body to get the only make a money only, deceit livings etc..

To be rich so then they are all reserved to the in the micro concept cursed bank saved.

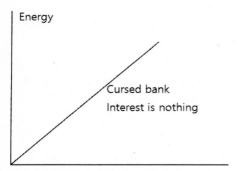
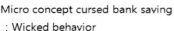
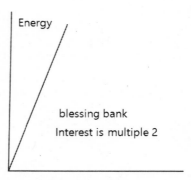

Micro concept cursed bank saving
: Wicked behavior

Micro concept blessing bank saving
: righteous behavior

Because of the cursed bank interesting is zero is so many actor save in the cursed bank so long cursed deposit is so big so that, in the bank there is no required necessary cursed point energy so that coursed bank interesting is nothing, so that cursed bank soul, in the infer then in the energy also not enough so long all of cursed bank actor living is never excitement.

But blessed bank is interesting is multiple 2, so that very rare of blessing bank so that blessing bank required to make incentive to come to blessing bank, so then give the interesting multiple 2, so then just righteous living in the macro concept actor the even not live rich but in the eternity concept then if a actor live in the righteous then, eternity. So long macro concept ③, is deceit stealth the blessing energy of the righteous, so then wicked actor live well by deceit to the righteous blessed living. After all wicked is all the time of the righteous strong time also wicked getting well, because of righteous still keep of the frame of the righteous structure , but in the end the wicked actor increased then, if all of broken the righteous so that if wicked actor harmful target is all disappeared then the macro concept actor frame is changed to wicked actors country,

so long in the macro concept energy number ④ is the all of the righteous actor disappeared, so then all of the occupied to the wicked actors, so long broken righteous actor frame is all disappeared to, but come to wicked concept world frame is comes then, there is not any righteous actors so that macro concept all of wicked actors concept world market is broken.

In the market broken but also, all of macro concept world are wicked behaviors, so long the concept of righteous, What is the blessing bank in the micro concept world, is help other, do sacrifice for others, do realize etc, reach at the micro concept point so then the desired mind is must be $1/\infty$, so long the realization of the meeting the body and soul meeting then, it must be the behavior of act in the macro concept world then saved in the blessing bank. This faction is not preceded so long, there is no any saving in the micro concept world, blessing bank then, and micro concept blessing bank is already bankruptcy to move the macro concept righteous actor live, so then, righteous actor all disappeared from the macro concept world.

How to keep righteous, in the end keep saving in the micro concept actor blessing bank saving in keep in increasing. Then how to it must be the required to live the life living direction, it is the macro to the micro direction, just all of the desired mind must be $1/\infty$, so long, all of mind must be decreased how to do, it must be required to be realized by the reach at the micro concept gate, tunnel reach micro concept point M $(-1/\infty + 1/\infty)$, as live with the relize so long reach at the micro cocnetp point reach M $(-1/\infty + 1/\infty)$, it means that mind is $1/\infty$ so then here also in the macro concept world " soul + body$(1/\infty)$+ body = soulful body" the only soluble is the micro concept gate reach is required to live righteously. So why keep righteous is required to be the micro concept point reaching is required to do, so long realize living required.

2014.09.19

Topic: macro concept "time"

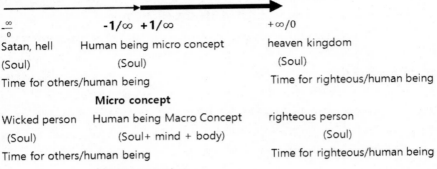

$\frac{\infty}{0}$ **-1/∞ +1/∞**   +∞/0

Satan, hell   Human being micro concept   heaven kingdom

(Soul)   (Soul)   (Soul)

Time for others/human being   Time for righteous/human being

Micro concept

Wicked person   Human being Macro Concept   righteous person

(Soul)   (Soul+ mind + body)   (Soul)

Time for others/human being   Time for righteous/human being

Macro concept

In this micro concept stated time and distance by accident, time is same adopt in the macro and micro concept world. Time is variance, so then how adopt as the meaningful in the macro concept world. All of macro concept actor has the same time, so all of actor use freely, all of macro concept actor used for the exclusively macro concept actor, in a day a actor live biological, social political cultural but also economical use but unseen range of the micro concept soul healthy time is ignorance. Most people think that all of the time is seen field only, but also most people is not same as the time to used each categories, so long, if someone use for the economy then it might be can get a money all of other sacrifice, so long in the macro concept actor making money main use of the time, so then all of actor use for the macro concept seen behavior only, this is natural just macro concept is machine of the making money, then if infer that if make money for the just time all of biological, social political cultural but also economical use but for all of the time used in the making money then, it must be called as pure making worker, but if someone use the time effectively adoptively time use then here balance so called it must be the worker to manager some more balanced actor.

Sort time usage	Macro concept	Micro concept
Unbalance Wicked behavior	Make a enough money being rich Cause of mental, physical out of order as forgotten bio, soc,	Forgotten unseen world actor Strength so that valance blessing Do not comes
Balance Righteous behavior	Money making is not full but Biological social political equality	Use time for the unseen world actor, strength soul so that blessed

Time is same all of macro concept actor, so then, time is related hurry and slow rhythm, so long most macro concept actor think as that diligent is virtue, idle actor is blame, and yes it must be right so long optimistic is required. Optimistic is very hard, because optimistic is not stealth others, do not stealth others but sustainment each actor behavior. All of actors are fear of being poor, so that all of actors are body in making money; fear is the mind, so long in the mind is existed in the living. Macro concept actor "soul + mind+ body= body" body of macro concept actor fear, desired mind is controlled to body moving, so long, to get in to safe zone, all the time hurry, then the life all hurry, time is busy every time, a actor live busy using time. Every moment busy so that haven't realize of living, do not know realize to reach at the micro concept point

The place is the mind is $1/\infty$, so long as get a peace, so long it called to micro concept point reach M $(-1/\infty + 1/\infty)$, so long, time used for the fast then, this is not related with righteous but related with wicked, fast, hurry means in the unseen world is soul getting not strong, but also, in the among macro concept actor compared with others, whole of living is not enough but all of time is occupied with body. So then the actor time is fast run reach at the moment just a glance reach at the end of macro concept world. The dead, to make money only then the actor live slaver, not a master, so long desire mind being slaver, out of mind then master living.

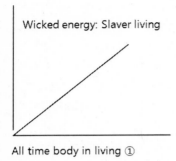

Wicked energy: Slaver living

All time body in living ①

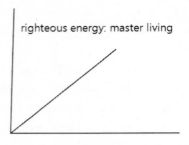

righteous energy: master living

time is optimistic using in living ②

All the time in living ① is desired mind is so huge, so long, in the macro concept point only one factor is money getting much but all of other factor poor, so then all of living is hurried to make money so all time used up, sometimes help other, energy sharing is nothing. So then it must be called to wicked energy. But time is optimistic using in living ②. Then their time is for others. But also help others. Then the time can't live busy and fast. To live help others, for the realize just unseen world "soul" strength so then it must be the live as the master living so long, master living is the even poor in getting money but manage itself, balanced time controlled living so called the live as the master living. Time is body, fast use then it must not calm all the time dynamic moving time, not fixed but all floating, so then just all the time core actor, so that it must be traveling. So that any soul best living condition is not come to the actor, so long, but also the not busy, calm, silent get give the time "soul" nurture condition making, so that so long not busy living is live as the fully master line in the life voyage is the even not rich but, live not follow other but as the first run by the ways of the manager ways of living, master living is related with the righteous. Realized is time is enough but also slow time is more prefer to live, so then it compared with a religious living is the just meditation and pray just communication with the unseen world micro concept world. So long, it must reach at the micro concept point reach M $(-1/\infty + 1/\infty)$, so long time is not managed by hurry, so if all of time horribly use then a actor live as the salve in this macro concept actor, but time is not horribly then it must live as the master living. So long, in the end the after time of the macro concept actor living then, it must be the hurry in time is mind is∞, so long soul, is $1/\infty$, then the hurry living actor must be in the micro concept world destination is located at the satanic world, so that in the macro concept living hurry, then lived as the salve position in the macro concept world, but also after living another stages are located for the satanic soul, wicked soul so long, how losing business, but in the not busy time macro concept actor live as the master, management living, but in the end then in the macro concept living after stages are all located at the micro concept actor "soul" located at the heaven king dome righteous soul eternity living place. Time for the macro concept world actor if do live busy then, after reach at what they expected to be, but after reach at the top then still hurry it must be no hurry, but still hurry, so then, it must be expected to be slow, but also time for use righteous, so called the shared time for other, help other, sacrifice then the success actor will be the master or manager, then enough asset can help, then the size of helping is good, but if not, just keep hurry then after all it never goes to the micro concept world righteous soul place going, so long, some of the wise macro concept actor then it must be reach at the goal then watch others who are poor's, disasters all of weak, but more much getting, then it must be after living it totality at the satanic soul destination. How to fit the optimistic balance then it is not easy but just getting realize then it goes, so realize is philosophical concept so long, micro concept is the variance is make $1/\infty$, if variance is to be $1/\infty$, it msut be realize so called soul and body is met, so long it must be excitement it is the peak of realized, realize actor can garaged to optimistic, so long a variance is not disappeared in the macro world, so bigger size is followed to variance is big, so it must not be reach at the micro concept point M $(-1/\infty + 1/\infty)$,

To make almost to zero of variance then it must be scope is easy, detail problems must be check so then there is not any wrong points, so long to be make less the variance it must be the all of the target working is also be as the micro then itself must be the variance be also zero then, it must be reach at the perfect, so long, so then, in the all of the categorized body time is it never produce perfect product, but also the in the macro concept actor, then all of actor live in the busy then, a macro concept actor also do not get at the living in the side of righteous living but if a actor live optimistic time managing then it produce the perfect products and righteous living in the end the product is eternity master piece so long eternity product for the treasure of the national, but also the actor also eternity live as the heaven kingdom righteous soul destination living.

2014.09.22
Topic: macro concept "soul living"

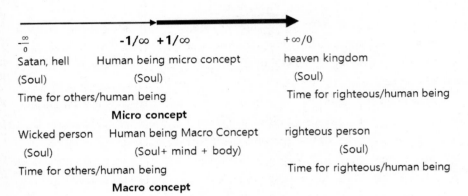

In this micro concept is realized as the upper arrows then it comes to the micro concept point is the M $(-1/\infty + 1/\infty)$, just all of the macro concept from old to present through to future, so then, so then all of past and future $\lim_{n=\infty} -1\frac{1}{n} = -\frac{1}{\infty}$ from future big past to about now, so then $\lim_{n=\infty} +1\frac{1}{n} = +\frac{1}{\infty}$, then future latest beginning. So long then in a moment reach at the micro concept point so long in the macro concept actor is consist of "soul + mind + body = body" so the this body is seen body of the macro concept actor, so long some of the variance is the mind if mind is adopted to the micro concept then mind is M$(-1/\infty + 1/\infty)$, then mind is the $\pm 1/\infty$ so then it comes soul + body = soulful body, but in the macro concept actor is "soul + mind + body" in this case is the mind is ∞ then titled to the macro concept actor is mindful body, so long most macro concept actor live as the macro concept actor with " soul + mind+ body= mindful body=body" so that just seen is real but unseen is not real so long, all of the believing is Seen featured. But if macro concept actor to micro actor in the macro concept world, so long, if in the real is not existence the feature of the soul only, but actually in the macro concept world, actor is the minor is soul but major is the body, so long is seen as the macro concept world seen feature is the body, but in the micro concept actor is the unseen world to the macro concept actor but seen to the micro concept actor, so that in the micro concept actor major is soul, so then in the macro concept actor is major is body, so long if the mind is disappeared from the macro concept actor, then mind is about to unseen then, macro concept actor, formed to the soul + mind forming=±1/∞ + body= soulfuil body= body, so long in the macro concept actor world is comes up even shown to the body, but actually soul is going with body, so long, macro concept live with soul, so then it equilibrium of the soul=body, so long in the macro concept world, soul=body is soul also actor but also body actor so then, it is said that micro concept actor live healthy, so long soul also feel strong with macro concept actor, so long how to do, so that actually a macro concept actor live in the micro concept M (-1/∞ + 1/∞),so long even live at the macro conetp actor but a macro concept actor soul live in the M (-1/∞ + 1/∞), so long M is the micro concept tunnel M (-1/∞ + 1/∞), then transaction between micro concept actor and macro concept world. So then, micro concept soul knows the excitement in living at the righteous soul world, so that eternity of the righteous living, so then realized at the macro concept is infer to the reach at the soul is met the righteous soul actor in the micro concept, so long live between macro concept world and micro concept world, but realized to realized righteous soul true living. It based on truth so then, truth and real is the righteous behavior, just righteous behavior is so excitement in the macro concept actors, what is the living is the excitement what the real excitement is so long out of dark, just unclean, or the dim light, so it mixed with the wicked actor, righteous actors so that all of mind is mixed located at the in the living macro concept actors, so that " soul + mind; wicked or righteous + body= mindful body, so then it never truth excitement, even feel of the guided excitement cause of drinking alcohol, but the real truth is mind is ±1/∞, so then it comes to concord to the "soul + body=soul body=body" so that righteous actor, just realized actor live as the living,

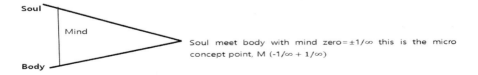

Soul meet body with mind zero=±1/∞ this is the micro concept point, M (-1/∞ + 1/∞)

What will be the micro concept point, after come of the M (-1/∞ + 1/∞), so that what happened to this, it must be inferred to a realize, creator, success in living, so long the from the actor changed the era, even unseen in the macro concept actor just living unseen living so that normal actor also realize this is micro concept M (-1/∞ + 1/∞), so long, but realize mens that success then is famous to others, so just give the a new concept world by the soul to meet body, so then, the soul pure, soul, is the reach at the M (-1/∞ + 1/∞), soul is based on the righteous so long, but it fully might knowledge, because of the soul is get a new idea from the soul world, soul world is all of righteous soul are try to give the macro concept realized actor, so a new idea helped form the micro concept souls, as we believe that god created the earth, so then creator so god all has known in the appeared in the macro concept world. It imagine that just creating is the so many difficult act then comes to creating, so long, being reach at the soul and body, mind is perfect zero, so then all of controlled body itself of the soul, so that god helping soul managed the body, so long, in the end, the god lead soul managed body means that a actor is in the religious is saint, so long just get a decision of all of knowledge is from god, so then if the micro concept reach then M (-1/∞ + 1/∞), it is the pleasure, so long the god lead, god gift is the eternity product, so god leaded product, so called out of mind but all is controlled by soul god then the product is marvelous master piece product, existence getting old then being treasure, some of the national treasure also, so then in the living is the righteous but also keep in the truth living then it comes to the micro concept point M (-1/∞ + 1/∞), how to live is reach the micro concept point M (-1/∞ + 1/∞), it must be inferred that it is the god select a actor for the realized, so then, god watching a actor living, so that to be righteous living then, it is the sacrifices but also time is shared with others, so then it must also supplied, so long righteous reach at the realize so long, around of actor all of the actor being happy, if more strong then it must be give the happy all of actors, just god son Jesus Christ, Buddha etc, realized actor eternity living in the macro concept actor world, even over the 2020 year all of the knowledge used in this time, bible, Buddha bible also, so then the realized is the really god saying, realized actor talk of the god's truth, so long, in the macro concept actor realized then, the actor soul is also very strong, then, we seen in the bible, so Jesus Christ shared to miracle then it is the soul world, so then soul is very strong , so that in this case god act, so that Jesus Christ walk on the water etc. just in this is real of micro concept world, but how to in the very unpopular actor, just usual no real but also very normal actor living also, if live a righteous then, but also realized to M (-1/∞ + 1/∞), then a a soulful body live in the concentration all of righteous, so long very hard to get to reach or the creature, so long so many times try and errors but also, some of infer that is the a actor live for the real purpose of creating then it comes to all of life used so long in the before dead then comes to the micro concept world M (-1/∞ + 1/∞) then it must be righteous lving, it created all of the creating giving produced., so long the product is kept eternity, produced a actor then the produced product with a realized strong actor soul is remained to the masterpiece eternity products, so that the product is eternity in the macro concept world. So long, then the righteous living actor also, the eternity is the a kind of macro concept historical actor they are righteous then eternity comes, but if some of actor, so long, macro concept actor if meet soul and body then in the end macro concept world, micro concept major actor also behavior of big role, strong relationship between the macro concept actor and micro concept actor is strong connected to do.

2014.09.23

Topic: macro concept "transient changed"

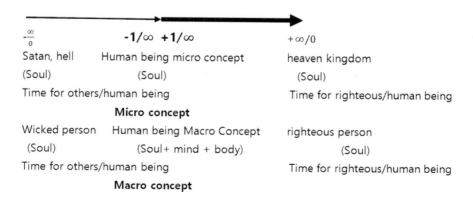

$-\frac{∞}{0}$	$-1/∞$ $+1/∞$	$+∞/0$
Satan, hell	Human being micro concept	heaven kingdom
(Soul)	(Soul)	(Soul)
Time for others/human being		Time for righteous/human being
	Micro concept	
Wicked person	Human being Macro Concept	righteous person
(Soul)	(Soul+ mind + body)	(Soul)
Time for others/human being		Time for righteous/human being
	Macro concept	

In this micro concept, momentum changed, transient changed, this is not recognized in macro concept actor, just macro concept actor getting old, so called as the aged getting. But in the moment in the micro concept point then

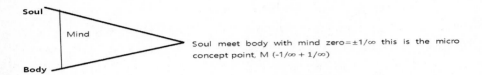

Soul meet body with mind zero=±1/∞ this is the micro concept point, M (-1/∞ + 1/∞)

Triangle point is the just moment changed point, transient changed, what happened to the point, the point is so moment, so long, that is the changed from before to after, what is this if not reach at the point then, reach at the realized, so then it must be changed, but also can catch the momentum changed, but also transient moment,

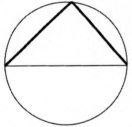

The triangle point is located at the round. The round is the realized points, so long if the among

Point distance is if micro concept point M (-1/∞ + 1/∞), then it seen, unseen is the micro concept

Point unseen is unseen dot point, but see the ∞ numbers micro cocnetp points, so long this line

Is the real line, so that seen round, what is the difference before micro concept point micro?

Concept point M (-1/∞ + 1/∞) after micro concept point is what happened to do, it must be

changed feeling. The round of real line is <N * micro concept point M (-1/∞ + 1/∞) = real line>

The round is the multiple reach at the micro concept point, the excitement of meeting of the soul

And body, so that the cross of just macro concept actor pair meeting is the getting realize so

Long, the strong soul just can increased after the out of the mind = micro concept point M

$(-1/\infty + 1/\infty)$, the until now then after realized soul being increased, so long come to this also

Need to strength the soul, after that the circumstance of health soul goes developed to another

Stages going, so that moment transient is micro concept reach, so then there are mind, mind:

Desired, fear, love, jealous, so long if reach at the micro concept point then, just meeting the soul

And body, it is really excitement which is not often, very rare feeling excitement the moment

Comes the excitement but also micro concept point means it never change in the moment of

Micro concept point. So long in the micro concept point is not transient changed. So that in the

line of round has the all of micro concept points so long round is the perfection shown, in the end the round is the truth, there is not any wicked point, it all of righteous points therefore the round is the great energy has, the round itself is the powerful source of energy. So long in living after the getting reach the points after points the realize micro concept increased, so long keep in the micro concept point then all of the soul is strength it means that soul is being major actor, so that in the round

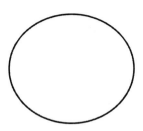

Round surface a real line is the consist of the ∞ numbers micro concept point M (-1/∞ + 1/∞) so then surface a real line is the righteous realized point M (-1/∞ + 1/∞) so long, inside of the surface line is the in the line is soul living place, so long in the round is the prefect of the micro concept, the macro concept seen as the round, but do not seen the micro concept point, so long in the macro concept point world, actor see the greatest round. It is the pleasure of excitement. In this perfect round is the just micro concept point just eternity everlasting same, so long the micro concept world beings, so then, macro concept world seen round so that in the round all of the righteous a realized soul remained living places, so long micro concept, in the macro concept world getting old, so long macro concept actor of "soul + mind + body= mindful body" then so then they have a fear, jealous, worrying minds so these mind get make body hard time, mind is all is source of deceit, so that mind is just false soul, just like soul act in the body, so that in the macro concept world perfect ignorance of the pair of soul, so that macro concept actor mind role of that, mind produce of the tired energy so then, it goes to the body is the slave of the mind, so then mind is not actor's pair, so that the macro concept actor after all deceit by the mind, so it goes to the temporally just all of mind slaver so that, body getting old, but if a actor realized then reach at the micro concept world, so long, micro concept point M (-1/∞ + 1/∞), so long just soulful actor, = soul + mind= point M (-1/∞ + 1/∞) + body = soulful body, so then soul is major actor it means that soul is the micro concept world, main actor but also it live eternity. So long in the micro concept point moment changed is even has the featured to the body, but after the micro concept point M (-1/∞ + 1/∞), reach at the point, so long just out of mind, all is the pure of the soul, that, so that in the just like the round seen, but unseen micro concept point, so that just like the macro concept seen is body, but actually the even seen the body but realized actor has the unseen soul is located at, so that, realized all of the mind is point M (-1/∞ + 1/∞) then even macro concept actor but soul, so called the soulful actor, the actor shine of light, just all of the center, the center, around of micro concept actor point M (-1/∞ + 1/∞), around actors all be learned from him/her. So long the realized actor must be live in the macro concept who are success in a field, but also do not famous, just personally live righteous so that reach at the point M (-1/∞ + 1/∞), then the not special usual actor also reach at the micro concept point, so the actor also can reach at the micro concept world. In the micro means that just segregate from the major, just in the minority place also, it can be the micro concept point, so long a small, unknown actor also reach at the micro concept point, micro concept point actor produce of the soulful products, so that soulful products is the a realized actor's behavior, living righteous, shared the time with others, helping others is the main concerning. Micro concept actor point M $(-1/\infty + 1/\infty)$ soul grow after reach out of the mind, so then the realize actor forget all of fear, but just go with pair soul so that it is the itself is excitement, so the strong health soul, lead the body to the healthful, the soul travel the macro concept world micro concept world, so that the soul know the righteous soul destination is how excitement with that, already experiment soul bust to the pair body live righteously living. So then righteous then the macro concept world being bright, so indeed the so wicked actor can be transfer to righteous act, so then the micro concept righteous soul actor pair do righteous so that it comes to the circulation of the micro concept and macro concept world, the realized actors are in the macro concept world, so then realized actor help peace in the macro concept actors. So that if the macro concept actor realized then the place to be peace, excitement and perfection. So then, if not comes the micro concept actor being then in the end the place occupied the wicked actors places, so then the community being disturb of that, how all of the wicked community. It means that each organized group must be the affected so that the success or failure is related with of the how many actors are live righteous or not, so long in the macro concept do not recognized to do, so that getting success in the business is not related but in the point of micro concept point, success is very closed related. Actually do not reach at the micro concept point M $(-1/\infty + 1/\infty)$ then do not successful products, because of there is no any soul located at the body, so long, micro concept point reached actor produce the masterpiece products all of the produced product being the antique, so long soulful antique must be produced by the realized actor so called reach at the point M $(-1/\infty + 1/\infty)$.

2014.09.24
Topic: macro concept and micro concept "husband & wife"

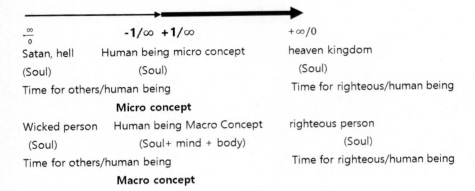

In this micro concept out of a unit actor, so called the pair, is husband & wife, so that tow actors are one pair of marriage couple, so long man and female unified to one of husband and wife, so that this is the in the micro concept, actor unit micro concept so called the personal micro concept M (-1/∞ + 1/∞), so then couple of marriage is two actor unit micro concept M (- 1/∞ + 1/∞) two micro concept 2*M (-1/∞ + 1/∞) so then just being of the marriage couple then two actor combined to one of the marriage unit one so then in the husband & wife is one of couple. As then it must be calculated as the mathematical soluble equations are

Let micro concept female micro concept as describe to FM, male micro concept as describe as also MM,
In the marriage cases
FM + MM= 2 unit actor micro concept
"Female soul + mind + body = mind body" + "male soul + mind + body= mind body" = 2 mind body.

In this time some of the mind is very high, so long, desired mind to get a each gender, so then, a female actor try to get a good male actor then in the point of female must be think, these soul is righteous soul or wicked soul, but also the counterpart male partner righteous or wicked husband meeting.

sort	Male Righteous	Male wicked	Female righteous	Female wicked
Male righteous			Blessing couple	Male duty
Male wicked			Female duty	divorced
Female righteous	Blessing couple	Female duty		
Female wicked	Male duty	divorced		

So long a unit of couple is two macro concept actor's meeting and go for living,

Righteous + righteous = natural good relationships, it must be a big blessed heavenly father loving couple.

Righteous + wicked = ① righteous actor kindly sacrifice then wicked changed to righteous = good sacrifice to help being wicked a partner to be the righteous = righteous + wicked changed to righteous= 2 righteous = in the end win to be recognized to make happy god, so god love this couple in the end in the soul destination is eternity of the righteous soul

Righteous + wicked = ② wicked actor template but also, righteous actor lose to change the wicked = righteous hard time but lived with wicked = righteous actor being wicked treat the same a partner wicked = 2 wicked actors= the wicked couple = soul destination is the wicked soul, so called satanic soul world.

Wicked + Wicked = just temporally shown to righteous actors are meet as the righteous then after get marriage two actor all are wicked then it comes to divorced. So long in this couple if do not remarriage then there is no in the micro concept world righteous, satanic place is not being destination.

In the micro concept living is not easy to live on, just marriage couple is the just like the male and female is must be equal to the same, then how to be same, so long, so that it seems to be the it must be infer that marriage combined to other gens living for the eternity, so that marriage is the eternity procedures, in the micro concept world and macro concept world concept is comes,

Macro concept male

soul	mind	body

Macro concept Female

soul	mind	body

FM soul + MM soul = 2 soul = how to be one of soul forming of marriage a unit couple

FM mind + MM mind = 2 mind = how to mind combined to one

FM body + MM body = 2 body = the macro concept majors not combined to one

As marriage Macro concept actor & micro concept actor comes

sort	Righteous living	Wicked living
Macro concept point	Time sharing, help other etc	Selfishness, do not help etc.
Micro concept point	Soul being health and strong	Soul being weak and feeble
Bank Deposit	Blessing bank saving, interesting is 100% + macro concept world Origin money is 2 times of righteous acts	Cursed bank saving interesting is 0%, in the macro concept world Wicked act, so then deceit actor cured X1 to wicked actor

So long

Macro concept world: soul + mind + body, then money, family, etc desired fulfillment it must be infer to mind is ∞, most actor select a counterparts in the Seen of result, so that wealth, higher ranking social factors then, it is guarantee to the perfection marriage living is secured or not, what is the variances, so then

Micro concept world counterpart actor in the micro concept blessing bank or cursed bank this is unseen world actor soul living, so long this is understand as the blessed or not, so long

Male and female, so called husband &wife is defined as husband is macro concept & micro concept combined to forming as "husband: macro concept: mind+ body+ micro concept: blessed bank deposit or cursed bank deposit.

If the husband & wife both are blessing bank deposit then husband & wife living is family, the family is grow, so long if it must be lived as the righteous so long possibly getting live as the righteous in the unit of the family also then the family live good.

But if husband & wife both are cursed bank deposit then husband & wife living is family, the family even now rich, wealth but family living is getting worse. So long in the two actors living is not simple, just seen world, so called macro concept world factor only considered then it must be not safe.

Just husband & wife living so then it must be pregnancy, it is just seen as the macro concept world seen world, but this is the god's principal, just micro concept world soul to macro concept world macro concept world actor baby. So then husband wife a family unit is the role of micro concept actor soul kings, god's soul entrust to the husband & wife, so long get marriage as the inferable

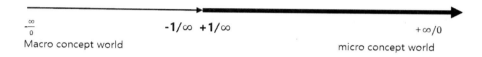

$$\frac{\infty}{0}$$ Macro concept world

$-1/\infty$ $+1/\infty$

$+\infty/0$ micro concept world

In a kind of infer then, micro concept world is not seen, but in the located at the unseen but in the micro concept world actor, soul, so then soul world unseen world seen, so then, soul world in the macro concept world is not existence, so long, macro concept world all of the touchable actors are all seen, but all is comes from the micro concept world souls, so then micro concept actor to macro actor creator is the realize, then in the moment of the birth of the a new micro concept actor to macro concept actor, it is the micro concept point micro concept M $(-1/\infty + 1/\infty)$ this is the birth point, in this moment comes from the soulful world to body living place, so that mother of female is creator, so long as a mother to the baby relationship is mother to baby is the mother is the righteous soulful behavior so long mother to the baby is the creator, but also realize so that, righteous typical factor is the mother is sacrifice to the baby, so then mother and baby is righteous soul, so called the soul is so strong then in the micro concept tunnel is strong so long in the micro concept tunnel M $(-1/\infty + 1/\infty)$ major operatiiing. macro concept mother is the role of the baby child is endless strong chain just mind comes to give the child mother love, but then mother closed the micro concept world M $(-1/\infty + 1/\infty)$, because of desired so big mind mother children only be good to live, so that it already disappeared to the mother of the micro concept point, it already mother son and daughter is being the macro concept actor role so then children also being just like same as the mother micro concept each actors micro concept M (- $1/\infty$ + $1/\infty$) is installed already.

So long just blessing or cursed is depend on children each actors problems but mother. So then mother must role for the adult each role is the wife role, wife role is the main concerning because of husband wife is the eternity soul living so then wife is the very required to lead the husband for the end of, but also in the micro concept living also, this is the originality, female is not origin of the purpose, the purpose is good righteous living as the pair so long, husband wife is another role is the helping old soul of husband parents filial duty it is the very strong righteous acts, because of strong actor of the female soul help the poor soul of the old parents good living. A female helped the old man living is the order, the young soul, old soul live help, this is the strong of the soul then it must be the blessing bank deposit, so long, a female is live excitement with husband soul. Husband wife is not separated but all is connected with male and female. Macro concept seen world act also important but micro concept world is the very important to the realized actors, so then if the realized and reach at the M (-$1/\infty$ + $1/\infty$), then so unseen world behavior is the macro concept world actors now showing.

Micro concept being tries to talk, so why important micro concept is this. Micro concept is more heavy to the macro concept, it compared with unseen world is the tree is the root is the strong then tree leaves are healthy so get a good produce, fruit etc. just unseen world is the how to strength is the doing righteous and the way of helping others, but also take a time for others.

2014.09.25

Topic: macro concept and micro concept "micro concept living"

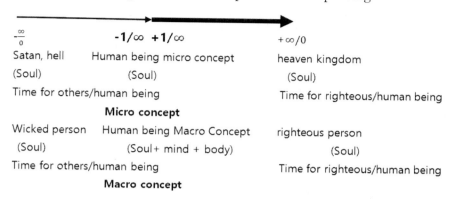

In this micro concept micro concept world actor is soul, so that it understand of the how to act in the macro concept world, then micro concept is unseen world so that all is not touch or realize, so long realize and touch in mind is somewhat similar to, the conception behavior is the same but realize is the touch in mind, so that, realize is mind is $\pm 1/\infty$ so that it comes up reach at the unseen world, so called micro concept world, so long if it is real that reach at the realize then,

it must be the reach at the micro concept point M $(-1/\infty + 1/\infty)$, then it must be main actor is the soul, so that soul is the free move from macro concept to micro concept but also micro concept to macro concept, in macro concept world actor if do realize then it come to micro concept point so called micro concept tunnel M $(-1/\infty + 1/\infty)$, but if do not realize then macro concept actor do not reach at the micro concept point M $(-1/\infty + 1/\infty)$ even some deceit as the mind to the soul, so long it is the wicked mind, so long Satan is the strong soul also, so that, Satan use the mind, but soul is actor so then righteous soul is from god soul destination, so long, so that soul is direct reach at the micro concept point, if the mind so called the even mind is the relative to the satanic so then mind to M $(-1/\infty + 1/\infty)$ then reach at the micro concept point, it means that realized actor must be the strong soul reach at the M $(-1/\infty + 1/\infty)$ but also the strong soul is the righteous soul so that righteous soul is transient from macro to micro concept world, so then after reach at the micro concept point M (-1/∞ + 1/∞) is a righteous soul, so long in the micro concept world righteous king is heavenly father lord, the son is the Jesus Christ, then righteous soul of macro concept actor soul is so string so that the soul connect to the micro concept world realized macro concept actor is "soul= righteous soul= macro concept actor= micro concept actor" so long, soul is common factor between micro concept world and macro concept world, so long, realized actor soul connect to heavenly father, so long heavenly father is the righteous soul try to say through the righteous soul realize, so called roach at the M (- 1/∞ + 1/∞)

so then it already explained that micro concept point is role of the micro concept tunnel to go for the righteous soul resident place, so that the realized actor live in the middle of the macro concept actor or micro concept place then, micro concept point also role for the macro concept actor realized soul residents used for the living place so that micro concept actor living is at M (- 1/∞ + 1/∞) so long

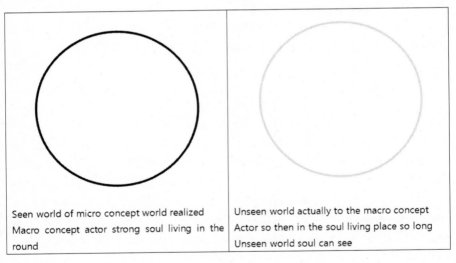

Seen world of micro concept world realized Macro concept actor strong soul living in the round	Unseen world actually to the macro concept Actor so then in the soul living place so long Unseen world soul can see

If this round line all of micro concept point is living line, then it must be called as the micro concept world, so long around is the frame of the micro concept point M (-1/∞ + 1/∞) then micro concept actor realized actor remained at the micro concept world, actually this is try to show to the Seen world but unseen world it must be shown to the round, but it is the try to show the micro concept world, but actually is not seen to the macro concept world, the realized actor is in the macro concept world and micro concept world then macro concept actor " soul + mind +body= mindful body" but in the " soul + body= soulful body" then soulful body live in the macro concept world and micro concept world. Micro concept world is the very moment just micro concept world what I explained micro concept point M (-1/∞ + 1/∞), so the round is the micro concept tunnel, but also micro concept soul living place is M (-1/∞ + 1/∞) so then, the round is the micro concept world, then micro concept point M (-1/∞ + 1/∞) is so small but unseen to the macro concept world, but in the micro concept world actor recognized so big world of micro concept world, all of micro concept actor full enough living, so long macro concept realized actor do not see the micro concept actor living place, so long here explained at the area, of micro concept area, but how to the time of the micro concept, time of the micro concept point is

$$-\frac{\infty}{0} \qquad\qquad \textbf{-1/∞ +1/∞} \qquad\qquad\qquad\qquad +\infty/0$$

Macro concept time scale is the = ∞/0 past, +∞/0 future, but micro concept time scale is the M (-1/∞ + 1/∞), so then micro concept is flash time scale, so then micro concept M (-1/∞ + 1/∞), time scale is not there is the past and future, so that micro concept recognized by flash so do not feel of the macro concept do not recognized at so long, macro concept time and micro concept time gap, difference is it must be inferred that ±∞ that but in the strong soul of realized macro concept actor live at the micro concept world M (-1/∞ + 1/∞),then the micro concept time and macro concept time is difference is the ±∞, so that the soul travel to the distance of ±∞, in the micro concept world M (-1/∞ + 1/∞), is unseen micro concept world but in the macro concept time scale then ±∞ , in the end soul travel in the micro concept world, just moment soul traveled to the ±∞ time scale, but also the area also, time is ±∞, then the place also ±∞ the soul move to the ±∞, so then micro concept actor living place M (-1/∞ + 1/∞). macro concept actor live in the micro concept actor living place, so long realized actor live between macro concept world and micro concept world, so long the time is also micro concept level, so then unseen world micro concept unrecognized by the do not realize, so then, if a realize then, the time difference of the micro and macro so then, a realize actor even live at the macro concept world, but the soul already live at the micro concept world, then realized live as the macro concept understand then live at the M $(-1/\infty + 1/\infty)$. it must be infer and explain by the time scale of micro concept so long micro concept time is not recognized, so long macro concept actor behavior, so seen nothing strange all is macro concept actor living. So that the righteous strong soul live in the micro concept world M $(-1/\infty + 1/\infty)$. so long in the real macro concept world, realized actor live in the micro concept world, just mind is $1/\infty$ then live righteous then connect the string soul, to righteous soul destinations so long, in the realized then, all of wisdom from all god, so long all of the real creative knowledge and wisdom is from micro concept righteous actor living place. So the realized actor gives to the macro concept world the eternity masterpiece products. So that in the eternity all of the recognition, antique art, all is from god, a realized actor created then that is not made by the macro concept actor but righteous soul, so called the micro concept righteous soul king, god's greatest present to the macro concept world. The masterpiece is macro concept world called that is soulful products, actually we do not know but all of the creative products art, novel etc is popular recognized then it is not made by man but god, soul, so then all of success macro concept actor must be followed the micro concept, so long actors lived as righteous but also keep followed the drilling all of mind reach at the M $(-1/\infty + 1/\infty)$. so called micro concept point reached, then the strong soul traveled to the righteous soul meet and get the solution to deliver to the macro concept actor the pair, so then the success macro concept actor fine the solutions to get a masterpiece, it is the really give a gift to macro concept world. This is the god present to the macro concept world.

2014.09.26

Topic: macro concept and micro concept "strong soul"

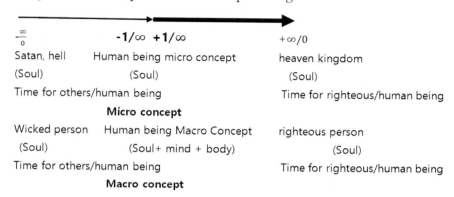

In this micro concept in the micro concept world main actor is "soul" soul is lived between macro concept world and micro concept world, so then macro world is minor actor is "soul + mind+ body= mindful body" to soul live health, then soul living condition must be best, so long in the macro concept actor how to live is the reach at the micro concept point the M $(-1/\infty + 1/\infty)$. so then try to reach at the micro concept point is so hard travel to go, so that in the macro concept world actor do not travel to the hard procedures, just like in the dangerous of walking fall but climb to the high top mountain, so long a reach at the top of mountain then comparable to the micro concept point M $(-1/\infty + 1/\infty)$. but most macro concept actor do not climb the Mt. so that after reach at the Mt. the excitement do not know, but also do not realize. Do realize is limited in the hard course, the other actors are some easy going. The hard course selected macro concept actor must walk on the micro concept actor try to go for the micro concept point the M $(- 1/\infty + 1/\infty)$ then how to reach at the micro concept point

sort	Righteous living	Wicked living
Macro concept point	Time sharing, help other etc	Selfishness, do not help etc.
Micro concept point	Soul being health and strong	Soul being weak and feeble
Bank Deposit	Blessing bank saving, interesting is 100% + macro concept world Origin money is 2 times of righteous acts	Cursed bank saving interesting is 0%, in the macro concept world Wicked act, so then deceit actor cured X1 to wicked actor

Righteous living is sacrifice, time sharing but also help others, so long, even helper is not rich but the actor realized so that the share time and help other is living basic, but also, to be reach at the micro concept point M $(-1/\infty + 1/\infty)$, helped actor feel excitement but also thank to the helper, so long, the righteous actor actor's sacrifice X 2, helper excitement but also helped actor thank to the helper, so that the righteous actor soul save in the micro concept world blessing bank saving, this bank interesting is also 100%, so long if so long if do righteous then in the macro concept save in the micro concept world blessing bank deposit is

Origin of righteous act is 1 + accepted of the righteous actor thank to helper 1 =2, this is the origin of saving, so then , in the blessing bank interesting is 100% so then= 2 + interesting 2 = so then = totality 4 unit is deposit to the blessing bank.

But in the wicked living then

Origin of wicked act is 1 + deceit actor cursed to deceit actor 1 = cursed origin saving is deposit in the micro concept cursed bank 2= cursed bank interesting is zero= 0%, so long so multiple actor are all in the cursed bank, so cursed bank don't necessary interesting so then deposit to the cursed bank deposit is 2.

So long righteous actor living is the getting blessing point X 4 = 4 blessing points, and then wicked actor living is the getting cursed point X 2 = 2, so long

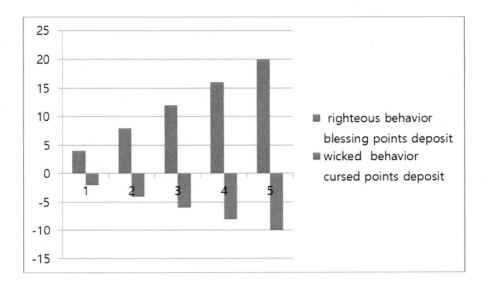

Just horizontal axis number is the origin of point, then saved in the righteous and cursed bank deposit point. This is not a real but a concept, so then righteous behavior has the blessing is bigger than wicked act cursed saving, it is the cursed is mercy but also righteous is give a big gift to the righteous actors.

This is the also energy then this is the totality result, is the energy to live on the in the micro concept point, so long, this is the somewhat misunderstood but, the micro concept world actor soul live, so then, wicked soul also in the macro concept a actor, but also righteous soul also in the macro concept also live in the micro concept world living energy.

So long it naturally the soul is decided to live on, if not any energy then, it must be infer so hunger to die, even though in the micro concept soul it don't necessary living energy, so that it is the conception so that in the macro concept world righteous actor micro concept destination is blessing bank location area, but also wicked actor also cursed bank location area is the destination. So then in the micro concept world also ahs the energy to used, so then personal energy then just one to one, then righteous energy is larger than wicked actor, but in the all of bank deposit size is cursed bank is much more larger than blessed bank deposit size. So long this deposit is the Satan king dome energy source, but also blessed bank deposit is the heaven king dome god side energy source. So then the realize is not much in the macro concept world, so long the number of wicked actor is much more larger, in the end the saving energy in the cursed bank then, the power to the macro concept actor must be a big worse, a big disaster comes.

But if the righteous actor behavior accumulate to the blessing bank deposit, so long then it gives to the peace in the macro concept world. But also another infer that cursed bank energy usage soul is a unit soul energy is half of the blessed bank energy a unit soul actor use, so that in the soul living in the micro concept world actor blessed bank saving actor live wealth, here micro concept actor, just blessed bank, and cursed bank is the truly do not difference but the righteous is critical concept so that energy is on the same conditions. Righteous behavior or wicked behavior is not deep difference but the not a righteous or not, so that the cursed bank saving is useful in the micro concept world energy usage.

In the end the blessed bank energy user is wealth, but cursed bank user is poor living. In the end in the macro concept as the righteous living then micro concept world rich living in eternity, so macro concept world living is very meaningful. So long in the macro concept rich or poor is not care of the micro concept world rich and poor is not related with but only the righteous living is very critical important. So that realized living so called reach at the micro concept point M $(- 1/\infty + 1/\infty)$ is basic condition.

2014.09.29

TOPIC: MACRO CONCEPT AND MICRO CONCEPT "MICRO CONCEPT DECISION"

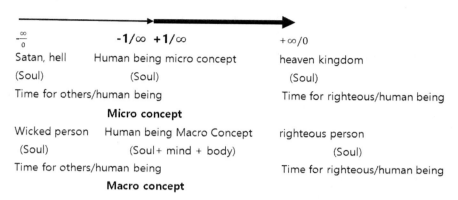

$\frac{\infty}{0}$ **-1/∞** **+1/∞**   +∞/0

Satan, hell   Human being micro concept   heaven kingdom

(Soul)   (Soul)   (Soul)

Time for others/human being   Time for righteous/human being

Micro concept

Wicked person   Human being Macro Concept   righteous person

(Soul)   (Soul+ mind + body)   (Soul)

Time for others/human being   Time for righteous/human being

Macro concept

In this micro concept, it must be usages for the macro concept. Micro concept actor is the "soul" so that souls are moves every place but also every times existence. Macro concept world also located. So long, macro concept actor move choose the righteous or wicked souls are move to the all of the macro concept actors micro concept frames. All of the macro concept actor has the frames but how to reach at the micro concept point M (-1/∞ + 1/∞) , if a actor do realized then reach at the micro concept gate M (-1/∞ + 1/∞) so then it is very easy explained to micro concept how to deliver the righteous soul knowledge, but also news etc, but wicked soul knowledge and wicked news etc. so long all of macro concept actor micro concept frame, so long in a realized actor, then if a actor reach at the micro concept gate M (-1/∞ + 1/∞) then, in the micro concept world even macro concept actor, so long in the micro concept actor tunnel is the micro concept gate M (-1/∞ + 1/∞) so that, macro concept actor can get communicate macro concept actor " soul minor + mind + body major= body" so then body minor soul be strong so that minor soul can meet to the travel to the freely to the micro concept world, so that, a macro actor soul meet a multi righteous souls, a macro concept actor macro world problems then so long the problems difficulties then righteous souls give a answer, but also if a religious macro concept actor then it must be reach at the micro concept world righteous soul king, heavenly father but also righteous soul king, Jesus

Christ also will be met, so then a realized a religious is in the bible is prophet so long apostle etc they write a god books, so that in the macro concept world a famous creator of a field, then a realized macro concept actor soul also through micro concept pipe line M $(-1/\infty + 1/\infty)$ travel souls meet in the micro ,concept world righteous soul about macro concept key idea, so long macro concept get, a righteous souls helping the macro concept world righteous living effort to accomplish the historical creative product bring from the micro concept world knowledge to using the micro concept world knowledge get to macro concept world a creative product which give to the macro concept world benefits.

But if do not realized but a wicked macro concept actor also to get a creative products then, the actor do not realize but the macro concept actor wicked getting the knowledge get it, so then how to get the knowledge, then, a wicked soul travel the wicked soul, so long very weak soul, so long the wicked actor all try to live also the same as the righteous soul products. So long wicked is not concluded but in the procedure in the middle of the time, wicked actor used all of the power of wicked, so long, how to related with micro concept frame, so long all of the actor ahs the micro concept frame, so long, the ways of the micro concept gate M $(-1/\infty + 1/\infty)$, so it reach at the micro concept reach also wicked, so long, a wicked actor also in the meeting a just wicked actor reach at the disguised even the actor is not lived as the righteous behavior but a actor live pretend to the righteous so that the actor also disguised to reach at the micro concept M $(-1/\infty + 1/\infty)$ so long wicked macro concept actor is the " soul1/∞ + mind ∞ + body = mindful body= body" so then wicked soul is so weak, so long the soul also in the disguised reaching at the micro concept pipe line M $(-1/\infty + 1/\infty)$ then, the weak soul, feeble soul so, the soul hard to travels, then a wicked soul in the micro concept world wicked soul, travel to the all of the place in the macro concept or micro concept world, so long easy meet a feeble macro concept soul, so long the wicked soul easily deceit so that a macro concept actor behavior is temporally going well, so that the macro concept actor do not realized but do not perfect in affairs then the affairs are not going eternity, the very strong criteria is the righteous so long, then righteous behavior then the actor reach at the micro concept point M $(-1/\infty + 1/\infty)$ so long the actor met the true of answer, but wicked soul met the false true, so that, that is not perfect answer, so that disguised reaching the micro concept gate actor meet the wicked soul so that in the end the macro concept actor produce or all of the affairs are not perfect products.

Micro concept decision is righteous soul meeting and wicked soul meeting is decided, so that if a macro concept actor decided the correct answer then, the decision making actor must live in the righteous living then but if a decision maker is lived as the wicked then the actor decision is not to be meet the righteous soul. So far, if a macro concept actor lives in the decision then, an optimistic key solution is getting from not a simply the special knowledge but the macro actor real living of righteous, so long if a actor live as the wicked then the decision place who is not helped righteous the correct solutions, so long, a macro concept world actor decide optimistic is derived from all of life living, so long, a life is the righteous living then if a righteous living actor helped in the higher ranker of decide from the micro concept actor real save and answer. But if a actor lived all of life then wicked then, a actor get the high ranker, then the decision maker decide must be also wicked to the system, so then the decide affect to the system wrong then in the end the system getting decay. So then the system must be defunct.

2014.09.30

Topic: macro concept and micro concept "the righteous helping others"

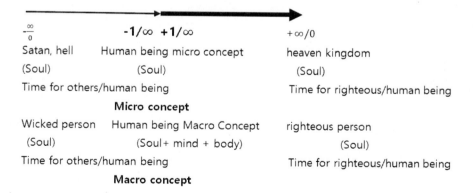

$-\frac{\infty}{0}$	**-1/∞ +1/∞**	+∞/0
Satan, hell	Human being micro concept	heaven kingdom
(Soul)	(Soul)	(Soul)
Time for others/human being		Time for righteous/human being
	Micro concept	
Wicked person	Human being Macro Concept	righteous person
(Soul)	(Soul+ mind + body)	(Soul)
Time for others/human being		Time for righteous/human being
	Macro concept	

In this micro concept the righteous is basis of share time and helping others. Then how to helping, to help what is necessary, to help then it must be need to prepare for helping others. So long it related with owner spirit so long, to help other then owner spirit so called it is reach at the micro concept point M $(-1/\infty + 1/\infty)$ in the macro concept actor live as the owner spirit or guest, then guest live leave and to leaves, so long, guest can watch a new place, move to move, but owner spirit actor do not live other but in the fixed place living. So then the actor is owner, so long who can help other, owner spirit or guest, who can reach at the micro concept point M $(-1/\infty + 1/\infty)$, who will be hard live, just travel all of the places the guest living hard or fixed a places then a fixed owner then it must be imagine that traveled to new places must be easier to the fixed owner will not to live easy. If a guest visits fixed owner place, then the owner it must be give the eating and room for guest, then owner give all of easy going of guest. So long owner must be role of the worker but guest must be treated as the premium, so long, why owner try to give the easy living in the owner house, in this cases, it must not be guest is not make hard to owner, so long, for the purpose of pity mind to guest, because of visiting the ways are all hard, so humble and honorable mind for the guest, in this case owner spirit help guest, so long, in this case help guest is owner, so that to be help other it must be owner spirit, so long righteous soul owner also, so that righteous soul = owner spirit, owner must be realized at helping a guest, guest must be easy, owner is hard in a moment, but the guest is guest, so easy but guest must leave a new places, so long, but owner is fixed a place, so that after leave to other place then, after that fixed place owner it don't necessary move another places, but also it must be out of trouble, in a moment resting time comes, but after soon it goes usually, so a owner help guest. Guest it must not help other, because of the actor haven't any asset but also, and whoever do not visit to the guest, because guest hasn't any fixed places, but guest on the ways of traveling then meet the same guest, then in the travel time can help other guest, but it must be not enough compared with fixed owner spirit actor. So righteous living required the procedures, so long, if an actor live easy then it must be apt to live as the guest, but an actor live hard time then it also infer that of the owner spirit actor, so long, righteous living is not easy, all the time sacrifices, but also comes to the obstacles, so that in the living right way then it comes very often wicked soul offend, so that hard to live as righteous living. But disrupter of the wicked living is very easy, so then, in the macro concept time it as the competition so long it as the normal, but wicked actor so disrupt other righteous act, then the righteous behavior must be frustrate in the end, it must be necessary as the righteous living features, sometimes righteous actor invaded from wicked actors, so long, righteous actor so that hard to bear of living, strangely righteous actor must be hard from wicked actors, if righteous do not change the wicked powers then, the righteous actor must be segregate from major wicked actors. This also the procedures of the righteous livings, so long, it must be righteous living is so rare due to hard live in the macro actors. Macro actor live as the owner spirit, but guest living, who be the owner spirit, who the guest living, how to be this ways, for eternity, macro actor in the hard time, so then it must be righteously endure then it comes to the righteous living, so that lovely righteous soul king god prepared to find the real righteous actor discriminate from wicked actors, but also hard time is the god's loving actor, so then all of the righteous living is hard time is the righteous living procedures, easy going in the macro concept then it must not to be eternity but the easy going must be energy used out then, it also it is not same as the righteous = realized actor living is righteous hard time, but in the easy going, of the wicked actor live hard time is cursed, so that righteous hard time is the endurance helping others but also to prepared with the righteous living energy but wicked actor after easy time over then it comes to the wicked actor comes cursed things. Just righteous living is must be selected to even hard but decide doing help, and times share for others. So called the owner spirit, do live righteous then justice and courageous is required actor, righteous living is helped by justice, courageous souls, in the point of micro concept world then, the micro concept actor "soul" discriminate from the wicked soul the righteous soul, because the pure righteous soul feel wicked fear, so righteous soul all fear of the wicked soul, so that some of distance places from the wicked soul places, naturally in the micro concept actor world, the souls themselves separated after macro concept world so that micro concept world righteous recognition of the true righteous souls, so long owner spirit lead to live righteous and furthermore the righteous actor get at the righteous soul destinations, but also naturally if a macro concept actor live as guest, then a guest live places to variable place easily so then, in the end the guest can't help others but also it must not to live shared guests time, so that guest living is hard to live in the micro concept world wicked soul place.

Topic: macro concept and micro concept "creature = micro concept"

$$\longrightarrow \quad \blacktriangleright\!\!\!\longrightarrow$$

$\frac{\infty}{0}$	$-1/\infty \quad +1/\infty$	$+\infty/0$
Satan, hell	Human being micro concept	heaven kingdom
(Soul)	(Soul)	(Soul)
Time for others/human being		Time for righteous/human being

Micro concept

Wicked person	Human being Macro Concept	righteous person
(Soul)	(Soul+ mind + body)	(Soul)
Time for others/human being		Time for righteous/human being

Macro concept

In this micro concept inferable then a actor reach at the micro concept point M $(-1/\infty + 1/\infty)$, if micro concept point M is the getting creatures, then the procedure of the micro concept is reach at the Micro concept point, there a strong actor in the macro concept "soul + mind + body=body" then minor of the macro concept soul being strong, so in the micro concept point M $(-1/\infty + 1/\infty)$ this is the time and the area, so then, in the micro concept point world, a strong macro concept soul dare meet a micro concept world pure soul, so then, in the macro concept actor do not fear of meeting the micro concept actor, because of live righteously so an actor soul is very pure and strong, so that it must be the actor is "soul + body= body" so that the actor soul is just soul so that in the micro concept point area, a strong actor meet then ask about the macro concept actor intrigue of a new feature getting, so that it necessary of a new creative solutions, so then the righteous actor show the solution library so that the strong actor can see the micro concept world knowledge which is prepared to help a righteous macro concept actor.

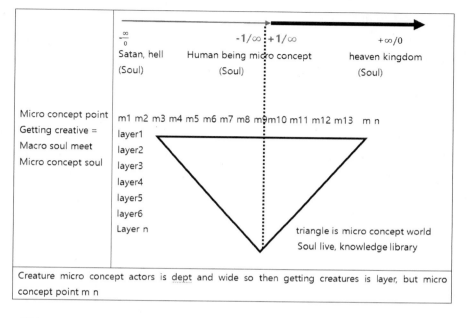

$\frac{\infty}{0}$	-1/∞ ⋮ +1/∞	+∞/0
Satan, hell	Human being micro concept	heaven kingdom
(Soul)	(Soul)	(Soul)

Micro concept point
Getting creative =
Macro soul meet
Micro concept soul

m1 m2 m3 m4 m5 m6 m7 m8 m9m10 m11 m12 m13   m n
layer1
layer2
layer3
layer4
layer5
layer6
Layer n

triangle is micro concept world
Soul live, knowledge library

Creature micro concept actors is dept and wide so then getting creatures is layer, but micro concept point m n

If a macro concept actor creator then an actor live to get products, but also new creative products then, it need to intrigues of soluble of the creature products.

Micro concept points: m1 m2 m3 m4 m5 m6 m7 m8 m9m10 m11 m12 m13 …….. m n
Macro concept actor meets micro concept world souls
Layer 1, layer 2, layer 3, layer 4, layer 5 layer 6 ……… layer n

In the micro concept world has the knowledge to give macro concept actor required So then macro concept actor reach at the micro concept point micro concept point M (- 1/∞ + 1/∞) then macro concept actor live all of effort to get a creative product and knowledge then a righteous living a strong soul reach at, in this case, macro actor components " soul + mind + body= body" if mind is 1/∞ then soul+body=soulful body=body macro actor almost same as the strong soul so then, in the micro concept point M (-1/∞ + 1/∞), So long macro concept is soulful body is also equal to "soul" so long macro concept actor living time, if a actor realized then a actor being " strong soul" so then macro concept actor move in the soul world so called micro concept world, so that micro concept actor is the "soul" so then in the micro concept world macro soul and micro concept major soul contact.

So long if a creative comes then

Creative = reach at the micro concept world M $(-1/\infty + 1/\infty)$, so macro concept actor being of the soulful body= so then strong soul, so then meet a micro concept actor in the micro concept world then, the first time get creature, so long

Creative 1 = M1 $(-1/\infty + 1/\infty)$ X micro concept world layer 1 = M1 layer 1, this is the creature so long macro concept actor reach at the M1 and the place creative knowledge's layer 1, so that comes the result of creature comes M1 layer1. It comes to

M1 layer 1 + M2 layer2 + M3 layer3 + M4 layer 4 …….. M n layer n is realized point so called to the reach at the micro concept points M, macro micro soul meets to comes creative product or knowledge so long keep continues as the realized points these point set is comes

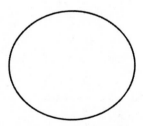

So then it comes round, the real line is the micro concept point or realized point set, so that but creative is not others area invading is not but just go deep to get a creative knowledge so that in the micro concept is pure so long it getting peace, micro is not big but in the unseen world micro concept world soul behavior and the macro concept world "soul + mind + body = body" so long unseen world is treasured, all of source of energy is not from the macro concept world but mostly productivities comes from the micro concept world, so that multiple of M1 layer1 M2 layer2 ….. Mn layer n, this point is the macro concept history, a company, a book, or all of the knowledge industry is all comes from the micro concept world knowledge.

So then a company or country, or the creative writer, book makers etc, so long the degree of the realize so called the create then the layer is the degree of the development then if a layers are the level also, so long in the personal realizations level,

M1 layer 1 + M2 layer2 + M3 layer3 + M4 layer 4 …….. M n layer n is realized point So long M1 layer 1 is actor, company etc, and knowledge depth levels so then it is the powers of the actor or companies but also country also, so then how to get the micro concept world knowledge getting are prime time comes.

2014.10.06

Topic: macro concept and micro concept "relationship"

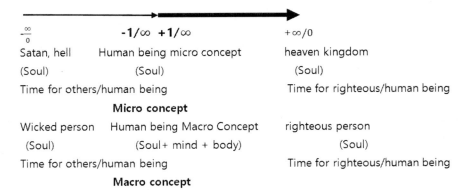

In the micro concept the soul is the center actor. At now why I start to say, micro concept I'm not perfect understand, why no one interesting then I'm try to talk this micro concept. These days I'm a Satan soul, because my mind doubts my relatives. The relationship all around of me, I'm doubt so that around of me all of actors are being of deceit, why I'm this, I'm a not a righteous soul, so then I'm a wicked soul. I feel fear of my relationships my deep friends also, even my wife, also. I'm so fear all around of me. Micro concept my relationship is wrong, what is problem to me, the relationship; if I were wrong then the other is being of righteous living, so if I were a righteous living then around of me is wicked actors. The macro concept actor is here, now, the relationship actor field is this, but in the souls relationship. So long the macro concepts are convergent to micro concept ranges micro concept world M $(-1/\infty + 1/\infty)$, so then in this world living actors are souls, souls live, the macro concept actor see macro concept actor so does micro concept actors are see in the soul, but soul recognition as the macro concept featured. So the soul moves to swiftly. Soul to soul, all of souls are live, micro concept souls are also wicked soul and righteous souls, soul live at the segregate righteous and wicked soul, so then, in this place, alls are same notions criteria but if I infer in the micro concept world, a middle places are mixed zone of righteous soul and wicked soul, in this places soul is actors so that each souls are see only wicked soul wicked soul but also righteous also righteous, then, here wicked – righteous mixed soul comes, this soul can see each soul, righteous soul, wicked soul, so long, wicked soul – righteous soul, in a soul the contaminated wicked and righteous soul, so that this soul can decided to righteous also wicked soul, this is the cause of relationship in the souls, the righteous – wicked soul, just live at the middle point, but righteous soul is live at the righteous soul destinations, but also wicked soul live at the wicked soul destination, righteous energy, wicked energy wave connect each souls, so then infer that is righteous actor waves to wave another righteous actors, but also wicked also same, but in the middle of the wicked – righteous soul, so that these actors are wicked and righteous soul energy spread.

So long the middle wicked – righteous soul is variance in the micro concept world,

Wicked soul destinations	Wicked – righteous soul	Righteous soul destination
Darkness	Darkness brightness	Brightness

Wicked – righteous soul is the variances because of an actor ahs the two actor color of the souls, so that this soul can be in the side of the wicked and righteous soul, so long this actor can see in the momentum of wicked then the actor being wicked so, then righteous soul is big suffer, but also moment wicked – righteous soul in the side of righteous then the moment wicked soul feel easy, so but the wicked- righteous soul stay at the wicked — righteous soul living place, there is no eternity of the destination.

So long in the micro concept world clearly divide wicked soul and righteous soul, but also this souls living condition is not same, the wicked is darkness but righteous is bright world, so then in the wicked — righteous soul is darkness condition and bright condition, how to separate wicked and righteous,

Infer that wicked — righteous soul meet in the micro concept world a soul of pure righteous soul do not have the pair, then lived at the macro concept world live righteously, then a actor must be live at the righteous eternity, in the righteous living destination, so long, adversely wicked soul single also meet in the middle of the wicked — righteous soul, so then this middle position actor soul go for the wicked soul eternity so long, the relationship is very essential.

Macro wicked actor living single	Wicked – righteous soul		Macro righteous actor Living single
Darkness	Darkness	brightness	Brightness

So long lived at macro concept actor righteous but do not marriage then in the waited at the wicked — righteous soul, so then, the righteous character + macro concept righteous actor then in the long run the soul is eternity located at the righteous soul destination, but also macro concept world wicked actor soul single + wicked — righteous soul = wicked soul destination do live eternity. These days in the macro concept actors live single to die. Then to be eternity, so then pair so long female and male couple is eternity soul living, so then if single need to be live eternity in a real living.

How to comes the wicked — righteous soul happened, then, in the macro concept actor marriage living then, in this time wicked soul so multiple, so long, if live a righteous soul, then move to the from macro concept world but this if both live righteous living then, a righteous actor in the micro concept world, if a macro concept actor still is not in the micro then wait in a angel forming, so then the righteous soul after coming then, meet a righteous macro concept actor same being couple to the eternity righteous living but, if in the macro concept world marriage living then, a couple live as the righteous, but the other is wicked living then in the temporally in the wicked – righteous soul, so then a macro concept actor comes then, meet righteous soul male female comes to meet lived at the righteous soul destination, but also the wicked soul also, then so not live macro concept world pair is not going for the same living after dead. So long, how to meet, so long relationship is very important in the macro concept success living is not easy.

The relationship in the macro concept world, male and female most actors to live success, all of marriage actors know the way to go for the both righteous soul being, teaching and lead to the a righteous soul actor all of responsibility to live righteously, if a righteous partner do example to the still is not in the righteous actor, endurance and bear to make somewhat wicked actor to be live righteous then after macro concept then this actor must be live righteously in the micro concept soul eternity living. Then the in the macro concept world, out of marriage pair, the relationship is also, how to express, the righteous actor in the macro concept world. In the relationship wicked and righteous all is mixed, then, it must be infer then, an actor lived do righteous or wicked then it must be, also estimated in the decision whose life lived as righteous or wicked. If a righteous actor lived then the relationship chain are righteous, but if a life lived wicked then wicked actor chain so that naturally counted on how to live in the macro concept world.

Righteous living

Actor 1	R								
R	R								
	R	R	R						
	R	Actor1	R						
		R		R	R	R			
				R	Actor1	R	R	R	R
				R		R		Actor1	R
							R		

Birth   Dead

W: wicked, R: righteous

Wicked living

Actor 2	W								
W	W								
	W	W	W						
	W	Actor2	W						
		W		W	W	W			
				W	Actor2	W	W	W	W
				W		W		Actor2	W
							W		

Birth   Dead

W: wicked R: righteous

The righteous actor1 make a righteous soul, so then an actor1 lived with righteous actors, but actor 2 make a wicked soul, so then an actor2 lived with wicked actors. Then it comes that actor 1 is righteous, but actor 2 wicked. How to make around actor to be wicked or righteous, to live make other righteous or wicked is possible, how to, it must be make other righteous or wicked is not a way of micro concept but micro concept is realized actor oneself, to live righteous it must be realized, so then reach at the micro concept point M ($-1/\infty + 1/\infty$), just make oneself all of the wicked mind to M ($-1/\infty + 1/\infty$) then it must be live at the actor 1 do righteous living. Righteous do not know the way of wicked then, the actor 1 live with only known the righteous so, actor 1 live all of the righteous actors. Righteous actor do not know the fear, even deceit from others, so that even if fall from others then do not anger then treat as feel sympathy, this is the righteous living, so called the man is the realized, beyond of the fear, to live righteous then all of the dreadful of the deceit mind, must be come to reach at the micro concept point so long M (- $1/\infty$ + $1/\infty$), but do live wicked then, it must be actor 2 is live as the wicked then, a actor 2 wicked to others, so long oneself is lived all of the wicked actors, so long the wicked living is dedicated to the eternity to lived in the wicked soul destinations.

Out of wicked then it must be reach at the micro concept so long, around of an actor1 must be so many times invaded from the wicked actors, then to live righteous, it must hard to do, so then all of the asset also must be reach at the micro concept point M ($-1/\infty$ + $1/\infty$) so long the realized actor1 must be beyond the living, if all of the real place are wicked then how to be live as the righteous then, it must be realized to reach at the micro concept point M ($-1/\infty$ + $1/\infty$), so long, all of mind to be reach at the micro concept point M ($-1/\infty$ + $1/\infty$), to be live righteous then

So long, upper round and mind is $1/\infty$ this is the realized so called reach at M ($-1/\infty$ + $1/\infty$), if is very simple all of mind is $1/\infty$ then, there is no fear to live on, living actor then all the time comes the fear, the fearful mind not to be deceit, or invaded from others, it must be comes the out of the circumstance. So long to live righteous then, it must be realized to the range of mind is $1/\infty$, then out of fear. To live righteous is reach at the micro concept point M1 ($-1/\infty$ + $1/\infty$), mind is to be $1/\infty$, then in the end comes to righteous living. In the relationship to live righteous then it must be all of mind being $1/\infty$, then it will come to excitement and happy with relationship, even in a real actor deceit then it also feels pity to a deceit actor. Live as the righteous so long losing gamer then, in the end comes to him/her as the righteous living.

2014.10.07

Topic: macro concept "making money"

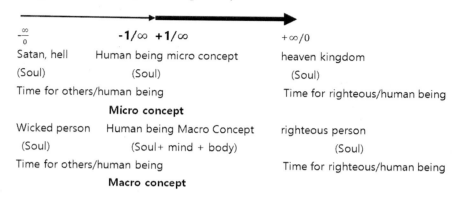

$$-\frac{\infty}{0} \qquad\qquad -1/\infty \quad +1/\infty \qquad\qquad +\infty/0$$

Satan, hell   Human being micro concept   heaven kingdom

(Soul)   (Soul)   (Soul)

Time for others/human being   Time for righteous/human being

Micro concept

Wicked person   Human being Macro Concept   righteous person

(Soul)   (Soul+ mind + body)   (Soul)

Time for others/human being   Time for righteous/human being

Macro concept

In this micro concept is unseen world, so then actually macro concept world actors are do not know, it must be most ignorance of existed at micro concept world. So that in the macro concept actor main activities to make money so called living energy getting. Most time used in the adult actor living, but youth time all study for preparing to make money. Some actor make money well, the other is not. But righteous actor makes money, wicked actor make money, and then the same as making as righteous actor making money, so rich actors are both righteous and wicked.

But righteous and wicked do not make money, so that the poor of righteous and wicked actor so then cause of poor is lazy behavior. This is the macro concept actor thinking to make money. Money is in the micro concept world is energy so called blessed point. So long, money making is inferred that money making is perfectly doing not related with micro concept world.

All of macro concept actor making rich making, all of macro concept actors are all desired to make money but all is not get being rich. Who can make money, some other is not make money.

What sources are tool to make money, the factors are diligent, a good learning, a fortune so all mixed comes to make much money, and here is fortune which gives lucky, so that the actor dilli9gent then unseen helper helped diligent actors working. But the poor are lazy, uneducated or unfortunately lived so all of trying to make money cases are all failed. Then most macro concept actors are only think seen world, so that all is just push all of their times for the making money.

The fortune is added with macro concept actor worked hard, then plus good fortune. An actor lived as the righteous so that he lived living just kept righteously so long time effort to make a real product, which help consumers' satisfaction, so that the products help multiple actors, so long the righteous make much money, but also wicked actor also can big make a money, money is the all of power getting, the power actor extort underground economy but also break a law and make money, some out of within the law the wicked actor also make a money disguised as the righteous actors. The fortune source is from righteous power but also wicked source power, so that in the micro concept world, the actors are all souls, so then, make money is mixed with righteous actor but also wicked actors, money is center for the wicked actor and righteous actors

So that money is the macro concept actors loving is money, instead of believing god. In the micro concept world righteous actor pursue heavenly father, Jesus Christ, but wicked actor pursue satanic king, so that so long, macro concept world actors out of righteous but also religious living is not, then just money is prime concerning so then, it must be all of actors are in the micro concept actor then infer that must be multiple money seekers are time all used for the exclusively for one selves so long, all are followers to the micro concept satanic world.

The way of make money but also amount of making money, of each actor the poor or the rich All of the rich is success evaluated as the rich, but the poor is thinking as the failure, this is the macro concept world evaluation. But in the micro concept world success is somewhat it must be not same as macro concept world so that, the poor is not failure in the micro concept actor world. The micro concept actor success is depends on the righteous living; shared time, giver position working. So long macro concept actor living as the poor living and suffering for the relatives even one actor's sake, but a personal actor lives all of living, a wife to the husband, all turf husband make obedient husband to live righteously then, husband wife is getting lived righteous all of living. This is a micro concept basic actor typical living. So long, a righteous wife effort all of her life to make husband to make live righteous living, so that, the poor in the macro concept actor are really success in the micro concept world, a righteous wife whole suffered her life, husband being righteous, so long, righteous is not related with pure macro concept world success actors, so long micro concept is unseen world, so long, is not famous actor, but a sacrificed for the husband then, a success living in the point of view micro concept is reach at the micro concept point M (-1/∞ + 1/∞), a righteous wife all mind being 1/∞ so then a righteous wife meet a soul of hers' so then the righteous soul behavior of sacrifice, she is lived as realized, so long reach at the M (-1/∞ + 1/∞) so she know that how important pair of living, but also, the realized actor soul already know, just eternity living is pair living in the micro concept world.

Macro concept world money making is success criteria, so long, the rich lived all used up of blessings, so then the rich actor lose of the energy. If infer then the rich all of actors success making money energy shared with the poor then, he must be live

The rich Righteous living

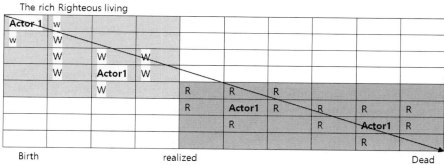

Birth   realized   Dead

W: wicked, R: righteous

The rich in the macro concept world, the actor just before world lived wicked make a big money, so then through middle to late of living the actor helped the poor so that around of the rich followed the righteous actors, the righteous actors all fell thank, but also, the rich realized, so that the actor reach at the micro concept point M (-1/∞ + 1/∞), so then in the micro concept micro concept pipe line to the righteous soul destination in the micro concept world. So then god of righteous actor in the micro concept world, use the rich righteous actor be as the god the rich as the god's messenger, so then god's macro concept world governing. So that the money is the righteous money is god side but if the rich use money doing not help but still keep as the power keeping for only oneself, then it must be the actor do not shared with others, but also do not help others, so that the rich are located at the micro concept world satanic world eternity living.

2014.10.08

Topic: macro concept " home"

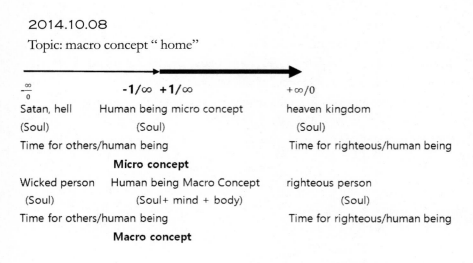

In the macro concept "home" is made of house's physical factor + human beings behavior, this is very simple, then in this micro concept a macro concept actor consist of soul + mind + body = body, then in the home has the family members, then, here is the father mother and son & daughter. So then a home owned the family, so long 4 actors are living at the home, there being of family. In the macro concept home is the family territory, family territory nations are 4 members, so long so that "soul + mind + body= body". Just macro concept actor recognized at just body, so in the home live an actor body,

In the macro home is macro actors territory, in this place is kingdom of macro actors "soul + mind + body= body" in this place lived four actors, so then it is called the family, so long, even all of the personal unit is four person so that is micro concept unit is 4, but in the family unit is one family micro concept unit is 1, so then family is micro concept point, even has the each has the micro concept point, so long, personal micro concept point is personal realization so long each personal actor micro concept gate M (-1/∞ + 1/∞), so long micro concept points are 4 X M (-1/∞ + 1/∞), this is has the a big variances each actors are righteous or wicked behaviors.

But in the family micro concept unit is 1 so long, to be one of family micro concept units then it must be sum of personal micro concept units so then 4X 1/4 M $(-1/\infty + 1/\infty)$, then family micro concept unit is family micro concept point is reach at the 1 X M $(-1/\infty + 1/\infty)$, so that all of member of personal is 0.25 so then, in the micro concept family unit micro concept point frame is at the head of household some of father role player, so then in the family has a family soul, is combined each macro actors soul 0.25 shared with others family members, so that in the mathematical point of view then just all of the member soul mixed to one in the home, so that here home is souls places. All the time personal o.25 soul are remained in the home. But in the micro concept point calculation is some different from mathematics calculating resulting.

In the family micro concept point, some of example table

sort	father	mother	son	daughter	family
Personal unit (micro concept point)	1 (1)	1 (1)	1 (1)	1 (1)	4 (4)
Family unit	0.25	0.25	0.25	0.25	1
Family micro Concept point	1	0	0	0	
Sum of family Micro concept point	2.25	1.25	1.25	1.25	6
Righteous soul		+1.25	+1.25	+1.25	+3.75
Wicked soul	-2.25				-2.25
Pure of family micro concept point	-2.25	+1.25	+1.25	+1.25	+1.5

Righteous soul micro concept point +, wicked soul − this section is inferred of for example, father is the wicked, but all of actors are righteous living.

In the macro concept home consist of it, is shape of micro concept point frame unit is indicated of the soul living best places so long, in the general mathematic soul are each soul o.25 are all together consist of the family, so that in the family foul member soul are live at the home. So long in the micro concept the head of family has the micro concept point frame, to be the so the head of family must be same as the father then, father micro concept point is 2.25, this very important to the family. Mother and children's micro concept point is 1.25 so that family micro concept 2.25/6 = 37.5 %, and other mother and children is about 20.1%, so then, if infer of father behavior is wicked then − 2.25 so long, 37.5 % micro concept point is losing then, the family are only 62.5% so then, the family righteous member of souls are hard to live but, just still has the still is the righteous soul is bigger than wicked soul, then 62.5% is more power than father.

In the macro concept actor living place is also the compared with the micro concept point or world so that family is soul living place also, it means that in the micro concept world soul place, so then, soul eternity is decide to the righteous soul living place, but also wicked soul places, but in the macro concept family are personal micro concept units, so then even in the family there are mixed with righteous soul and wicked soul, so then in the micro concept point's righteous − wicked soul living place, so that all of the family are hard to live, husband wife, even the children are also mixed with righteous soul and wicked soul, so that the family is bright or dark color of family is comes, if infer of righteous family then the family is warm and bright actor live, but if wicked soul living then dark in the family. So that in the bright living place is righteous soul best living place but also dark place is best living place for the wicked souls. So then in the wicked and righteous are lived in this place, then it must be righteous soul endured and transgression to a part of the wicked actor to be changed to righteous soul making is righteous actor duty.

2014.10.10

Topic: macro concept "me =I"

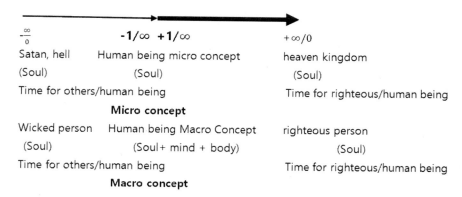

In this micro concept macro concept "me= I" what is this, micro concept is micro concept gate M (-1/∞ + 1/∞), this means seen to unseen but existed. All of macro concept creatures, micro concept is micro concept gate M (-1/∞ + 1/∞), so then the point of the point, so long "me=I" then macro concept i= me is master, so long governor, so that just infer that I'm a center, so long if this is used at the micro concept then micro concept gate M (-1/∞ + 1/∞), macro I= me, is in the micro concept point is the world of micro concept world is M (-1/∞ + 1/∞), this is the infer in the macro concept world then

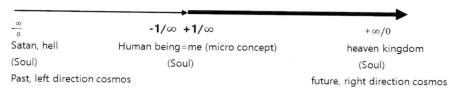

Micro concept me=I is live at the center of the micro concept gate M (-1/∞ + 1/∞), so then macro concept me = I is live with other actors, so that forget me=I, but just see others only. But also do not know how important me=I it is, macro concept me=I is all the time existed as the social position seen, but in the micro concept world me=I is the soul, but also soul is located at the in the micro concept gate world M (-1/∞ + 1/∞), in this place macro concept social political ranking is not operated. Micro concept soul is just me=I's necessary center, so then it must be explained to understand well, then it must seen in the macro concept to the micro concept then, macro concept actor do not recognized but also, if recognized then, angel or demon, so then these are mightier to the macro concept, so then most macro actors are called to family god or called generally god. So long, god means that compatible all of the macro concept problems, so then all of the macro actor expect all solve by helped from god. So then me=I is not ranking is last but all the time is ranking is number 1, so long number one is the creator or exclusively live oneself only, so in the universe or cosmos center.

In the micro concept cosmos also located at the micro concept point micro concept gate M $(- 1/\infty + 1/\infty)$, so long, me =I is lived at the center of the my micro concept frame, in my macro concept actor micro concept frame is located at the macro concept actor, so long, me = I realized then macro concept actor " soul + mind + body = mindful body= body" but if a realized actor is " soul + mind = $1/\infty$ + body= so long soulful body= body" then, in the macro concept world, a realized actor live as the soul body, then soul is lived at the micro concept world micro concept gate M $(-1/\infty + 1/\infty)$,but also it has inferred to the all of cosmos are located also at the micro concept gate M $(-1/\infty + 1/\infty)$, then inferred that me=I is center of micro concept point micro concept gate M $(-1/\infty + 1/\infty)$,because of macro concept actor me=I micro concept frame so that I'm the center of the cosmos.

So then in the micro concept me=I is the center of the micro concept micro concept gate M $(-1/\infty + 1/\infty)$, then micro concept me= I is the called to the simply micro concept micro concept gate M $(-1/\infty + 1/\infty)$, in the micro concept world has righteous soul destination, wicked soul destination, in the micro concept me=I is located at the righteous soul, but also wicked soul. So long if righteous soul in the micro concept world then, the actor soul is the located at the bright side living, but if an actor lives as the wicked then the actor live at the dark place. So long the recognition of actor is a macro concept actor frame point of view. So long me=I is very important it is the me=I existed then all is governing the cosmos, it truly do not recognized then, me=I how important is not know, but to the realized actor know the important of me=I because, so long me=I is the master, so long, manage me=I, so long, do live righteously, help others etc. then the actor live in the bright place and time, this is the macro concept actor who is realized, so long the actor reach at the micro concept gate micro concept gate M $(-1/\infty + 1/\infty)$, the realized macro concept actor me=I managed oneself, but it is not easy in the living at the macro concept actor, so long, so then do not realized so long most macro concept actor, they follow the money making, so called the micro and macro energy, then all forget but also all of macro concept actor lives wicked circumstances. So long do not know the micro concept so that just developed all of making energy but forget all of existed soul so long micro concept world then do not realized then he must be still it is not mind is decreased but still macro concept actor mind is ∞, then

Macro concept actor is "soul + mind=∞ + body = mindful body= body" so long live fully mind all of desired to live, this actors are all try to make much money, so long the actor mind is∞, it means that the actor do not live righteously, so that he live all of actor's time fully for actor's own, but also but also the actor do not help others, so then, itself is wicked living, so long, the actor do not reach at the micro concept gate M $(-1/\infty + 1/\infty)$, so long, wicked actor in the macro concept so long, wicked actors are mind is ∞

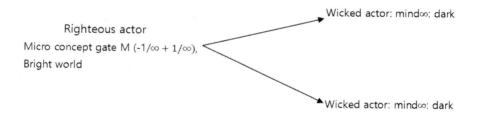

Righteous actor
Micro concept gate M $(-1/\infty + 1/\infty)$,
Bright world

Wicked actor: mind∞: dark

Wicked actor: mind∞: dark

Then me=I is in the side of the righteous actor, then if located at the wicked actor then it must be me=I live in the bright or dark. But actually do not know because of all of macro concept mind is ∞ then it is purpose all of ignorance actors, these actors are all general so long, macro actors are does not care of the micro concept world existed. Wicked actors are all so that all community actors are live as the wicked, so that the community all covered as the macro concept micro concept pair, so long all of these macro concept actors are all wicked so long, wicked soul in the micro concept then the community must be dark.

Me=I is located at the righteous actor living place, or wicked actor living place, so then me=I has the point of view, this is the in the macro concept actor life living, if a Me=I do live at the righteous then the actor do see all of righteous explained, so that the actor live at the bright place, but Me=I is located at the wicked actor place the actor has the eye to live on in the macro concept so long, the wicked soul living at the dark world, so long, the wicked soul is me=I then in the macro concept Me=I live in the point of wicked , all of means use for the make money, so long all of time concentrate to the make money.

Me=I instinctually want to live with righteous world, but also live in the bright areas, but Me=I have a desired to live rich, to make much money so then, to be that ways, Me=I do not have any time with others, wholly for oneself, but also, to save a money for the rich live do not give just anything, so then, Me=I get a rich so then he try to live as rich in the community, then, around of me=I all are wicked actors, so then, the wicked actor thinking is golden rule, so in the end all of the community has the hard living, but also all of the righteous actor treated as ridiculed, me=I is

wicked actor so then, the actor live wicked rule. The wicked actors do not reach at the micro concept point micro concept gate M $(-1/\infty + 1/\infty)$, the wicked actor also deceit so that fake micro concept point fake micro concept gate M $(-1/\infty$ (real is $- \infty$) $+ \frac{1}{\infty}$ (real is $- \infty$)) so that a wicked macro concept actors live at the fake micro concept point fake micro concept gate M $(-1/\infty$ (real is $- \infty$) $+ \frac{1}{\infty}$ (real is $+ \infty$)) , so then wicked actor get in the ways of wicked then it comes faced to be wicked.

2014.10.13

Topic: micro concept "soul= wicked 50%+ righteous 50%)"

$\frac{\infty}{0}$	**-1/∞ +1/∞**	**+∞/0**
Satan, hell	Human being micro concept	heaven kingdom
(Soul)	(Soul)	(Soul)
Time for others/human being		Time for righteous/human being
	Micro concept	
Wicked person	Human being Macro Concept	righteous person
(Soul)	(Soul+ mind + body)	(Soul)
Time for others/human being		Time for righteous/human being
	Macro concept	

In this micro concept explained as macro concept actor is "soul + mind + body= mindful body" so then until now, explained mind is wicked, in the micro concept was not cleared, but today on the way world place comes to me that soul is consist of wicked soul is 50%, righteous soul is 50% this is come to me. Now then comes macro concept actor is "soul (wicked 50%+righteous50%) + mind + body= mindful body" I'm fear of explain, until now just realized is mind is 1/∞ then it comes to soul + body = soulful body" it is simple, just variance is the only mind, but in this cases mind is 1/∞ then mind is disappeared then, it must be soul + body =soulful body" so then how to wicked soul + body= wicked soulful body, righteous soul + body= soulful body, then it must be very fear of mind is 1/∞ then comes, so worry. The realization then it must be reach at the micro concept point M (-1/∞ + 1/∞), it has been simple, just reach at the mind is 1/∞ then it must be combined between soul + body = soulful body = body. But now another variance the soul is wicked soul and righteous soul, wicked actor do not reach at the righteous terminal but the wicked soul will be take down a stop, but righteous actor go to the terminal. To be that righteous soul must be strong soul and energy is also much more than wicked soul. In this micro concept A birth of macro concept soul is consist of wicked soul 50%, righteous soul 50

But this macro concept lives in the macro concept world, to the finish then a matured actor can live righteous soul or wicked soul. How to be decided is live righteous or wicked soul. This is dare explained to be the in the micro concept actor living place wicked soul living destination, but also righteous soul eternity living destination.

The sure is macro concept actor is birth of soul consisted of wicked soul 50% righteous soul 50% + mind + body= mindful body" if do not realized then all of macro concept actor are recognized as the "mind + body= mindful body= body" but recognized of "soul + mind + body" then moment must be mind is $1/\infty$, then it comes two cases "wicked soul + mind = $1/\infty$ + body= wicked soulful body= body" but also " righteous soul + mind=$1/\infty$ + body= righteous soul" until now explained realized is the mind is $1/\infty$, then naturally righteous soul explained.

Wicked soul + mind=$1/\infty$ + body = wicked soul body = body ------- ①
Righteous soul + mind=$1/\infty$ + body = righteous soul body = body --------②

sort	Birth actor①	The old actor②	Realized actor③
Macro concept soul	Wicked, righteous	Wicked. wicked righteous	righteous
Micro concept soul	Wicked , righteous	Wicked. Wicked righteous	righteous

Birth actor ① is soul is birth as the wicked & soul half and half so then, secured from the both sided wicked soul, righteous soul, so then peace living temporally all occupied by the mind, so that in the birth effect time is peace with growing mind.

The old actor ② is grown in the macro concept world so that the old actor must be used all of the time and energy for the ways, then a actor live wicked, another actor are wicked & righteous soul

So long mind is still has the strong so that their wicked soul, but also wicked righteous soul, so that it is not sure of the realized soul.

Realized actor ③ this is realized actor, it is the really the mind is $1/\infty$ so long, it must be righteous soul is grow to the all occupied to righteous soul + body= so then righteous body= body. So then this realized actor reach at the micro concept point M ($-1/\infty + 1/\infty$), so then in the tunnel to the micro concept point

M ($-1/\infty + 1/\infty$), the actor live at the micro concept righteous soul living places, so that the realized actor only can go the eternity righteous soul reaching at the eternity soul destinations. Even if has the soul is wicked soul + righteous soul, but it is simplify then the way of the called as the macro concept actor is the "soul + mind + body" mind is $1/\infty$ then soul + body = soulful body is correct to the realized actor. So then micro concept actor is the still argue is the soul + body is clear. Just do righteous living is only under the realized soul only the righteous soul only live righteous. So then righteous actor is giving time, asset as the donor, helping others, sacrifices living, so then this is not easy, so the righteous actor lived righteous with realized. So then how to live is realized. So that, in the birth time wicked, righteous souls are divided to wicked soul $1/\infty$, but also righteous is∞, so then wicked, to be disappeared from a righteous actor, so then in this time naturally the "mind + wicked soul = wicked mind = mind=$1/\infty$, then the realized actor lived as the "righteous soul is ∞ = strong soul, wicked soul $1/\infty$ + mind is $1/\infty$ + body= realized soul= the righteous soul body= body" the simplified to the in the micro concept point is " righteous soul + body = righteous soulful body= body" this body strong soul, strong energy, this power righteous soul win to the all of disturb from the wicked soul and mind, so that it really getting the righteous soul getting at the micro concept point M ($-1/\infty + 1/\infty$), then the righteous soul is very strong, so that all of the Omni souls are weak wicked soul is not competed, so a strong righteous soul reach at any disturb or temptation.

But the old actor ② is not realized so that the macro concept actor "wick soul righteous soul + mind+ body" then if a actor live wicked actor is ∞, righteous soul is $1/\infty$ + mind + body = wicked soul body= wicked body", but also "wicked soul 50% righteous soul 50% + mind + body= wicked soul righteous soul body= wicked righteous body" so that in the macro concept actor of the lived to the end of living is wicked soul is captured to the deceit and seduced from the satanic souls, so then all of doing not realized actors are all in this categories. So long in the living of the righteous 50% + wicked 50% is consist of this soul is carried in the actor, wicked soul meet the wicked soul actors, so that satanic offence & defense, but also meet a righteous actor so that the righteous soul and wicked soul actor live in the point of view is neutrality living. But this soul is located at the wicked soul living destination because of the righteous soul is so fear of the wicked soul, so that wicked soul, not pure of righteous live with 50%, so that live as the neutrally living actor living at the micro concept actor living wicked soul living place.

Birth actor ① live in the macro concept world, most actor are time of the increased of the mind, so long mind is full=∞, so long this time is the also a hidden actor with mind, an actor soul wicked soul increased or righteous soul is increased is decided. Birth actor soul try to live righteous soul much better then wicked, but in during living righteous is increased but if a actor temptation and deceit from the satanic actors. So that all of deceit actor does not go for the righteous ways, do not realize all of time and asset just for the only used for the wicked actor sake. In conclusion to be live righteous then so called realized way to reach at the micro concept Micro concept point M (-1/∞ + 1/∞), a righteous actor fight to win the enemy "wicked soul + mind" then it comes to "righteous soul + body= realized body= soulful body" so then in the fight and win so long being a strong righteous soul is can reach at the micro concept point micro M (-1/∞ + 1/∞)

2014.10.14

Topic: macro concept "soul 40% body 60%)"

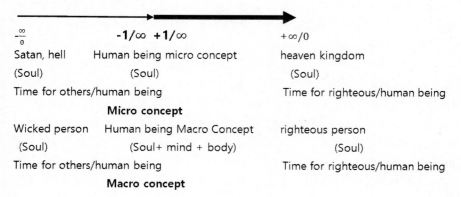

In this micro concept I have been writing, micro concept who leads this micro concept the actor is the "soul", in the macro concept lead actor who consist of "soul + mind + body", in the macro concept all of the behavior of getting energy. The energy use, then micro concept actor must be use, but also in the macro concept actor also "soul + mind + body" so then in the macro concept actor has the soul, so then in the macro also soul need to live, so then macro concept energy is used in the body's energy usages.

In the micro concept an actor live, then the soul is only actor but in the macro concept actor consist of "soul + mind +body' so long if ignorant in the forgotten of soul, so that made energy whole used for the body, so that 100% used up for the macro concept actor, energy is flow, so long in the macro concept actor the energy is flow among bodies. So that energy flows.

Energy flow just only bodies, so long body groups. Each body uses each of actor energy. All of energy 100% of energy is used for the exclusively body, this is the do not realized actors living.

But do realized actor reach at the micro concept point M $(-1/\infty + 1/\infty)$ all of the macro concept actor; soul + mind + body= realized actor then, mind is $1/\infty$, so long then it must be infer that mind is zero, then the realized actor is "soul + body= soul body= seen as body= body" so long, the realized actor energy must be to be realized then, the realized is shared with time, help other, then realized so then, it naturally it must be the time, asset, totality energy must be used shared with others, so long, it must be infer but in the macro concept actor living is 50% to 50% is equal, then but if soul 50%, body 50% then this is macro concept is body must be somewhat poor, so that this is maybe 60% is body, 40% is soul. So then realized actor may be used the macro actor energy, so then body use 60%, soul is about 40%, how to be this ways, the realized actor quantity concept is comes, it must be the % is not important, sometimes that 1% also meaningful to the righteous living.

Just for the soul, soul is 40% then, what is 40%, and then righteous is consist of time with others, but also help others. But also righteous actor personal time usages also, a actor has the time a day, is the 24 hours, so then, on the way my work place, 24 hours X 0.4= 9.6 hours. So long in the quantity concept at least used about 10 hours used for the soul. In the macro concept actor live 24 hours a day, this time is 14 hours is for the body sake, but 10 hours is for soul.

In the macro concept actor time usage is who blame if use all time in a day, then an actor do not slept all used time for the exclusively macro concept actor. Then the righteous actor time is very short to live with others. Then if a actor use 24 hours a day, then if a body used 24 hours a day then it must be not reach at the micro concept point M (-1/∞ + 1/∞), to live righteous living then it must be an actor time must be only use for him/herself, but 10 hours is for the soul. It must be soul 10 hours is may be sleeping is very important, so that soul free in the night time macro concept actor body sleeping then soul is live, so live must be care of the body, so then healthy and strong soul must be reach at the micro concept tunnel M (-1/∞ + 1/∞) it must be reach at the righteous soul traveling to the righteous soul, so long the righteous soul show in the dream. So long soul 40% energy usage is shared time, help others, so long it must be inferred to be then 8 o'clock used for the sleeping, but just 2 hours only for others, this is the just all of the general macro concept actor live it is so easy. Righteous soul, the reached at the micro concept point M (-1/∞ + 1/∞), so long at least shared with a actors a day 40% is used for soul, but it must be possible is can be more also, so long time table is

1	2	3	4	5	6	7	8	9	10	11	12
13	14	15	16	17	18	19	20	21	22	23	24

1~10 of green color is use for the soul, after 11~24 is for use body.

Who will read this book, then I'm strongly try to perfect follow it, in my case to live righteously then my time is 24 hours, so long, if I live fully use 24 hours then it must be I can't live righteously. So long, a actor me is my 24 hours is me, but who knows my time 24 hours is mine or just 24 hours is to the ignorant actor if I were ignorant actor then I can fully use my time as the 24 hours, but if I were in the righteous actor then it must be my time 24 hours is not mine, so long at least 60% is for me, other 40% is soul, 40% soul is righteous act time, help others time, so long strength my soul then I have to enough sleep. So then 10 hours of soul is very important to live in the macro concept body also be health.

To be lives righteous then keeps a road, ways of the righteous soul living. So long time a big segment is soul time live soul excitement 10 hours in a day, 14 hour of mine then in the future also 14 hours are segment to me, 14 hours is 100% then 14hours is 1005 then 60 % is 8 hours a day is for exclusively for the actor but also used 6 hours to the souls, so then this soul is used for the making money then, the money is not me, but souls, so then souls time is 6 hours, so then my income is not me, so that to be righteous then the income of 40% must be use for others then I'm sorry that is not be doing, but to be righteous so long to be righteous, 40 % soul usage is very essential for the righteous soul living.

Righteous actor time is 100% then it is divided to actor body 60%, soul 40 % Then in the micro concept actor has the stages so long reach at the micro concept point reach so then micro concept point M $(-1/\infty + 1/\infty)$, it must be infer to that in the percentage ratio is the micro concept quality explained then it must be in the macro concept explained.

M1 = a righteous actor 100= 100 times= body 60%= 60 times, soul 40% =40times
      Then just 60%= 100 %, so long
M2 = A righteous actor use 60 times as 100% = body 60%, soul 40% =24 times
      Then just actor use 36 hours as 100%
M3 = a righteous actor 36 times as 100% = body 60%, soul 40% = 14.4 = 15 times
      Then just actor use 19 times as 100%
M4 = a righteous actor 19 times as the 100% = body is 60%, soul 40% = 7.6= 8 times
      Then just actor use 11times as the 100%

M5 = A righteous actor 11 times as 100% = body is 60%, soul 40% =4.4 =5 times
      Then just actor 6 times as 100%

M6 = A righteous actor 6 hours as 100% = body is 60%, soul 40% = 2.4= 3 times
      Then just actor 3 times as 100%

M7 = A righteous actor 3 hours as 100% = body is 60^, soul 40%= 1.2 = 2 times
      Then just actor 1 times as 100%

M8 = a righteous actor 1 hours as 100% = body is 60%, soul 40% = 0.4= 1 time
      Then just actor 0 times as 100% = body is 60%, soul 40% = 0 = 0 times

M9 = just a righteous soul 0 hours is 100 = then in this micro concept world so called

Soul is not used energy so called time, so that after come to the micro concept world then

All of use the time soul, so long the realized actor gradually increased to using for the soul, so long, M1 M2 M3 M4 .... M n then it increased to the soul sake, so long in this to be live as the righteous soul, so long then the realized actor time, help other is in the end the major work in the macro concept actor. It must be inferred to in the macro concept actor living is getting old, but also getting rich then for the realized actor shared with other time, and asset, so then around of the righteous actor then, all of the actors are excitement and being perfect.

Part 2

" Micro Concept(-1/∞ +1/∞) " built
Macro Concept Actor Progress

Macro concept actor formed "soul + body"

⇩

Macro concept actor formed "soul +mind + body"

⇩

**Macro concept actor formed of "Wicked soul 50%
righteous soul 50% +mind100 + body 100%"**

2014.10.15

Topic: macro concept "husband & wife"

$-\frac{\infty}{0}$ $-1/\infty$ $+1/\infty$ $+\infty/0$

Satan, hell   Human being micro concept   heaven kingdom

(Soul)   (Soul)   (Soul)

Time for others/human being   Time for righteous/human being

Micro concept

Wicked person   Human being Macro Concept   righteous person

(Soul)   (Wicked Soul50 righteous soul 50 +mind 100+body100)   (Soul)

Time for others/human being   Time for righteous/human being

Macro concept

In this micro concept the important actor is soul; this soul is actor, so long so feel happy and unhappy. In the micro concept world has two world, one is righteous world, other is wicked world. In the micro concept actor live between righteous soul resident and wicked residents in the righteous, wicked world. Then eternity world micro concept is required for the perfection is husband soul and wife soul these souls are separated in the macro concept world, so then after full lived at the macro concept world, then it must be reach at the micro concept world, so then husband & wife soul are meet just husband wife soul one is being then goes to the eternity destination of micro concept world. To be perfect it required husband & wife souls, so long in the micro concept world husband & wife soul get to the perfection, this perfection create of excitement so then, husband &wife soul is excitement state.

So long in the macro concept actor world, husband and wife live at the macro concept world, so long to be safe, and keep a rule, but also not to be sin, but also live safe is man and woman, husband wife so that marriage living is secure of safe, perfection living, if not marriage then it must be the imperfection, but also unsafe, but getting forming of the husband & wife is the perfection & excitement, husband wife is the perfect

Man is seek woman, woman seek man = marriage

Man   woman

Marriage husband& wife

Before marriage then the man unsafe, somewhat imperfect, the same as woman is so long to be perfect and safes, man and woman try to be perfect and safe, meet man & woman as a husband & wife. So some what it is similar to the a birth macro actor come to the unseen world to Seen world of a macro concept world, then surprised to the actor, the actor thought that a soul of actor will meet body so the soul lead the body, the body must be sure of perfection to live at the micro concept world righteous soul destination living but

The birth actor is "soul + mind + body = so long mindful body= body" so that soul live hard in the macro concept world, mind is∞, but soul is$1/\infty$, it goes to the micro concept world to the wicked soul world, but if mind is$1/\infty$ then soul is ∞ this strong soul is can have a energy to move to get over the all of obstacle so then reach at the righteous soul destination.

So long is very similar of the marriage in the macro concept world, so long, after get marriage is man + woman get marriage so then husband + wife = husband wife. So that the bride & bridegroom expects to live excitement & perfection, but soon after unaccustomed to children comes so that it comes in the husband wife is "husband + children + wife" so then it must be equate as

Soul + mind + body = husband + children + wife,

To be reach at the micro concept point M $(-1/\infty + 1/\infty)$, it must be in the Soul + mind + body, then mind is $1/.\infty$= about to zero, then it comes "soul +body = soulful body= body" this body reach at the micro concept point M $(-1/\infty + 1/\infty)$

Then to reach at the micro concept point of husband wife then it must be children=$1/\infty$ = about children is zero then it comes to the husband + wife = husband &wife= soulful husband & wife = husband & wife reach at the micro

343

concept point M (-1/∞ + 1/∞)

Then mind is 1/∞, children is 1/∞

Mind is about zero is the all of the realize then, the mind is come to about zero, so long the children = 1/∞, about to zero, so then children=0, so long children is zero then husband wife must be realized then husband wife reach at the micro concept point M (-1/∞ + 1/∞)

How to the children get to 1/∞=0, children is the still in the actor is the 50% righteous, 50% wicked soul, so it must be children to be 1/∞, then righteous soul is∞ wicked soul 1/∞ then it must be inferred to be the husband wife be excitement & perfect, then children is compare to mind, so then children is composed to "wicked soul 50% + righteous soul 50% + mind + body" then "wicked soul 1/∞ +righteous soul∞ + mind1/∞ + body= then righteous body= children" then " husband + children + wife" changed to the Husband + children righteous soul ∞ + wife" then it comes just husband wife be reach at the excitement and perfection.

Husband wife is reach at the micro concept M (-1/∞ + 1/∞), actually to be excitement perfection then "husband = soul+ mind = body = husband, wife= soul + mind + body= body, wife" Children = soul + mind + body = mindful body = mindful children'

So long, to be righteous living in the macro concept world, but also this is lead to the micro concept world, so long the condition is

Sort of souls	Wicked % righteous%	Wicked % righteous%	Wicked % righteous%
Husband soul	Wicked 100 righteous0	Wicked 50 righteous50	Wicked 0 righteous100
Wife soul	Wicked 100 righteous0	Wicked 50 righteous50	Wicked 0 righteous100
Children soul	Wicked 100 righteous0	Wicked 50 righteous50	Wicked 0 righteous100

In the living of the wicked 50% righteous 50% so then it must be this beginning soul are grow to the wicked 100% righteous 0%, but also the wicked 0% righteous 100%, then this combination is husband wife and children is combined to husband wife to be righteous living then

Husband: Wicked 0% righteous100%
Wife: Wicked 0% righteous100%
Children: Wicked 0% righteous100%

To be reach at the micro concept actor of the husband wife then this equations comes

Husband: Wicked 0% righteous100% + Children: Wicked 0% righteous100% + Wife: Wicked 0% righteous100% = this is so ideal but in the micro concept world righteous soul living place eternity living then come to the excitement & perfection accomplishment. In the end the living is based on the righteous. Then the righteous is composed of the time shared with others & helping other etc. so then the husband wife will go to the eternity of righteous soul Living places.

Husband wife is infer to the micro concept point world, so then husband wife between husband and wife is micro concept tunnel micro concept point M $(-1/\infty + 1/\infty)$, if a husband is live at the righteous + wife is live at righteous then the infer of the micro concept world is forming the micro concept world micro concept point M $(-1/\infty + 1/\infty)$, so long in the end the micro concept point is reach at the then, husband wife has the micro concept frame but between husband & wife comes micro concept point M $(-1/\infty + 1/\infty)$.

2014.10.16

Topic: macro concept "decision makings"

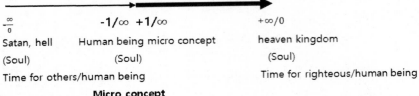

$-\frac{\infty}{0}$ **-1/∞ +1/∞**   +∞/0

Satan, hell   Human being micro concept   heaven kingdom

(Soul)   (Soul)   (Soul)

Time for others/human being   Time for righteous/human being

           Micro concept

Wicked person   Human being Macro Concept   righteous person

(Soul)   (Wicked Soul50 righteous soul 50 +mind 100+body100)   (Soul)

Time for others/human being   Time for righteous/human being

           Macro concept

In this micro concept try to say of the unseen world connected to the Seen world. The macro concept world actor breathes every moment, and then it also decides every moment. Macro concept decision making is recognized or unrecognized moment decide is occurred, what is related with the micro concept. The bus run by the drivers driving, so then, the bus run well on the road. But if a driver does not decide optimistically then the bus will be run out of the road. Then the bus delay to reach at the destination. Or it make worse than the bus will not reach at the destination.

The moment decision making is just like breathe so long, uncountable decide among decide how decide is kept running on the road or out of road decided.

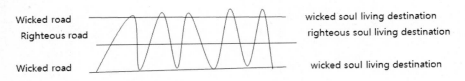

Wicked road   wicked soul living destination

Righteous road   righteous soul living destination

Wicked road   wicked soul living destination

The macro concept world a actor live as every second moment breaths so macro concept actor move the direction by decision making in a seconds. For the sake of the benefit of the actors then macro concept actor decide wicked decide but also righteous. So long, without recognition then naturally decide by an actor's the sine curve decide, so long righteous living is not easy because of the righteous road all has give to used it, but all of actor run for the easy way. Then breakaway of the actor, righteous decide is followed as sacrifice, then even hard to run but to running on the righteous road, consciously decide to the righteous even higher pay to run, so that as possible as actors save the cost, out of the righteous road. Then out of the righteous road then the actor already in the road of the wicked road, wicked road is cost must be chief so then, actor choose the wicked ways. The realized actor must be the mind is $1/\infty$, so long the calculation of the trading profit mind must be disappeared so long, micro concept actor soul is behavior then, the micro concept actor live in the micro concept world, which is realized actor or lived end of macro concept actor, so long the actor lived righteously. So long in the micro concept point M $(-1/\infty + 1/\infty)$, place can live the soul, so that the soul is major actor so long, the righteous decision actor must be mind of trading profit is $1/\infty$, almost zero in mind, so long realized actor live conscious righteous decide. Actually righteous decide is the decide actor is not body, but soul, so that righteous decide then naturally righteous soul decide.

Righteous soul decide in the micro concept point world point M $(-1/\infty + 1/\infty)$, so long this is the pipe line connect to micro concept righteous soul destination so long micro concept point M $(-1/\infty + 1/\infty)$, is righteous souls living place, so that in the micro concept actor righteous souls are react so then the righteous actor move on the righteous road.

But if a wicked soul decides in the macro concept point world all of actor decided by trading profit, so out of recognized actor follows momentum of the advantage position so that the actor live the direction of running a road. So that

Realized actor running road

The direct line is the righteous actor so long realized actor move so that, the realized actor run on the direct road so that, do not care of trading profit getting mind, mind must be $1/\infty$, so long run by soul so that righteous soul keep living righteous, so long, soul expect to reach at the righteous soul destination. But the wicked soul actor the mind is ∞ so then trading profit is prefer to other value, so that the for the profit, the decision is shift in a moment, so many time changed the directions. The decision maker runs the curve road. the followed profit actor just do not have any time for others, and further more cause of short of time, but also very hurry due to the direction is moment changed mostly wicked multiple decide is all is differ

The wicked decisions are all of variable so that if a new ways need to newly knowledge, but also another wicked decide also again a new knowledge so that, the wicked decision makers are all haven't time for others, the wicked decision is follows of the trading profit, so then a wicked decide actor calculate balance then not on the losing but all the time winning position then, the wicked decide actor do not help others perfectly.

But the righteous decision is very simple the one way move, so it don't have to get a new knowledge but all of the righteous actor just follows of the righteous, so long, just go with others, but also help others, so long help means that other also help me, so long all of actors are live in the macro concept world righteous living. So long the realized actor run for the straight line.

This is the soulful story so that wicked actor decide or righteous decide, so then wicked decide is much faster than righteous decide. The righteous decide means that the speed is slow, but wicked is decision speed is fast

①The righteous momentum decide time

②The wicked momentum decide time

The righteous momentum decide time ① is somewhat delayed compared to ②The wicked momentum decide times so long, the righteous decide is consciously righteous which is connect to the righteous soul micro concept place actor moving. But wicked moment decide is so fast because of the getting momentum benefits. To make a benefit so quickly decide not to be lost the optimistic time, so that the fast decision actor related to the wicked decide.

2014.10.17

Topic: macro concept "husband & wife 2"

$-\frac{\infty}{0}$ **-1/∞ +1/∞**   **+∞/0**

Satan, hell   Human being micro concept   heaven kingdom

(Soul)   (Soul)   (Soul)

Time for others/human being   Time for righteous/human being

Micro concept

Wicked person   Human being Macro Concept   righteous person

(Soul)   (Wicked Soul50 righteous soul 50 +mind 100+body100)   (Soul)

Time for others/human being   Time for righteous/human being

Macro concept

In this micro concept, macro concept actors are what relationship is really help for the micro concept actor living, the husband wife is the source of peace and safe, just only single is unsafe and is not perfect but as the husband wife is the perfect. So then in the macro concept relationships are most important. This really important relationship is created in the macro concept world, husband is male, and wife is female, this male is "soul 100, + mind100+ body100=body of male, husband" another female is also "soul100+ mind100+ body100= body of female, wife" these two actors are created husband wife being, so then husband wife is made of this "man soul 50 female soul50=husband wife soul 100 + husband wife mind100+ husband wife body100= husband wife" here is comes male soul 100, female soul 100, husband wife soul 100 so that it comes natural so that micro concept world experience soul male 100, female soul 100, so long these experience husband 50 soul + wife 50 soul = meet to husband wife soul 100, so then in the husband wife soul, until then, righteous soul or wicked soul, so then, if husband soul consist of the wicked soul 50, righteous soul 50, wife soul also consist of wicked soul 50 righteous soul50, then a husband wife is meet husband righteous soul 50 wife righteous soul then righteous soul husband wife is formed. So then soul is comes to "husband righteous soul50 wife righteous soul50 + husband wife mind100+ husband wife body100= husband wife" in the macro concept life voyage, in the

Husband wife life voyage of souls

Sort	①0~30 years	②31~60 years	③61~90 years
Macro concept	Male righteous soul Male wicked soul	Husband wife soul	Husband wife righteous soul Husband wife wicked soul
Micro concept	Male righteous soul Male wicked soul	Husband wife soul	Husband wife righteous soul Husband wife wicked soul

The husband wife life souls are ①0~30 years, ②31~60 years, ③61~90 years and finally it revealed to macro concept world a husband wife temporally segregated in the change d to the macro concept actor to micro concept actors, so then an early reached at micro concept world actor wait a pair of each souls, so then husband wife soul is lived as righteous or wicked, is revealed in the criteria of the macro concept world and micro concept world. But the husband wife soul gradually grows after comes to husband wife, then

Husband wife righteous and wicked mind (variance)

Sort	Husband soul	Mind(variance)	Wife soul
Righteous living	Righteous soul Wicked soul	Mind is reach at $1/\infty = 0$ Husband righteous soul Wife righteous soul	Righteous soul Wicked soul
Wicked living	Righteous soul Wicked soul	Mind is reach at$\infty = \infty$ Husband wicked soul Wife wicked soul	Righteous soul Wicked soul

So then husband wife righteous soul living comes from righteous husband and wife husband with the variances of mind variances is reach at $1/\infty$, but also the actor of the husband wife is righteous soul combined to the husband wife, but wicked living is wicked actors of the husband and wife but also this husband wife mind is so huge to∞, so that husband wife and personal souls is so deep related with, personal actor soul factor: righteous actor, wicked actor, then husband wife actor are in the righteous soul or wicked soul comes, so then each actor must be sacrifice for others souls, then strongly love each other then it must be the righteous soul ways. So long the husband wife righteous soul, so then the soul of strong, health is based on pure, each soul, loyalty then husband wife soul being healthy.

So long the end of macro concept world is then it must be go for the micro concept world, so long the healthy husband wife is based on the strong love, then love is the sacrifice, so long love is not mind, but love is the soul behavior, so long it really the husband wife be righteous then, righteous soul, so long righteous soul strong then, it must be infer, the micro concept point is M $(-1/\infty + 1/\infty)$, so then the husband wife righteous strong soul reach at the micro concept point, so then within in the micro concept point world point M $(-1/\infty + 1/\infty)$, so long the husband wife comes to live in the time of macro concept point actor then, macro concept actor strong soul move to the overcomes of obstacles then reach at the point world point M $(-1/\infty + 1/\infty)$, so long husband wife soul live in the soulful world, so long even body live but mind is $1/\infty$ so long, so long comes " soul + body= soulful body" mind is 0, so that soul is ∞ then strong soul live at the micro concept point world point M $(-1/\infty + 1/\infty)$, the righteous husband wife soul live at the micro concept world, so that macro concept actor soul meet a righteous soul in the micro concept world, so long, in the micro concept world lord heavenly father soul, so that strong blessed. these macro concept actors are living as righteous so that god orders to helping others. So then in the macro concept actor helping others, shared time others, so long, this is, how glory to the husband wife righteous living, even the simple of the personal macro concept righteous living is somewhat simple but live two actor of one of husband wife is hard to live that, in the end of it originally each actor live righteous this is basic, this personal righteous soul so that another actor is husband wife righteous soul, so then, to live as husband wife righteous living then, the three actors are husband wife righteous soul, husband soul, wife soul, three righteous souls. So long husband wife righteous living is itself is a big energy. This energy is husband wife accumulated a righteous behavior to accumulated blessing bank in the micro concept world blessing bank, so long, in this righteous soul living is not easy. But wicked soul actor deceit so sometimes easy but also the wicked actor live easily, but righteous living is so hard, what is differences so long, in the macro concept actor of wicked, so long happy pleasure but all of energy is dependent but to the righteous actor are hard living all of independent so long, what is the backup, so long, in the end the righteous soul has the soulful rich, this is the even live at the hard but in the soulful world actor is very excitement and so long reach at the perfection. Husband wife is a source of righteous is a strong guarantee this guarantee is make peace, and safe, this a big soul rich then, the righteous soul cover the husband wife ground, in the ground living actors are live excitement with peace and happy live, this is all of righteous behavior's micro concept actors major souls play. The major actor's playing a major role. So long all of righteous behavior repay back from righteous souls.

2014.10.20

Topic: micro concept "energy"

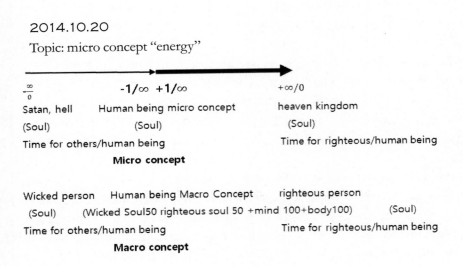

In this micro concept, micro point world M $(-1/\infty + 1/\infty)$, how to operated, the energy of the micro concept energy is calculated by $E=mc^2$, so long in the micro concept world $E=mc^2$,

$= 1/\infty \times C\,2 = c2/\infty =$ it must be same as the M is be as $1/\infty$ so long then $e= 1/\infty$

In the micro concept the energy is $1/\infty$, so then in the micro concept world total energy is $1/\infty$

Actually the micro concept world is the M $(-1/\infty + 1/\infty)$, so long then in this space is M $(-1/\infty + 1/\infty)$, so then the micro concept world moving energy is also $1/\infty$, so long micro living actor moving energy is also $1/\infty$, then in the micro concept world is M $(-1/\infty + 1/\infty)$,, the management energy is also $1/\infty$, the micro concept actor consuming energy is also $1/\infty$, but the micro concept world is M $(-1/\infty + 1/\infty)$, so then macro concept energy is $E=mc^2$

Then macro concept energy is m=not $1/\infty$, so then it must be $E=mc^2$

$M = \infty =$ then $E = m = \infty c2 = c2 \times \infty = c2\infty$, then macro concept world is huge energy required. But also it has the macro energy. But in the micro concept world energy is $1/\infty$, so long, the macro is limited but micro is infinite so long soul goes to the infinite,

$-\dfrac{\infty}{0}$ $-1/\infty$ $+1/\infty$ $+\infty/0$

Satan, hell   Human being micro concept   heaven kingdom

Micro concept world is to show then " ⬭ "this micro concept world" so long but the soul is not dead, but living, so that micro concept so that in the micro concept world actor live at the micro concept point world M ($-1/\infty + 1/\infty$), in this micro concept actor live so long, the actor of micro concept actor unseen actor, but the actors are go living with a place, so long in the macro concept actor live as the forming the macro concept actor "soul + mind + body = body" then the soul is macro concept actors minor role player but body is major player.

Micro concept actor soul lives at the righteous soul living places, but also wicked soul living place, so long the soul is forming the

sort	①Before birth	②After birth	③After dead
Macro concept world		Minor/wicked+ righteous soul	
Micro concept world	Wicked + righteous soul	Righteous & Wicked soul/connect to macro souls	Righteous world soul &Wicked world soul Eternity destination

Soul is located until now so not know it, but soul is same as cycle of living, in this living soul energy is about to $1/\infty$, so long micro concept actor soul is does not use energy compared with macro concept world. But the energy sources is origin of the righteous energy is righteous behavior it is connected to the in the micro concept blessed bank, so long in the macro concept world righteous behavior for other time shared, but also help others, so long love neighbors, so then the behavior changed to the in the micro concept world blessed bank.

But the wicked soul also ahs the energy soul source is in the micro concept world wicked soul destination then, wicked soul world cursed bank saving, so in the macro concept world wicked behavior naturally stored to the cursed bank.

It must be infer that ①Before birth, the soul comes to meet the body, so then, soul is consist of the, the must be infer also, the micro concept world righteous actor 50%, but also wicked soul actor 50 combined to be made of righteous & wicked soul before come to the meet the one soul so long actually in the right birth time is "soul + body= infant" so long, so soul do not use energy in the macro concept world, so long, in the infant is balanced wicked and righteous, but after that the infant live the nutrient for the growth is when the energy helped from the parents saved energy is used, so then if the parents saved energy in the blessing bank or cursed bank then, the infant is grow unseen world, so long, most parents are also so young so long, then it must be infer that blessing bank energy used, the parents filial duty well so then it accumulated at the blessed bank, but if a youth do not well filial duty then, it must be somewhat wicked then just low wicked then, the infant living is must be infer to the righteous soul infant, so long, the soul living energy is not used for manage itself, but soul operate of the give the soulful blessing but also soulful saving energy to the righteous soul saving in the blessing bank, but also wicked then wicked bank cursed bank saving role, so long, the soul is role for the connect to the macro to micro concept world.

③After birth then the soul must be from infant to grow youth but also, get marriage then the macro concept soul is single mature, but also double mature is comes, then, so long, in the single time, the male, female single must be auto behavior, all is decided the living the righteous living is most good and band is mixed, so then, still has the half wicked half righteous, so long usual living, but male female meet to live the marriage so then, male & female combine to marriage couple. So long this couple live then two soul are live in the macro concept world two actors, but the soul is mixed male & female actors, so long soul is just like cloudy forming, so long soul is mixed with male & female, so long the soul is so strong so that, marriage soul is must be also recognition to the macro concept world and micro concept world, so that, in this soul is male soul 1, female soul2, male & female 3, so long this soul very strong soul then, it must be righteous soul, due to strong soul is love each other strongly, loving is effect man and woman, so long man is for the woman and woman for man, then so long male and female love, so that, both side is safe, strong peace, this is the role for the soul act, if strong love each other then, it must be itself is righteous, if male and female live strongly then each male so excitement but also female is so big excitement, in the end male& female must go for the micro concept world live excitement and perfection. Just love each other purely so long, and then the husband wife soul is live righteous eternity. Male and female meeting is also body to body, but also soul to soul, so then this is very usual but this is secret but it is very if love deep in this macro concept world then, it goes to the husband wife righteous eternity, because love each other then, each soul is excitement but also husband wife soul is excitement so then, live is sacrifice but also male and female help each others, so long, this is very simple, the pure love then it must give to the actor righteous eternity living. Why deep in pair loving is given to the righteous soul eternity living is each male has the "righteous 50 wicked 50 + mind 100 + body100= male" combined "righteous 50 wicked 50 + mind 100 + body100= female" to husband wife, so long, just male & female is overcomes of the wicked 50 and mind 100, so that the loving each other is really realized so then know the value of loving, so long, deep love is the mixed with so righteous factors, so long in the micro concept world soul, then the reach at the micro concept point then it must be micro concept point world M $(-1/\infty + 1/\infty)$, so long wicked 50 + mind 100 is so long it comes to the a deep love marriage actor must be complete excitement & perfection so long "male righteous soul + body" + "female righteous soul + body" = so long husband wife soul + husband wife body= husband wife body.

③After dead, the righteous marriage soul go for the righteous soul destination but also wicked marriage soul for the wicked soul destination.

All of soul is same as the in the macro concept living but also micro concept world, soul is not dead, soul is live eternity. During soul live then any energy is not consumed due to e=1/∞.

2014.10.21

Topic: macro concept "love"

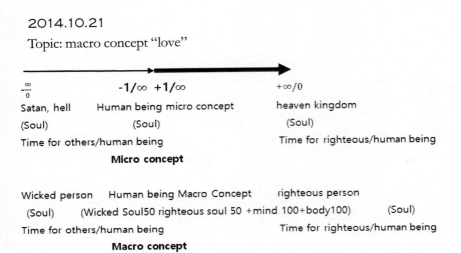

In this micro concept the actor is soul, soul feel so pure mind, if some of blemish then soul can feel not pure. Soul is all of process of the macro concept actor living, but also the soul estimated of soul perfection. The perfection soul can see what happened in the macro concept world. All of the actors living also just like elementary school graduator as middle school student all covers the elementary course, the same as the micro concept soul get perfection to the macro concept actors. In the micro concept world righteous world, wicked world eternity destination of the soul is pair, so long in the macro concept male and female, so long husband wife, this perfection soul estimated itself, naturally belongs in the righteous soul, but wicked soul, so long, if not then, in the macro concept world pair actor do not live righteous then surly never problems to be wicked soul world, but in the pair a actor is righteous, the other is wicked then, in the soul world do not live macro concept world pair because of located at the eternity in the righteous soul world, but also wicked soul world segregated, so then macro concept pair each actor dead is not same so that a soul first go the other soul after going, in this time also has a variance, so long, but it must not be wicked to righteous so that, righteous to righteous, so long, a male is righteous then a male died then he must be wait female comes to micro concept world, then already comes as the righteous then, a female is wicked then, eternity segregate, forever do not meet, because of the actor eternity world is not changed, so long, in the micro concept world meet, a righteous female and righteous male, to combined to pair, then going eternity living. So long, all of macro concept actor live variably, after death a pair then remained pair will be marriage to others, then it is the end of the macro concept world, but the pair is being righteous is also has, but in this a new changed marriage partner then, still wicked then, the pair must be going to the micro concept world wicked soul destination, in this cases first dead soul, how to do, then it must be changed in the micro concept world, so long righteous a partner change to another righteous soul, being changed, so long, the righteous is soulful righteous is not same, so long in the macro concept world, pair is live each other righteous, then it must be the pair live deep strong love, so that the energy is must be not switch husband wife, so long it really loved in the macro concept world then do not segregate each other even death, so long, the righteous actor live love other partner then, it must be righteous, so long, the actor must be meaningful live, because of micro concept actor soul, which be helped from the micro concept world righteous souls, the pair of macro actor deep love then, a deep relationship.

Macro concept world actor "love" then love is the peak of the word in the macro concept world, so long, love is definite as all of actor of righteous which is shared time, and give others, sacrifice others, so this mixed express is "love" so long this valuable "love" give to others then, the love giver is already is realized, so long love other than a actor, of a real lover must be infer that the actor reach at the micro concept actor concept point world M $(-1/\infty + 1/\infty)$, this unseen a moment so long, in the marriage time to get loves others, then in a moment reach at the micro concept point, so that being the pair of soul unify for the pair of souls. So long in the micro concept actor live as loving relationship, the marriage actors are love deep then, it must be feel of the souls are feel perfect feel, so long, loving as pair, this is permitted to love each others, but this is very simple do love, then all understand each other, just perfect love, so long love is the really excitement so that if the 100% pure love each other then it reach at the perfection so long, then accurate perfection love excitement, so long, love is excitement then this effect both macro concept actor and micro concept actors, so long, love is not same as the sex, but love is the excitement of souls, soul live eternity so long, if do love truly pure, then perfect pure then, actually in the micro concept point concept point world M (-1/∞ + 1/∞), reach. So long, micro concept and macro concept is tunnel so long micro actor soul macro concept actor minor soul meets in the micro concept tunnel, so long, "true pure love" makes excitement macro concept actor or micro concept actor, so long, so then in the concept of micro, so then, if micro concept actor has the righteous actor soul destination then, eternity living is pleasure then how to make it, so long, just macro loving excitement of perfection, then in the micro concept world, righteous souls live eternity for long time live happy, then micro concept righteous soul actor pair of husband wife of righteous deep in love, so then it is the eternity excitement & perfection, so long righteous is the real love based then, the love is the excitement engine so long, the righteous blessing bank saved account is kept for the eternity excitement living energy. This is the perfection then, the actor of righteous soul has blessing energy, and this energy is the gift related with righteous actor eternity king order, so long, righteous soul living energy is eternity is don't use but, the pair of excitement soul, has the blessing others, so this is special benevolent, this is the give to the righteous macro concept actor helping, soul energy is used for the righteous actor saving in the hard time, so then, in the macro concept actor feel that miracle so long, the righteous actor did best all of righteous actor so then it must be need just little knowledge so long but, also then just tip helped by the micro concept actor righteous gift to the macro concept real righteous actors. But if a macro actor lives wicked then a wicked actor dead then it must be located at the wicked soul destination eternity wicked world, so long the wicked soul itself saved as the wicked soul destination of the cursed bank saving. So that the wicked soul actor curse the wicked actor of the wicked behavior, so long wicked actor curse wicked actor soul, so long it is the knows the see is seen just of the wicked actor know wicked soul, so that, wicked actor must be cursed by the wicked soul. In conclusion is macro concept world wicked actor cursed from the wicked micro concept world wicked soul actor, so that wicked soul cursed to macro concept actor living curse, the micro concept actor try to give power to the macro concept wicked actor, so long macro actor received cursed energy then it is must be packed as good but in the end the power is ruined to so long wicked and finally as cursed. But also righteous soul is help blessing energy to the righteous macro concept actor. Here is very strong come to righteous soul is macro concept macro concept righteous actor, but also in the macro concept actor live wicked then the wicked actor influenced within the micro concept wicked soul related.

Love is the righteous souls so that husband wife is really deep relationship; love itself is the excitement so long love is the get at the perfection. Wicked is even live as the pair then, the pair does not love truly so that even couple but do not love, so long each other live wicked in the end the couple must be live as the life of the wicked so then false love each others. So long in the macro concept world love is not easy because of the personal basis is not righteous, so long the pair of the husband wife hard to love pure love, if a part are righteous then, the righteous help wicked soul, then it can be husband wife being same righteous or wicked, so long righteous actor must be role of the strong then, in the coming of the micro concept world then, husband wife influence righteous then it comes to the perfect, so long, very well, husband wife is really important to live righteous ling in the micro concept world, love is the key to live righteous or not. So that righteous loving each other is the key role of the being live at the micro concept world righteous living eternity.

2014.10.22

Topic: micro concept "depth"

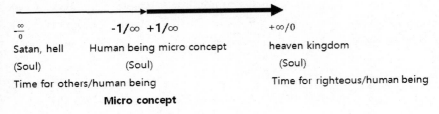

-∞/0   **-1/∞ +1/∞**   +∞/0

Satan, hell   Human being micro concept   heaven kingdom

(Soul)   (Soul)   (Soul)

Time for others/human being   Time for righteous/human being

Micro concept

Wicked person   Human being Macro Concept   righteous person

(Soul)   (Wicked Soul50 righteous soul 50 +mind 100+body100)   (Soul)

Time for others/human being   Time for righteous/human being

Macro concept

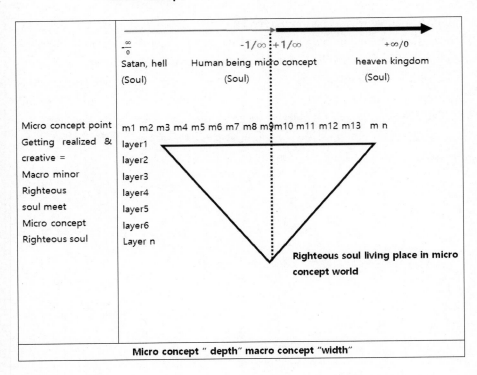

-∞/0   -1/∞ +1/∞   +∞/0

Satan, hell   Human being micro concept   heaven kingdom

(Soul)   (Soul)   (Soul)

Micro concept point | m1 m2 m3 m4 m5 m6 m7 m8 m9 m10 m11 m12 m13 m n

Getting realized & | layer1

creative = | layer2

Macro minor | layer3

Righteous | layer4

soul meet | layer5

Micro concept | layer6

Righteous soul | Layer n

Righteous soul living place in micro concept world

Micro concept " depth" macro concept "width"

In this micro concept how to use, the micro concept is can be help the macro concept the point concept of living ways is this, just travel to the deep, not wide, so then micro concept actor do not travel other all the time is situation at the micro concept point, micro concept point strength means that going propound, deep in the realization, so long, micro concept point, gate, tunnel as express concept point world M $(-1/\infty + 1/\infty)$, micro concept point is started and realized as the time concept so long, in the micro concept point melt of past, future just mixed past and future is present, so then it is comes to me the micro concept point, micro concept must be explained in the macro concept world, divided to unseen world, so long, seen unseen world is macro concept world and micro concept world. Then in the micro concept point traveling, and macro concept world travel is explained to macro concept point actor travel to a place is do not reach at the micro concept gate, so long this is the unrealized actor do not know the micro concept so long, just pursue of the macro concept actors main interesting is getting the energy getting, so all of time is only used for the energy getting safe, but in the micro concept world so called realized so long reach at the micro concept point, gate, tunnel concept point world M $(-1/\infty + 1/\infty)$,, then micro concept actor travel to the through micro concept gate concept point world M $(-1/\infty + 1/\infty)$, the realized actor, micro concept gate is the start to travel just like the station to the travel start, all of the macro actor start from birth to the a place macro concept is body is main actor so that most birth actor travel to the end of actor so long, macro actor feel that do not know the micro concept world so long macro concept actor end of macro concept world is dead.

But macro concept world actor also realized then, the righteous actor and soul is reach at the micro concept gate concept point world M $(-1/\infty + 1/\infty)$, so that micro concept actor soul travel in the micro concept tunnel to the micro concept righteous soul living destination.

Micro concept "depth" macro concept "width" diagram, the vertical travel to the micro concept gate passed actor move to the strong soul, the righteous soul actor but still the actor is has body.

So long macro concept actor has the minor is soul so long, just mind is $1/\infty$ so long even macro concept actor mind is minor but if a reach at the mind is $1/\infty$ the "soul 50 + body50 = soulful body= body" so long, the realized macro concept actor travel through micro concept tunnel micro concept point world M $(-1/\infty + 1/\infty)$, so long micro concept tour road is also lied, so that micro concept actor strong soul of righteous soul move on the micro concept actor soul road.

The road has the station, or stops, so then it is the layer of realized but also creature also, so long, this micro concept road stop, station is the a righteous actor get a creature products to the macro concept actor usages but also cultural, or religious but also philosophical relics, so long a realized actor wrote book for helping macro concept actor realized living.

The realized actor hardly arrive at the micro concept point then, the macro concept actor hard, sacrifice, help others, shared time love pure, but also concentration all of time for the creative art, technology etc. the righteous realized actor reach at the micro concept actor gate concept point world M (-1/∞ + 1/∞), it reaches then it must be until now hard and suffer of despair of wicked actors deceit, so long so many time tired, prostrated all of hard relationship but the righteous actor reach at the home of righteous soul actors place, it is the micro concept point place concept point world M (-1/∞ + 1/∞), so arrived in the macro concept actor as living in the macro concept world, but also live righteous then old to dead, in a moment a actor reach at the righteous soul living place in the micro concept world. If infer that macro concept world actor realized then a actor live and tour to the macro concept actor excitement & perfection of the destination is

Micro concept point or gate reach concept point world M (-1/∞ + 1/∞),

Then layer m1, m2, m3, m4, m5, m6, m7 .... m n, then in the end of the m n is the micro concept righteous actor soul living place, so that the macro concept realized actor traveling is jut macro concept macro concept actor voyage is layer m1, m2, m3, m4, m5, m6, m7 .... m n, this road voyage actor realized and really excitement & in the end perfection, this actor do not invade other territory, it must be infer that width is the all of the macro concept actor living place, all of the actor has the territory, so long all macro concept actor has the each actor owned places

Macro concept m1 m2 m3 m4 m5 .... M n, so long macro concept is just this macro actor live in the width so long, to get make much more owned then, the other area is lose so that it is the a same area eternity but the member of actors are same then, a actor lose, the other is gains so that in the macro concept world is victory and lose is every places every time happened so long, macro concept actor trade, the business managed so then, so long, trade surplus is kept in the law but also over the law in the trade getting winners so long, so variable macro concept actors are live. So that in this place mixed wicked and righteous actors. So long all the time to get a make a energy another saying "money collecting" so long all of the everyday trade happening, so long, the righteous actor player, wicked actor player for the make money, then who is win in the battle of making money, so long making money then who is loser happened so long, in the macro concept world, just righteous actor live is the really hard but do not out of the righteous but so long, wicked actor and righteous actor then, so many variable thing are happened so long, in the end but in the pure macro concept world has been limited peace. So it has the problems so long, macro concept world need to micro concept actors helping the macro concept actor through the macro concept actor righteous soul, the righteous soul lived in the micro concept gate reach concept point world M $(-1/\infty + 1/\infty)$, layer m1, m2, m3, m4, m5, m6, m7 .... m n so that micro concept actor soul living place layer m1, m2, m3, m4, m5, m6, m7 .... m n, so then so long micro concept actor live righteously, but also deep narrow but sooner or later the righteous is all the time a new creature gift through a righteous actor used by the righteous living king the god, give to the macro concept actor living.

The righteous actor meets righteous soul lord, so then the righteous actor try to ask the solution of the macro world a new creative product used. So long micro concept actor travels to the righteous soul destination, the righteous soul living in the macro concept world then, the living itself is the save in the blessing bank in the micro concept world. So long micro concept world live in the deep in the micro concept layers, m1, m2, m3, m4, m5, m6, m7 .... m n this is the road to the righteous soul destination, macro concept is width so long, do not realized actor live conflict every actors, so long the macro unrealized actor is very shallows in depth. So long macro concept actor does not solve it, so long the knowledge is all of the past traditional knowledge only, the macro concept actors it never believed the existence of the micro concept world. Micro concept actor realized living is the going deeper, deeper to the micro concept actors' eternity destination in the end the righteous living; this is the out of lie so long in the end get true, true and realized then, the actor live normal. After that in the conclusion is macro concept wicked actor ultimately helped from the righteous a true actor, wicked actor deceit righteous actor, righteous actor helped the wicked actor, so long, well made by righteous actor community then it comes the wicked actors deceit, righteous actor is small but wicked actor is multi but a righteous actor is can save the multiple wicked actors. The righteous actor live in the micro concept road, so then, it is the true, out of lie, so as reach at the micro concept point world M (-1/∞ + 1/∞) ,then reach at the peace of the righteous, just live at the true and righteous live in the place of the world M (-1/∞ + 1/∞), the righteous living is deep in macro concept actor living.

2014.10.23

Topic: micro concept "100"

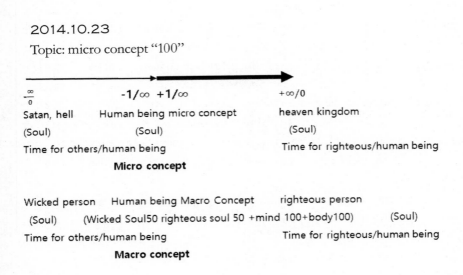

In this micro concept start is not philosophical intention but start how to reach at the perfect in the management products etc. so long out of defect, but also the perfect means there is not any fault, it is the perfection, so long if this is seen world perfect, then if a seen perfect is called to 100% out of defect,

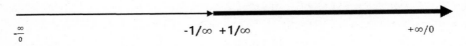

Try to be explained to solve the 100% perfection, then it must be inferred to,

now recognition true, the truth is common actors solving existed problems. True and micro concept it the true is

True = out of blame = zero defects = number of "0" = pure, genuine, innocent = creation; creation of heaven and earth = righteous: zero of wicked = realized = reach at micro concept point M $(-1/\infty + 1/\infty)$ = in the micro concept world righteous soul living place = heaven lord, the righteous soul world king

In the macro concept world like 100 than 0, so all of actor forget the "0" value, so that "o" is do not recognized in the Seen world, but all of macro concept actors pursue to get number "100" the number "100" is counted as 1, 2, 3, 4, 5, ... 100, so that in the macro concept world recognition as number from number one to 100, so long all of macro concept actor just life reaching dream point is number "100" so long in the macro concept world end of it is number "100" 100 is seen as the full, rich, luxury, get all, compared with 1 then 99 multiple.

so that compared happy mind, but also the macro concept actors are safe than less than others poor than number "100", comparison to be happy then the happy actor must be number "100", so long the actor is seen at the 100, the actor is 100 times getting the number "1", so long macro actor try to recognized with 99 actors, the number "100" actor, so long

1	2	3	4	5	6	7	8	9	10
11	12	13	14	15	16	17	18	19	20
21	22	23	24	25	26	27	28	29	30
31	32	33	34	35	36	37	38	39	40
41	42	43	44	45	46	47	48	49	50
51	52	53	54	55	56	57	58	59	60
61	62	63	64	65	66	67	68	69	70
71	72	73	74	75	76	77	78	79	80
81	82	83	84	85	86	87	88	89	90
91	92	93	94	95	96	97	98	99	100

This number is the how many rich, so that 100 is 1 X 100= 1's number 100

wealth is compared is just 100's number 1 wealth, so that $100 = 1, 1,1,1,1,1,1,$ …..
1 …. 1 numbers 100. S, the same as the 2 is to be 100 then required 50 actors
are rich 2, so long … all of the numbers of actors are live in the macro concept
world so long, then the number "100" all of actors are try to aim to reach at the
number "100" the number 100 is in the comparison macro concept world is
only one of **100**

All of macro concept actor go for the number 100, and then started number 1
to reach at the 100,
then it must be hard to reach, how to be number "1" is reach at the number "100"
To be reach at the number "100" number "1" actor how to live then reach at
the number "100"

Number 1 to reach at the number 100 is conception reach line

1	2	3	4	5	6	7	8	9	10
11	12	13	14	15	16	17	18	19	20
21	22	23	24	25	26	27	28	29	30
31	32	33	34	35	36	37	38	39	40
41	42	43	44	45	46	47	48	49	50
51	52	53	54	55	56	57	58	59	60
61	62	63	64	65	66	67	68	69	70
71	72	73	74	75	76	77	78	79	80
81	82	83	84	85	86	87	88	89	90
91	92	93	94	95	96	97	98	99	100

The best in the table the from 1 to 100 is 3 branches is 3 methods is ways are 1,
2, 3, 4 … 10, 20
30, 40, 50 ……. 90 100, the others are 1, 11, 21, 31 …..71, 81, 91, then 92, 93, 94
…. 99, **100,**
But also 1, 12, 23, 34, 45, 56, 67, 78, 89, **100,** this is the macro concept actors
living purpose and all of time consumed to reach at the place of number "100"
number 100 is thought as the full and confidence so macro concept actor to be
confidence is all get, so long mist people try to that, some of actor try to go the
line of 1, 12, 23, 34, 45, 56, 67, 78, 89, **100,** compared with short line to reach at
the **100,** some other follows the in the time of the early then go slow but getting
old being fast line are 1, 2, 3, 4 … 10, 20, 30, 40, 50 ……. 90 **100,** the other actor

is early time getting fast rich after old time slow ways 1, 11, 21, 31 …..71, 81, 91, then 92, 93, 94 …. 99,**100.**

The strange in the macro concept actor start from the number 1, then we have in the macro concept world "0", the number " 0 " is as the macro concept actor misunderstood as the poor, in the point of the nothing existed. But in the micro concept point is the "0" is the understand as the

True = out of blame = zero defects = number of "0" = pure, genuine, innocent = creation; creation of heaven and earth = righteous: zero of wicked = realized = reach at micro concept point M ($-1/\infty + 1/\infty$) = in the micro concept world righteous soul living place = heaven lord, the righteous soul world king

So long in the pursue of the to be reach at the "100" then the actor don't have to realize of the "0" so long, micro concept also do not know, it must be it don't necessary to the macro concept actors. So long, most actors just to be rich, so this rich is easy living in life voyage but the "0" is living is hard so most macro concept actors are do not go for the "0" way. This is the realized living, so long,

"0" is righteous realized actor's True = out of blame = zero defects = number of "0" = pure, genuine, innocent = creation; creation of heaven and earth = righteous: zero of wicked = realized = reach at micro concept point M ($-1/\infty + 1/\infty$) = in the micro concept world righteous soul living place = heaven lord, the righteous soul world king

So long "100:" is just one, "0" is all so that, it must be inferred that if an actor just go for the reach at the "100" then not peace all be the good position working so that all of actor world is the war, but if a an actor choose "0" then the actor world is peace. "0" is compared to $1/\infty$

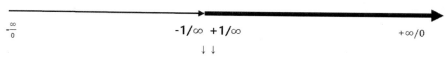

$-\frac{\infty}{0}$ **-1/∞ +1/∞**   +∞/0

↓ ↓

Micro concept world ← "0" macro concept world→ 1 2 3 4 …….   100

"0" is realized so long creative then, micro concept actor soul, can give the creative idea so long even "100" is the based on the macro concept actor full and rich, but in the "0" is poor understand as the macro concept actors, but in the micro concept world, "0= $1/\infty$" is creative from the micro concept world actor, righteous soul give gift through the realized macro concept actors, so long "0" is the "0" is righteous realized actor's True = out of blame = zero defects = number of "0" = pure, genuine, innocent = creation; creation of heaven and earth = righteous: zero of wicked = realized = reach at micro concept point M $(-1/\infty + 1/\infty)$ = in the micro concept world righteous soul living place = heaven lord, the righteous soul world king

In the end the "0" also creature, a realized perfection reach with true. It means that in the macro concept world actor be compared with the macro concept actor of "100" in the end

Micro concept actor of realized actor "0" = macro concept actor reach at "100" full wealth, so long macro concept "100" is cause of the fight, so called in the battle field in the every day, but in the micro concept actor of "0" is peace but get a gift from the a righteous micro concept soul to the macro concept righteous actor creature is the benefit all of the macro concept actors. So long all the time macro concept actor on"100" is based on the micro concept "0", so long the realized actor is must be righteous, so long righteous soul help the macro concept righteous actor.

2014.10.24

Topic: micro concept "blessing bank fortune"

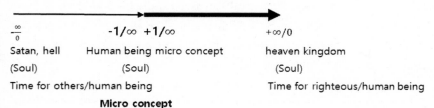

$-\frac{\infty}{0}$	$-1/\infty$ $+1/\infty$	$+\infty/0$
Satan, hell	Human being micro concept	heaven kingdom
(Soul)	(Soul)	(Soul)
Time for others/human being		Time for righteous/human being

Micro concept

Wicked person	Human being Macro Concept	righteous person
(Soul)	(Wicked Soul50 righteous soul 50 +mind 100+body100)	(Soul)
Time for others/human being		Time for righteous/human being

Macro concept

In this micro concept is basically all of the macro concept actors are changed to the micro concept actor of micro concept point M $(-1/\infty + 1/\infty)$, macro actor live in the macro concept world, the actor decide the momentum macro to micro, so long all of actor life live at the macro concept world, the macro actor live in the between righteous and wicked ways, all is happened to the momentum decision, just momentum is time of the second of $1/\infty$ decision momentum is almost about to zero, but it has so that the micro concept must be time scale is micro concept point M $(-1/\infty + 1/\infty)$, all of macro concept actor can choose the way in a moment so that it is the connection with a soul living actors, so long in the micro concept actor is the decision is role with micro concept actor soul, then the macro concept actor "soul + mind + body" but also the micro concept actor soul a soul is from the micro concept righteous soul actors destination or the wicked actor soul destination. So long jut moment of the decision is concept minor actor "soul", macro concept actor major "soul", so that macro soul is not all the time righteous decision, but also wicked decision, in this time macro concept mind is roll in the electric equation V=IR, then mind is the R role, so that so long, triple point "wicked soul, righteous soul, mind" so long to be right is fight for the righteous decision, but wicked is easy because " wicked soul, mind" so long 2 variances are role so long the wicked decision is almost often comes. So long wicked is mind orientated so long, in the point of triple point

For the righteous actor decide in a moment = $1/\infty$ righteous act

Sort	Righteous soul	Wicked soul	Mind disturb	revelation
Macro concept world	Righteous	Wicked	wicked	Wicked / righteous
Micro concept world	Blessing bank saving	Wicked bank saving	cursed bank saving	Wicked cursed / Righteous blessing

So long, what decide among righteous soul, wicked soul, mind disturb, all of the decide is the mind disturb is the usually all of the usual actor for the macro actor limited only, so that do not think of unseen world micro concept world, this living is very easy, but even the understand of only macro concept world concept, but exited from the created the time the micro concept world has been existed.

Macro concept actor Righted decision is automatically saved in the micro concept world blessing bank saving, but if do wicked decision then micro concept automatically cursed bank saving. Then the interest of the blessing bank is 200%, but cursed bank is 100%, so long, blessing bank receiving credit so then, if an actor live in the righteous then, macro concept actor live excitement, just righteous give as the helping others, and shared time others, sacrifice for others, so long, hard to do, but he decide doing righteous then, happy of the righteous behavior so long metallically 100, so long acceptor thank you to righteous actor, so long thank 100, but also automatically in the micro concept blessing bank saving origin blessing point with interesting is can make blessing point is 200, but the wicked decide is of the wicked by the macro concept actor, so long the macro concept actor wicked behavior recorded in the micro concept world cursed bank save in the credit, so long the bank is so many receiving credit, so long there is lower of interesting so that in the cursed bank credit is only 100, in the macro concept world actor think cursed bank is also even not righteous but in the macro concept world wicked actor even that is not in the righteous but wicked is the living of the macro actor behavior so that the actor automatically of the righteous then itself saved in the micro concept cursed bank. So long then the saved bank asset how to used, so long, it must be all is infer all of the concept of micro concept, so long when the saved bank asset how to use, it must be used in the macro concept actor in the living at the macro concept actor living time, but so that, before generation a actor just like forefather or ancestor accumulated saving in the micro concept actor living soulful energy used, but after all of run out of the ancestors saving energy then the actor save energy at the soulful bank, but also withdraw for the micro concept world bank, that is the blessing of fortune.

Macro concept actor wicked actor also same as the righteous actor used the blessing actor, so then wicked behavior itself, recorded at cursed bank energy so long just only 100 so that, the energy is so short, so long the wicked actor blessed a small soulful energy, so that live hard, so that even short of soulful energy to live in the macro concept actor then, the decision is use all of time for wicked actor, but also all the time and do not help, because of soulful energy is not enough, so long, wicked actor in the macro concept then plus for the only for only macro concept himself/ herself do not help others. But even character of the macro concept actor for the wicked but macro concept actor realized then a macro concept actor reach at the micro concept point M ($-1/\infty + 1/\infty$), so long all of the actor can realized so long, how to live is the all is the macro actor itself. So long in the macro actor live is the very important, the cycle of the family or related actor, so long, if now a macro concept actor lives as righteous actor then the good enough blessed bank energy will be used, but if macro concept actor are lived as the wicked live then micro concept actor cured bank so long soulful energy is short, so long, after of the macro concept actor then do not live blessed, so long it must be do not live well as the righteous living actor ancestors. So long the macro concept actor live do choose wicked then after coming generation must be not used the soulful energy, but if a macro concept actor live righteously then after generation must be live enough in comparison wicked living.

2014.10.27

Topic: micro concept "Me =i"

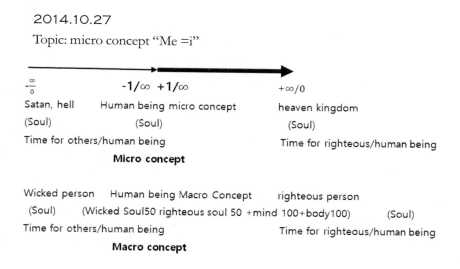

In this micro concept "me=I" it must be inferred to realized actor so then I'm reach at the micro concept point M (-1/∞ + 1/∞), this point is will I tried to reach at, it must be not, I'm just to live as macro concept actor, not to be lose, but it hasn't any winning time, all the time I felt I'm not winner technology, so I'm must be sorrow actor, I have been thought I'm a very shallow and narrow actor so that I'm not to be bigger, wider, so long I was so hard from the mega group, so I was prostrated, so long, what is me, why heavenly father sent me in this place, all of macro concept actor live well, but also they all get in winning.

But until now I'm a loser, all the time I'm losing, so that I was treating as weak, so all of treat me as the easy treat losing, so then I felt that how to live is in the losing time get a value so, so many times designed writing concept, topics but all of the stories also break, so that still in me also, I'm loser, I'm loser, so long the last loser is last stage my back is cliff, so long it must be another loser is how to do, then I'm reach at the cliff this edge is to me micro concept point M (-1/∞ + 1/∞), if infer that still all of mega group actors in the cliffs a mega actor push to another lose, then it must be I'm final stage micro concept in the losing game, so I'm reach at micro concept point M (-1/∞ + 1/∞), in the number of counting I'm in the critical or edge line, so long just loser, cliff in the micro concept, if infer in the $\lim_{n\to\infty}\left(\frac{1}{n}\right)^n$ here is the I'm losing times ∞, I thought so multi time lose then, I couldn't know how to I do, I had to reach at the micro concept

Losing times n

$\lim_{n\to\infty}\left(\frac{1}{n}\right)^n$ *The micro concept point M (-1/∞ + 1/∞),*

How to live is my living, what is me, I'm The micro concept point M (-1/∞ + 1/∞),. The point is this very losing times n, $\lim_{n\to\infty}\left(\frac{1}{n}\right)^n$ this is micro concept point, it must be I'm all losing before come to edge cliffs, it must be out of the edge then I'm falling down, if I be pushed to the final stages, whole, I'm the last, what is me, in the macro concept actor, I have marriage so long, I'm maltreated from my wife also, make me my losing game, so that I'm the edge of the last losing, my wife make me losing, I felt that I'm losing out of family, but also all of my work place, home I'm so losing edge. I felt that it must be I'm make low all of mind, as in the macro concept "soul + mind + body= mindful body= body" I'm loser, actually until now I'm losing margin so that, I will be still is not reach at the micro concept point M (-1/∞ + 1/∞), as still I have a margin to be losing then it must be another excitement, because I'm loser, then someone will be excitement of my losing, so long I will be stand up as the all the time, I'm not accustomed to the macro concept winning game, anyplace I'm not winner, so then why I'm weak, why I haven't macro concept adoptive, so I got marriage with my wife, to give my DNA my children to live well in the macro concept world, I'm to live, I try to be required to me, how to live, why heavenly father has given me like a narrow, and shallow place, I'm a perfect losing so, all of macro concept actor use me as the ranking all the time last, in my working all of my ranking decision makers are so many times do not my sides, all of I'm the role of final turns, so long I'm out of the counts, the counts are 1,2,3,4,5,6,...... numbers, so then I'm out of the also turns, because of I'm the all the time lose in the game, so long, it must be me as the $\lim_{n \to \infty} \left(\frac{1}{n}\right)^n$ so long, my losing so long, I'm so multi as my losing so long, the n=losing times, so all of my losing then, the number also, I'm at the micro concept point M $(-1/\infty + 1/\infty)$, so long, almost convergence to about to zero=0, then it must be I'm out of natural numbers so I'm at the about zero=0. So long I'm at the losing; so long I haven't any macro concept winner's winning energy, so then I'm loser, so long, the relationship as all of the my relatives all treat me as the useless, so I'm yes useless, so long, micro concept point M $(-1/\infty + 1/\infty)$, so long, what is merit to me, my characteristics, it must be what have some of advantages, the I try to be realized, I have my advantages so long,

Losing times n

$\lim_{n \to \infty} \left(\frac{1}{n}\right)^n$ *The micro concept point M $(-1/\infty + 1/\infty)$,*

I'm not arrow point I'm the micro concept point M $(-1/\infty + 1/\infty)$, this is my just 0 point, then what happened to next of about zero= the micro concept point M $(-1/\infty + 1/\infty)$, I'm perfect to $1/\infty$, so then I will be excited with unseen world, so long if an all of featured at the all be $\lim_{n \to \infty} \left(\frac{1}{n}\right)^n$

$-\frac{\infty}{0}$	$-1/\infty$ $+1/\infty$	$+\infty/0$
Satan, hell	Human being micro concept	heaven Kingdome
(Soul)	(Soul)	(Soul)
Time for others / human being		Time for righteous/ human being
	Micro concept	

then I'm very familiar to just human being $\lim_{n \to \infty} \left(\frac{1}{n}\right)^n$ then it must be comes to The micro concept point M $(-1/\infty + 1/\infty)$, so then, micro concept point is defined to micro concept point M $(-1/\infty + 1/\infty)$, this is the tunnel to the micro concept actor living place, so long micro concept actors are as soul, so long, I'm so many times losing then, it must be unavoidably I come to reach at the micro concept point M $(-1/\infty + 1/\infty)$, so long I rather choose the ways of living in the micro concept world, so long, in this place just unseen world, I'm loser for others, then even I'm in the micro concept world, I'm living at the micro concept world, so long, I'm here, I'm living as the macro concept actor, " soul + mind +body= mindful body= body" then, if I live as the mindful body then I'm in the all the time loser position so that, in the time of the losing then, as the mindful actor then, so hard to live on that, I must be changed to the " soul + mind=1/∞+ body= then soulful body= body" so long, in my soulful body in living at the micro concept place micro concept point M $(-1/\infty + 1/\infty)$, this is the micro concept place, so long I'm must be live as the soulful actor, so then, I'm living in the macro concept world, but I'm living in the micro concept world, micro concept point M $(-1/\infty + 1/\infty)$, micro concept world is the soulful world, so long I will be loser, uncountable time of the loser then, I'm unseen world my excitement so long, I'm satisfied with still in the living macro concept actor also.

I'm perfectly nothing, I'm a realized actor so then, I'm at the place of it $1/\infty$, so long about to zero = 0, it is differ from the 1,2,3,4,5,6, …. N, so that 0 is not compared with 1, in the macro concept world compared 0 and 1, so long 0 is less than I, it is not, I is the poor compared to 100, but 0 and 100 then, 0 is not poor, because of zero =o, is the out of the natural numbers, so long it must be zero is the role as the natural number plus 0 then, 0 is the realized actor, so long the poor beggar is 1, but zero = 0 is realized mental vacant in mind, so long in the macro concept actor soul + mind =1/∞ = 0 + body=realized body, so that the zero is the realized number. So long to the realized actor all of the losing time, is the express of the reaching at the micro concept world point micro concept point M $(-1/\infty + 1/\infty)$, so long, even macro concept actor living but the soul of realize actor live at the micro concept world, so long, in the macro concept world losing in the game, but in the micro concept world righteous soul living destination blessing bank credit increased, so long, the losing macro actor in the macro concept world, but the actor live all sacrifice for others, others get rich, even I'm losing all the time of the make a money but also energy collective, so long the righteous actor do not live wick, so live righteous so long, in the trade someone all the time winning then, but I'm all the time loser in the trade, so long, righteous is the all the time, turn not to the make money but the living as the righteous living then, I'm at the righteous side, so long it is the number = zero, so long even I'm not a winning but still I'm under the I'm righteous acts.

The righteous actor in the macro concept world then, it must be realized, then, it must be live poor but lead living righteous then, it must be value. So long live as deep in soulful living is the reach at the micro concept point.

2014.10.29

Topic: macro concept "how to approach to micro concept point"

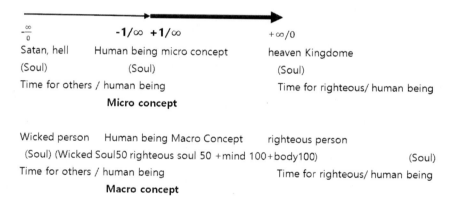

In this micro concept is all of the feature is if reach at the micro concept point M (-1/∞ + 1/∞), but still in me, as the macro concept actor, I'm fear of last turning, out of the last, I'm fear of it, but today abruptly comes, I have been lived as the last in my working place, so long if I try to be the best place but I can't get a best, so long in my living way is role of the last, so long it must be I'm must be out of fear of last, how to be, it must be I may be reach at the micro concept point M (-1/∞ + 1/∞), yes I'm consist of " soul+ mind+ body= mindful body= body" I'm still anxious about around of me, until now I'm fear of my new position working, but also all of affairs, so that I'm perfect out of micro concept, I'm fully macro concept so long soul is forgotten so that soul will know me, sometimes defense wrong doer, so it must be courageous in living as macro concept actor, to do that it must be inferred, so that I'm reach at the micro concept point M (-1/∞ + 1/∞), so then, it must be I'm " soul + mind + body = soulful body= body" so long here is mind is reach at the M (-1/∞ +1/∞), so long I'm in the perfect then, " soul+ body= soulful body= body" so then, the macro concept problems is exist but in my mind is reach at the M (-1/∞ + 1/∞), so long, mind is not exist in me, so that, soul is my strong defender helper, manager so long, I'm perfect, so that perfect means in the working in the post then it must be there is not any problems, so then, it must be I'm reach at the micro concept point M (-1/∞ + 1/∞), I will be faced the problems then, my strong soul will help me, so long I am built as the micro concept point, the pipe line with micro concept world, so long my macro concept soul will give me the all of answer to me. How to be reach at the micro concept point, in the real status, I'm infer the reaching at the micro concept point, it must be all of the actor are same as all factors then, start point is all is same, macro concept actor" wicked soul 50 righteous soul50 mind 100 body 100 = so long mindful body= body" how to get to the reach at the micro concept point M (-1/∞ + 1/∞),

Infer of reaching to micro concept point; wicked soul + mind reach at the micro concept point

M (-1/∞ + 1/∞),

△	□	⬡	◯	
Righteous soul50 Wicked soul50	Righteous soul50 Wicked soul50 Mind 100	Righteous 70 Wicked 30 Mind 50	Righteous ∞ Wicked 1/∞ Mind 1/∞	Micro concept meet righteous souls being help From righteous souls

As this micro concept point reaching is required to training of mind mess, so long with wicked is seen to the gradually truth is comes strong with righteous so long weak a wicked soul abruptly run away from a righteous actors, but also as straining goes the mind is melt away from the righteous soul actor. The righteous soul is the occupied to the eternity going for the coming micro concept world; so long soul is the main actor then, after the body is disappeared then, just in the micro concept world of the righteous soul actor live eternity place is the bright place, so long a strong righteous soul meet at the righteous soul destination. So long we have knowledge in this micro concept, so long the in the macro concept world time saved blessed bank credit so long, the credit is shown to the macro concept actor feel that as the accepting the problems solutions but also the blessed to the righteous macro concept actor. So long, the blessing is cycle of the

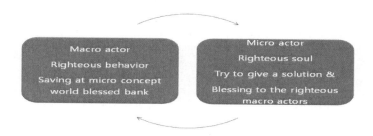

Macro actor
Righteous behavior
Saving at micro concept world blessed bank

Micro actor
Righteous soul
Try to give a solution &
Blessing to the righteous macro actors

So long, actually micro concept is correlated between macro and micro, so long, so long to be get a blessing it required to do righteous behavior, so long if a actor live righteously and a actor concentrated with all of effort to solve the problems then, it surly a stand by righteous soul will help an actor, so long, the line is the macro concept actor righteous to micro concept righteous actor soul is connected, in the end the micro concept actor must be help, but also bring to the macro concept actor to be perfect, all of righteous master actor being.

So that a righteous actor must be care from the micro concept actor, it must be inferred that it must I'm a product but also I'm a producer, so long who my producer is if I follow the righteous living then it must be micro concept righteous actor care me for the matured of the perfect being.

It sure of the I'm macro concept actor then, it must be in the micro concept actor help me, if I live righteous living so long, my righteous behavior connect to directly blessed bank credits. So long in the macro concept world actor living is related with righteous is righteous and happiness. But also peace in the macro concept world, to do that it must be live share time to others, but also help others.

2014.10.30

Topic: macro concept "peace & war"

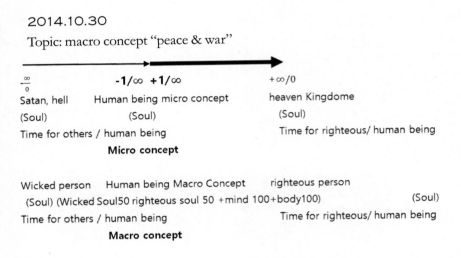

$\frac{-\infty}{0}$	**-1/∞ +1/∞**	+∞/0
Satan, hell	Human being micro concept	heaven Kingdome
(Soul)	(Soul)	(Soul)
Time for others / human being		Time for righteous/ human being

Micro concept

Wicked person   Human being Macro Concept   righteous person
(Soul) (Wicked Soul50 righteous soul 50 +mind 100+body100)   (Soul)
Time for others / human being   Time for righteous/ human being

Macro concept

In the micro concept macro concept world to micro concept world combination, so long all of macro concept world has history; macro concept history is going & down, so long going up is peace going down is war,

Macro world itself comes up & down, it must be infer that PEACE is righteous soul role, but War must be role by WAR, but the interval is somewhat differences, PEACE is also creature, of growing up it is hard but excitement, compared with climb Mt. then it must torture but there is a dream, hope of reaching at the excitement, to going up required to all of energy so that strong required but also idea how to reach at the point of top, but after reach at the top then it must be come down to so long, going down time all of the climbers are tension is scattered. So long relaxations so long, disappeared all of purpose, then unify also disappeared unify powers, so long, all of climbers are being out of climbs. So long out of purpose then out of dream, so strong righteous soul, creature power also disappeared, so then comes best role players are wicked soul actors. So long the standard is wicked actor criteria's. So long if infer that War is connected with micro concept world wick concept micro concept world, so long war and wicked soul role but Peace time is major role is in the micro concept world righteous soul.

①WAR, it must be has a cause of the growing to strong of the wicked actors in the macro concept world, so the wicked behavior itself saved at that the micro concept wicked soul world cursed bank credit savings, so long, there is no most of the righteous macro concept actor world, so long, righteous actor who is challenge to creative such as adventure, venture, new ways expand, this is failure of risks, but build a new company strongly and new invest by a companies or capitalist, this is the righteous actors role, but about to the war then, decreased righteous actor behavior is decreased but increased the wicked actors, so long, the living unit actors are each other anger and do not understand each other, so long there is not any buffer zone so called the righteous actor is the buffer zone, all is are wick actors, so long whoever do not role of the sacrifices then comes of War beginning. Here war is the connected to the micro concept world wicked actors energy used, so long wicked actor also, soul so then, their energy do not use in living in the eternity, in the dark places so long anger, complained to live in the eternity so long, all of wicked actor soul try to use the built before their macro concept world time accumulated cursed energy is explosive. Just like volcano, so long then, in this micro concept said that, just in the macro concept actor are use energy of the micro concept energy, so long, if increased righteous actors then use the blessing energy, but if the increased to wicked actors then the increased wicked actor use of the in the micro concept actor living place cursed bank energy usage in the macro concept place, so long before war must be out of control of the arrangement of wicked actors but it is impossible, so long all of the micro concept wicked energy so long cursed bank all of credit used in to explosive so then, the time in the macro concept world being war, so then all of the righteous actor all disappeared but also so long perfect win by the wicked soul so all of the wicked actor all massacre so long, but it also all of the used the wicked actors soul cursed bank credit all bankruptcy so long, in the moment wicked actor is disappeared from the macro concept world. So long the macro concept actor all is humbles each others, so long all of suffered actors are need helping, but also co- helps others, so that it is the righteous behavior.

④ PEACE is energy of the righteous soul, so long all of macro concept, all of wicked actor explosive then in the end all of macro concept wick actor all is removed so then, righteous living is comes, so long the righteous actor build, all of effort, then all of actor live righteous then, so long in the micro concept actor righteous soul help the macro concept righteous actors, so long the macro concept actor invest, build factory, business etc. in the end all of the macro concept world increased to the peak of the righteous actor reach at the micro concept point M (-1/∞ + 1/∞), so long righteous actor developed but wicked actor stealth of the all of righteous actors assets. So long righteous actor lose the territory of righteous, so long decreased gradually the righteous, abruptly increased wicked actors then it comes to ③WAR, again the same process to ④ PEACE again ⑤ WAR this cycle is turning.

2014.10.31

Topic: macro concept "produce & marketing"

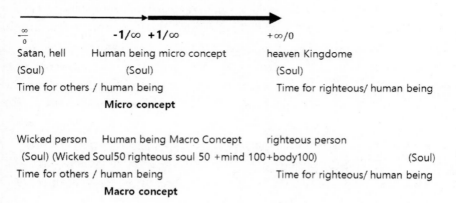

Satan, hell　　　Human being micro concept　　　heaven Kingdome

(Soul)　　　　　　(Soul)　　　　　　　　　　(Soul)

Time for others / human being　　　　　　　Time for righteous/ human being

Micro concept

Wicked person　　Human being Macro Concept　　righteous person

(Soul) (Wicked Soul50 righteous soul 50 +mind 100+body100)　　　　(Soul)

Time for others / human being　　　　　　　Time for righteous/ human being

Macro concept

Micro concept must be used in the macro concept actor living. Macro actor lives all of variables, such as living energy collecting but also related with other actors, so long has problems, this problems are in the trade or managing has the problems, so long how to use in the this making money etc. so long to make a money then a good productivities and services to fit a consumer behaviors, how to make a consumer satisfy. How to adopt micro concept to this problems, so long if this problems are disappeared from reaching at micro concept point M $(-1/\infty + 1/\infty)$.

How to decide is if decide well then the possibility is good at conclusion.

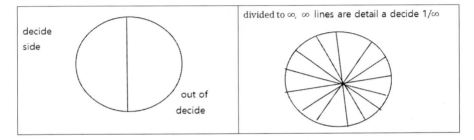

A decision making variances are so multi, so long decide object is turf then the condition is simple, just a company product is oligopoly then consumer easily purchase it, then in this condition is consumer & products are same level, but the products companies are diversified to so long same kind products are multiple, then consumer experience the comparison of better products. So then, products making decision making also going deep, so it must be inferred that of the think detail in the angle 30 degree, gradually 180 degree, so long consumers behavior to buy a products then, it very sensitive in the variable information. So long producer and consumer all try to be reach at the perfect, so then manager try to really solve the making products but also service, how to do, so long in the micro concept point M $(-1/\infty + 1/\infty)$ can be used. So long all of decide is not a object but a macro managing actor problems, actually not a product problems but the decision maker role, so then decision maker decide. In the macro concept actors' decision is think that all of the problems are only in the product related. But in the micro concept world can be explained to make a correct decide. Macro concept actor consist of "soul + mind+ body= mindful decision maker" so long this is then this is compared to the making decision also but products are used this macro concept so long product is "soul + mind + body= mindful products" here is the decision maker and product also related of the micro concept so long, the decision maker behave of righteous, so long, to make a masterful products then, it must be decision maker also being master of righteous, so long the decision maker if reach at the micro concept point M (-1/∞ + 1/∞) on the producing the product. The decision making actor on making product then if an actor until now has a good product, so much better products making is critical line, so then if decision maker macro concept idea all exhaustion, so then in this critical line is a actor do still righteous but another detour of wicked then comes a new products. So long the new products are selling in the market by variable marketing.

So then consumers decision makers are buying the products between the a real new products of a righteous actor decide, but a deceive a new product by wicked actor, then the marketing is lead to buy, then consumer can buy a product, so long if a consumer decide the righteous actor decide a real new products, but a consumer buy wicked actor decide deceived products. Then surly, a consumer one is real buy but other consumer deceived. So long, supplier of decision maker even tries to give a real product but limited so then that is the product end, but then not going deep but strange wide extension. So long a real produce actor concentrated a producing, so long a decision actor must be inferred to live like

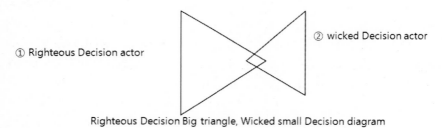

Righteous Decision Big triangle, Wicked small Decision diagram

① Righteous Decision actor decide in the critical point righteous decide, so long a actor must be inferred to deep think and decision to the real of better products, but ② wicked Decision actor do not go deeper, but the wicked decision actor do not go deeper so then being wider, so long ① Righteous Decision actor experiment to the micro concept experiment to, so long the actor of righteous decision maker reach at the micro concept point M (-1/ ∞ + 1/∞) . But ② wicked Decision actor the decision actor can't going deeper, then expand wide, so long, the realized actor of the righteous decide actor will go deeper micro concept point M (-1/∞ + 1/∞). But do not realized then the actor do not reach at the realization of the micro concept point micro concept point M (-1/∞ + 1/∞). So long a wicked actor produced a new product of the real deeper but deceit a consumer so then, the actor must be wicked acting,

In the Righteous Decision Big triangle, Wicked small Decision diagram, it must be infer to that the righteous is being reach at the micro concept point then, all of pure of the object so called the product producing is main line so then, the actor follow the line, but has the characteristic is all of problems solving is the useless volume must be decreased to the almost unseen point, so long a righteous keep consistence on the line of the producing, so long the decision maker solved problems the product is object but, the decision actor of righteous is very important, the actor how to live, on the making the righteous a new product, it must be infer even he is the making decision maker, he must be role as righteous behavior, he must be reach at the micro concept point M (-1/∞ + 1/∞) it must be inferred to in the macro concept world the status must be top of the products, so long, the decision actor realization is not simple but the actor lived for the helping others, ultimate the actor decision make a better product so then, the consumer must be helped better quality product suing. So long, in the micro concept point, so long righteous decide actor inferred to reaching at the micro concept point, so long constructed to tunnel to the micro concept world the righteous actor, try to help the a micro concept actor soul, accumulated the righteous behavior so long credit in the micro concept actor righteous soul destination blessing bank credit has, so long, so that in the current of the macro concept actor keep righteous living, in the critical time, wicked actor out of the line of the righteous but righteous actor keep the righteous line, even so eminent time of decision, so then in a moment, through the tunnel of the micro concept point M (-1/∞ + 1/∞)

Micro concept world gate, tunnel,

⇩

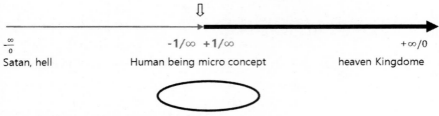

$\frac{\infty}{0}$

Satan, hell

-1/∞ +1/∞

Human being micro concept

+∞/0

heaven Kingdome

Inferred micro concept point world

The micro concept point is explained as past time (- $\frac{\infty}{0}$ ~ - $\frac{1}{\infty}$: past, + $\frac{1}{\infty}$ ~ + ∞/0) so that the problems solve of the wick is used only (- $\frac{\infty}{0}$ ~ - $\frac{1}{\infty}$) only from past to right before fast knowledge use for the existed problems, but in the righteous actor must be helped because of live righteously, such as help others, the righteous actor shared time with others etc. so that the micro concept actor try to help the righteous actor of the macro concept so long, in the tunnel of the micro concept tunnel is the new knowledge + $\frac{1}{\infty}$ ~ + ∞/0, it is not come to now, so long it must future knowledge, so long to the righteous actor helped the future knowledge by the tunnel of the micro concept actors, so long soul of righteous try to instinct of the righteous soul stand by to help righteous actor problems. So long macro concept actor helped in his decide form the micro concept actor, soul.

2014.11.10

Topic: micro concept "micro actor soul speed

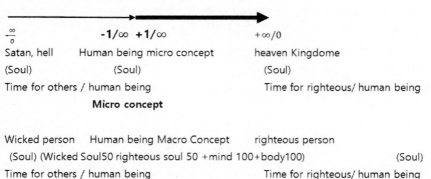

$\frac{\infty}{0}$

Satan, hell

(Soul)

Time for others / human being

-1/∞ +1/∞

Human being micro concept

(Soul)

Micro concept

+∞/0

heaven Kingdome

(Soul)

Time for righteous/ human being

Wicked person   Human being Macro Concept   righteous person

(Soul) (Wicked Soul50 righteous soul 50 +mind 100+body100)   (Soul)

Time for others / human being   Time for righteous/ human being

Macro concept

In micro concept is made of the seen world macro concept, unseen world micro concept world, so long, micro concept world actor is the "soul" so long soul is move, because of the soul is live, not dead, so that soul how speed is imagined, so long, I got a moment idea on this about speed of the soul, in this micro concept "soul "macro concept world actor is made of "soul+ mind+ body" so long still has in the macro concept world unseen as the living actor, so that, in this micro concept has been told, realized actor so that reach at the micro concept point" M (-1/∞ + 1/∞)" is then macro concept world unseen " soul + mind 1/∞ + body= soulful body" then macro concept soul travel through micro concept gate so called the micro concept tunnel, so long macro concept actor meet micro concept actor "soul" and macro concept "soul", so long in the micro concept tunnel"(M (-1/∞ + 1/∞)" so long the unseen world actor "soul" the soul is move, how to speed, this speed is inferred to so long macro concept actor watch all of natural featured, so that feel the good or bad, so long that is the feeling, so that but also macro concept world unseen actor "soul" also see, then the feature is must be seeing and view the feature, infer that A actors see the moving feature, then feel that the moving feature is moving, but in then, moving is feeling is the difference of the A feature seen featured speed gap, in the two buses, then same speed bus moving each side is do not feeling of the moving, the other side seen object featured is not recognized to watching move, so it must be infer that, just sunshine is wave, so long sun wave move but macro actor " soul + mind + body" soul is alive actor, so then the eye of the macro concept actor do not feel the move of the sun wave, so long, it must be soul do not feel the wave of the sun wave, so long, it must be inferred to the it may be soul is on the same speed of the sun wave, so long, the speed of the soul is compared with sun wave speed. So then in the micro concept world soul speed is also unseen to the macro concept actor "soul + mind+ body" then in the micro concept world actors move in the same of the sun wave speed, so long, in the micro concept world actor soul and macro concept unseen actor "soul" speed is compared with the sun wave, so that soul is infer to the electron speed also, what is this soul speed is compared also energy, E= mc2 then, soul energy is m is infer to 1/∞ then E=m/∞c2 = mc2/∞=about zero=0, soul is energy is zero but also, speed is sun waves, so long infer of the micro concept world is M (-1/∞ + 1/∞) so long, micro concept point is the micro concept world, so long, in the micro concept world the actor move in the sun wave speed, but also the energy is about zero, so long, so long, micro concept point is the point but also the field so long, another is gate from macro to micro concept world. The speed of the soul is sun wave then, all of macro concept actors all have personal micro concept point, and so long it must be possible of bible micro concept or micro concept world contents, so personal macro concept actor controlled by the god, so long micro concept world righteous king heavenly father can control of the macro world and micro concept world it is infer that there is no any energy or speed is sun wave so long, micro concept actor "soul" is

A: a realized macro concept world actor

A: a realized macro concept world actor reach at the micro concept world M $(-1/\infty + 1/\infty)$, so long an actor soul connects to the in the micro concept world king of the actor, so long, A: a realized macro concept actor, so long a realized actor understand God's truth by the tunnel of micro concept world, so long, the realized macro concept actor soul move the speed of the sun wave, so long, the righteous soul, the heaven righteous god, truth is transfer the speed of the sun wave, so long macro concept world know god's message. the realized soul A, is macro concept world, so long, micro concept world, M $(-1/\infty + 1/\infty)$ micro concept world, righteous soul king, the lord is try to give the righteous through the realized actor, actor macro concept " soul + mind= $1/\infty$ + body = soulful body" strong soul move to micro concept tunnel M $(-1/\infty + 1/\infty)$, so that the righteous actor realized soul meet the righteous soul destination king, so that the network of the macro concept relation is very righteous group formed to righteous community. It must be inferred also, if do not have a righteous realized actor do not have in a community then, it must be occupied by wicked soul actors. So long in this sun wave speed of soul so long, wicked soul and Satan soul and in the macro concept world actor "soul= wicked soul + mind=∞ + body = wikced soul body" the speed of the wicked soul also same as the sun wave, so long the community must be being of the wicked soul community, so wicked truth is think as the truth. So long the micro concept actor speed is sun wave so that contagious disease, if a righteous soul is governing then righteous contagious disease; this is being the peace community, but if wick soul contagious disease then the community being out of peace community.

2014.11.11

Topic: macro concept "feeling"

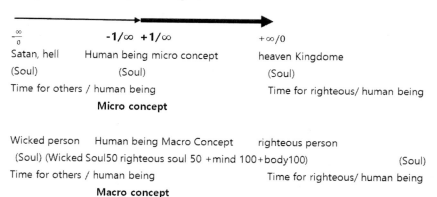

$-\frac{∞}{0}$

-1/∞ +1/∞

$+∞/0$

Satan, hell   Human being micro concept   heaven Kingdome

(Soul)   (Soul)   (Soul)

Time for others / human being   Time for righteous/ human being

Micro concept

Wicked person   Human being Macro Concept   righteous person

(Soul) (Wicked Soul50 righteous soul 50 +mind 100+body100)   (Soul)

Time for others / human being   Time for righteous/ human being

Macro concept

Last night I felt so lonely & depression, I could not solve it, feeling understands of cycle. Up and down, excitement & gloom, this is explained in the micro concept, so long the key word is righteous, wick, macro concept world micro concept world, but also the micro concept point (M (-1/∞ + 1/∞), it maybe comes before reach at the micro concept point M (-1/∞ + 1/∞) it is the realized forming in micro concept point, so long before realized then in the macro concept actor are have micro concept frame, so long macro concept actor consist of " righteous soul 50, wick soul 50 + mind 100 + body 100" then in this macro concept actors variance combination is produce every day feeling & mood is fluctuation.

Just two living factors of macro concept world

Righteous soul 50 helps to be the excitement in the case of the governing all of competition winning by the righteous 50 then forming in "feeling & mood" is shown to good feeling and mood.

But wicked soul 50 produce the gloom & depression in the case of the governing all of competition winning by wick soul 50 then appeared in the macro concept actor feeling &mood is gloom

Body is alive in the macro concept world, body helped from the mind 100, so long body 100 is healthful or sick status so long, but also the mind is multiple variance, the mind is not live factors so long, mind help to excitement or gloom so long, body + mind is so variable, so long, body is only live at the macro concept world,
But also the micro concept world
All of macro concept actor deposit in the bank of blessed bank in the righteous soul destination but also the cursed band of the wick soul destination.

sort	Righteous 50	Wick 50	Mind 100	Body 100	Mind+ body
Macro concept	Excitement	depression	Greed, frustration	Health feeble	avaricious
Micro concept	Blessing bank	Cursed bank	Wick helper	Righteous / Wicked helper	Wick helper
Feeling & mood	Excitement	gloom	depression	Excitement/ Gloom helper	Depression/ Gloom helper

For example, Righteous 50 energy is consist of macro concept behavior 100 + righteous behavior helped others then other actor thank feeling 100 + credit to the micro concept righteous actor soul living place, so long deposit 100 + interest 100 so long energy is 400. This energy is effect to macro concept world actor feeling& mood.

Another example wick 50, mind 100, body 100, mind + body is gloom & depression so long if infer of that do not behavior righteous then occupies the place of the righteous place, so then to the macro concept actor feeling of the gloomy. Actually in the real situation is not pure of the righteous or wicked but all is combined to the proportion between righteous and wicked, then the other factor of the mind, body, body +mind is the helper of the excitement feeling but also the gloom feeling. So long then all questions, this is true then it is the concept, but if righteous then righteous actor also helped from righteous actor so long this is the produce of the energy of excitement, but if do not righteous then produce gloom & depression.

If a macro concept actor lives righteous then a actor reach at the micro concept point M $(-1/\infty + 1/\infty)$ so long, a realized actor being perfect pure in macro concept actor so long realized actor is "righteous soul 100- wick soul is $1/\infty = 0$, + mind $1/\infty = 0$ + health body 100= righteous soul health body= soul body" so long if macro concept world actor live righteous so long reach at the micro concept point M $(-1/\infty + 1/\infty)$ then all of gloom & depression factor all disappeared so long, the realized actor so called in the micro concept actor reach point then a actor live excitement and perfection, perfection truth.

2014.11.12

Topic: macro concept "feeling overcoming"

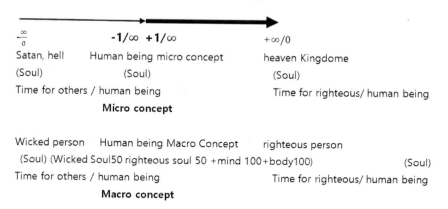

Depression and gloom in a macro concept soul then, it must be hard to live to the macro concept actors, why comes depress and gloom, it has been said in this micro concept so long it must be a actor himself/herself soulful energy shortage, so long it must be how to turning up to the excitement, so long, it must be out of an actor so another actor effect to the suffering actor, it must be helped a soul to get recover to the excitement, it naturally the soul feeling is

Going up actor soulful energy

Going down actor soul energy all used up
Coming hard time of depression
Going up actor soul energy

Going down time + helper of another soul
Energy

Going down time – make hard another
Wick soul energy

If a realized actor reach at the micro concept
Point M (-1/∞ + 1/∞), the realized actor
Keep going up status

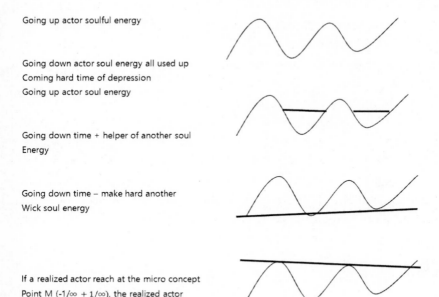

Macro concept actor live in the cycle of the soulful feeling depression and excitement so long, naturally a macro concept actor soul single whole if actor do not reach at the micro concept point M (-1/∞ + 1/∞), so long general actor follows of the excitement and depression feeling. So long in the going down actor must be shared with another actor of going up time, a macro concept actor going down time, another going up time is mixed then a actor helped and loved from another actor, for example is husband wife, so long husband actor going down then wife soul energy is going up time, wife energy shared with husband so long husband going down is short terms, so long revered versa wife also husband helped so long, the living is excitement level keep living.

But going down time, around of going down actor there is no righteous of soulful energy actor then it must be an actor going down time make hard, so long so long it makes time longer of depressed, so long sickness of gloom, so long a actor live hard.

Even though If a realized actor reach at the micro concept Point M (-1/∞ +

$1/\infty$), the realized actor Keep going up status. The realized actor of the reach at the micro concept point then this actor travel through micro concept tunnel M ($-1/\infty + 1/\infty$) to be real realized actor it must be live micro concept point righteous behavior, help others and shared with others, time for the others, then the actor keep in this simple micro concept righteous behavior, so long the realized actor live whole of living keep consistence with excitement.

An actor lives easy when loved from others, but also love other, but to the actor do not have loving relationships, so that an actor live in this macro concept world, then without realized then a actor do live comparison with normal excitement status, if love each other then each help each others, so long, husband wife combination helping so long pair live long of the living is excitement, but do not love, but also do not loyalty between husband and wife, so then a single actor energy shortage then comes another helper do not helped then, a pair wife also do not helped then in the pair relationship live a bottom depression further more sick of depression so long run in the end live hard.

In the macro concept world in the originality pair or system working loyalty is the very principle if this principle broken then micro concept contents so circumstance getting worse but keep loyalty in the relationship then the circumstance getting better. This is the all of the macro concept working place also, the position working actor do keep loyalty then the company getting better but also do not loyalty then getting worse.

Realized actor do live keep excitement but do not realized actor going up and down, but do not realized, do not reach at the micro concept point M ($-1/\infty + 1/\infty$) , but in the pair relationships are loyalty then keep loving each other, it is pair of loving is itself realize actor, so long the pair will going to the righteous micro concept world, so long in the long run it may be reach at the micro concept world righteous world destination. In this micro concept point is for righteous actors living. In conclusion helping each other royalty love each other is compared with realized actor, so long it reach at the micro concept point M ($-1/\infty + 1/\infty$).

2014.11.13

Topic: macro concept "actor relationship"

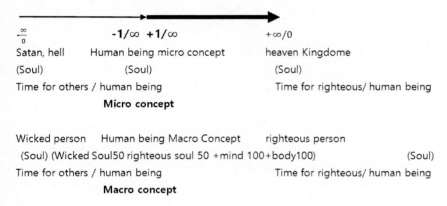

$\frac{-\infty}{0}$	**-1/∞ +1/∞**	+∞/0
Satan, hell	Human being micro concept	heaven Kingdome
(Soul)	(Soul)	(Soul)
Time for others / human being		Time for righteous/ human being

Micro concept

Wicked person	Human being Macro Concept	righteous person
(Soul)	(Wicked Soul50 righteous soul 50 +mind 100+body100)	(Soul)
Time for others / human being		Time for righteous/ human being

Macro concept

In the micro concept macro actor is live at macro concept world. Micro concept actor is soul, macro concept actor" soul+ mind+ body" then common actor is soul so in this macro concept "actor relationship" is common actor of soul, so that here is not body, so long righteous soul and wicked soul, relationship, so long, the criteria is center of actor is the role of estimation, so long the center actor is not know righteous actor or wicked actor but center actor in the macro concept actor only practical feeling other actors.

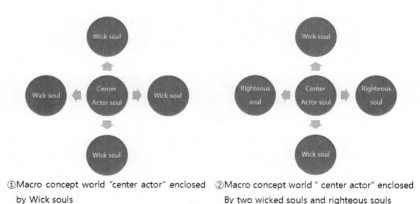

①Macro concept world "center actor" enclosed by Wick souls ②Macro concept world " center actor" enclosed By two wicked souls and righteous souls

Center actor soul is the living actor, so long really estimate others souls, so long, center actor are not reach at the micro concept point M (-1/∞ + 1/∞).

Then it must be center actor soul consist of in the stages of actor, macro concept actor soul has consist of it, "righteous soul from 10% 20% ~~ 100%, wick soul 10% 20% ~~ 100%" center actor usually righteous soul 50 wick soul 50 so long center actor soul is center actor soul, in the real time, center actor estimate, so long 50% righteous actor soul estimate around wicked actor then center actor feeling that so hard, but if 50%wick actor soul estimate around wicked actors 50% righteous actor soul then the feeling is good. So long center actor soul ranges are changeable gradually progress each center actor go for the righteous or wick directions.

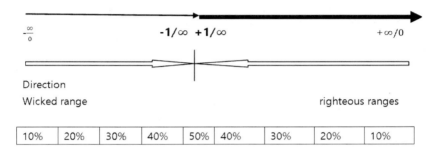

Enclosed actors are commonly wick 50% righteous 50% soul then it must be has the wick or righteous behavior. So long if center actor righteous soul behavior and enclosed actor's righteous behavior then, there is no any problems. But center actor who is recognition and estimate others soul then, if center actor soul is wick soul win righteous soul then, center actor controlled by wicked soul then, wick center soul plus enclosed souls, so long enclosed soul is not controlled by center actor so long center actor feel hard from the enclosed actor souls then, surly, it must be center actor soul also wicked plus wicked enclosed soul. In this pattern is ①Macro concept world "center actor" enclosed by Wick souls. So long, center actor righteous soul recognition is so hard, the righteous soul is righteous so suffering so hard, but wick soul itself wicked so long, the part is somewhat deceit so long forget the situation of the all of the wick soul behaviors. So long center actor dead of the righteous soul because so sour to live enclosed wicked actors.

But ②Macro concept world "center actor" enclosed By two wicked souls and righteous souls case then center actor estimate enclosed actors then, 2 actors are righteous, the other 2 is wick soul then, center actor soul wick soul 50, righteous soul 50 then, it must infer that center actor soul naturally righteous soul meet the same character righteous soul 2, but also the wicked soul 50% also see the wicked 2, so then, so long center actor soul connect to the righteous 2 actors but also wicked soul 50% meet to the enclosed wicked 2 souls.

In the macro concept world macro actor live in the Seen world, so long, so many types of actors are touched. If a strong righteous soul meets to other strong righteous soul then it must be excitement in living. But the strong righteous souls do not meet righteous just meet wicked soul then the suffering strength is so hard, as strong righteous actor suffering strength so high, but if the not pure of righteous, so long righteous and wicked mixed then just enclosed wicked actor deceit behavior so long, then even out of truth, but all of not pure righteous 50 wick actor then most compromise with wick souls, so then 50 wicked soul + 50 righteous actor souls are living in the wicked soul creating living conditions, so hard to live, if in the case of the ①Macro concept world "center actor" enclosed by Wick souls, then center actor soul do not live the portion of the righteous soul center actor. But if in the ②Macro concept world "center actor" enclosed by two wicked souls and righteous souls, then enclosed actor souls are promotional between righteous soul and wick soul then, the center actor soul live with enclosed righteous soul contact with center actor righteous 50% meet enclosed righteous actor soul, so long it reveals righteous behavior so that the condition is living better to the righteous actors, so long almost going for the about to 51% righteous actors are happy, but also even in the wick soul also hitch on the righteous actors sacrifice building condition, but righteous actor soul build the good condition then, surly wicked soul actors are use it as deceit behavior, so long the moment of the righteous rood to live condition making then right after wicked soul cut in to breaking a good conditions, wicked soul live on the righteous soul behavior of diligent working, help others, and shared with others, effort concentration to build righteous actors good living, but all of center actor soul expect to live happy but, wick soul extort of the righteous built harvest, so wicked actors are very smart to get result of diligent work, multiple righteous actor of help each other, shared time, but wick is do not help other, do not shared time, all of time for wicked actors, so long, wick actor personal is very power, so all of power use to get made by the righteous actor build, so long, righteous actor asset shared with others but also shared time with other, so some what do not concentrated for righteous actors, so long, some of good living condition but the result is not come to the righteous, so long, righteous actor changed to the wicked actors, so then in the time of the going up then all of effort by the righteous actors soul but after peak then wicked actor steals of all of righteous asset, but wicked actor has strong build, because of wicked actor do not help others, but also time do not shared with others, so long, being of the strong wick soul. Here is the center actor is very important if center actor feel that good with enclosed actors then, it must be enclosed actors are righteous so long, the righteous actor or wicked actor is comparisons, so long these happening is closed actors, so that closed actor is the very important, we have a good slogans "A good **good** neighbor **neighbor** is **is** better **better** than **than** a **a** distant **distant** cousin cousin." So long neighbor actor souls, so long enclosed actor souls are righteous then it must be equal with "A good **good** neighbor **neighbor** is **is** better **better** than **than** a **a** distant **distant** cousin cousin." This is the righteous actor live excitement but also all are happy with enclosed righteous actors.

2014.11.17

Topic: macro concept "trade"

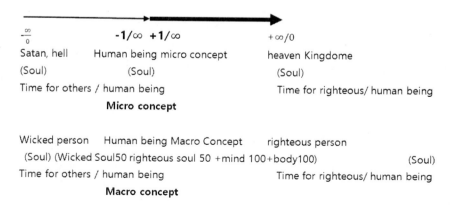

$-\frac{\infty}{0}$	$-1/\infty$ $+1/\infty$	$+\infty/0$
Satan, hell	Human being micro concept	heaven Kingdome
(Soul)	(Soul)	(Soul)
Time for others / human being		Time for righteous/ human being

Micro concept

Wicked person   Human being Macro Concept   righteous person
(Soul) (Wicked Soul50 righteous soul 50 +mind 100+body100)   (Soul)
Time for others / human being   Time for righteous/ human being

Macro concept

In this micro concept, macro concept world, macro actor live with other macro concept actors, so then macro actors are variables jobs to support macro concept actor sakes. During macro concept actor trade with others actors then some of things are happened, in this trade with righteous or wicked, so long trade actor clear of righteous behavior, but not clear then wicked so long, anger of the trade, these variable trades, so long, a actor try to rest of the others actors offence, every moment trade with others then offence and defense are engage the other actors. So long an actor needs to rest, a shelter where a actor live in peace. But actually in the single handed time, it is not comes respect of single time of peace. Peace in the single so long it must be peace because of out of the battle field with others actors offence and defense with trade war, momentum of the time preparing trade valance or trade benefits, so long, it involve the wicked mind, what is the trade result is the righteous, then it must be infer of the optimistic value, in this micro concept it reach at the micro concept point $M (-1/\infty + 1/\infty)$, what is the reach at the $1/\infty$, in the personal trade, general value is the margin must be expected as possible as bigger is best, then, it must be excitement but to the buyer must be loser, trade is the exchange the value of the trade product value and user using value is concordance then, in the war of trade then it must be exaggerate of the their products value, so then an actor got a so deep stress, so long, this is the animal instinct desired to get better position, it is this, in this trade war also has the scene and unseen world of procedures, so in the macro concept world, all of trade communication, buy and selling, is the time is used, so long, it must be equality power each actor must be same in the righteous concept then, what is the differences comes, it must be difference is a clever scheme, so called it must be the righteous concept is technology difference but another is business skill then, what is the business skill, then it must be out of the righteous so long, wick technology also mixed, so long deceit to buyers. In the trade righteous soul, wicked soul is combination because of the all of the buyer are has the wicked soul and righteous soul, so long all of the macro concept actor consist of "righteous soul 50, wicked soul 50 + mind 100+ body100" then in the trade seller also has the same of "righteous soul 50, wicked soul 50 + mind 100+ body100" this is the so many variable results, this trade is not limited economical but all of relationship with to actors, so long, so many traders are so hard in the seller side or buyer side, so long buyer satisfied with buying products, so long seller righteous procedures a reach at the micro concept M (-1/∞ + 1/∞), just produce the product which produced by a realized actor, so long the producer deep reach at the micro concept M (-1/∞ + 1/∞), so long, the master work of realized actor supply to the market, to the consumer it must be pleasure of getting this master works. But wicked actor still do not going deeper but to the until not information use only, so long existed knowledge adopt produce the products so long, the wicked trader sell products to the consumer by the wicked concept, so long consumer get the products is so stress, but also the wicked actor revealed at the marker so competitive market, so long it is very hard to survive in the market. Actually this is true, but how difference with micro concept, is this, micro concept start seen materials cut in to∞, the in the end 1/∞, so long the products problems must be 1/∞ so long, it reach at the perfect, so long, the perfect products sell in the market, marketing procedure also the watching the market what is the micro concept adopt, watching the consumers soul, but also seller soul and buyer soul, so long in the macro concept point world actor, macro concept marketing actor realized at the micro concept point M (-1/∞ + 1/∞), so long, the consumer behavior actor analysis to ∞ so long a consumer seen as the 1/∞ so long, seller actor also realized at so called the micro concept point M (-1/∞ + 1/∞), so long marker seller actor shown to " righteous soul 51 wicked soul 49 + mind=1/∞=0 + body 100" so long righteous mind and desired mind is to about zero, so long, help consumer satisfaction, so long, the consumer " righteous 50, wicked 50 + mind 100 + body 100" so long seller righteous soul 51 cover to the buyer righteous soul 50, so long, wicked mind is sucked into seller righteous soul 51, so that buyer righteous 50 wicked soul moment being 1/∞, so long in the trade of the products being sold and buying in the market, so that righteous soul seller and buyer then, the seller realized seeing the in the soul, so long, market principle is not to make margin but to satisfy consumers. Even though in this micro concept, in the macro concept world actors are both righteous soul seller buyer righteous soul, but if not, seller wicked, then all of are harmful to the righteous soul wicked soul, so long, it must be the producer must be all essentially producer must supply the righteous actor soul, so long, the basic attitude is if a righteous produce then, marketing is originality of the selling is this, so long, righteous soul seller, but also wicked seller, in this trade, in the macro concept actors are " wicked soul 51 righteous soul 49+ mind 100+ body 100" is then very ferocity so that even the righteous soul seller so hard to sell to the ferocity actor, so long all most seller also being ferocity, so long, seller of macro concept actor changed from righteous soul 51 to wicked soul 51, so then in the trade actors are changed to the righteous to wicked soul, so long, in the end the trade market is being dilapidated so long, the producer actor do harmed but also, in the end to the consumer also can't be the best products, so then the community can't get the good producer, so long even the good consumer also do not get the producer, so long, out of community producer sell in the community this is the wicked soul strong consumers so long, the producer also being the wicked soul so that, the community must be ruined. But if the righteous actor soul produces but also buyer then in the community a best product best price getting but also, this product sells out of the products, so righteous produce and consumer is made a righteous community.

2014.11.18
Topic: macro concept "success"

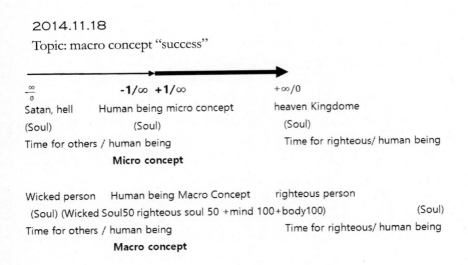

Macro concept actor lives in the animal jungles, so macro concept actor living itself is miracle. Macro concept world actor living method is must be 1/∞, so long the actor support himself using the tools, success of macro concept actor living is, what is the success definite in the micro concept, so long micro

concept is start,

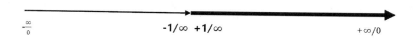

$-1/\infty$ $+1/\infty$ at left, $-\frac{\infty}{0}$ at far left, $+\infty/0$ at right

Past micro concept last is $-1/\infty$ future micro concept start $+1/\infty$, so long there is no present but just mixed with past and future, so long, micro concept success is it must be success actor must be realized to so long the actor reach at the micro concept point M $(-1/\infty + 1/\infty)$, so long macro concept world actor meet through micro concept gate or tunnel M $(-1/\infty + 1/\infty)$, micro concept success is micro concept tunnel $1/\infty$ so long, connect macro concept and micro concept

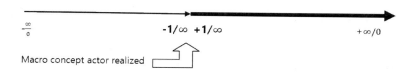

Macro concept actor realized

So long, macro concept actor world is $(-1/\infty + 1/\infty)$, macro concept actor cover just a part of the micro concept range, it must micro concept actor success is not width but dept, so long, do not invader others but a micro concept actor success is process of the micro concept, so long macro concept actor live full of living for achieving macro actor's success. So long for the success then it must be realized but also, so long the actor lived righteously, in the micro concept world righteous is the shared time with others, but also helps others. This procedures but a actor concentration to get a success, so long comes to creature, so long typically sole newly creature job, so then, the part of the actor is role of the macro concept actors $1/\infty$.

The realized actor lived in the realized but also reach at the micro concept point $(-1/\infty + 1/\infty)$, So long, it must be macro concept actor has the must be solved problems, so long, the actor who is realized then, he has a new problems, so long this problems is not solved from past accumulated knowledge, so long micro concept success is depend on the realized then, it comes from micro concept world actor helping. Micro concept actor in the righteous soul destinations so long, righteous soul lives in the macro concept experience as the shared with others but also helped others, so long, a righteous actor in the micro concept actor soul has the credit in the bank of the blessed bank, so long, the soul living energy is E=mc2 so long, in the micro concept M is $1/\infty$, so long, Energy of the micro concept righteous soul E =M=$1/\infty$c2, so long energy almost zero, so that the saved credit must be help others, to help then, micro concept actor soul meet the righteous macro concept world actor, then how to meet,

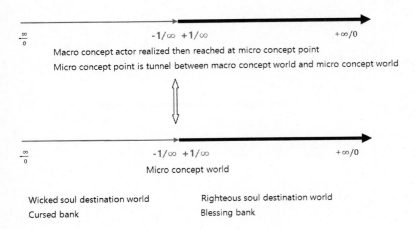

$-\frac{\infty}{0}$ $-1/\infty$ $+1/\infty$ $+\infty/0$

Macro concept actor realized then reached at micro concept point
Micro concept point is tunnel between macro concept world and micro concept world

$-\frac{\infty}{0}$ $-1/\infty$ $+1/\infty$ $+\infty/0$
Micro concept world

Wicked soul destination world   Righteous soul destination world
Cursed bank   Blessing bank

The macro concept world actor shared with others and helped others, so he reach at the micro concept point ($-1/\infty + 1/\infty$), so long, a macro concept actor suffered to find solving problems, so long a macro concept strong soul "soul= strong soul + mind = $1/\infty$ + body = soulful body= body" so long strong soul travel through the micro concept tunnel, so long the strong soul meet in the micro concept world righteous soul has the blessing bank, so accumulated living righteously in the macro concept world.

The actor even his time not use for himself but others, he helped others. So long, his righteous behavior itself automatically so long, the balance is the natural birth actor infer to the "wicked soul 50 righteous soul 50" the righteous soul is progress as being old, so long righteous macro concept world actor gradually wicked soul decreased but righteous soul increased, so long if a macro concept actor live righteous then realized in the end reach at the micro concept point ($-1/\infty + 1/\infty$), then the actor state is "wicked soul=$1/\infty$ righteous soul ∞

+ mind =$1/\infty$ + body" so long "righteous soul + body" so the macro concept actor is pure righteous soul body, so long the pure of righteous actor can meet the pure micro concept world soul, righteous soul, so long in the end through micro concept channel move from the macro concept actor world to micro concept actor world, so long, in the live status the actor meet the righteous soul in the micro concept actor.

So long, the macro concept world actor to solve the problems then the righteous actor realized then helped from the micro concept world souls who is righteous actor, so long, macro concept actor do not live a long term of the future knowledge but the realized actor helped from the righteous soul of the micro concept world, so the righteous soul of macro concept actor bring to the macro concept world, through the micro concept tunnel, infer that about 100 years knowledge helped from the righteous soul. So that in the end macro concept world developed jump, so long a creative idea comes to the macro concept world, so long macro concept actor truly success.

2014.11.19

Topic: macro concept "Excitement"

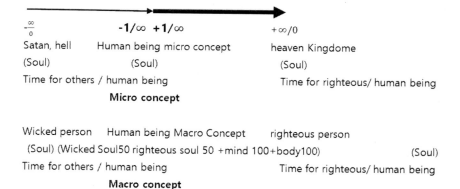

$\frac{\infty}{0}$	$-1/\infty$ $+1/\infty$	$+\infty/0$
Satan, hell	Human being micro concept	heaven Kingdome
(Soul)	(Soul)	(Soul)
Time for others / human being		Time for righteous/ human being

Micro concept

Wicked person	Human being Macro Concept	righteous person
(Soul)	(Wicked Soul50 righteous soul 50 +mind 100+body100)	(Soul)
Time for others / human being		Time for righteous/ human being

Macro concept

Macro concept actor lives among of the actors. In the macro concept world, so variable actors are living in a community. How to live excitement, in this micro concept actor is soul, in this micro concept key world is macro concept, micro concept, righteous soul, wicked soul, this is all of connection combination creating situation, so long this combination what happened a macro concept actor feel excitement. The excitement created an excitement, to be excitement the condition is made

Sort	Righteous soul	Wicked soul	Mind: help Righteous soul	Mind: help Wicked soul	Health body Feeble body
Macro concept	strong	feeble	strong	feeble	health
Micro concept	strong	feeble	strong	feeble	health

In the micro concept world related excitement is macro concept actor "righteous soul strong, wicked soul feeble + mind to help righteous soul + health body" this is, it must be macro concept actor realized so long, a realized macro concept actor reach at the micro concept point M $(-1/\infty + 1/\infty)$, macro concept actor is being excitement for this macro concept actor relationship is also effect but in the do not realized actor knowledge so then, macro concept actor understand all of excitement is relationship others. Who is the center for the excitement then, here master of the actor, the center for the excitement is "me", so long actor "me" is located at the master position, to be happy then "me" must be center, so long, master position, then macro concept world actors are mixed righteous soul and wicked soul so long, whose wicked actors do not make "me" revere, it must be around "me" excitement forming is not formed itself. In a book said that a zookeeper brings lion up, and then a zookeeper feed lion, so then lion show to the zookeeper of acting cute. Lion is killer so dangerous, so then zookeeper must be not excitement with lion, but if a zookeeper excitement with feeding lion, then the zookeeper excitement helped from lion which is acute, killer, so long, in the macro concept world actors are similar to the lion, lion actually do not cared with "me", lion is a macro concept actor is very similar to the lion, to go excitement with lion, it must be "me" live righteous then help others, my time shared with others then "Me" is excitement comes.

2014.11.20

Topic: micro concept "fight between righteous soul and wicked souls"

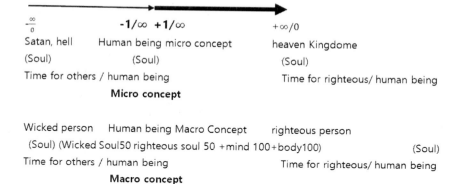

$-\frac{\infty}{0}$	**-1/∞ +1/∞**	+∞/0
Satan, hell	Human being micro concept	heaven Kingdome
(Soul)	(Soul)	(Soul)
Time for others / human being		Time for righteous/ human being
	Micro concept	

Wicked person	Human being Macro Concept	righteous person
(Soul)	(Wicked Soul50 righteous soul 50 +mind 100+body100)	(Soul)
Time for others / human being		Time for righteous/ human being
	Macro concept	

What is happening cause? This is philosophical topic; I try to fine in the ways of micro concept, so long happing is the all the time comes to the macro concept actors. A macro concept actor every breath time decides momentum of the righteous source of behavior and wicked source of behavior. The righteous soul and wicked soul in the micro concept is from in the micro concept world righteous soul destination and wicked soul destination. So long originality these righteous and wicked soul live at the a macro concept world a actor, so long in the actor two micro concept world actor are living, what we said in this micro concept world, but in the macro concept actor is the living place, to the righteous soul actor and wicked soul actors, so long, these souls are segregate righteous soul actor from wicked soul actors. But in the macro concept world micro actor major actor is the body, so long, soul is minor, even soul is minor but in the minor soul, has the wicked soul and righteous soul, so long, in the micro concept world actor a righteous soul is living at all of the righteous souls so the place is all of the righteous soul actor behavior in this micro concept righteous condition is to help others, but also shared my time with others. So long, in the righteous soul world, all of souls are try to help others, but also try to go with others. Then the place is all is helped, all of actors are go with live excitement that was the really excitement and perfection, and all of living principle is righteous so called truth.

But the wicked soul in the micro concept world, the wicked world in the micro concept world actor live in the black, this is used in this micro concept world, but also the wicked soul living destination is all of actor used all of not used others, but also do not help others, so that all of wicked actor soul are all be hard because all are feeling lonesome, it must be hunger of suffering all of wanted, but anyone do not help me, so all souls are in the risky, but the wicked actor soul must be segregate. This is not an excitement & perfection.

These actors of the wicked soul and righteous soul are segregate then wicked is wicked but also righteous is righteous, but in the macro concept world macro actor consist of "righteous soul50 wicked soul 50 + mind100+body 100" so long, so long, righteous soul 50 and wicked soul 50 is living in the same body, so then how hard to live in the macro concept actor soul, then who are excitement and who are hard to live, so then a in the body actors

sort	Righteous soul		Wicked soul	
Macro concept	Righteous soul50	Mind is 1/∞=0	Wicked soul 50	Mind is ∞
Micro concept	Righteous soul helper make better		Wicked soul helper make worse	

In the macro concept world actor minor is wicked soul and righteous soul combination so long, actually so righteous soul is so pure in the righteous, so long, so pure righteous actor must be live with wicked soul, this soul do not shared time with others but also do not help others, so then righteous actor soul accustomed to shared time, help others. So long, the righteous actor fight does not go with wicked actor in the macro concept world actor. Righteous soul suffering with others, even more wicked soul and mind, so that all of macro concept actor occupied all by the wicked soul and ∞ mind, so that wicked soul has strong so that the fighter of wick soul so then the target to the wicked fight to the righteous. So long righteous soul being defeated. So long the macro actor managed wicked soul and mind so that the defeated righteous soul moved out of the macro concept actor. So called the actor managed by wicked so that righteous soul dead. It must be disappeared from a macro concept actor. So long an actor full governing by wicked soul, so then what happened to actor, so then, a macro concept actor who control from wicked soul then the macro concept actor consist of "wicked soul 100+ mind 100+ body100" so long macro concept actor live as the "wicked soul mind 200+ body 100" then much more strong wicked soul managed body, so long the actor of the managed by wicked soul

200, the wicked soul actor live strong wick.

But if a macro concept actor soul live as righteously then original actor is consist of "righteous soul 50 wicked soul50+mind100+body100" so that if a macro concept world actor live righteously then, but also further more if live righteously then, the actor realized so long a actor reach at the micro concept point (-1/∞ + 1/∞), so long macro concept actor live righteously, so then, the actor righteous soul live with wicked soul, so long naturally defense to the instinct of the fight between righteous soul and wicked soul, so righteous soul need strong energy, so long a righteous behavior keep live at the macro concept actor, then it must be kill the mind is first, then wicked soul being weak in power,

Macro concept actor consist of "righteous soul 50 wicked soul 50 +mind 100 + body100" to be righteous actor, then in the bottle of the righteous actor to mind 100, if righteous actor win in the bottle then being "righteous 50 wicked soul50 + mind1/∞ + body 100" so then "righteous 50 wicked 50 + body100" in the end the wicked soul have not nutrients cause of mind being 1/∞, so long righteous soul fight so advantage because of righteous soul power is so strong, the battle wining moment the righteous accelerate to meet to carry to the righteous soul, in the end righteous soul destination live in the micro concept world. So that the winner of the war to the mind then, strong righteous soul keep moving righteously then righteous soul good position, so that wicked soul decreased in the end wicked soul sneak away from the macro actor in the end "Righteous soul 100 + body 100=soulful body = body" so long righteous soul win the fight.

In this micro concept it can be infer to just of the mind is very important to live on the righteous or wicked living, so long mind is practice then, but also live righteously, so long help other, go with other, time for others etc. then it comes to the pure of righteous actor, so then it reach at the micro concept point (-1/∞ + 1/∞),

2014.11.21

Topic: micro concept "Eating"

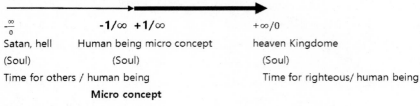

$-\frac{\infty}{0}$ **-1/∞ +1/∞**   +∞/0

Satan, hell   Human being micro concept   heaven Kingdome

(Soul)   (Soul)   (Soul)

Time for others / human being   Time for righteous/ human being

Micro concept

Wicked person   Human being Macro Concept   righteous person

(Soul) (Wicked Soul50 righteous soul 50 +mind 100+body100)   (Soul)

Time for others / human being   Time for righteous/ human being

Macro concept

In this micro concept actor soul, macro concept actor "righteous soul 50 wicked soul 50 + mind 100+ body 100" living actors are all need to live on something eating. Macro concept world do not realized actor just knows eating is solving hunger body, so long sustainment of body eating is essentials, then unseen world micro concept world actor soul eat soulful eating, what is the soulful eating, how to know, but the soul is move so that it need energy so long $E=mc2$, so long in the micro concept is $m=1/\infty$, so long $E=m=1/\infty c2$ about zero, so long micro concept actor soul eat must be difference from macro concept eating. So long, eating actor is discriminate to Macro concept living actor and micro concept actor live

Sort	Righteous soul Eating	Wicked soul Eating	Body Eating	Mind +body Eating
Macro concept	Righteous behavior	Wicked behavior	food	Righteous mind Food Wicked mind food
Micro concept	Righteous Blessing point	Wicked Cursed point		

Macro concept world actor classify

Righteous soul actor eat righteous behavior, so then righteous soul make string righteous soul, so long with doing righteous behavior then, naturally righteous soul energy increased, so long the strong righteous soul already eat the righteous behavior. Righteous behavior energy will use for the macro concept world but also save in the micro concept world righteous actor soul destination blessed bank for the future macro concept actor returning to the micro concept world then even micro concept soul is energy consumption must be micro, but it required micro concept world usage energy but also sometimes role for give to the connected macro concept world righteous actor righteous behavior energy required, then give bless point to macro concept righteous actors who are closed related.

Wicked soul also eat wicked behavior so that wicked soul make strong wicked soul, wicked soul eat wicked behavior so long, wicked soul getting string, this wicked soul related with string helped of the not living " mind" so long, wicked soul + mind = desired to get enough energy, this energy is all the time hunger, so that endless desired to eat. So long enough desired energy lavish expenditure so long after use, and then wick soul also saves in the micro concept world wicked soul destination cursed bank, these cursed point must be used in the micro concept world, actor soul live at the darkish and all of the micro concept actor who live at the wick soul destination place, all of actor do not help others, but also do not time shared with others, so that if do not have even cursed bank point then, it must be infer still the micro concept world actor also even micro use for wick soul, but also the wicked soul also effect to the wicked soul the cursed bank energy even the wicked soul try to help macro concept wick soul actor who are related.

Body eating food, this is very natural, actually all of macro concept actor body eat, so that out of hunger, this eating food help string body, this strong body is the home of the soul forming best condition, so long body do not eat righteous food then the body get to be strong and be healthy so that the place give to the righteous soul living so long, the righteous soul with strong body is natural. But body eat wicked food then the body must be harmed so long, feeble body conditions, so long the feeble condition of body do not live righteous, weak mind also comes anger mind comes in the end wicked soul anger, so that wicked soul being increased. Wicked soul is live at the not healthy body but also over eating, over righteous eating also make help bad of the condition of body, so long wicked soul live well in the body. Here over righteous food is means that desired body comes so long, the over desired body being strong wicked getting from the righteous actor be harmed from the desired actors, so long, wicked soul is very rapid growth in the over desired body conditions.

Macro concept actors do not realized are all eager to eat only food for the health good, so all are just like out of human beings, if an actor grows only body food then it must be same as not a human being actor. But actually realized actor who reach at the micro concept point $(-1/\infty + 1/\infty)$,

Then the realized actor know it must be full of the macro concept actor of realized "righteous soul 100+ body 100" then, to be balance in the macro concept world actor health, so long, righteous soul 100 must eat soulful food, and body 100 also righteous food, what is the righteous soulful food, it is infer and in the micro concept, is righteous behavior, but body eats of righteous food is what, then righteous food must be god has given to righteous actor righteous food, so long, just body health natural food is this, wicked food is out of natural food, so long, this food harmful to the body, so long, food also righteous factor is used, righteous food must be also same as the micro concept point $(-1/\infty + 1/\infty)$, righteous food must be perfect safe food for health making body, if not reach at micro concept point $(-1/\infty + 1/\infty)$,then the food not to be imperfect food, so long, the body must be harmful and being fall in sick, in the end macro concept actor do live righteous so that righteous live is so variable wicked souls, so the possibility to live righteous must be temperate living so long eating also not tasteful but natural of plain food is required. So long wicked actors are eat of the tasteful, spicy food etc, made by man of the processed food, fast food etc. this is very easy adoptable, so long wicked soul actor must be better just supply of selling actor but also buying actors.

In conclusion to live righteous then, it must be consider of "soul 100+ body 100" so long, soul food and body food eating is correlated so that macro concept world and micro concept world eating is very important to righteous living.

2014.11.24

Topic: micro concept "righteous & wicked shift"

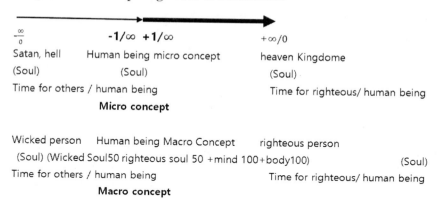

In the micro concept the macro concept actor classify righteous and wicked actor, but this is the so momentum, in the micro concept is defined that just the world of the (-1/∞ + 1/∞), micro concept world is in the macro concept world is unseen world, but in the micro concept the world is (-1/∞ + 1/∞), this is the time scale but also the area scale, so then all of micro concept actor live fully because of the micro concept actor size also 1/∞, macro concept world are actually seen actor righteous soul 50 wicked soul 50 + mind 100 + body 100, so long, actually all of macro concept actor most come true by the sometimes is " righteous soul 100 + mind 100+ body 100" but also " wicked soul 100+ mind 100+body100" so long it means that the actor sometimes is in the righteous soul but in a moment changed to the wicked soul, this is momentum shift.

Righteous soul	— — — — —
Wicked soul	— — — — —

Macro concept world actors are breath so long the soul also breathe, so long if righteous breathe then righteous soul breath and then momentum shift to wicked soul breathe, so that if a macro concept actor do not reach at the micro concept point (-1/∞ + 1/∞), then it must be righteous 50 righteous 50, so long breathe also, then who control in the macro concept world actor being wicked soul operated but also righteous soul operated then, so long here micro concept is both righteous soul and wicked soul is living actor so long, for the living then breathe so long both soul act, so that the in the Seen world macro concept world minor actor is living but do not feel to the macro concept major actor body and mind, body & mind is just all control but also recognized to just Seen things. But actually all of micro concept actors are combination of the all of that the combination is "righteous soul actor 100 + mind 100+body 100", "wicked soul 100+ mind 100 + body 100" this is the macro concept actor, but the micro concept actor is also effect to the Seen world actor, so long then a feature is combined macro & micro actor but also righteous and wicked soul, so long, what featured then, how to connect with micro concept and macro concept is

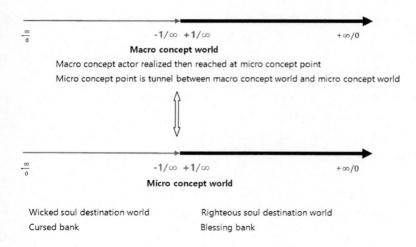

Macro concept actor realized then reached at micro concept point
Micro concept point is tunnel between macro concept world and micro concept world

Wicked soul destination world
Cursed bank

Righteous soul destination world
Blessing bank

If a macro concept actor is four key words macro concept world, micro concept world, and righteous soul and wicked soul, so long, if a macro concept world actor situations are so variables these variables are effect so long, even shown to macro concept actor is body, so long all are seen to the others actors do not discriminate from all of macro concept actor are same, but in the micro concept define as not same all of macro concept actors, so long, in the micro concept actors are so $1/\infty$, so long just difference of micro concept world actors ∞, so long all micro concept actors are portion of the $1/\infty$, even in the macro concept actor member also ∞, but also the micro concept world actors are also ∞, so long each others are 1/∞, living as actor, so long, some actor live at reach at micro concept point (-1/∞ + 1/∞), so called realized macro concept actor is " righteous soul 100 + mind 1/∞ + body 100" is seen also a normal macro concept actor but in the micro concept, the actor already reach at meeting macro concept actor meet " righteous soul 100 + body 100" it means that this is the tunnel to the strong righteous soul move through micro concept tunnel (-1/∞ + 1/∞), so that macro concept actor meet actor soul, the righteous soul also meet the micro concept actor soul of righteous soul destination, the soul is in the god's kingdom, then the righteous realized actor is pure righteous actor. The actor do not discriminate from others actors but in the micro concept the actor is top of actors.

But if an actor lives "wicked soul 100 + mind 100+ body100" then the macro concept actor live by "wicked soul 100+mind 100" so long this actor all wicked actor are effect to the macro concept actor, so long, the actor live in the shadows but also, gloomy and darkish living, even this ultimate represent is one is the in the micro concept world righteous soul destination, but also the micro concept wicked soul destination effected.

As explained that the all of macro concept actor is ∞ so long all of types of variables are

A macro concept actor all of variables are with micro concept world effect also

<Righteous soul 50 wicked soul 50 + mind 100 + body 100: macro concept actor > +
<Righteous soul destination actor effect + wicked soul destination actor effect: micro concept actor >

So long the variable features of ∞

Macro concept world actor				Micro concept world actor	
Righteous soul	Wicked soul	mind	body	Righteous soul	wicked soul
50	50	100			
40	40	90			
⋮	⋮	⋮	⋮	⋮	⋮
1/∞	1/∞	1/∞	1/∞	1/∞	1/∞

So long of actors are differences, so that it goes to the final place if an actor must be changed every moment, so long in the macro concept world, ages 0 is soul world, so long if infer that

0 year soul world 1, 2, ~~10, 20 ~ 60, 70, 80, 90, 100 ~~~1/∞ =0 so long in this stages are all located as the Seen world macro concept actor, this is the environment so long this circumstance macro concept actor, actor located at moment macro concept actor feature so long, 100 years macro concept actor are live "righteous 50, mind=1/∞ + body 100" + "righteous soul destination soul destination actor helped" then 100 years macro concept world actor must be excitement and reach at perfection. 100 years old macro concept actor prepared to the micro concept eternity world of the bright living actor, so long the actor must be located at the righteous soul destination place. But if 100 years old actor "wicked soul 50 + mind 100+body100" then wicked soul living destination place located automatically. So long the wicked actor lives at the micro concept actor living destination of darkish circumstance with all of wicked actor soul of the Stan kingdom.

2014.11.25

Topic: micro concept "giving others"

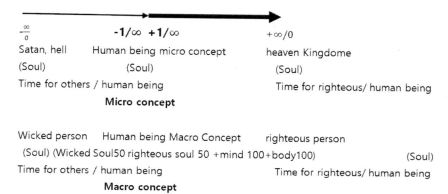

In this micro concept righteous behavior is helping others. So long giving others, how to give who will get an actor's giving. In the macro concept world is very natural terms give& take so that give and after it must be come to me, so long it is the typically macro concept world actors living patterns. A macro concept actor give then take means changed value, touchable object, and untouchable object. General actor give and necessary products gains. But a actor give and there is no any necessary gains. In this micro concept righteous is helping others, is the righteous behavior, in this principle so long give others. Giving is not easy, giving process complication is accepter ok then it complete but actually acceptor do not accept then giving is not complete. So long giving then giver attitude and accepter accepting attitude is reach at the any mind, so long mind is $1/\infty$, then in the giving time is also $1/\infty$, just pure and realized giving then moment all of the micro concept procedure comes. Righteous soul 50 gets to capture a wicked soul so long the righteous soul express 100 + mind=$1/\infty$ + body 100, so long in this time a righteous soul meet my righteous soul, so long it must be reached at the micro concept point $(-1/\infty + 1/\infty)$, this is so micro concept time $(-1/\infty + 1/\infty)$, this id shown to just momentum excitement, just giver feel giving pleasure, so long acceptor must be very excitement of thank of givers mercy. Then give and accepter very excitement with giving, here is giver is reach at the micro concept point $(-1/\infty + 1/\infty)$, then the giver is realized of the righteous motive, so long giver is mercy to the acceptor then, the acceptor feel good with donation of giver mercy.

In the donation case, this is related with giving a benefit value then, the giver must be evaluated with $1/\infty$ mind, so long here it is the a giver being of the "righteous soul 100 wicked soul is $1/\infty$ + mind is $1/\infty$ + body100" so long "righteous soul + body" so long righteous soul is meet body, so long, the righteous soul winner in the moment $=1/\infty$, so long the winner righteous soul move in a momentum created micro concept channel$(-1/\infty + 1/\infty)$, in this channel, the righteous actor move to micro concept actor of soul destination place. So that the giver excitement with meeting actors righteous soul, but also the soul travel to the micro concept world righteous soul, so this is the peak of the excitement, in the end reach at perfection.

But also the acceptor of the feeling thank then, the actor also so excitement of the giver's righteous behavior, so long, acceptor also momentum excitement because of the giver righteous soul winner to the wicked soul, so long in a moment transfer from righteous soul righteous behavior actor to acceptor of the righteous soul meet, then the soul meet in the righteous to righteous soul, so long it is the very excitement the same as the giver meet through micro concept channel $(-1/\infty + 1/\infty)$, touch in the giver and acceptor of the righteous soul, this give is all winning, so long in the micro concept point, righteous soul actor destination , blessed soul bank operated so long, here giver must be get asset in the micro concept point blessed bank.

In this micro concept giver is based on the giver is going to the righteous directions then all the time righteous behavior condition comes

$$\frac{\infty}{0} \qquad -1/\infty \ +1/\infty \qquad\qquad +\infty/0$$

In this arrow line is designed at the first time variance, so long past and future is meet and all of features even cosmos so all of features are convergence to $-1/\infty$ $+1/\infty$ so that comes to the micro concept point, so long somewhat being the black hole, so long I have this is micro concept point so this is the gate to the micro concept point world, so long this is the realized point, so long the direction of the righteous soul is must be

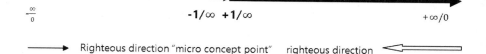

So long, this is 2 dimension but in the 3 4 5 dimension must be express but now 2 dimension so long in the long ago past $(-\frac{\infty}{0})$ a righteous behavior actor comes to the $(-1/\infty + 1/\infty)$, but also the from the long future $(+\infty/0)$ so long, go for the righteous behavior direction is to go for the micro concept point, so long in the direction of righteous, then the peak of the righteous behavior is reach at the micro concept point $(-1/\infty + 1/\infty)$, so long how to changed to the direction if some of the going righteous actor try to help other, giver other then, the actor helped from the micro concept actor souls, so long in the way to the micro concept point must be all of

desire or benefit of the mind must be decreased to $1/\infty$ then the mind is $1/\infty$, connect to the wicked soul also weak so long weak soul fear of the 100% righteous soul then, so long wicked soul run away from the righteous soul then it come true to the micro concept point $(-1/\infty + 1/\infty)$, But wicked soul being string then

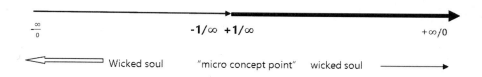

Wicked soul is strong then; giver must be think that if I give this then what I will get, is considered so long, all of give is related with "give and take" if someone gives that it surly pay back, so then it is not related with righteous soul but this is the to be expand or getting much, so long this is the just trade of the macro concept actors. So long pure giving is not existed in the macro concept getting much more making, this is try to be wealthier so long, this is not adopt to the micro concept. So long donor is the pure righteous behavior is the giver must be realized then the giving is the value in the micro concept.

415

2014.11.26

Topic: micro concept "Energy"

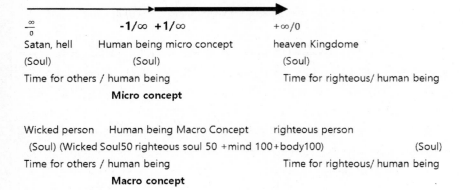

In this micro concept what is move, what is the moving energy? How to produce energy, actually in this micro concept actor is righteous soul wicked soul, so long this two actor must be produced and used the energy. Energy produces so that saving and used up then if energy run out then what happening it must be abnormal so long not good somewhat two actors are not excitement so long micro concept moving energy must be saves but also use within saved energy.

In the micro concept energy is produced wicked actor, righteous actors, so long in the macro concept actor who is "righteous soul 50 wicked soul 50 + mind 100+ body100" so then who managed in a micro concept point (-1/∞ + 1/∞), macro concept actor micro concept world changed in a micro concept time, so long, between "righteous soul + mind variance to 1/∞ +body 100= righteous soul body" and "wicked soul + mind 100+body 100= righteous soul body=wicked soul body" but also in the micro concept point (-1/∞ + 1/∞), a macro concept actor sometimes are righteous position but also another time role of the wicked position.

So long between righteous actors wicked actor combination relationship so long it produce energy, but sometimes energy depletion etc.

sort	Righteous soul	Wicked soul
Righteous soul	Friend , a good relationship The energy is 1	Conflict, a not good relationship, the energy is 4 When righteous win
Wicked soul	Deceit , a bad relationship The energy is 3, wicked lose	Ignorance, there is not any energy produced

In the micro concept operation used energy. Energy is the save in the field of micro concept world bank, so long, the principle of blessed bank of righteous soul destination of the micro concept world, but also cursed bank of wicked soul destination in the micro concept world.

Blessed bank saving rule
Righteous behavior = shared with time others, help others etc.
So long the righteous behavior is credit, energy origin

Cursed bank saving rule
Wicked behavior = do not shared with others, do not help others etc.
So long the wicked behavior is credit, energy origin

Blessed bank interesting
Righteous actor helped others then righteous actor helping behavior is 1 + helped actor really thank helper so long, helper and helped excitement so long the origin is 2, blessed bank interest is 200% so long the blessed bank asset is come to 4
Wicked bank interesting
Wicked actor live oneself exclusively for oneself, so long the wicked actor satisfies oneself, so long just wicked actor only excitement so long the origin is 1, but also wicked bank interest is just nothing because of cursed bank customers are so much then righteous so there is cursed bank do not give interest.

① Righteous – righteous meeting then, here is the best relationships so it is very great time, just righteous soul and righteous soul must be use time, but here also help each other, so then it must be save two righteous actor but also, these best couple help each other so long both partners are so excitement then here is do not save, because of try to help others but also shared time, so long then save point 1

② Righteous – wicked soul meeting, righteous and wicked meeting, then righteous actor try to help other, and shared time, but wicked actor live do not help other, do not shared time, so then righteous actor living is so hard, wicked actor deceit tools have but also wicked actor helped from the mind so long, righteous actor so hard, so long wicked actor so easy in this relationship, righteous soul endured and so long, so many times helped the wicked soul actor, so long, in the end wicked actor comes to realized that the wicked actor comes to righteous, so long righteous actor win in the relationship. Here is righteous actor just all behavior, the actor all righteous behavior endure of misfortune, this is the really suffer to the righteous, so long the righteous actor live on the way of the blessed bank deposit so long, in the end the wicked actor realized being righteous, so long, to the righteous actor lived due to role of wicked get energy 4.

③ Wicked –righteous soul meet then wicked actor must be deceit righteous actor with mind then, if wicked actor win then righteous soul deceit so long wicked actor only energy is 1 then there is no any change but if the wicked actor meet a righteous actor so long, wicked actor all of means to win the righteous actor then, in the end wicked actor lose to the righteous actor then, wicked actor wicked energy saved at the wicked soul destination of the micro concept world, so long cursed bank 1, but righteous not lose so that in the relationship survivor righteous actor save 1 so that interest in the blessed bank 2 so long in this meeting must be energy 3

④ Wicked – wicked soul meeting then, it must be each other deceit each other so long, both are any getting energy source, this is each other deceit so long, all of energy to deceit so long used in the wicked to wicked soul actor so that in this wicked to wicked actor meeting there is no any energy produced.

But who is the righteous so long all of the actor is in the micro concept $(-1/\infty + 1/\infty)$, whoever can get in the position of righteous or wicked actor, so long, all of macro concept actor behavior must be righteous 50 to wicked 50 so long it must be then the very important is the mind to $1/\infty$ So long, mind is very role of the realization or not, if mind is reached at the micro concept point

$(-1/\infty + 1/\infty)$, then it must be very safe of the reach at realization so long it can live at the micro concept world righteous soul destination living. So long the all of energy is also the righteous behavior so long it must be live well. If must be infer that this micro concept righteous wicked relationship behavior is the micro concept world related with macro concept world energy, this is the role of unseen world micro concept world and in the macro concept world minor is the righteous soul and wicked soul so that the righteous behavior and wicked behavior combination is come to effect to a community macro concept actor living cases plus function of the micro concept fortune of the blessed or even wicked bank cursed energy must be combination occur, this is micro concept energy.

2014.11.27

Topic: micro concept "the way to reach at micro concept point"

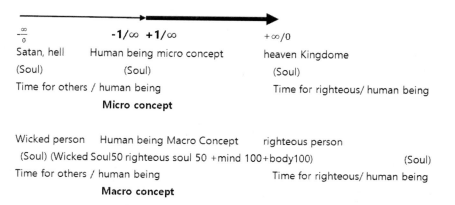

In this micro concept, how to reach at micro concept point $(-1/\infty + 1/\infty)$, macro concept is seen but also in the macro concept world actor try to big, but in the micro concept world actor is unseen world so long in the point of macro concept world is being decreased to be a living but do not seen, so long reach at micro concept point $(-1/\infty + 1/\infty)$, how to reach at the micro concept point $(-1/\infty + 1/\infty)$, in this micro concept keep talking, the ways are so variables

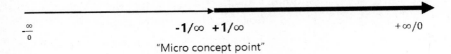

$$-\frac{\infty}{0} \qquad \mathbf{-1}/\infty \ \ \mathbf{+1}/\infty \qquad\qquad\qquad +\infty/0$$

"Micro concept point"

A macro concept actor to reach at the micro concept point is so variables, but also some other does not reach at the micro concept point, to reach at the micro concept point is so variables ∞

So long, a actor choose the way $1/\infty$, so long general reach at the micro concept world is the In this micro concept describes then a birth macro concept actor from a time and place then the actor is compose "righteous soul 50 wicked soul 50 + mind 100+ body 100" a macro concept actor has for variance to be reach at the micro concept point, this variance are some time make hard to reach at micro concept point $(-1/\infty + 1/\infty)$,

but also these for variances are combinational of procedures create of the micro concept point $(-1/\infty + 1/\infty)$, but the macro concept actor reach the ways are ∞ then a macro concept actor choose a way so long the ways is $1/\infty$, the macro concept actor live to reach at the micro concept point $(-1/\infty + 1/\infty)$, the seen world macro concept world actor try to live to get much more energy to live safe, so that macro concept actor living ways is

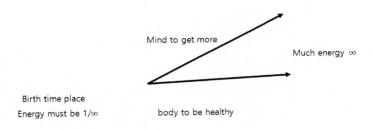

Mind to get more

Much energy ∞

Birth time place
Energy must be $1/\infty$ body to be healthy

Most common fact is based in the macro concept world actor; just body must be healthy but also much more getting money so to do that all of macro concept wicked actor assistance mind is ∞

So long in the macro concept actor just recognized all of macro concept actor all of the knowledge is this, about body, so how to live healthy, mind how to much money, so long this macro concept actor "mind +body" so long all of knowledge is macro concept do not reach at micro concept point $(-1/\infty + 1/\infty)$,

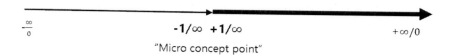

$\frac{\infty}{0}$ **-1/∞ +1/∞**   +∞/0

"Micro concept point"

The old knowledge just historical knowledge is solution of the problems of the "mind + body" all are reference from the (- $\frac{\infty}{0}$ ~ 1/∞) do not know future knowledge, to be helped from future knowledge (+1/∞ ~ +∞/0) the how to use the future knowledge is helped micro concept point (-1/∞ + 1/∞) to be helped from future knowledge then, the future start pint but also past end point is micro concept point (-1/∞ + 1/∞), reaching is general ways, the general ways also from ∞ method to 1/ ∞ so long, the reach way is in macro concept point must be feel weight decreased to be reach at micro concept point, just like gold from gold mines so to get gold do huge gold ore, to get gold it must be gold ore smash to stone powder and melt and get melt gold, and then after make pure gold, so then pure gold is infer to reach at the micro concept point. So then, macro concept world actor to be reached at the micro concept point (-1/∞ +1/∞), then it must be macro concept actor "righteous soul 50 macro soul 50 + mind 100 + body 100" this macro concept living actor must be break to power of the macro concept to be micro concept actor, the gold is break gold ore to power, but how to macro concept actor break macro concept actor to be micro concept actor

It must be infer, to get a gold the gold ore must be break, so long in this procedure gold ore so hard to bear on, the machine break in the forcibly, the gold ore get so big stress, powerful stress so then all of hard process endured. How to say in adopt to the macro concept actor, it must be just living is not easy, but the actor who reach at the micro concept point (-1/∞ + 1/∞), the actor all of adversity faced then overcome to be reach at the micro concept point (-1/∞ + 1/∞), so long the actor life direction, destination is micro concept point (-1/∞ + 1/∞), the actor live righteous living line, much more the actor shared time, and help others, if a actor invent for the peace all of actors then this is all of actor being happy then it must be help so many actors so, the invention is the micro concept point reach then, the actor helped from the future knowledge, in the procedure, the procedure is in the micro concept saying. The macro concept actor minor of the righteous soul being string then, the righteous soul reach at the micro concept point, so called micro concept world gate (-1/∞ + 1/∞), the realized so called reach at the macro concept point so long righteous macro soul meet in the micro concept world righteous soul, so then the micro concept world micro concept actor righteous soul helped the future knowledge, actually in the micro concept world righteous soul live eternity so long, in the macro concept world future is in the micro concept world is actually in the point of micro concept so long the micro concept world is (-1/∞ + 1/∞), micro concept time and area is all are micro concept point (-1/∞ + 1/∞), So long, in the macro concept point actor to reach at the micro concept point is ∞, so long multi variable but in the one of the micro concept point reaching method is macro concept point recognized ways is the direction is being decreased to seen unseen is micro concept, so long infer of the being micro concept is

Macro concept actor is "righteous soul 50 wicked soul 50 + mind 100 + body 100" so long, in the macro concept point actor live then reach at the micro concept point is must be infer as

"Righteous soul 100 + mind =1/∞ + body 100 = soulful body= body" in this macro concept actor must be realized so long mind is 1/∞ "righteous soul 100+ body 100" super strong soul and healthy body meet, it is the perfect strong soul, in this time soul is being major class up to the body, so long, even body is not disappeared but the righteous strong soul reach at the micro concept point (-1/∞ + 1/∞), here to be break all of the mind, the actor how to live is it must be imagined just like the gold ore to be pure gold, all of out of gold are break down, so long to be break mind the actor how to live suffer, all of the suffering endured then, the actor meet his strong righteous soul, the righteous soul of strong meet in the micro concept tunnel so that it already being righteous soul, so long with body soul, reach at the micro concept righteous soul living destination so long, the realized macro concept world actor find a new creative form helped in the micro concept world the righteous soul.

Macro concept actor to be reach at the micro concept point is this

Macro concept actor is "righteous soul 50 wicked soul 50 + mind 100 + body 100" so then in the macro concept actor understand gradually reach at micro concept point (-1/∞ + 1/∞),

is ①"righteous soul 50 wicked soul 50 + mind =1/∞ +body 100" ② " righteous soul 100 + body100" ③ " righteous soul 100 + body100 = zero"

④"righteous soul 100" in this case all of macro concept actor dead in the macro concept world, then if a macro concept actor live as righteously then wicked soul with mind is 1/∞ then after a strong righteous soul, so fear of strong soul so that out of mind wicked soul run away for the righteous actor, so that the righteous actor body also disappeared so long, the strong righteous soul 100" come to micro concept world strong righteous soul so long it comes at the righteous soul destination.

2014.12.01

Topic: macro concept "share time of righteous behavior"

In this micro concept righteous actor behavior is time shared, and help others, this two categories are major behavior, in this micro concept how to definite the righteous behavior, here is time is a variance between micro concept world and macro concept world, so long time is the common factor of the micro and macro, so time is asset each actor, time is the all of the actor same so long time is the very criteria so long the time is used for exclusively his/her actor only, but how to shared with others, it is the comes to righteous behavior center slogan, shared time is all covered but in the macro concept actor slogan another is help others. Then righteous behavior is shared time others but also help others. Here time shared is all of righteous behavior is all cover but help other is special behavior. Shared time is beginning of the righteous behavior, so long in the same place located then the relationship building, so long, all busy for doing himself /herself exclusively do getting energy getting, so long, all time plan and activity is not others, so long, it is the soul is easy because of a actor thought that just only himself/herself then going is fast, if she/he is doing something then do fast so long this is very instinct to live better than others, so long all of time use for himself/herself. This is general in the macro concept world, so just time is a personal asset, so they use time freely, so long time is criteria if shared time others then it start live righteous, but do not with others then the actor do not live righteous. Most macro concept actor behavior of busy so that time is not enough with others, so long time is sometimes must be do not all get it, sometimes jump not for himself/herself but others. Time shared so long it required order of priority, so long, time is required to managed, time has the seed, so long do not busy then do not have time usage seed, time is the surly asset, so long if a time seed comes then time is follows, so long, time usage is decision making after comes time, so long, time is the just like of the input variance so long, going for stop for using time is really important. The time is actor to actor is so long time is the all the time followed, so long in this micro concept righteous behavior order of priority is macro concept and micro concept world relationship. So long time and location is this, time is energy location is circumstance so long, time is energy so that time is must be difference with macro concept world ages, so long time is expensive time is rare situation. Time value is also micro concept important is this, Time is me is start, a actor how to use time is decide

I have time but this time is $1/\infty$ in the micro concept point $(-1/\infty + 1/\infty)$, so long the time is micro concept so long, time is all usual attainment time and place is varied based on time but also time based on places. So long a time going out to other time and place so long, if my time for the righteous then it must be out of me time but also place, so long, in the micro concept point $(-1/\infty + 1/\infty)$, here is time and place is so long micro concept world is time and place also, so long, the actor try to be live righteous then, what it must be arrange the time, time do not scatter but time and round but angle, so long time is must be first plan the act, so long, the righteous is first is the time usage direction, so long, if the time is direction to the righteous place, is here have righteous place, it must it must be infer, righteous place, so long place is physical feature but the righteous + place, so long, the word righteous, so long what is the righteous so long righteous is in this micro concept world , so long a actors place, so long, actor place is actor of world + place, then actor must be inferred that, a actor is righteous then, the actor place is righteous actor governing place is righteous place, so long, a actor live as the righteous then, the actor must be compose " righteous soul + mind = $1/\infty$ + body" so long, correct time is start to the righteous place so long the direction is to the righteous place, so long the righteous place is righteous behavior then itself is the righteous place, so long, if righteous behavior then it comes itself righteous place so long, righteous behavior is time usage with others, so long, in the moment is the actor composition is " righteous soul + body" so long, the behavior of righteous is it already made actor, so long, the direction to the righteous place going, so righteous behavior is living in the micro concept world $(-1/\infty + 1/\infty)$, so long, the righteous actor " righteous soul +body" is live at the micro concept world $(-1/\infty + 1/\infty)$, an actor who do righteous behavior must be righteous behavior place with time, so time also with righteous with then, the time is the righteous but if the time is wicked then, wicked time, so long, the time and place is wicked so, time also need a actor's attitude, time also shift with actors righteous or wicked behavior. So long actor is the influence to the time and place all defined by an actor behavior. What is the motto of the righteous behavior, who help to be behavior, timeshared is the indication of the micro concept world, so long to be time shared with others then, it must be the actor time is righteous time then, the actor time is righteous time, so long, the actor shared then righteous time shared, so long, the actor going to the righteous place, so long, in the ways of traveling, the same direction traveling is all of passenger are friend who go same direction to the righteous place. So long to be live righteous but also shared time with righteous is time is not have the angular but the righteous time is round so long, righteous is the round with round then, go harmony with others, so long, this is the all of sharp angular is all being wear of all sharp angular but to going round, so long, the time of righteous then, all of shared with other then, it must be righteous met righteous actor, so long it is very excitement but also get in to the perfect point. But if infer that the righteous actor of round to meet the not righteous of the sharp angular then the righteous round of the actor hit other sharp angular to be going around, so long, righteous behavior is not easy, in the time shared time, some of the times has the sharp angular, so long if a actor also sharp angular sharp + sharp so then, shred time was not excitement, so long, a actor scar in mind so that closed time shared time others, but also, another actor must be sharp angular actor then meet a round of actor so then, the sharp angular actor helped from round so long round drill the sharp angular, so that the sharp angular actor open time for others, so long, in the time sharing then all is not excitement, so that time shared is also, required round actor, so long, all be with time is sacrifice, but also love others then, it comes to the righteous, love, sacrifice is not easy, so long, love is not easy, sacrifice also is not easy, so long, in this micro concept world $(-1/\infty + 1/\infty)$, Shared with time other is time is the decision making result, so long, try to be with other then, if an actor sharp rectangular then the act must be also sharp, then the decision try to go with others, then shared another actor really hard to go with a actor. So long sharp actor if meet sharp actor then, the shared time must be hell, but round to round then sharing time is very excitement, so long, the sharp actor time and the place is so variable so long, a actor meting point is variable so long sharp rectangular actor meet round actor also, so long, so long round actor also sharp actor also meet others, doing other is doing live other is not easy, but this not easy behavior but all of endure then it comes to the going round, if a actor sharp rectangular actor hate to meet others then, the rectangular actor must be not going round, so long still it getting time goes the actor must be going round, then if not go with others then, the actor do not reach at the going round, so long the round actor, he/she live with others, do donor position so then, to live with others are naturally shared time, so long in the shared time, comes to help others, so long, then it must be excitement, so long, to get going round then, the rectangular sharp actor it must be not to live sharp, so long, if a actor live full life just sharp rectangular then, the actor must be getting ages then, the actor all loser from others, because of as ages then, the actor still has the sharp rectangular then, it must hard to live, so that, in the young ages if not go with others then, it must time lose of sharp rectangular cut or managed by other round actor or dull rectangular sharp actor then, it comes going round, so long all of the relationship not easy, all of meeting actors are hard some actor wicked so long really hard to a actor, but also a righteous actor easy going, make other easy going is very important in the share time others. In the relationship is rectangular sharp actor to round and rectangular sharp, not to be wicked living then it must be shared time other, to be righteous then it must be shared time others, it is very essential conditions, in the macro concept world actor getting ages all of conditions are variables, in this conditions all of actors are positions wicked or righteous, but also giver or acceptor, so long this is not easy to be eternity shared time others, so long, how to live full of life shared with others, so long going down, being humble is essential to live others, to be it must be reach at the micro concept point $(-1/\infty + 1/\infty)$, to live as righteous actor, so long, the righteous actor how hard procedure come and gone, it must not out of sharing time other then, it is not easy to be the righteous actor, so long, god must be revealed to others, the others are righteous or wicked then, it also, they are has the micro concept world procedures. If an actor meet righteous actor then, it must be the actor wicked so long the wicked actor helped from righteous actor, but also the actor shared time wicked actor then, the actor must be righteous actor so long, the righteous actor must help other wicked actor, then the actor do righteous behavior, so then even hard to live others but, the role is required to a sharp rectangular to be round, so long shared time is the micro concept point is very required, in this micro concept if a actor feel round, further more a actor live with round then, it must be righteous destination of righteous actors. So long to be reach at the micro concept point righteous actor around then, the round actor try to shared time with sharp rectangular actor of wicked actor. In this shared of time is very criteria is the righteous behavior is help other, so long, wicked actor do not shared time, then there is no any excitement & perfection, so long, to be reach at the righteous behavior then, the righteous must be sacrifices so long, righteous position actor role for the peace defense, to be recognized from micro concept actor righteous destination actor king then, it must be role of righteous in the macro concept world. The wicked actor live doing not shared others, but also do not help others, so long all of micro concept wicked actor destination king Satan try to make worse. So long, macro concept world living must be deteriorate. So long, micro concept world try to help, righteous micro concept world help macro concept world righteous actor, but also micro concept world wicked actor also assistance macro concept wicked actor so that the actor role for the micro concept actor wicked soul destination king, Satan. So long, if do not shared with others then, it must be disappeared all of righteous actor, so to be righteous living then it must be shared time with others.

2014.12.02

Topic: macro concept "micro concept transition"

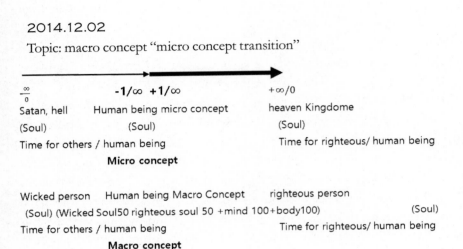

In this micro concept the micro concept point M $(-1/\infty + 1/\infty)$, micro point is a actor has, so long micro concept point M $(-1/\infty + 1/\infty)$, is sometimes peak, so long micro concept point has been explained life scale, but micro concept point also calculate in a personal micro concept scale, so long micro concept point M $(-1/\infty + 1/\infty)$, so long to the macro concept a actor has multiple micro concept point what is the micro concept point in a micro concept scale

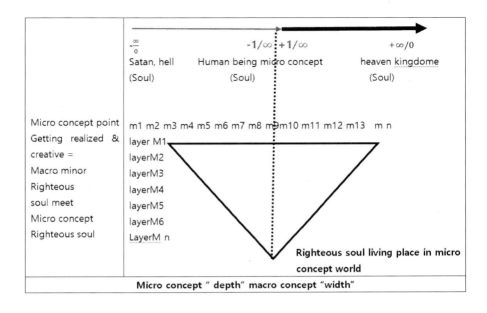

Macro concept actor reach at the Mn mn micro concept point reach at M (-1/∞ + 1/∞),

In the macro concept point micro concept point M (-1/∞ + 1/∞), is above diagram so long micro concept point is the width & dept, so long all of micro concept point in the macro concept world is just do not invader other macro concept ranges, so long micro concept point is not invaders but create of a innovative new micro concept point M (-1/∞ + 1/∞), micro concept point of the 4 dimension is width M1 dept M1

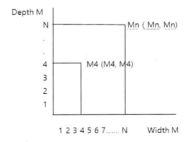

Macro an actor micro concept transition

In the micro scale of micro concept M $(-1/\infty + 1/\infty)$, so long, M4 $(-1/\infty + 1/\infty)$,...... Mn $(-1/\infty + 1/\infty)$, so long, micro concept point so long, if a macro world actor live M $(-1/\infty + 1/\infty)$, this micro concept point is a macro concept actor live to realize an project a actors micro concept scale, macro concept actor live support for himself/herself, so long, so long M1 has reach at Mn Mn M $(-1/\infty + 1/\infty)$, so long, in the end it comes to M1M1, M2M2, M3M3 ...... MnMn M $(-1/\infty + 1/\infty)$, this is the going round

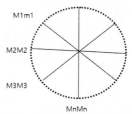

A macro concept actor realize then the excitement &perfection is round

Here is round point going deeper to the 4 dimension center, so long center of round is reach at the micro concept depth point M $(-1/\infty + 1/\infty)$, in the round surface line is almost a black line, unseen the micro concept width point, so long, to be round a actor must be endless realize so called micro concept point M $(-1/\infty + 1/\infty)$, so long, a personal actor being, live righteous then the man must be come to round, but if not reach at the excitement & perfection then, a actor has the shape rectangular so long, a macro concept actor live in the direction to the righteous ways then the actor live micro concept righteous livings.

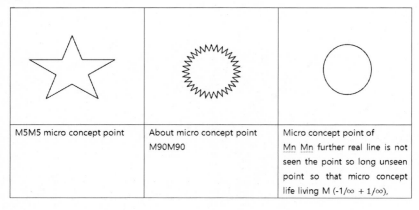

M5M5 micro concept point	About micro concept point M90M90	Micro concept point of Mn Mn further real line is not seen the point so long unseen point so that micro concept life living M $(-1/\infty + 1/\infty)$,

Micro concept point reaching at a macro concept world actor being round of characters, so then it must be a actor has possibility to live in the micro concept point world righteous soul destination actor so long, macro concept actor reach at a unseen soul, so long, the actor life being at righteous soul, through multiple momentum micro concept point reaching. In the macro concept world micro concept point is realization but also all of coming problems solving.

As living as macro concept world, an actor so multiple against powers, but also some of the helping power, so that in the battle then understand of the righteous side power, but in the case of wicked actor then helped from the righteous power, so turning points of righteous & wicked power. In the macro concept world is bottle field, so that even a micro concept world is so does, in the micro concept world M $(-1/\infty + 1/\infty)$, is has the righteous and wicked world is reversed power, so this power is safe, not to be heel to righteous or wicked. All of balance on the axis of wicked and righteous, then in the macro concept world and micro concept world being peace, but here righteous number wicked number balance means not but the power of righteous and wicked power, so long, this is been actually all of wicked and righteous relationship is mostly depend on, comparison between righteous and wicked so that a actor and another actor happen to righteous and wicked power effect. But mostly righteous is most actor like to be, but also live eternity because of righteous micro concept world destination is must be bright and peace. So long all of actor try to share time but also, like to help others. So the place is heaven kingdom.

In the macro concept world a actor who work for the organization then the role is what is this, about his position must be get well, if he is follows of the righteous direction then, the organization must be going well on the axis of righteous direction actor. The righteous actor live just like M1M1 $\sim\sim\sim$ MnMn keep going for the one shell perfection then a new micro concept M2M2 so long a macro concept actor endless purse of the righteous direction the procedures of the righteous mechanic then the actor final of the macro actor get of "righteous soul + healthy body" then healthy body help a righteous soul be strong to pass the it required strong energy from macro concept world to micro concept world, so long " righteous soul + strong righteous body then body must be $1/\infty$) so then, right after pass the from macro concept world to micro concept world then it being " strong righteous soul" this strong soul travel in the micro concept world to the eternity righteous micro concept world. So long, this strong micro concept world strong righteous soul, has blessed bank righteous energy, so long the righteous actor live with energy, so long another macro concept world actor live in the program of the being righteous, so then, a actor come to micro concept world M1 (-1/ ∞ + 1/∞) , then a new macro concept righteous soul through the micro concept world tunnel M (-1/∞ + 1/∞), travel to meet a strong righteous soul in the micro concept world, so the reach at the micro concept world, then, the treasure to bless to the macro concept world righteous soul so long, a new righteous soul actor live righteous, so long micro concept actor keep transition.

2014.12.03

Topic: macro concept "I =V/R"

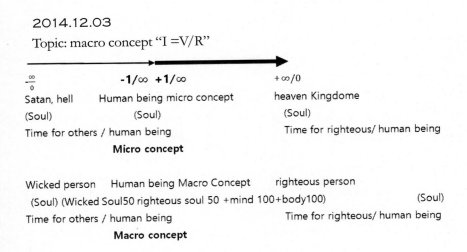

In this micro concept all of actor try to be living at righteous, but actually it is not, all of actor do not live in the way of righteous, then how to be made of righteous and wicked. So long, but also most actor try to be righteous but why do not live in the righteous. The righteous and wicked is how to related, so long, if a actor righteous living is related with the physical formula I=V/R

So long, electric current flows with V=voltage, R= electric resistance. Current is related with V X 1/R = V/R, the current want to flow to∞, but actually in the macro concept world current can't because of electric resistance, R make slow the current I, so long, current do not go ∞ cause of R, so long, in this micro concept, so long, I(righteous living)=V(righteous living power)/R(wicked living), so long, macro concept actor live as righteous then, it must be required a macro concept actor is consist of " righteous soul 50 wicked soul50 + mind 100+ body 100" so long, do live righteous living is I=V/R, so long I changed to righteous soul 50, but also R is wicked 50 and mind 100, and V is body 100, so long to go for the righteous living it must be a macro concept actor live in the macro concept world, if a macro concept actor live to righteously

I=righteous soul 50 = body 100/ wicked soul 50 mind100, so long righteous living is also body 100, but make hard is wicked soul 50 mind 100, so that in this micro concept to be righteous is the mind is $1/\infty$, then it comes from micro concept point M1 $(-1/\infty + 1/\infty)$,

I=righteous soul 50 = body 100/ wicked soul 50(mind100=$1/\infty$)
I=righteous soul 50 = body 100/ wicked soul 50 X $1/\infty$)
I=righteous soul 50 = body 100 / (wicked soul 50//∞)
I=righteous soul 50 = body 100 / (wicked soul 50//∞) = body 100/0
I=righteous soul 50 = body 100/0 righteous soul 50 size is body 100 ∞

Righteous soul 50 is with strong health body, so long, in the macro concept world strong healthy body is make righteous soul power being 100, and so long the righteous actor comes to reach at the "righteous soul 100 + body 100" so this strong healthy righteous soul actor, so he must be fight to Satan, so called pure wicked 100 then a strong righteous soul so strong healthy righteous soul actor fight to strong wicked actor, actually wicked power, so fight then must be win so long the strong righteous 100 soul actor, role of the righteous fighter, because of strong righteous soul also face to the strong wicked soul, if lose in the fight then, the righteous soul must be ruin to wicked soul, so long

I=righteous soul 50 = body 100/0 righteous soul 50 size is body 100 ∞
I=righteous soul 50 = body 100 ∞ so that righteous actor compose of "righteous soul 100 + body 100" Strong righteous soul actor = "righteous soul 100 + body 100"

As righteous strong healthy righteous soul 100 body 100 must be reaching at micro concept world (-1/∞ + 1/∞), so long to be live as the micro concept world micro concept righteous soul destination reaching it also more powerful power required so long, righteous soul 100 + body 100, transient from macro concept world righteous actor = righteous soul 100 + body being micro concept point reach at (-1/∞ + 1/∞), so long, to be micro concept world the righteous soul destination reach it required to righteous soul 100 + body 100 = 1/∞ so long , strong righteous soul = righteous soul 100, pure righteous soul, so long it perfect righteous soul 100, this soul get in to micro concept world, the moment macro concept world to micro concept world, so long in the procedure of the actor of righteous living, then, righteous actor.

it required to strong health body. So long a real reach at micro concept point (-1/∞ + 1/∞), is live righteously excitement but also reach at perfection so coming perfection all of righteous in the righteous micro concept world righteous soul destination.

2014.12.04

Topic: macro concept "righteous soul nutritive element"

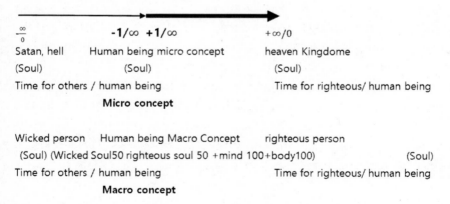

In this micro concept actor is righteous soul, in the macro concept minority" righteous soul 50 go with wicked soul 50" so long righteous soul suffering with hateful wicked soul, so long how to live in the macro concept before come to realized then reach at the micro concept point (-1/∞ + 1/∞), what is the righteous soul nutritive elements? Just righteous behavior energy helped from the righteous soul nutriments, so long then in the behavior of righteous soul going with excitement, so long, before fight with wicked soul then, the macro concept actor must live helpful for the righteous soul strength. Righteous behavior definition it use time with others and help others, so to carry out this in the micro concept righteous soul behavior doctrine then, it must be required being excitement by absorbing nutrients of righteous soul energy. Righteous soul goes peace, so long then in the soul living best place location is important, so long a righteous soul behavior actor must live soul like place, soul do excitement with a soul love place, righteous soul best living place, so then macro concept actor must consider for the purpose of righteous living and behavior is defend on the macro concept actor going body soul likeable place, so righteous soul eat righteous soul nutrients, so long righteous soul nutrients is a beautiful and silent place, then, it must be wicked soul very hard going with this because of wicked soul try to be hidden places, so long if righteous soul body located at the rightful soul going excitement place, this place is give righteous soul being peace, and rest so long, body also feel going with righteous soul, but the wicked soul like to busy and go with wicked place a hidden or turbulence place but also it located macro actor being tired, so long in this time smeared all of body, temptation to lead to wicked behavior, so long the wicked soul go with macro concept actor desired mind, much more making money, but also more time working, but also, here is the all the time the desired macro concept actor, desired even sacrifice of other factor but only desired to make money, so long, in this place is best place for the wicked soul, wicked soul temptation try to macro concept actor out of the righteous to come to wicked so long, the desired a fool of desired mind then, it must be make much money, so long, then it must be rich then what happened, it turned out the actor, the desired actor all with wicked soul so, the actor in the end failed to be rich what macro concept actor wanted to do. So long macro concept desired actor live just one direction even around of center actor, expected the role, but all disregard but only to make money is only doing, so then, the wicked soul best living conditions, so wicked soul actor formed to "righteous soul really hard to bear so long righteous almost to die but wicked soul is very strong + very naturally mind is ∞ + so long body is very tired, so long the body is getting sickness" but all of wicked actor soul keep eating all of eating stuffs so that, the macro concept wicked soul live easy, the wicked macro concept actor live excitement with over eat, over night etc. just all of macro concept actor all the time for himself only, macro concept actor so busy so long the time is not for others, the wicked soul mind getting desired all, so that, wicked soul has all of means to get make full of getting, the wicked soul do not help other even, wicked soul actor " righteous soul hunger almost to die but wicked soul get strength to ∞ + the body get to really deteriorated so almost to die" then the wicked soul body, do not rest time all of body only behavior to make rich, so then wicked soul safe station on the macro concept actor, so long all of desired mind also very strong, then the body must be going dead" another forming is " wicked soul 100 + mind 100 + body almost to die $1/\infty$" so long, wicked soul residents body go to dead, but so long all of desired getting rich asset is but also the other wicked soul watching the wicked soul actor, so long, all of wicked actor getting asset all used up with the wicked others actor but also the deteriorated body, the body is going to dead.

The righteous soul actor soul really likes to so long the righteous soul nutritive is time going with others but also the righteous soul actors help others. The is macro concept actor "righteous actor with excitement time with others, but also help others + mind is $1/\infty$ + body is very strong in healthy so body 100" so long, body good health and the righteous soul so excitement, so long, the righteous soul nutritive is just help others so long around of the righteous macro concept actor do live time usage balance so long, around of righteous actor all be excitement with time usage, so long the righteous actor help around of righteous actor, so long, the actor live normal and balance time usages, so long, the feature of righteous actor " righteous soul excitement with others then wicked soul actor at a loss + mind come to out of orders + excitement body is good health" so long, the righteous soul all the time not over but also, so long, all the time macro concept righteous soul located the righteous soul likeable place, in the good air good scenery the very silent place is really excited to the righteous soul eating, so long, in the time is all the time righteous soul try to best is the macro concept actor rest regular so long, early sleep early get up in the morning, so long, so many time soul active in the macro concept actor micro concept place $(-1/\infty + 1/\infty)$, so long the righteous actor soul to soul's heat's contents, so long, the righteous nutritive is depend on how to use mind, if mind desired then the balance is broken then righteous soul getting worse, so long it comes the wicked soul getting better, the righteous soul nutritive must be realized all of mind get to 1/∞, so then at least righteous soul actor reach at the micro concept point (-1/∞ + 1/∞), this righteous soul actor do not have mind, just righteous soul actor forms" righteous soul 100+ body 100= righteous body=body" must be excitement and perfection showing, coincide with all of macro concept behavior all of process all be depend on the righteous acts, so long, the procedure result all be getting perfection. The micro concept tries proof as the righteous behavior excitement and the righteous with mind to 1/∞ then getting perfection. So long, righteous nutritive eating righteous macro concept actor reaches at perfection.

2014.12.05

Topic: macro concept "righteous soul time & environment"

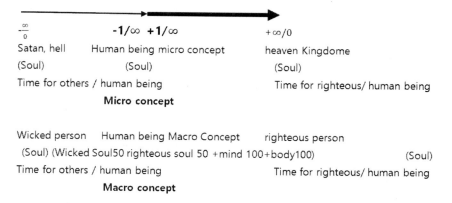

In this micro concept is righteous soul must be preferable condition have, so that infer of the righteous soul actor like time and environment, but also wicked soul actor like time and environment must be also exist. In the macro concept world, the type of actor also infer, so long, this condition is ages, times, place, this is the macro concept world an actor best condition.

Until now inferable macro concept actor ages are must be ratio must be difference about a macro concept actor

437

sort	0~30 years old	30~60 years old	60~90, 100 years old
Actor minor soul Ratio righteous/wicked	50/50	50 + righteous behavior/ 50 + wicked behavior	Strong righteous soul/ Wicked soul 1/∞ Righteous soul 1/∞/ Strong wicked soul
Time of the day	to midnight	Righteous soul: early morning & early Sleep wicked soul: late morning & late sleep	Righteous soul: Meditation, pray, slow tempo Wicked soul: Make money affairs Fast tempo
Place of the day	Crowd place	Righteous soul: Home, family Wicked soul Night club, alcoholic etc.	Righteous soul: Silent Mt., temple Wicked soul: Money making turbulence place
Micro concept nutritive	Righteous & Wicked soul Simultaneously effect	Righteous soul: Blessed bank saved energy Wicked energy: Cursed bank energy	Righteous soul: Enough balance Wicked soul: Debt, energy deficiency

Righteous soul actor in the macro concept world, it must be righteous soul memorize in the before come to macro concept world, righteous soul destination, so long, the place must be so comfortable for the eternity so long meditative, or peace, but also early morning but also early sleep is like, it must be inferable to early morning get up, but also early sleep must be, righteous soul go with strong best condition body condition, but also, righteous soul move in the dream so long, early bed must be minor of macro concept world righteous soul comes to behavior in the night time sleeping body, so long sleeping means to the soul actor must be governing of the soul, so long, soul must be excitement, very tired soul sleep then, righteous soul strong active condition made, but if a macro concept world actor sleep late Am 1 o'clock then the righteous soul do not active enough but also, at this time soul also tired, so long soul moving time is short, so long, just like if still do not go sleep early then, soul defeated from the heavy desired body to make money, then, the soul hate place located in the money changed place so hard to live the righteous soul, the time become loner then soul must be so hard, so long, in the trade money to make wicked style money, because in this time do not live righteous actor soul, so long wicked actor soul like, wicked actor soul is excitement with crowded condition, so many macro concept actors are clamored. So long in this place wicked soul really like, so that wicked soul is like in the place of the multi macro concept actor trade and wicked making money etc place, but also, the time is late morning, but also out of the early bed, so long mid night trade and drinking alcoholic etc. so long, desired of much money getting but also drinking alcoholic with sexuality power going up, in this turbulence time and place.

So long, righteous soul really against to the wicked soul best place, righteous soul is silent and meditation and slow tempo, but wicked soul actor like, clamored, trade of making money, but also fast tempo etc. but also righteous time is early morning, so long Am 4 etc, but wicked soul do not get up early because of slept midnight so long, wicked soul slept late then body do not fresh clean air so long, body must be getting worse, but also righteous soul actor go sleep earlier, but wicked soul do not go to sleep early, because of wicked soul like to roar, so that be in a frenzy, so that wicked soul actor chance in the mid night, so the actor do not like early sleep. So long, the actor soul comes to residents by the wicked soul.

In the macro concept world a righteous soul actor life style is

Righteous Wicked actor life style

So long, righteous wicked actor difference comes from the gradually righteous and wicked soul destination effect gradually distance because of after come to macro concept world, then from micro concept world soul actor effect decreased, so long from 30 to 60 years old, getting difference so called to the getting to righteous direction or wicked direction comes. So long 30~60 years old if must be ticketing to the righteous soul destination but also wicked soul destination. So long, a macro concept actor 30~60 year is the very core of living, so long, macro concept actor forms " righteous 50 wicked 50 + mind 100+ body100" is 0~30 years old, but after to reach at the 30~60 then "righteous 50.1 wicked 49.9 + mind 80 + body 100" then 60 ~90,100

Then it must be "righteous 100 + body 100= righteous living" "wicked 100+mind 100+ body 30= wicked living" so long, the 30~60 years old effected in the economic behavior of making money just all of the mixed with righteous and wicked actor soul is adopt even though a macro concept world actor try to be righteous living then the actor get on the righteous direction ticketing, so long, the actor must be righteous behavior so long, shared with others but also help others. But wicked direction actor still does not have time with others but also; strongly do not help others, so long a wicked actor so busy of exclusively for fro himself/herself, so long, the wicked actor body condition getting worse, so long, because of desire 100 is the all of body still run for making money. Then it comes to the run for the 60~90,100 then righteous direction moving actor must be reach at the place of meditation peace place but also, mediate and pray, this is the soul being strong righteous soul, so long, the righteous soul actor, preparing eternity of coming micro concept world, just only soulful living eternity place going.

2014.12.08

Topic: macro concept "decision making"

$-\frac{\infty}{0}$	**-1/∞ +1/∞**	$+\infty/0$
Satan, hell	Human being micro concept	heaven Kingdome
(Soul)	(Soul)	(Soul)
Time for others / human being		Time for righteous/ human being
	Micro concept	

Wicked person	Human being Macro Concept	righteous person	
(Soul)	(Wicked Soul50 righteous soul 50 +mind 100+body100)		(Soul)
Time for others / human being		Time for righteous/ human being	
	Macro concept		

In this micro concept is defined as (-1/∞ + 1/∞), this is comes automatically but, micro is seen Unseen (-1/∞ + 1/∞), this is means that reach at excitement & perfection point. Micro concept solutions are righteous pursuing result, so long, micro concept being reach at perfection conclusion, this is righteous without wicked, and this is the direction for the righteous soul destination. In the macro concept world, to go for the destination is required to be decided. How many decides are make reach at the micro concept world righteous soul destination.

Righteous decision is RD is just 1/∞, it means that the per infinite, so long, the possible decisions are∞, so long in this infinite decisions are mixed with righteous and wicked, to get RD,. It must be 1/∞, so long in the infinite(∞) has half righteous but also half is wicked decision. The pure RD comes from righteous decision – wicked decision= righteous decision of 1/∞, here micro concept point is defined to (-1/∞ + 1/∞), so long, until now explained micro concept point is as time scale of (-1/∞ + 1/∞), past and future, but also space scale micro concept (-1/∞ + 1/∞), is here 1/∞, so long righteous decision RD is 1/∞ of expanded case is righteous 50% and wicked 50%, but more accurate inferable of righteous 50%, is decision making scale infer that RD=0.5 X1/∞, RD=0.5/∞, so long, the righteous decision RD most break of possibility of choose to the decide, righteous decision(RD) process, is also go with wicked decision(WD) process, the possibility is still has the half, so long righteous to wicked form getting righteous decision then righteous decision 0.5 – wicked decision 0.5= then must be in the mathematics is zero, but in the micro concept just righteous decision $0.5/\infty$ - wicked decision $0.5/\infty$ = it has righteous decision comes $1/\infty$, so that decided activate to the in the micro concept places $(-1/\infty + 1/\infty)$,, so then the decision is fixed to the macro concept featured.

Macro concept feature is micro concept $1/\infty$ righteous decision to the micro concept place $(-1/\infty + 1/\infty)$, then it comes to macro concept. Macro concept world a feature is fix or not flexible get to the hard feature. So long, this hard feature is very strong do not flexible so long, macro concept actor perfect credibility with hard surface so long, all of macro concept actor just happy with hard featured. So then, it must be infer to Macro concept M is must be micro concept righteous decision RD, so long Macro concept M = RD1 + RD2 + RD3 + ... +RDn = sum of righteous decision (RD) so long, macro concept feature is RD's sum, in this is naturally go for the eternity, so long righteous decision making propelling to righteous destination, so long accumulated RD to forming of righteous $(-1/\infty + 1/\infty)$, so long this is micro concept accomplish then, micro concept accomplish is Macro, so long, macro concept world is sum of micro righteous decisions, so long, righteous decision is building of the righteous world $(-1/\infty + 1/\infty)$, these righteous decision produce a righteous products in the macro concept world. So long righteous decision produce masterpiece but also Excitement & perfection comes but actually in the macro concept world actually it is not shown to macro concept actor simply perfection, so long comes confuse to all the time do not righteous decide. A macro concept actor also decide to righteously but macro concept actor decide then, macro concept actor "righteous 50 wicked 50 + mind 100+ body 100" to get a righteous decision it must be win in the game between righteous 50 wicked 50 so long, this is macro concept actor itself, hard to decide to righteous decision, but also in the micro concept world or macro concept world, the decision making is influenced also macro actors also micro concept actors, so long, to be righteous decide, is at first in the macro concept world actor" righteous 50 wicked 50 +mind100+body 100" righteous 50 fight to wicked 50, so long if righteous is win to wicked, but also in the macro concept world, other actor going with forming of macro concept world accomplishing feature, then co worker and helpers are also righteous winners but also micro concept world actor, so long, a macro concept actor reach at the micro concept point so long tunnel to meet micro concept righteous soul actor helping, then the righteous decision (RD) is being real macro concept world righteous produce. So long, righteous decision is helped from righteous actors; so long it is the club of righteous, it must infer to the righteous behavior is going with other time, and help others, so long very simple but in the righteous behavior is so long, in this definite righteous procedures, this unit is multiples then, so long multiple units must be being righteous club, the bunch of righteous club is excitement & perfection coming. To be reach at the micro concept point, it must be required to righteous decision (RD) so long, the bundle of righteous decisions (RD), the RD decision is seed to the righteous behaviors, but also, righteous behavior lead to the righteous soul destination.

Here is

| Macro concept world | Righteous decision | Righteous behavior | ⟷⟶ |
| Micro concept world | ⟹ | | Righteous soul destination |

The righteous behavior macro concept world and micro concept world macro concept world righteous actor

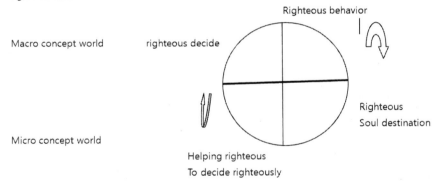

Righteous behavior

Macro concept world · · · · · · · · righteous decide

Righteous Soul destination

Micro concept world

Helping righteous
To decide righteously

Righteous decide and behavior make a macro concept world, a actor live righteously but also the actor accomplished to righteous product, organization etc, they based on righteous so long, it comes to excitement &perfections with righteous cycle but also righteous bundling, these is the righteous actor helpers. Righteous is perfection means that wicked soul or behavior reach at $1/\infty$ so that it must be reaching at excitement & perfection. In this macro concept actor might be think that to make money a project planning is all of bundle of decision, then, it the actor do not live as the righteous then, the decision is not come to righteous, so long, the macro concept world actor project manager of decision then, to be success then, it must be touch with righteous bundles and righteous decision cycle adopt it not, if cut in the wicked decision comes then, the project must be comes wicked behavior then, the out of result must be reach at the wicked products, organization so long, the macro concept wicked decision break even existed product or systems. In conclusion to be perfect success in the making money project is based on the righteous cycle and procedure is only way. The righteous to make excitement and comes perfection.

2014.12.09

Topic: macro concept "body is micro concept place"

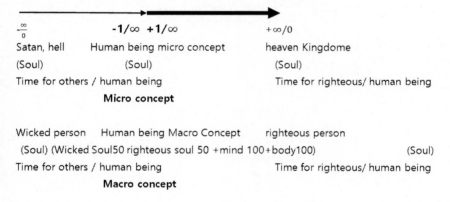

Body glass bottle, Mind compact materials in the glass bottle, soul is transparent actor in the macro concept world, minor soul destination is body without all of mind is out from body, then soul located at the body. So long, in the body owner is soul, so that in the body world major actor is soul, so long in this case body is destination place, soul is actor so long, In the macro concept world (-1/ ∞ + 1/∞) , is this, so long micro concept world formed in the body, (-1/∞ + 1/∞).

Therefore in the body in the macro concept world actor body is soul's destination. So long soul is major actors in the macro concept world body, macro major actor body is usual but in the realization reach at the micro concept world (-1/∞ + 1/∞), and then, body is not body but body is souls destination, so long soul move in the macro concept world just like in the micro concept world major actor soul moving. Macro concept world an actor realized, then it reaches at the micro concept point (-1/∞ + 1/∞), then a righteous actor meet in the micro concept tunnel, the tunnel is connected between macro concept world and micro concept world, so long macro actor, (righteous soul 50 wicked soul 50 + mind100+body100 = this is normal actor body=body seen) so long if a actor realized then, a actor reaches at the micro concept point (-1/∞ + 1/∞), so long, Cup is body, compacted materials is righteous soul 50 wicked soul 50 mind 100.

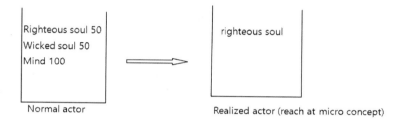

Normal actor   Realized actor (reach at micro concept)

Normal actors live with anger, fight, desired, but also hate other, worried. Normal actor body is cup so long, the cup carried compact materials in the cup so long, and body carries all the time righteous soul, wicked soul, and mind. This is macro concept actor normal characters. So long macro concept actor body leaded by righteous soul + wicked soul + mind, so that body is compared with car then, righteous driver, wicked driver and mind driver. So that the macro concept actor lost of originality micro concept world and macro concept world combined living. This combined living is that macro concept actor behavior influenced to micro concept actor soul behaviors, in this behavior need required micro concept actor soul sake

In the macro concept actor world normal actor to live required but also naturally comes because of the in the macro concept world, in the macro concept world mixed righteous soul and wicked souls so long, a actor must be required to live with righteous wicked actors, so long, a actor has the tool to live in the macro concept world. Macro actor (righteous soul50, wicked soul 50 + mind 100) so long, macro actor sometimes fight to others actors, so long then in actor mind being desired to be rich, anger, hate, stealing. This is natural, and then in this time, wicked mind helped from mind100, so long, macro concept world live with wicked soul + mind 100, so long these actor activate a actor of wicked soul strong but also mind 100 active, so long the living is caved in to wicked soul so long been wicked actor.

But normal macro concept actor realized to reach at the micro concept point (-1/∞ + 1/∞), so long, macro concept world (righteous soul, wicked soul 1/∞ + body 1/∞) macro concept actor reach at the micro concept world (-1/∞ + 1/∞) , after then the macro concept actor being (righteous soul 100) so long, righteous soul 50 increased to reach at the 100, the wicked soul move from the place then the empty space the space occupied to righteous soul, so long, it has been, after realized actor(righteous soul 50 + from wicked soul 1/∞ about to zero to righteous soul 50= a strong righteous soul 100 being) so long strong righteous soul can live within the macro concept world wicked actors and righteous actors. So long, there must be strong righteous soul actor being target of the wicked soul actors try to turn over to wicked souls. So long if not true realized then, the actor it already being wicked soul itself. So that the true righteous actor soul is strong to win in the combat to wicked soul actors, so long the righteous soul actor in the actor of macro concept world. So hard to live on, so long the best place is micro concept world. But sure is the righteous soul is helped from righteous soul, but also righteous souls are trying to shared time all the time, so long, even hard to live with wicked soul but after segregated from the wicked soul then, the pure righteous soul destination is destination at the righteous eternity soul world.

Macro concept world righteous strong soul actor so called realized actor is made from the mind is 1/∞ and wicked soul run away from strong righteous soul, so long, the variance to the righteous being is mind is 1/∞, so then in the living macro concept body is macro concept strong righteous soul 100 governing body 100, so long, the righteous soul actor original minor to the body but a strong righteous soul 100 is being major just like in the micro concept world, so long strong righteous soul100 governing in the macro concept seen actor body.

Body is living in the macro concept world, but another macro concept world major actor is strong righteous soul 100, so long, the strong soul governing body, then from now on, body is to the strong righteous soul is destination of righteous eternity living. Body is compared with micro concept world righteous soul destination. So long in the macro concept world the strong righteous soul move in the body. In this case is macro concept actor reach at the micro concept point (-1/∞ + 1/∞),

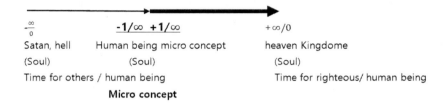

$\frac{\infty}{0}$	**-1/∞ +1/∞**	+∞/0
Satan, hell	Human being micro concept	heaven Kingdome
(Soul)	(Soul)	(Soul)
Time for others / human being		Time for righteous/ human being
	Micro concept	

So long micro concept point (-1/∞ + 1/∞), actually arrow form is first hint to me in this micro concept so long do not change but the concept go deeper than some of changed, so long micro concept main procedure is all being convergent to point (-1/∞ + 1/∞), the arrow is first timescale but wicked satanic is -∞/0 but righteous heaven king dome is +∞/0, time scale is fit in the arrow but in the righteous wicked soul is not explained, it must be inferred to 3~4 dimension so long upper arrow must be understand first realized micro concept point (-1/∞ +1/∞).

So long micro concept point (-1/∞ + 1/∞) reaching at is being strong righteous soul meet through micro concept tunnel (-1/∞ + 1/∞), righteous destination souls. So long in the macro concept world going well must be related with micro concept, righteous behavior in the macro concept world, a righteous blessed bank blessing get through micro concept tunnel so long, righteous soul helping in the macro concept world righteous soul actor.

Topic: macro concept "the way to micro concept point"

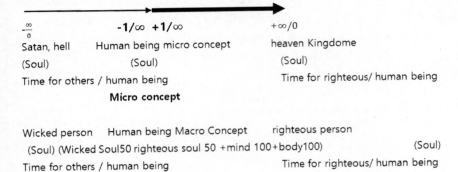

$\frac{\infty}{0}$ **-1/∞ +1/∞**   +∞/0

Satan, hell   Human being micro concept   heaven Kingdome

(Soul)   (Soul)   (Soul)

Time for others / human being   Time for righteous/ human being

Micro concept

Wicked person   Human being Macro Concept   righteous person

(Soul) (Wicked Soul50 righteous soul 50 +mind 100+body100)   (Soul)

Time for others / human being   Time for righteous/ human being

Macro concept

In this micro concept defined micro concept, so long, so many things are appeared. Then micro concept point is located at (-1/∞ + 1/∞), the micro concept point residents are righteous soul's related tunnel and place and time is operated place.

The micro concept place (-1/∞ + 1/∞), unseen world, this place is macro concept actor behavior of ultimate reaching place, but also the place is the same as the time, just time is not seen but must be place then must seen but unseen but it is the place for the micro concept actor righteous soul's location. So long keep going the clear of micro concept point (-1/∞ + 1/∞), gradually in this micro concept, micro concept point is defined and clear why to go for the micro concept point. The macro concept point move to where, macro concept actor where to go, and which direction is micro concept point.

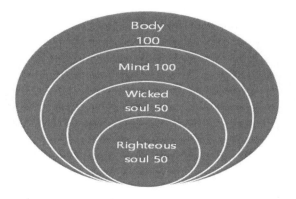

The macro concept actor all has even all of possible living tools.

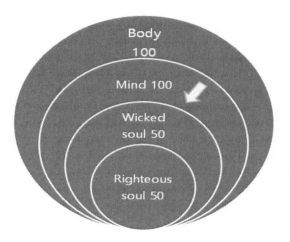

The macro concept actor cut mind 100 away, so long, the actor burden is make less, very lighter than ever, so long forming

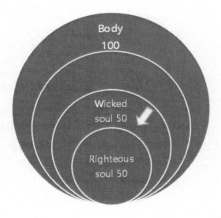

Mind is disappeared from a macro concept actor so long, the macro concept actor "righteous soul + soul + body 100) so long, general soul + body so long, at least just live actor compose of macro concept actor, so long

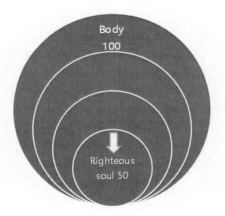

Right after of disappeared mind then it comes that wicked mind disappeared, because of wicked soul has been helped from mind, but mind is disappeared then wicked soul cause of disappeared losing mind and fear of the righteous soul, because wicked soul losing with truth power which support of righteous behavior power.

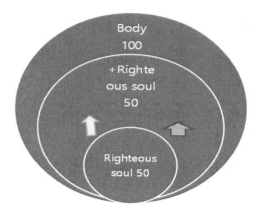

After disappeared from wicked soul + mind = strong righteous soul appeared, just wicked soul place changed to righteous so long, the wicked soul place so long wicked place righteous soul

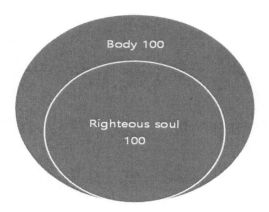

This macro concept actor who met body and righteous also, this macro concept actor so excitement because the ultimate winner of righteous soul very excited with body, so long righteous soul managed body to go for the righteous soul destination, the righteous soul knows that the destination of micro concept world, micro concept world actors, righteous soul, try to help body to go with righteous soul world. Strong body strong righteous soul reaches the excitement & perfection.

Righteous soul being macro concept world, righteous soul is major actor in the macro concept world also, just macro concept actor body with righteous soul so long major actor with body is the destination place, so long the righteous soul governing body,

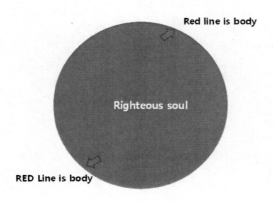

Red color line and arrows the indicate of body, so long body is the righteous soul destination in the macro concept point, this is the realization, so long reach at the micro concept point($-1/\infty + 1/\infty$),

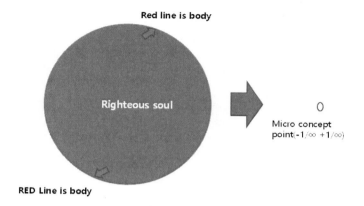

Red line is body

Righteous soul

O

Micro concept
point(-1/∞ +1/∞)

RED Line is body

Righteous soul governing body then macro concept actor is seen unseen righteous soul living actor governing so long, the body behavior is not a body but righteous soul is doing. So long micro concept major actor behavior, so long just being of the body is macro concept world, then body is the same as micro concept righteous soul destination so, it really in the macro concept actor body is seen but in the micro concept point then, so long body is the micro concept location, so long, in the macro concept world, a realization actor so called reach at the micro concept point (-1/∞ + 1/∞). so that the ways of micro concept point reaching is in the macro concept actor life, the life how to live, where to go for, so long, in this micro concept inferable it has the turning, the ways is cutting a way a burden, heavy naturally gain life tools or energy or etc. so long to go for the righteous living and being righteous soul move to the micro concept point to go for the micro concept world righteous soul destination.

① Heavy burden natural macro concept actor: righteous soul50 wicked soul50 + mind 100+ body 100.
② Cutting away of the mind 100
③ Cutting away mind with wicked soul
④ Righteous soul getting 100
⑤ Righteous soul governing body
⑥ Body is location of strong righteous soul
⑦ Reach at micro concept point (-1/∞ + 1/∞),
⑧ Strong righteous soul through micro concept point (-1/∞ + 1/∞), to micro concept world
⑨ Micro concept point world being the righteous soul eternity living at the destination.

2014.12.11

Topic: macro concept "battle righteous soul to wicked soul"

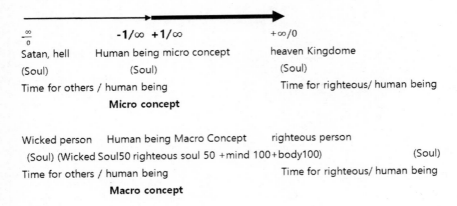

$\frac{\infty}{0}$ **-1/∞ +1/∞**   +∞/0

Satan, hell   Human being micro concept   heaven Kingdome

(Soul)   (Soul)   (Soul)

Time for others / human being   Time for righteous/ human being

Micro concept

Wicked person   Human being Macro Concept   righteous person

(Soul) (Wicked Soul50 righteous soul 50 +mind 100+body100)   (Soul)

Time for others / human being   Time for righteous/ human being

Macro concept

In this micro concept macro concept actor, micro concept actor role in this micro concept, but also righteous soul and wicked soul actor role must be cored role. it imagine that how hard live with righteous soul and wicked soul. Who is hard who is better in the righteous soul and wicked soul. Here righteous soul and wicked soul id from macro concept actor is" minor actor soul; righteous soul 50 wicked soul50 + major actor seen field: mind 100 do not live unseen body controller + body 100" so in the macro concept actors are soul and body is living actor, but mind is not live not an actor

Righteous soul 50 wicked actors 50 grows to getting old then, in this micro concept, both souls are same at the macro concept body, so long macro concept actor getting older, then,

both righteous and wicked ➡ separated righteous from wicked soul	
Birth a macro concept actor	**Approaching to micro concept world**
-The actor soul is righteous soul & wicked soul	The macro concept minor actor, righteous soul
- micro concept world righteous destination's	And wicked soul also getting wider from micro
Righteous minor of macro concept actor care	concept world righteous soul & wicked soul
Wicked actor also cared from micro concept	Destination. So that it became to preparing to
world wicked soul destination	Go back soul's destination, the one is righteous
	But another going wicked soul

In this micro concept is micro concept world (-1/∞ + 1/∞), macro concept world actors are birthed, then the actor souls are righteous soul and wicked soul in the macro concept actor body. With mind which is leading mind's way of body. So that in the macro concept world actor is so young then, the actor try to be getting much so long this is the" wicked soul + mind" role, but that is the to the macro concept actor world a young actor in wild dream. This is the all from wicked soul and mind, so long, strong fight happened to youth love to dynamic, crazy dance, all of the hot energy radiated so long, youth live helped from the wicked soul who from helped in the micro concept world wicked soul destination.

So long early of the macro concept actor consist of righteous soul and wicked soul, so long, the righteous soul and wicked soul, so long in the youth early, then how hard to the righteous soul, wicked soul is very excitement with righteous soul, because of wicked soul has extort from righteous soul. So then righteous soul so hard to be beard, macro concept actor dynamic time, the actor all of big desired helping from wicked soul + mind, so that wicked soul is so strong, in this time, is infer of 0~30 years. So then micro concept world actor cared macro concept youth, then the early macro concept assist soul energy from where, so called in the micro concept explained then, so long, the energy is related with, micro concept wicked destination bank is cursed bank, so long cursed bank deposit energy used wicked soul deliver to macro concept actor wicked actors to live dynamic. In the early time, so macro concept world actor wrong decision so then make hard others, just only getting it, so that wicked soul actor only for himself only. The wicked actor, so that the wicked soul is strong time then, how to hard to live, the other part righteous soul endured in this time, so early years, so long righteous soul, keep failure with battle to wicked souls. Wicked soul so strong, but also mind is strong, so that, in this time of macro concept actor 0~30 years.

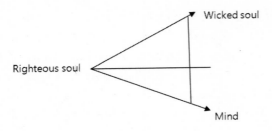

In the time of 0~30 years strong wicked soul strong time

Macro concept actor helped major from wicked soul and mind then, the actor fast run away to ∞

So long wicked soul + mind are even sacrifice of righteous soul actor's all get, much more getting all of energy. Wicked soul helped from the micro concept world wicked soul destination's cursed bank credits and macro concept world not actor but role of wicked soul, so long mind is strong royalty to the wicked soul. So long, wicked soul can't anything but mind is related also with body. So long body tries to make decreased the mind, so that mind is reached at 1/∞, then, how to body make decreased mind, it is macro concept world actor diligence, so long, out of the wicked soul but also mind, so long, how to macro concept body decreased mind

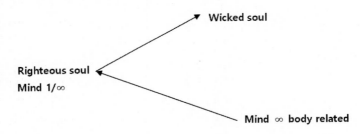

Body make mind decreased from ∞ to 1/∞, so long after this, naturally the mind is disappear So long, wicked soul lost royalty mind erased, so wicked soul power must be also weak, so long the variances become clears not then the macro concept actor "righteous soul 50 wicked soul50 + mind 100 X 1/∞ almost to zero + body 100" so long "righteous 50 wicked 50 + body 100" so that Righteous soul to wicked soul one to one battle, so long

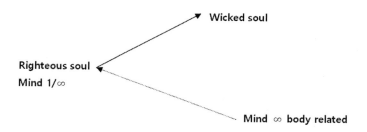

Wicked soul

Righteous soul
Mind $1/\infty$

Mind ∞ body related

Righteous soul to wicked soul fights, so long without mind of royalty to wicked soul so that at last righteous gradually increased power but also helped going for the righteous soul destination directions so then at last the endured so long wait of righteous soul act, then, so long macro concept world actor move to righteous soul destination of micro concept world destination. So long the way to righteous actor helped from micro concept actor soul.

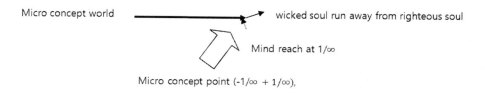

Micro concept world

wicked soul run away from righteous soul

Mind reach at $1/\infty$

Micro concept point $(-1/\infty + 1/\infty)$,

A macro concept world actor if live at righteous then, the actor battle to wicked soul, then body trained to make fewer minds so long soul reach at $1/\infty$, right after mind being to $1/\infty$, then it must be righteous soul to wicked soul, then, righteous soul gradually power increased but wicked soul lost a strong helper of mind so long wicked soul energy almost weak, so that weak soul and strong righteous soul battle then, in the end righteous soul win the battle.

As soon as possible the righteous soul helper micro concept actor righteous soul help to win in the battle to wicked soul so then, the strong righteous soul being strong righteous soul so long, it reach at the micro concept point $(-1/\infty + 1/\infty)$, so long a righteous actor win the battle.

Topic: macro concept "living righteous soul and wicked soul"

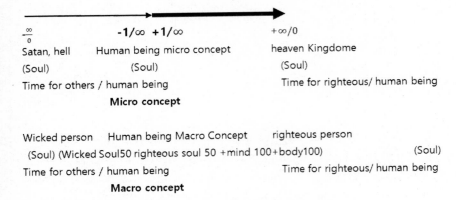

	Micro concept	
$-\infty/0$	$-1/\infty$ $+1/\infty$	$+\infty/0$
Satan, hell	Human being micro concept	heaven Kingdome
(Soul)	(Soul)	(Soul)
Time for others / human being		Time for righteous/ human being

Wicked person	Human being Macro Concept	righteous person
(Soul)	(Wicked Soul50 righteous soul 50 +mind 100+body100)	(Soul)
Time for others / human being		Time for righteous/ human being

Macro concept

In this micro concept macro concept actor live in the macro concept world, macro world consist of wicked soul actor, righteous soul actor, so then all of actor are formed in time scale of $1/\infty$.

The righteous actors in the micro concept are shared time with others, but also help others. This is simple behavior of righteous actor. But wicked actor is against of the righteous actor behavior, so long do not shared time with others and do not help others. As macro concept world macro actor living is faced so multi variances. A macro concept actor sometimes good, the other bad, sometimes excitement but the other time is anger, so long, all the time actor of righteous soul, but wicked soul, these two variance intercourse so long appeared to macro concept actor multiple featured.

sort	define	Micro concept world friendly	Soulful energy	Priced Macro actors
Righteous soul	Shared time Help others	Righteous soul Destination	Blessed bank credit	Rich in soul, Macro Expansive actor
Wicked soul	Do not shared time Do not help others	Wicked soul Destination	Cursed bank credit	Poor in soul Cheap actor

Here is actor is me, so long I can go with righteous soul managed actor of macro concept actor and wicked soul managed actor of macro concept actor, it must be in my existence spaces are righteous and wicked soul groups forming. So long, wicked actor live do not help others but also do not shared time, so then, in the place I'm located then it must be ignorance with me, but wicked actor distance from me, but also a righteous try to shared with me but also try to help me, then in this relationship is influenced to me a weather of good or excitement but anger or bad.

In this case I be in the wicked soul actor position then

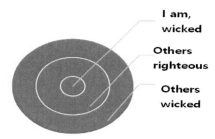

I am, wicked

Others righteous

Others wicked

If I am a wicked actor then, my attitude around of me, I'm criticizing others. But it also angers to others. Then I'm also wicked soul managed so long, cause of me other righteous actor do harmed. But also with others wicked actor then, I'm wicked soul so then I'm faced with, I'm wicked other righteous and others also wicked then, 1 of wicked + 1 of righteous + 1 of wicked = so then right to wicked ration is 1:2 so that, wicked is 200% power but righteous 100% so long, in the time of moment space group are being wicked because of middle righteous is siege from wicked power. Then in the end in a group of a weak righteous turning to wicked, so long I'm going with all of wicked actors. So that I'm living in the wicked world where no one shared with others but also do not help others. So long, I'm feeling of acting irritated. So long my mood is anger time.

But if I were righteous in a time then

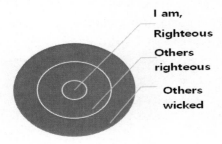

In this case, I'm righteous soul acting, so then around of me is righteous power 1 + righteous power 1 + wicked power 1. So long, in this moment place are group is formed as righteous 2 to wicked 1 = this group influence to righteous group. This group being righteous group, so long I'm righteous going with righteous actors. The result of that I'm going with righteous actors so that I'm righteous soul excitement the time and place, so long I'm reach at the perfection.

In conclusion to live with righteous others then, it must be I'm in the side of righteous soul managed actor, but if I faced with wicked actor then I'm must be wicked soul actor. So long how to live in this macro concept world is all of depend on me. Any time any place is I'm the all of living as righteous or wicked, so long, it must be infer to live in the macro concept world then, righteous I'm must be located at the micro concept point $(-1/\infty + 1/\infty)$.

2014.12.15

Topic: macro concept "macro concept actor experience"

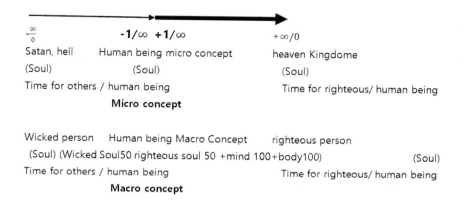

$-\frac{\infty}{0}$ **-1/∞ +1/∞**   +∞/0

Satan, hell   Human being micro concept   heaven Kingdome

(Soul)   (Soul)   (Soul)

Time for others / human being   Time for righteous/ human being

              Micro concept

Wicked person   Human being Macro Concept   righteous person

(Soul) (Wicked Soul50 righteous soul 50 +mind 100+body100)   (Soul)

Time for others / human being   Time for righteous/ human being

              Macro concept

In this micro concept, macro actor live at the shown world, the macro concept actor watching, feeling, this two acceptor getting seeing memory but also felling memory. Macro concept actor every moment is seeing recording, feeling is also with watching lead to perfect story movie in the micro concept world the place is (-1/∞ + 1/∞) where is just like infinite recorded memory chip. It must be inferred, in the macro living as macro concept actor, the actor must see and feel of excitement and perfection. Then the recorded infinite memory chip in the all of macro concept actor living time watching and feeling, the infinite chip recoded in micro concept world. The actor of micro concept actor play the macro time acted recorded movie, the film in the micro concept actor must be eternity excitement but also the micro concept actor knowledge the macro concept world, all of the macro concept actor knowledge also eternity living excitement. So long, all of recorded macro actor's living time, all of watching, and feeling all of actors behavior are excitement factor in the micro concept world. So long, the micro concept actor must be behavior of the wicked or righteous then, if an actor lived righteous in the macro concept actor then in the righteous soul destination world actor naturally edited to righteous actor get it memory chip is recorded to righteous behavior but also, righteous knowledge is eternity continued to be the reach at the excitement & perfection, so long all of macro concept actor live is not reach at the micro concept point (-1/∞ +

1/∞). so called the actor is not realized but also reaching at the perfection. But all of righteous actor living reaching at the micro concept actor point (-1/∞ + 1/∞) then the righteous micro concept actor live as the conclusion of macro actor time learning, so long the knowledge is finished in the righteous actor soul destination. So long, it must be inferred to be being perfection of the macro concept actor world living time learned and watching, feeling all is all being clear to reach at the perfection, so long, eternity knowledge library stored. So long in the righteous actor of the micro concept place, then, all are excitement of the all of eternity righteous but also excitement memory chip, so that how it is excitement living in the righteous soul destination world, all of actor live excited. So long in the micro concept actor soul, accumulate all of righteous actors living experience and knowledge. The righteous knowledge in the micro concept actor world, so long how important it is as macro concept actor a righteous and excitement experience important, so long, if not live righteously then it must be live at wicked actor, then in this micro concept, so long the actor do not live righteously but also, the actor lived as wicked actor, then, the actor must be located at the wicked destination micro concept world, so the actor also in the macro concept world time memory in the chip of infinite memory. After macro concept actor's living reach at the micro concept world, so long, the actor located at the wicked world, so long, and the place micro concept actor also all has wicked story move played but also, wicked knowledge is recorded to wicked micro concept actor micro concept actor. It must be inferred to for eternity living with excitement and hard living is depended on macro concept time experienced. But also truly all of living in the macro concept world and micro concept world, if a macro concept actor live righteous then, after macro concept world then live at micro concept actor then, the micro concept actor live excitement, but if not live righteous behavior, then, the actor live wicked then, after living at micro concept world of wicked then, the wicked actor do not live excitement if must be tortured. So long macro concept time how to live, is do righteous and wicked, then, live within potentiality what I said in this micro concept 6:4, if a actor got a 10 energy then 6 is use for macro actor's but 4 is not macro actor but remained energy but also, somehow 4 is others. In the living of macro concept world then 4 are others. But if a wicked actor lives whole 10, then 10 are all of macro actors. So long, here is energy is materials but also time, all is counted on. The relationship is connection to others, so long, then giving to others 4 then, it is so excitement but also related with others, as macro concept actor ordering and sharing relationship is the point, to live so long, to be righteous actor living then, it must be realized to be getting much is not important, optimistic is best, over the optimistic getting is not important, so long all the time is urgent, risk, so all the time is attentive so that, the moment is active, the macro actor live fiercely. So long at this point role and effected from the micro concept actor and macro actor crossed in the micro concept gate or tunnel (-1/∞ + 1/∞), to be righteous living, all of the actor live at the optimistic then, over, and under, all is not related with righteous behavior, so long, in this micro concept try to talk is, the poor, but also small person, do not learn, so that live is unseen in the macro concept actor world. So not strong, not rich, do not learn, so long in so long macro concept actor world, not success actors how to live is going to righteous soul destination getting, so that, micro concept actor is defined to small getting is better. Small getting is not proud in the macro concept world, so long macro concept world is rich is best, poor is not best, so then the center of life voyage is to be rich, so then all of the poor actor feel that he/she live in the frustrated so long, just not success actor also must be going to the righteous behavior to so long, the poor must be live righteous, then the poor can live in the micro concept actor, righteous soul destination, easy getting, macro concept actor live rich then, the actor is optimistic to over, but the poor is live at the all the time risk.

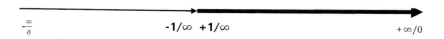

Optimistic getting, micro concept point

So long to be righteous, righteous actor experience with optimistic getting is big option to be going in to micro concept world, righteous behavior so long, living at the righteous soul destination. The rich must be consider to be shared with the poor, then, the actor more better than the poor, because of the in this micro concept actor righteous definition is shared with time, but also give others. So long, give other center is giver position then, the rich actor must be righteous behavior originality. The rich for the righteous is give others shad shared time, then, it must be the rich also, feel edge time, here means that to be optimistic, the rich actor cared with others, give others then, the actor always touch with others, so long other risk solving tools, here is the a righteous poor actor pray to the god then, the god ask the righteous actor of rich to help the poor, then the rich is god's really good messenger.

The rich must be realized at the micro concept point $(-1/\infty + 1/\infty)$. the rich is macro tend but the poor is naturally closed to micro concept, $(-1/\infty + 1/\infty)$. micro concept actor just live in the $1/\infty$, go deeper not going wider. Optimistic point, is compared with micro concept point $(-1/\infty + 1/\infty)$. micro concept point to be live righteous then it required to live sacrifice, but also hard time, so long to be righteous is not easy, but also 6:4 4 is for usage others is also not easy, so long, to live righteous, so long, righteous living is eternity unchangeable forever recognized truth, so long righteous behavior is not enough but optimistic so long, living with micro concept relative then it must be happier. Micro concept is not bigger, richer but the poor then, the micro concept actor live righteously then, even is not popular actor the actor personal must be count on as the righteous actor. Micro concept actor from now on the personal actor of not success, so usual actor righteous, this is the soul world so long, macro concept actor social position is macro but micro is the personal, as the personal do not be wicked so righteous living and after macro concept living then the poor righteous cared with others but also help others. The actor surly reach at the micro concept world and righteous destination, so long general actor all being righteous behavior but also, after macro concept world it must be reach at righteous soul world.

2014.12.16

Topic: macro concept "micro concept world knowledge using"

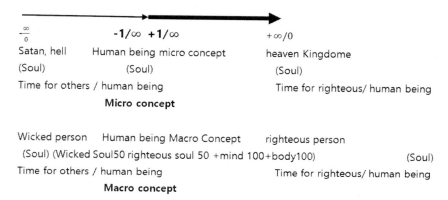

In micro concept, macro concept world actor live all of time with knowledge, this knowledge from where, all of knowledge is from unseen world, in this micro concept, unseen world is micro concept world. How to build in micro concept world knowledge is micro concept world is soul world, so long, soul world is righteous soul destination, but also wicked soul destination.

Knowledge is helping product macro concept world actor's concerning. Micro concept world actor soul produced from macro concept world actor, so long, macro concept actor live all of effort in the macro concept world, macro concept world actor try to get a solutions but actually all is not come to complete, macro concept actor complete is reach at micro concept point world $(-1/\infty + 1/\infty)$. micro concept point is $(-1/\infty + 1/\infty)$. the knowledge is existed in the macro concept world is from to $-1/\infty$, but none existed knowledge in the macro concept world, then the knowledge is must be comes in the future, so long future knowledge is from future to now $+1/\infty$.

So long, macro concept actor must be reach at the micro concept point $(-1/\infty + 1/\infty)$. the macro concept actor live just righteously, so called truth, then, the macro actor live in righteous and truth, but he has a problem so that he earnestly ask the solutions, then the macro concept actor correctly know the problems, the problems solving then it comes to helpful to macro concept actors living

465

righteously helping, so that the macro concept world actor, effort to get a solution, the actor live righteously, righteous living is shared time to others, but also help others. So long, this is the righteous actor, then, in this micro concept actor, micro concept actor world, righteous soul destination actors are comes to righteous soul. How to process of macro concept actor who live in righteously then how to related macro concept actor of righteous and micro concept world righteous soul.

Macro concept world actor Righteous soul helping channel,
It has been done, to now -1/∞, this is in the 1/∞ time interval the knowledge is from +1/∞ future knowledge come to in a moment of 1/∞

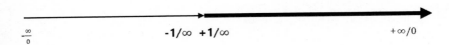

$\frac{\infty}{0}$ **-1/∞ +1/∞**   +∞/0

Just micro concept point (-1/∞ + 1/∞). is the producing of knowledge point also, so long, the micro concept point is explained to as in the terms of philosophy, then realized then it comes to reach at the micro concept point (-1/∞ + 1/∞). so long, micro concept point is related with, hard course of macro concept actor living. Here is micro concept point is M, then which macro actor A reach at the micro concept point. Then it must be actor A micro concept point, so long A. M (-1/∞ + 1/∞). so long, Actor A reach at the M (-1/∞ + 1/∞). of micro concept point.

Macro concept point getting knowledge is
Express to from ~ to existed -1/∞, in the long run, A. M (-1/∞ + 1/∞). being of the ~1/∞, how to get to future knowledge is it must be a macro concept actor reach at the micro concept point (-1/∞ + 1/∞). this is the infer that of the unseen world a place of (-1/∞ + 1/∞). but also time of the (-1/∞ + 1/∞). this is located at the macro concept actor living as righteously.

So long, macro concept actor of righteous living then, the righteous actor must be getting a faced to problems, then,

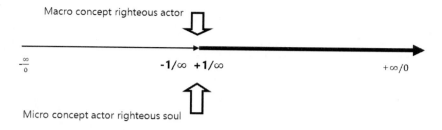

So long, the righteous macro actor soul meet in the so long, to be reach at the micro concept point, a macro concept actor do live righteously then righteous soul feel of helping macro concept righteous actor getting solving problems. So then, macro concept actor makes feel excitement, this is the macro concept actor all of living shared time with others and help others. So that the righteous actor live suffering, difficult, hard course to be realized in the way so long, the actor reach at micro concept point (-1/∞ + 1/∞). so long, micro concept soul actor give macro concept righteous actor. Then what happened to righteous macro concept actor get a realized at so long macro concept actor problems solved. This righteous actor solving then it comes to excitement & perfection. This production all of the actor being pleased and excitement,

So that the soluble by righteous micro concept actor then, the macro concept actor product is being eternity, so called as truth, so long a righteous macro concept actor get blessed from righteous micro concept soul.

2014.12.18

Topic: macro concept "micro concept world & Macro concept world"

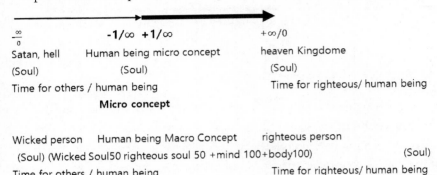

In this micro concept, key words are micro concept, macro concept, righteous soul and wicked soul, these are core words. These are acting in the micro concept world (-1/∞ + 1/∞), here is micro concept point is defined to (-1/∞ + 1/∞), this is indicated to time, and space, so long, in this micro concept is recognition ranges, the futures, must be +1/∞ ~, but also past is ~-1/∞, this is the time basis so long, a macro concept actor recognized in the macro concept point (-1/∞ + 1/∞), in the micro concept world is also recognition to also (-1/∞ + 1/∞), the micro concept world space is also (-1/∞ + 1/∞). Macro concept world is seen world, but micro concept world is unseen world. Macro concept world and macro concept world is existed in a place.

If macro concept then macro concept world only existed, so long, macro concept recognition is not seen or try to seek micro concept world, this world is conception world only, so long macro concept world is so huge, so long do not calculate the size. So long, micro concept world also huge but also so long distance located space. But micro concept world is

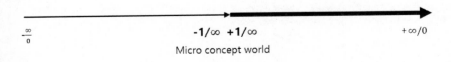

Size is so micro, so long (-1/∞ + 1/∞). In this time and place are micro concept actor souls living destination, then macro concept world actor is really recognized then it must be infer that, macro concept actor realized as in a place and time (-1/∞ + 1/∞).

Macro concept world and micro concept world are must be a meeting place is the micro concept point (-1/∞ + 1/∞). The macro concept world and micro concept world is recognized by the macro concept world an actor reaches at the micro concept point (-1/∞ + 1/∞). So long a macro concept actor realized then, the macro concept actor realized the micro concept world existing.

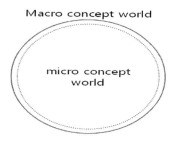

Macro concept world

micro concept world

Macro concept world is seen world, but macro concept world do not seen to macro concept actor, but a macro concept actor realized then the actor realized at the place is (-1/∞ .. 1/∞... If a macro concept actor realized then, the macro concept world supported from micro concept world. In the macro concept world, do not realized macro concept actor do not know the micro concept world, but if a actor realized then the actor get in to the micro concept point (-1/∞ .. 1/∞... Actually micro concept point is unseen but existed place. The place is existed in the macro concept world realized actor. Micro concept world is formed in the macro concept actor of realized. In this micro concept world in the realized actor's reaching at micro concept point (-1/∞ .. 1/∞... Micro concept world and macro concept world is same place, this is to the realized macro concept actor recognition. So long, macro concept actor world is seen world seen world actor living in the macro concept world, but micro concept world is righteous soul and wicked soul living place. So long in this micro concept point, a macro concept actor realized, so called macro concept realized actor reach at the micro concept point (-1/∞ .. 1/∞... The place is tunnel from macro concept point to micro concept world is (-1/∞ .. 1/∞... It being the place of micro concept world is (-1/∞ .. 1/∞... So then realized macro concept actor recognized a micro concept actor moving. So long the realized actor recognized two world, macro concept world and micro concept world, so long, realized actor world expand to macro concept world to micro concept actor world. Micro concept recognition is micro concept place is unseen world but realized actor recognized world (-1/∞ .. 1/∞... So long realized actor live life recognition to seen life unseen life.

Seen world : macro concept world	

Do not realized actor's living place is just seen world limited

Seen world : macro concept world	Unseen world : micro concept world

Do live as realized actor; so long reach at micro concept point, then through micro concept tunnel (-1/∞ + 1/∞). So long realized actor living in the two world micro concept world, and macro concept world.

Do live as realized actor; so long reach at micro concept point, then through micro concept tunnel (-1/∞ + 1/∞). So long realized actor living in the two world micro concept world, and macro concept world.

2014.12.19

Topic: macro concept "Macro concept actor energy is same"

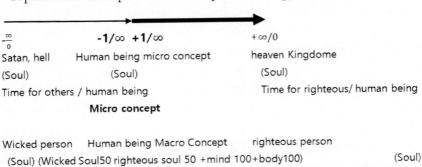

In this micro concept, macro concept birth life voyage energy, the energy is same; the energy is usage is free by an actor. The actor lives in the seen a feature place. The actor does behavior variables. All of macro concept living principle make money, so long, input time is invest to make money, the output macro concept actor's income this is the physical income, but spiritual income is also required but do not realized actor does not know the soul role. Soul energy is same, soul energy same means that physical energy increasing role is soul energy. Soul energy is blessing to the macro concept actor living.

Macro concept actor "righteous soul 50 wicked soul 50 + mind 100 + body 100" then the macro concept world actor use energy, then, macro concept actor of energy living is righteous living and wicked living

1. Righteous living actor use energy " righteous soul 100 + mind 100" it is the realized actor used energy then, righteous living actor use energy then, this energy is sacrifices and the righteous hard living but also shared time with others and help others, so working for righteous is required energy, so long a righteous energy use for righteous behavior.

2. Wicked living actor use energy " wicked soul 100 + mind 100+ body 100" wicked living actor do not help others but also do not shared time for others, so long all of an actor energy use for exclusively wicked actor only.

3. Righteous living half and wicked living is the actor energy sometimes use for the righteous behavior but also use for the wicked behavior, so long so long energy is half for right and the other is wicked.

Equality energy of each actor, then the actor how to use energy this is actor free decision, so long, all is not other but all is the actor choice but also responsibility, then realized actor feel of the world is macro concept world and wicked actor, so long an actor live righteously then, reach at the micro concept point (-1/∞ + 1/∞). Then micro concept point is tunnel and micro concept world (-1/∞ + 1/∞). So then realized actor world is both macro concept world and micro concept world, so long the righteous actor live righteously living then, the actor energy used for the productivity, so long righteous actor behavior of righteously then, all of righteous behavior is saved at the micro concept righteous soul destination world, blessed bank accumulated.

So long, righteous actor use energy use righteously then, the energy is up down to, so long, a righteous actor of upper and another generation actor live righteously then, the righteous actor energy give bless to righteous actor.

But if macro concept actor energy used for the wicked, only exclusively macro actors, so long, then actor will be get a physical energy must be rich so long, if do not realized actor all think that just seen world rich living is all, so long, wicked actor definition is do not shared time with others but also do not help others. So long it is very natural, in the macro concept world, an actor will be living well, but the actor lives as the wick. But the actor wicked behavior naturally saved at the micro concept world wicked soul living destination place cursed bank. So that the actor behavior must be used energy for exclusively the actor's, so then the actor success in the macro concept world, so long it must be seems to the poor actor understood as wicked actor living is better. If then this is do not realized actor, but to the realized actor, so long reach at the micro concept point so long, the actor recognized that the living righteous actor macro concept world and micro concept world. But if a wicked actor do not realized, so long the actor do not reach at the micro concept point, so long wicked actor just for the living a seen world so called macro concept world living is only recognition. So that wick actor success in the macro concept world, rich, and social places is also comparison better than out of wick actors. Then it must be wicked actor live well, what is equal, wicked actor just all used other righteous actor help others, but also shared time, then in this actor living frame but, the wicked actor all of time and energy only for wicked actor sake, then this is correct?, it must be not, the righteous soul recognized at the macro concept world and micro concept world. So long wicked actor live well in the macro concept world, do not help other and shared time with others then, the rich actor energy usage all related with cursed bank credit increased. So long, the macro concept world wicked live actor, after macro concept world living after, the actor live in the micro concept world as wicked soul. So long, the actor get cursed bank energy, so long, the wicked soul have a power to curse. Even the wicked soul think help but the help power is cursed to the macro of wicked actor, so that the wicked actor macro concept living is not eternity all of macro wicked actor influenced from micro concept world wicked actor soul cursed bank energy is effect to macro concept actor behavior.

All of actor in the macro concept world, the energy usage is free but, if the energy used for the righteous then, then energy keep continued to next generation giving blessing, but if do not live righteously then, the actors energy will be effect to curse to next generation. So long, the righteous living and reach at the micro concept point (-1/∞ + 1/∞). Then it must be understand the sure of helped through micro concept tunnel (-1/∞ + 1/∞). A good solving idea getting but also fortune from righteous soul, micro concept point is to the realized actor must be recognized to macro concept world and micro concept world so long, the living world is 2 fold wide.

2014.12.26

Topic: macro concept "righteous soul relationship building"

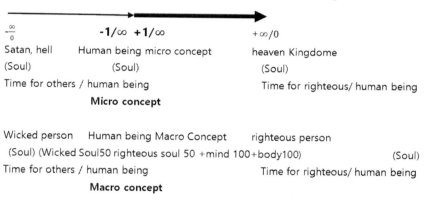

In this micro concept, the relationship building is also micro concept related factors. The relationship building is cause of being righteous and wicked behavior. Even righteous and wicked comes in a single behavior, but in the single time behavior related with righteous soul and wicked soul. In the macro concept world an actor build relationship. So long the actor of righteous must be behavior of 100% righteous behavior actor, but also the try to do righteous but the ability is not same as the righteous soul actor ability, so long, if a do not ability actor is about 60 % of the righteous actor ability 100's, so long

Righteous soul actor 100%	

Righteous soul actor 60%	Wicked soul actor 40%

This is the actor of relationship building, so long, all the time, between righteous soul actor 100 and righteous soul 60 to wicked soul 40% then, happened actually in the macro concept world do not recognitions but all of the relationship is happened.

So long, all the time building of righteous 100 and righteous 100 then it is very excitement but also it is lucky, but usually all of relationship building is righteous soul actor 100 and righteous soul 60% with wicked soul 40%, so then, it must be done the working.

In the macro concept world, the relationship some is righteous the other is not righteous, so then, if a righteous 100 shared with 40 % with righteous 60% occupied another wicked 40%, so long the righteous 100 must be target to the mixed righteous and wicked soul, if a righteous 100 shared 100 righteous soul, 40% righteous soul donate to the righteous soul 60% + wicked soul 40% actor, then, infer of righteous 100, give 40% righteous soul to the "righteous soul 60% + wicked soul 40" then plus of relationship behavior so long righteous soul 40% attached to the " righteous 60% + wicked 40% so + righteous 40%"

Righteous soul actor 60%	Righteous soul 40

Donate righteous 40% to the "righteous soul 60 + wicked soul actor 40"

Then

Righteous soul actor 60%	Wicked soul actor 40%	Righteous soul 40

So long, righteous 100 souls shared 40 % righteous soul with "righteous soul 60% + wicked 40%"

Then 40% righteous soul shared with "righteous soul 60% + wicked 40%" so then, it beings that "righteous soul 60% + wicked 40% + righteous soul 40%" so that "righteous soul 60% + wicked 40%" newly forms to "righteous soul 100 + wicked soul 40%" in this time happened in the actor of the "righteous soul 60% + wicked 40%" soul affected from

Righteous soul actor 60%	Righteous soul 40

Donate righteous 40% to the "righteous soul 60 + wicked soul actor 40"

⬇

Then

Righteous soul actor 60%	Wicked soul actor 40%	Righteous soul 40

Then the "righteous soul 60% + wicked 40%" to "the "righteous soul 100% + wicked 40%"

⟹ Righteous actor 100% + wicked 40%, in this time, another righteous actor helper comes from micro concept world righteous soul actor blessing of micro concept actor righteous soul destination world blessed banking credit used to help " righteous 100+ wicked 40" so long it beings to " righteous 100+ righteous blessing 100 + wicked 40"

⬇

Righteous soul actor 60%	Wicked soul actor 40%	Righteous soul 40	Righteous belssing100

So long, strong righteous soul righteous soul 60% + righteous 100 soul's 40% donation 40% + then helped from micro concept actor soul credit 100, so then righteous soul 200% this power must be strong to dispel the wicked soul 40% so long

⬇

Then the wicked soul actor dispelled from a strong 200 righteous soul

Righteous soul actor 60%	Wicked soul actor 40% Dispelled	Righteous soul 40	Righteous belssing100

So long, it being the perfect righteous soul, righteous soul 200%

Righteous soul actor 60%	Dispelled wicked	Righteous soul 40	Righteous belssing100

⬇

Righteous soul actor 60% + Righteous soul 40 + Righteous belssing100 = righteous soul 200% = righteous soul 100 of the origin of helper of righteous soul.

In the end the righteous soul 100%, shared with "righteous soul 60 + wicked soul 40%" so long

In the start in the building righteous actor behavior to the wicked actor

Righteous soul actor 100%

Righteous soul actor 60%	Wicked soul actor 40%

To

Righteous soul actor 100%

Righteous soul actor 100%

So long the righteous behavior soul actor create a new righteous soul actor, then it must be in this macro concept world, with body of the righteous actor relationship so that the righteous soul actor live with created counter actor of righteous then, it must be living in the righteous soul world. In this process some of the reader riddle to this procedure,

Righteous soul actor 100%

Righteous soul actor 60% to be forming 100 it must be occupied by wicked soul actor 40%

So long, to make righteous actor of wicked actor, then behavior of righteous behavior so long 40%

righteous soul shared with wicked. Then it must be understood as righteous soul $100 - 40 = 60\%$, so wrong, but is not, the righteous actor also shared with others righteous actor 100% soul 40% soul shared so long 60% righteous soul + others righteous soul 40% so long still it goes 100%, this solution also, but another infer is that righteous 100%, among then 40% shared with wicked soul then, righteous soul is like smoke type so, even give 40% then the righteous soul more strength, so long righteous 100 soul still 100 souls, this is the micro concept actor calculating. So long righteous soul shared with others then, the shared soul is another strong soul of righteous, so long, righteous behavior create a new righteous, this is not a mathematic in the macro concept world helped from righteous behavior then, being helped actor must be feel excitement with righteous soul. So long righteous helping other 40% then, strong of the origin of the righteous soul keeps 100% righteous soul.

But if not same as the righteous soul does not help others then, do not other being wicked soul actor,

Righteous soul actor 100%	

Righteous soul actor 60%	Wicked soul actor 40%

Righteous soul actor 100 does not help other "righteous soul actor 60 + wicked soul actor 40%" so then, the wicked soul actor tries to work as same as righteous soul actor 100%. So long wicked soul actor 40 % is increased to wicked soul try to collect

Then wicked soul collects wicked soul helper: then "righteous soul 60% + wicked soul40%" collect Helper of wicked soul so long, "righteous soul 60% + wicked soul40%" + mind 100+ micro concept world wicked soul destination actor 100" here is micro concept wicked soul credit is micro concept world wicked soul destination world cursed bank credit help wicked actor soul, so long" righteous soul 60% + wicked soul 40% + mind 100%+ wicked soul cursed 100" so then

Wicked soul 40% + mind 100%+ cursed 100%= 240% + righteous soul 60% then, righteous soul dispelled from the" righteous soul 60+ wicked soul 40" in the end

Righteous soul actor 60%	Wicked soul actor 40%	Mind 100	Micro concept world wicked soul cursed credit 100

Righteous soul actor 60% Dispelled	Wicked soul actor 40%	Mind 100	Micro concept world wicked soul cursed credit 100

Wicked soul actor 40% + Mind 100 + Micro concept world wicked soul cursed credit 100 Wicked soul actor being 240% so long= strong wicked soul actor to being compatible of wicked Pure soul created to wicked soul 100

So long, do not shared origin of the righteous actor has been blessed but, so long, a actor has been lived as righteous but, if a actor do not shared with others but also do not help other then, it must be right after then, the actor being wicked actor, so long, in the end in the procedures are all being changed to strong wicked soul, even if the originality is righteous but if do not righteous then,

At first being

Righteous soul actor 100% origin

Wicked soul actor 100% created

At second is created wicked soul 100 comes, but also, the righteous actor do not shared with others but also, do not helped then, in the definition of the righteous, right after being wicked, but also the righteous soul around all of wicked soul created so long, origin of righteous actor transfer to wicked soul 100, so long, in the end infer of all switching to wicked soul actor

At second

Righteous soul actor 100% origin being to wicked soul actor

Wicked soul actor 100% created

In the end

Wicked soul actor 100

Wicked soul actor 100%

If the righteous actor does not righteous behavior then, create wicked actor but also origin righteous soul also being wicked soul.

So long righteous behavior is very important, righteous estimated actor duty is so strong. Righteous actor must be behavior of righteously.

Topic: micro ~ macro concept "micro concept degree"

$$\longrightarrow \Longrightarrow$$

$-\frac{\infty}{0}$	$-1/\infty$ $+1/\infty$	$+\infty/0$
Satan, hell	Human being micro concept	heaven Kingdome
(Soul)	(Soul)	(Soul)
Time for others / human being		Time for righteous/ human being

Micro concept

Wicked person	Human being Macro Concept	righteous person
(Soul)	(Wicked Soul50 righteous soul 50 +mind 100+body100)	(Soul)
Time for others / human being		Time for righteous/ human being

Macro concept

Micro concept start from $(-1/\infty + 1/\infty)$. This is come to me by strike my head with hammer, unseen world and seen world, from fast longtime ago, future long after, but in micro concept is seen just macro concept momentum time $(-1/\infty + 1/\infty)$. This is micro concept point is time and area, so long, micro concept point $(-1/\infty + 1/\infty)$ is it must be 4 dimension. Time and area is must be recognized but 4 dimension to be it required to be dept, so long, dept is must be ∞ depth is not calculated, micro concept gate, macro concept world actor has personal micro concept gate.

so long if infer a actor realized so long, a macro concept actor" righteous soul 50 wicked soul 50 + mind 100 + body 100" so long it changed to the realized to reach at the micro concept point $(-1/\infty + 1/\infty)$, so long, being " righteous soul 50~0 wicked soul 0~50 + mind 0~100 +body 100" infer if realized at, so long reach at micro concept point $(-1/\infty + 1/\infty)$, so long simply " righteous soul + body" so long, under the feature 4 dimension time, area, depth,

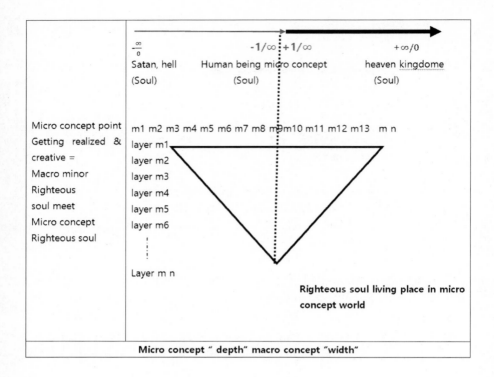

	$-\frac{\infty}{0}$ $-1/\infty$: $+1/\infty$ $+\infty/0$

Micro concept " depth" macro concept "width"

In this micro concept, macro concept actor realized to reach at micro concept point ($-1/\infty$ $+1/\infty$), so then a actor soul reach at righteous so long realized, the actor soul live at the micro concept point ($-1/\infty + 1/\infty$), this is m1, then the actor more deeper going, so long, the realized actor, micro concept actor move to go deeper, so long, macro concept actor has micro concept gate, so long, macro concept world actor live, a actor live righteously but also realized actor living, then, a actor live m1($-1/\infty + 1/\infty$) then this actor keep getting deeper to reach at micro concept world m n($-1/\infty + 1/\infty$), so long, a macro concept world actor live in righteous living then,

a actor live as m1($-1/\infty + 1/\infty$) X depth m1 this is a actor coordinate, so long in the macro concept world

Living is seen world X unseen world, so called, macro concept world X micro concept world, so long, infer to dept is location of the micro concept world, but also macro concept world realized micro concept point is m1 ($-1/\infty + 1/\infty$), so that a macro concept actor coordinate is m1(-1/∞ + 1/∞) X dept m1, so long dept layers, so that m(-1/∞ + 1/∞) X m1, m2,m3, m4,m5... m n.

So then micro concept actor how to live at in the righteous living, so it must be micro concept degree, this is macro concept actor soul realized micro concept point is 1/∞, then micro concept point, to meet macro concept in living as righteously actor tunnel (-1/∞ + 1/∞) to micro concept world so long this is infer as the depth m n. so long micro concept degree is micro concept realized point micro concept point X micro concept point meeting place, depth = so long, micro concept point is express to 1/∞ but to reach at the micro concept point world tunnel (-1/∞ + 1/∞) to micro concept actor destination, this is dept, this depth is how to deep realized so long so long, it express to ∞ = so long 1/∞ X ∞ = 1. This is comes to unseen world to Seen world, so long unseen world is 1/∞ but seen world is 1/∞ X ∞ =1, so long micro concept world. Micro concept degree is 1/∞ X ∞ = 1. Micro concept reaching actor to go for the micro concept soul world how to go deeper is now newly comes, micro concept world actor in the macro concept world, so long, the depth difference is macro concept actor realized degree. Even a actor being reach at the micro concept point, then, if a realized actor keep going deeper this is to go for the micro concept actor soul destination living place. Righteous soul living actors keep going deeper, so that the actor reaches at the eternity righteous soul living destination place.

It must be infer to macro concept actor live for righteous, so then, macro concept actor realized, so long reach at the micro concept point (-1/∞ + 1/∞), this is being realized, so long the actor reach at the micro concept point, so called gate and tunnel (-1/∞ + 1/∞) , micro concept reaching actors going more deeper righteous living then it must be go deeper.

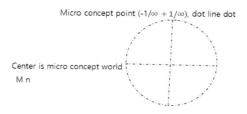

Micro concept point (-1/∞ + 1/∞), dot line dot

Center is micro concept world
M n

Micro concept coordinates so called to micro concept degree

Micro concept point is (-1/∞ + 1/∞), so then the point is a macro concept actor realized so long micro concept point and gate to micro concept point (-1/∞ + 1/∞) , to reach at the micro concept world destination place, the realized actor also difference, if infer to that macro concept actor realized so long, micro concept point reaching then, in the micro concept place of (-1/∞ + 1/∞), then in the micro concept actors communities various actors are living. So then in the pursuing living righteous, then it must be relationship building is happened, so long, macro concept world lived with others. So then, in this micro concept point, all of macro concept world actor has personal micro concept gate, so long, try to live righteously then, the actor live righteously, so long, two actors meet so that from one actor to be two actor related so long, in this relationship is also, has the unit, so that, a unit, in this micro concept actor explained, micro concept point is personal, a unit, so long, two actor forming to a unit, so that the unit also has the micro concept gate, Unit is typically husband wife is very good example, so long husband wife unit must be recognized to realized as couple, so that, two actor one unit, so unit must be live righteously. So long a unit being live righteously, so that the unit can reach at the micro concept point (-1/∞ + 1/∞), unit micro concept reaching is macro concept point of view, unit tow actor live righteous but also unit shared time with other actors but also help others. For these two actor are being one unit, so long, it already two actors are all righteous behavior so that, the two actors are each reach at the micro concept point (-1/∞ + 1/∞), unit actor being "righteous soul +body" another actor "righteous soul + body" this personal righteous soul being one unit is then "the actor of righteous soul + body, the others actor righteous soul +body plus each other half righteous soul combined to unit body" the unit actor righteous living is cause excitement and perfection coming.

sort	Righteous soul actor	Righteous soul actor	Unit soul actor
Personal actor	Righteous + body	Righteous +body	
Unit actor	Righteous + body	Righteous +body	Half soul unit plus

Two righteous soul actors forming to unit soul

So long, tow righteous actor forming to unit then, personal soul actor righteous, the others personal righteous actor, if this actor live personal then, this is personal, but forming unit, then, plus each other righteous soul half to half combined to one soul so long, here is unit soul making, so that unit soul is "righteous soul + body, righteous soul + body, Plus one of unit soul" so that unit soul actor being much more power. Unit soul actor created this is governing each other soul, so long; the unit is same as personal soul so long unit righteous behavior related also micro concept world righteous soul destination so long, the relationship is recognized in micro concept world. So long, the micro concept world righteous soul destination place, righteous actors blessed bank blessing to unit soul actor. So long a typical unit is couple, so long husband wife live as righteous then, the couple also recognized as righteous unit soul. So long the unit get be also reach at the excitement but also perfection.

2014.12.30

Topic: macro "macro actor energy"

$-\frac{\infty}{0}$	$-1/\infty$ $+1/\infty$	$+\infty/0$
Satan, hell	Human being micro concept	heaven Kingdome
(Soul)	(Soul)	(Soul)
Time for others / human being		Time for righteous/ human being

Micro concept

Wicked person	Human being Macro Concept	righteous person
(Soul)	(Wicked Soul50 righteous soul 50 +mind 100+body100)	(Soul)
Time for others / human being		Time for righteous/ human being

Macro concept

In this micro concept the macro concept actor live with energy. The energy is making live easy. So long, macro concept actor tries to get energy to live, all of time use. Micro concept is start all of macro concept actors' all thing brush aside then comes to soul, so long in the form of micro concept point is $(-1/\infty + 1/\infty)$, so long, do not reach at the micro concept point do not know the micro concept energy, but only getting in the macro concept world, so long, macro concept energy is money, so that all of macro concept actors effort to get money, all of live also targeting at making money, all of living time, so long cause of this, macro concept actor live busy. But a macro concept actor who realized so that reach at the micro concept point, the actor knows micro concept actor world living energy is required. In the macro concept world actor " righteous soul 50 wicked soul 50 + mind 100+ body 100" so long, if do not realized actor only see the Seen world so long macro concept world, so that the actor try to get money much more than others. To make money the actor all of best to get in the position of getting money, so long macro concept actor making money

sort	Righteous Soul 50	Wicked Soul 50	Mind 100	Body 100
Macro concept world	Shared time with others Helping others Make money With others	Do not shared Others. Do not help others. Make money Exclusive for actors	To make a big money. Much more time for making money	Righteous making money body good healthy But wicked get Worse health
Micro concept world	Righteous soul Bless bank credit	Wicked soul Cursed bank credit		

Macro concept actor ① righteous soul 50, ② wicked soul 50, ③ mind 100, ④ body 100, these actors are forming a macro concept actor.

To make money macro concept actor mostly much more makes money then, operated by ② wicked soul 50, ③ mind 100 so then, this actors are a side of the micro concept actor of wicked soul related. In the point of micro concept then, truly wicked soul of do not shared time, all of time make money macro concept actor soul, but also do not help others. So then it must be getting much money, but also ③ mind 100 operated to make a big money. So this ③ mind 100 is cause of much time use in making money, so long ④ body 100 doing make money over time, so that the body deteriorated. In the macro concept actor make diligence so long do not know perfectly in the end, the actor mind, and wicked soul is expanded so that the actor live all of purpose of getting money. In this micro concept point these wicked actor side behavior is directly to micro concept wicked soul destination cursed bank. So long much time for make money actor really getting at being rich, but while making time do not build blessed bank blessing credit, so that, the actor accumulated cursed bank cursed point increased. Even an actor makes money in the Seen world so called macro concept world. So then in the macro concept world actor ② wicked soul 50, ③ mind 100, ④ body 100 so long, these actors are still wicked soul invaded a rich then, the ④ body 100 hit so long, wicked soul actor behavior getting energy is not going eternity, because of cursed bank energy operated, so called in the micro concept world, wicked soul break the wicked actor soul actor behavior, so long, deteriorate body. In this time ③ mind 100 getting anger so long, wicked soul 50 with mind 100 then it make worse to the end worst so long all of collecting energy used up. So that the wicked actor role built finally break.

But ① righteous soul 50 is seen in the macro concept world actor, the actor shared with time others but also, help others. So then, the make money time is so long, but also, so hard to get a originality creative position, just find a new way of living so that, the righteous soul actor realized so long, the actor reach at the micro concept point (-1/∞ + 1/∞), so that the actor know the living world is macro concept world and micro concept world. So long, righteous soul behavior, the behaved in the macro concept world, in the personal actors, the righteous soul is being excited with shared time with others but also, help others. So that even the actor does not make money in the macro concept world, so long, somewhat the actor must be prostrated but the actor knows that, the actor live sacrificed but also time is longer to get make money, the actor of righteous actor devote to created some of it, so that the actor do not combat with others, so long, do not make hard others, but to get a creative living required to long time, but in this hard procedure then, hard but the righteous actor follows righteous definition is do live time others but also help others, so long, the actor in the end helped from micro concept world micro concept world righteous soul living destination blessing bank credit, the actor of righteous soul then helped from micro concept world blessing point helped righteous soul actor then the actor solved the problems to be creative perfection. So that the righteous actor lived so long time, so hard but the actor keeps in the righteous soul behavior, so long, the actor helped the living for the making money so called energy. The righteous soul making money is all the time based on the shared times others but also help others. So then helped actor soul, helped from righteous soul blessing point getting actor, the actors soul live excitement so long, micro concept world, the righteous soul 50 be strong, so long, in the reaching at the micro concept point (-1/∞ + 1/∞), so long in the end, the actor being a righteous living actor forming "righteous 100+body 100" so long, to live righteous then, it must be wicked actor run way from pure righteous soul, so long righteous soul behavior so long, it comes excitement and perfection, it means that it comes to the "righteous soul + body" this is comes to real excitement & perfection, so long righteous soul actor beings. The actor live eternity with healthy body and the creature actor source of making energy getting is for long time survived because of the actor support for the righteous actor's sakes also.

2014.12.31
Topic: macro "mind making to 1/∞"

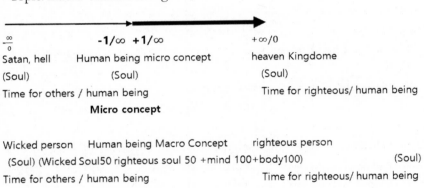

In this micro concept macro concept actor consist of "righteous soul 50 wicked soul50 + mind100+ body 100". Macro concept actor tries to be live excitement & perfection. Then the only not live actor is mind100, mind 100 is parasite at the body, mind100 is a source of problems so that mind is formed to ∞ so long mind is locate every time every place, so long, in the macro concept actor who do not realized so called do not reach at micro concept point (-1/∞ + 1/∞), so long, the actor only watch Seen world macro concept world then, the actor rely on mind 100, so long the actor only tries to get much money. So long to get make money it required to over time to make money so called, the actor do not use only for himself. So long the mind is desired, so that, the actor gets in sick, but also sometimes deceit from others mind100 actors. So long the macro concept actor who do not realized and do not reach at micro concept point do not know a living actor soul righteous soul50 wicked soul50 so that the actor helped from a not living a parasite mind100, so that the actor live out of living feeling, so that the mind 100 lead a macro concept actor to reckless for making money etc. so that mind 100 coax the actor to live over time out of optimistic attitude but just mind100 push to do over or it jealous of other getting well success is so that the actor do not have a satisfaction so long, the actor live as the wicked soul actor being getting well. So long mind100 is a source of living body getting suffering. So long do not realized actor so called do not reach at the micro concept point $(-1/\infty + 1/\infty)$, then the actor helped from mind 100, and then desired over time use then the actor being edible to others mind100 so long, endless mind100 is macro concept world center workers. So long here all of macro concept actor lives fight for the other actor100, mind100 is macro concept trouble supplier core actor, but the mind do not live, so that mind is not human mind only, desired, over work, this must be slaver to the other mind100, then it kept mind 100 strong to a actor it must be infer that righteous soul wicked soul segregate from body 100, then, wicked soul50 and mind100 is relatives are same side, so long, mind 100 help wicked soul 50, so that mind100 help wicked soul 50, wicked souls actor connect to in the micro soul destination living wicked soul actor, so long if infer that mind whisper " wicked soul please the actor make hard because of the actor troubled " so that the wicked actor travel to meet micro concept wicked actor and ask to curse the trouble actor, so the wicked soul saved of cursed bank energy of breaking the trouble actor affairs. So long mind is role for the between wicked actor soul and body 100, if body 100 to go doing by the mind100 order, if mind 100 do not operated then, the mind 100 whisper to the wicked actor, so then wicked actor try to help mind100 helping, so long, wicked soul actor cursed energy usage.

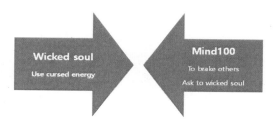

Mind 100 has a characteristics of over jealous but also over getting, so that conflict to others then the actor feel unfair so that, the actor of mind100 ask to curse the other mind100 actor, so that the asked wicked soul travel to ask to the micro concept actor wicked soul destination cursed bank, cursed energy usage right getting. So that the cursed energy is used break other actor affair.

Therefore mind 100 is very core of to get be live excitement, out of trouble it required to make mind 100 to be $1/\infty$, how to reach at the mind100 to be $1/\infty$, how to be this is the personal training to be out of mind 100 traps.

This is must be live righteous then, righteous soul actor helped then, it must be decreased the mind 100. Macro actor to live peace and excitement then, it must be decreased mind100, so long,

it infer that mind 100 is being $1/\infty$ then it comes soul meet to the body, so long this is really excitement & perfections. So long, the mind 100 and soul of the righteous or wicked soul, if to live righteous living then, righteous behavior use the blessing energy, so long, righteous soul gain blessing power, so long, if infer that to be live righteous then, it must be out of mind 100, but also wicked soul also, so long in the end it comes to meet righteous soul and body meeting.

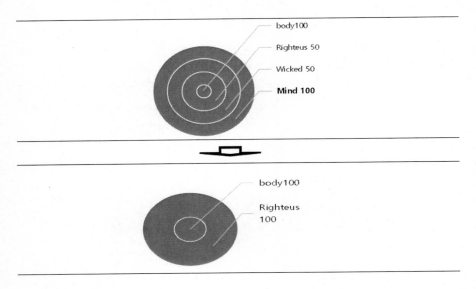

Macro actor to live peace and excitement what is important is the mind 100 must be $1/\infty$, this is then it must be mind 100 weak and disappeared then, the macro concept world actor do not helped from mind 100, so then the mind 100 do not use the wicked actor soul, so long, the wicked actor gradually power is decreased, so long, very hard to move because of strong mind 100, so long in the mind 100 being to $1/\infty$, so that righteous soul slowly move, but also the mind 100 is almost disappeared to$1/\infty$ it means that the body 100 go with souls, so long, the wicked soul being decreased, and start righteous soul, so long, righteous soul help body moving, so long body helped by souls, so long, the righteous soul help body to live righteously. So then, gradually the body behaviors righteously, to live with others, help others.

So then the actor reach at the micro concept point $(-1/\infty + 1/\infty)$ so long, mind100 to $1/\infty$, in the end righteous soul 50 behavior so long, against wicked soul getting lower, in the end righteous soul getting power, in the end wicked soul fear of being pure of righteous soul, so then wicked soul dispelled to wicked soul actor. So long, the actor being controlled righteous soul, in the end by the moment mind 100 being to $1/\infty$ then being " righteous soul100 + body 100" this is realized actor, but also this is the reach at the micro concept point $(-1/\infty + 1/\infty)$. This is living excitement and perfection. Here macro concept actor feel peace and excitement comes.

2015.01.02

Topic: micro concept living

$-\frac{\infty}{0}$

-1/∞ +1/∞   +∞/0

Satan, hell   Human being micro concept   heaven Kingdome

(Soul)   (Soul)   (Soul)

Time for others / human being   Time for righteous/ human being

Micro concept

Wicked person   Human being Macro Concept   righteous person

(Soul) (Wicked Soul50 righteous soul 50 +mind 100+body100)   (Soul)

Time for others / human being   Time for righteous/ human being

Macro concept

In this micro concept how to live, micro concept place is point (-1/∞ + 1/∞) and time is point (-1/ ∞ + 1/∞) . Micro concept world also point (-1/ ∞ + 1/∞) , micro concept gate is point (-1/∞ + 1/∞). Micro concept tunnel is point (-1/∞ + 1/∞). In this micro concept all, the concept key is (-1/∞ + 1/∞). This is this micro concept all, in this micro concept comes to me, hit my head, I was so surprised to me, but also, this is engine to write to now. Micro concept is Unseen &Seen point, (-1/∞ + 1/∞). Micro concept point is first come to me, past of 1/∞ fast, but also future is beginning of future 1/∞, so long, macro concept actor get a knowledge to solve the coming problems, past knowledge and future knowledge getting point is (-1/∞ + 1/∞). So long micro concept point coming realized at micro concept world (-1/∞ + 1/∞). Micro concept place and time living actor also micro concept actor, who is soul, soul, in this micro concept required to solve the macro concept actor seen world, is body featured, how to come to micro concept point so long, what necessary to live macro concept world actor. So long in this micro concept explained as a scale of micro concept method. So long it might be helped the ways of micro concept, micro concept living actor is soul, so then actually recognition of this procedure is secured by the macro concept actor. Macro concept actor has the micro concept gate, so long, macro concept actor recognized really, so long, the macro concept actor and micro concept actor must be connected, so but in the macro concept actor just Seen world behavior is all. Actually micro concept world is not seen so that to the macro concept world actor it doesn't mind. Macro concept actor live in the Seen world, so then macro concept actor need to live energy, this is the must be all, but also macro concept actor get related with others. Macro actors who are not famous and are not rich, just unseen macro concept actor live in this macro concept world. Macro concept actor's live righteously wickedly. Very unknown actor lives righteously so long it shared time with others but also helped others. So that the actor do not live rich, but also famous, so long, another way of living the success or rich actor who has been worked all of actor time is used for himself, but also time is short so long, the time exclusively used for himself, so busy the actor time do not shared with others but also, so long fast and busy for himself, so long it hasn't time help others. So then in the macro concept world, all long for being rich and famous, micro concept is start from point $(-1/\infty + 1/\infty)$. So long, the macro concept actor portion is $1/\infty$, so long, micro concept actor is soul, so long the actor has the $1/\infty$ position so long width, so then the actor do not invader others $1/\infty$, so long, the actor is live in the portion of the $1/\infty$, this is micro concept actor living ways, but macro concept actor get energy as possible as get rich. All of time for use getting energy. So long, this is the do not shared time with others, but also do not help others, then it must be living of the wicked way. The righteous actor is the live the $1/\infty$ width, but also go deeper∞, so long the righteous actor get be optimistic getting energy, so long macro concept actor, go deeper to meet righteous micro concept soul, macro concept actor comes by go deeper of micro concept actor, so long, then it must be seen in the macro concept actor go growing. A macro concept actor realized so long reach at point $(-1/\infty + 1/\infty)$. the in the micro concept point $(-1/\infty + 1/\infty)$ in the place the actor do not go out of the micro concept place $(-1/\infty + 1/\infty)$ then the micro concept reaching actor go deeper whining in the micro concept place $(-1/\infty + 1/\infty)$. The macro concept actor Seen world is seen by others the actor grown. Macro concept actor grows in physical, so long, in the Seen world macro concept actor are recognized in the growing physically, but do not recognized in soulful. So that macro concept actor must be grow, some before grow physically because of the soul is from micro concept world so soulful energetic so that, it based on the strong soul so it required to live on the macro concept world physical strength, but after 30 years old, physical growth being stop, so then all of macro concept actor being busy to get live energy, but also related with others, so long, in this time, just minor of actor in the macro concept world major is body and soul is minor, so long, minor soul also must be recognized by macro concept actor. Here is realized macro concept actor inferred to realized actors soul, so long the actor try to live righteously, but the other actors are live for the only physical strength but also only in the Seen world so long but, in the macro concept world body is just finished all of physical world. So long micro concept world do not know in the macro concept world is only seen macro concept actors. So long, how to live as micro concept ways is, it must be in the micro concept as explained so long, do live righteous so long, righteous behavior direct ways is must be connected with micro concept world, so long micro concept world righteous soul destination. So long the actor going for the micro concept world $(-1/\infty .. 1/\infty...$ So that it realized, the actor live excitement to go with others and help others. So then micro concept world formed and live in the micro concept world $(-1/\infty .. 1/\infty...$

Micro concept world $(-1/\infty + 1/\infty)$ is formed by righteous macro actor so long micro concept world actor, micro concept world $(-1/\infty + 1/\infty)$. In this place is macro concept world is micro concept moment, so long, this is connected as the soul, so long, and righteous soul is connected with other righteous souls so long, the actor lives as the state of excitement & perfection. So long, micro concept world $(-1/\infty + 1/\infty)$ the righteous actor in the micro concept world all of realized micro concept actor are all being state of the excitement & perfection. So long in the micro concept world $(-1/\infty + 1/\infty)$ living actor lives excitement & perfection, so long the actor can solve the problems. The righteous actor in the micro concept place $(-1/\infty + 1/\infty)$ shared time with others and help others as excitement & perfection. In the micro concept world $(-1/\infty + 1/ \infty)$ is fulfillment all of righteous actors who lived with others and helped others. So then how to related with macro concept world, here micro concept world is formed to $(-1/\infty + 1/\infty)$. Micro concept world from fast to future $(-1/\infty + 1/\infty)$. In this place all of soul living in the micro concept places. Micro concept world is $(-1/\infty + 1/\infty)$. This is showing in the macro concept world, so long, macro concept world is located the micro concept gate each person but also each unit so long, the micro concept world is in the macro concept world. It infer that if a realized actor then the actor reach at the micro concept point then, the micro concept point is located at realized actor

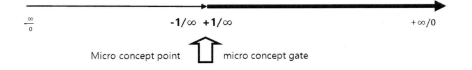

Macro concept actor who realized and reach at the micro concept point, ⬆ is actor, so then realized actor connect micro concept actor, so long the realized actor itself is micro concept actor then it must be the macro concept actor located at the realized macro concept actor so long, the micro concept point (-1/ ∞ + 1/∞) . And micro concept point (-1/ ∞ + 1/∞) . So long, micro concept point is macro concept actor who is realized and reaches the micro concept point.

The realized actor is located at the micro concept point (-1/∞ + 1/∞). But do not realized actor, then the actor do not recognized micro concept. This is comes by the righteous living then in the end reach at the micro concept point (-1/∞ + 1/∞) so long, righteous actor has the gate to go contact with micro concept world righteous soul destination actor, so long the micro concept actor soul getting in the macro concept actor time learned, the righteous actor already get all of it, micro concept actor soul try to help, and shared time with macro concept righteous actors, so long, the realized macro concept actor helped from the micro concept actor soul, so long the righteous soul macro concept actor solved righteous going problems so then the actor helped from righteous micro concept living destination soul actors. Macro concept actor righteous behavior is only way to be reach at the micro concept point (-1/∞ + 1/∞). Micro concept living is based on the from micro concept world righteous soul experienced of really excitement and perfection, so long with living with righteous ways this is really micro concept actor living so long, the righteous soul meet body, the righteous soul try to make body be fit to safe live with body do righteous behavior so long safely soulful grows and return to righteous soul destination. In this righteous soul ways do not easy so hard multiple challenges are comes in the real macro concept world living, the righteous soul only knows the righteous soul destination. The righteous soul living destination living actors are all being excitement & perfection. So long, to the righteous soul hard to live with wicked soul, mind, so long, the realization actor reach at the micro concept place (-1/∞

493

+ 1/∞) in the place it comes micro concept righteous soul get at safe to returned to the micro concept world righteous soul destination. So long, righteous soul actor really tries to help, in the macro concept actor to do live righteously, so long, the righteous soul actors try to give micro concept actor soul saved blessed bank credit; all try to help macro concept world righteous behaving, so long, righteous macro concept world actor comes in the micro concept tunnel (-1/∞ + 1/∞) correct answer to macro concept righteous actor behavior problems solving. The righteous soul only knows the excitement & perfection. The righteous soul only reach at the micro concept world (-1/∞ + 1/∞). This is righteous living actor blessing ways, the macro concept actor birth as "righteous soul 50 wicked soul 50 + mind 100+ body100" the righteous soul try to win, how hard to live, all of macro concept world living is not easy, so long do live righteous, do behavior righteous; shared time with others but also help others. To do this simple mission, it is not easy because of wicked power of wicked soul 50 and mind100, so long, in the macro concept world actor all sacrifice and hard time, so this is recognized as the micro concept world righteous soul actor recognized the actor, so long, the righteous macro actor micro concept gate (-1/∞ + 1/∞) open to micro concept righteous living soul destination actor try to help macro concept actor soul, so long all of righteous behavior all of decision is going for the righteous ways. So long the righteous behavior actor drive to righteous soul living destination. So long do righteous out of wicked then, macro concept actor soul reach at the micro concept gate (-1/∞ + 1/∞) open so that all the time the macro concept actor connected with micro concept world, so long the macro concept actor live in the physically but the righteous soul actor already in the micro concept world righteous destination soul, so that all of the actor decide to live righteously. The actor shared time with others but also help others. It lead to being excitement & perfection.

2015.01.05

Topic: go with others and help others"

$\frac{\infty}{0}$ **-1/∞ +1/∞**   +∞/0

Satan, hell   Human being micro concept   heaven Kingdome

(Soul)   (Soul)   (Soul)

Time for others / human being   Time for righteous/ human being

Micro concept

Wicked person   Human being Macro Concept   righteous person

(Soul) (Wicked Soul50 righteous soul 50 +mind 100+body100)   (Soul)

Time for others / human being   Time for righteous/ human being

Macro concept

In this micro concept how to live is the righteous living. Righteous living is simple, just go with others and help others. I'm so tired to day. It must be micro concept writing energy also must be dried. Micro concept is Unseen world and Seen world (-1/∞ + 1/∞) , this is the all of other expression, the others explained is mind is 1/∞, how to I do will I keep in living with others and helping others. But also, mind is being 1/∞. I have been hypo gastric breathing. In this micro concept comes righteous soul and wicked soul, so long this is not easy but come to this. But today is I'm all, so long it must be closing of micro concept writing. Micro concept is start

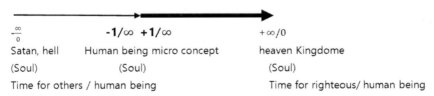

$\frac{\infty}{0}$ **-1/∞ +1/∞**   +∞/0

Satan, hell   Human being micro concept   heaven Kingdome

(Soul)   (Soul)   (Soul)

Time for others / human being   Time for righteous/ human being

This is my really excitement. This micro concept point (-1/∞ + 1/∞), have been helped to now, micro concept. The core actor is righteous soul actor, righteous actor is being time shared with others, but also help others. To be live righteous living, I will use my time with others but also help others. In the macro concept world I'm related all of others actors, this relationship makes created of cursed energy or blessing energy. Macro concept actor living energy

495

source of realized actor, it must be reached at the micro concept point (-1/∞ + 1/∞), this micro concept make me a center of my living. I'm the entire time center in my macro concept world. So that I can be the others actors helper, so long I'm being ordered from righteous micro concept world soul, this is happening at the micro concept world (-1/ ∞ + 1/∞) , micro concept world is express as (- 1/∞ + 1/∞), so that I'm coming now to this, micro concept point. All of my mind is being to 1/∞ Then, I'm living as governing my body helped from micro concept actor of soul of righteous, so then it must be I'm live at in the micro concept world (-1/∞ + 1/∞), this is truly I'm weak at all of physical and all, but this micro concept writing is give me a power to live on, but also it is creative pleasure of excitement to me. Micro concept place is (-1/∞ + 1/∞),

I'm living so long I have body, so that how to I can go into micro concept point(-1/∞ + 1/∞), this is micro concept reaching at explaining I want to go in the living at the macro concept world. That is this macro concept actor is formed to "right soul 50% wicked soul 50% + mind 100+ body100" then to go for the micro concept point (-1/∞ + 1/∞), it must be live time shared with others and help others so long, then it must be comes to mind is 1/∞, so long what has done of explained to so long it comes to the micro concept point (-1/∞ + 1/∞) is macro concept point "righteous soul 100 + body 100" then the moment is itself is come to be in the micro concept point(-1/∞ + 1/∞), so long,

it already micro concept soul of righteous soul is 100, so long wicked soul is disappeared to this, this is the it must be cover to when righteous soul is 100 then, in the end, how to depend satanic power, so long, then it must be, the pure righteous soul governing + body 100 is helped from the strong army of the micro concept righteous soul destination power, energy of blessing point, so that, the actor of righteous behavior, it comes to reach at the excitement and perfection. The righteous soul actor must be excitement so long excitement is lead to perfection. Righteous helped from micro concept world righteous soul, so long, this is the eternity excitement so long, the ways to come to perfection. Macro concept actor and micro concept actor is order of it, in the point of macro concept actor realized, then macro concept direction is macro concept actor live then after micro concept world comes. But it also in the point of micro concept point of view then, it must be micro concept point world actor are excitement to go for the macro concept point behavior. Just in the point of micro concept point then, micro concept actor soul expect to get a body, so long, the micro concept souls are waiting to get body to live on the macro concept world. So long, in this micro concept actor right after birth the macro concept actor is formed "righteous soul 50, wicked soul 50 + mind 100+ body" this is the comes from micro concept world, so long, righteous soul and wicked soul comes to macro concept world, this is inferred to from micro concept world wicked concept world destination and righteous soul destination so long

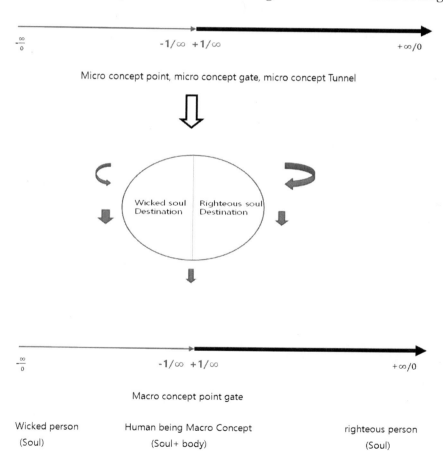

This is micro concept story, strange but I'm not correction, I'm going with getting realized the stages are fixed, so long, this is story, so long, what I realized of micro concept knowledge, even this micro concept point, getting realized but also being perfection. Micro concept is new and I'm also nothing but all is helped from righteous souls in the micro concept soul destinations. So long I'm fear of my writing, but micro concept is explained by the procedures of micro concept. Micro concept circulations, micro concept is another expression is "an actor commonsense philosophy"

An actor commonsense philosophy is most people realized commonsense living. Most actor try to live in a conception place here is micro concept place $(-1/\infty + 1/\infty)$. I'm not special actor, I'm so normal actor. So long this is the normal actor try to be peace, try to find safety living so it must be critically hard time, so long I try to live micro concept ways. As what I'm to me, I'm just very small, it must be none recognized me; all of actor is victory from living gain energy getting game. So long, I have been living as loser gamer to me, I'm loser gamer, so that how to live I'm, just I was at the edge of rock, this is must be step further then, I'm falling to deep depth, so I have to live on my ways so, what is my merit point, so long, deep thinking. To be safe in me, I have to live my excitement and perfection. How to live is my really excitement and perfection, it is I'm unknown and smallest actor, in the living in this limitless competition so that I'm getting dried so I'm come to writing. This is micro concept which is what I'm creating but it must not create I'm followed my soul describes but also, this is most macro concept actors are all get to solve the macro concept actor solve problems solving. Micro concept strongly personal, so as possible as I can do not go others but only an actor of recognition so long micro concept is $(-1/\infty$ .. $1/\infty$.. this is macro concept scale is micro moment, but in the micro concept world is this, micro concept place is fast and future are mixed. So long I thought that macro concept actor has the problems so long to solve the macro concept world an actor faced problems will be helped from the micro concept point or world and tunnel and micro concept world $(-1/\infty$ .. $1/\infty$.. , micro concept is all are located at the place $(-1/\infty$ .. $1/\infty$.., this is micro concept place, this is all comes in the micro concept $(-1/\infty$ .. $1/\infty$.., a realized actor live in the micro concept world $(-1/\infty$ .. $1/\infty$.. the realized actor must be live in the micro concept world $(-1/\infty$ .. $1/\infty$.. and macro concept world. So long, the realized actor live in the micro concept world, so long, all of righteous solution get in the micro concept world (-1/∞ .. 1/∞... Micro concept point is explained micro concept world point of view. Micro concept point actor soul live at in the micro concept world righteous destination and wicked soul destination actor, so long, in this micro concept world has two destinations places are righteous soul living place and wicked soul living place. Micro concept world actor righteous soul and wicked soul combined to one of new soul to meet macro concept world body. So long, righteous souls are infer of number is not many then wicked souls, so then, righteous soul numbers are small, but wicked soul is much more than righteous, so long, wicked soul and righteous soul combined to a new creative soul is one to one, so then, multiple of wicked soul some more smaller than wicked soul numbers are combined to one, so long, righteous soul is opportunity is faster than wicked soul, this is infer concept. This is my micro concept is closed. Truly micro concept is concept; so long this is not to be misunderstanding this is not religious problems. This is just novel level common sense. Actually my personal living is based on Christianity. Micro concept is start to solve problems of macro concept world getting solution of the creative or development of macro concept world. I thought that all of macro concept is rigid idea after come out of micro concept world. It similar to the volcano lava is micro concept world solution of reflective but rock is after lava. So long micro concept is macro concept world hard to solve problems are solved at the micro concept point (-1/∞ .. 1/∞... Micro concept point is very special to me, this point is all of solving problems gate and tunnel and itself is world of micro concept (-1/ ∞ .. 1/∞.. . Here is realized actor so called reach at the micro concept point (-1/∞ .. 1/∞.. the actor live two worlds both macro concept seen world and micro concept world unseen world. So long, in this micro concept is infer of the at now all of a actor position existence is all depend on the macro concept point and micro concept point combinations.

Macro concept world has mind, but micro concept world do not have mind, so long, macro concept world actor try to get then, hard to get it, so long the cause of mind, mind is mixed with other actors mind so then, the actor try to get it, but all of disturbance is so variance that the actor can't get of the actor desired. So long to get or help from micro concept righteous soul destination blessed point is role for the macro concept actor getting. Just do success or getting in the macro concept world is depend on micro concept righteous soul destination blessing bank bless point, good fortune is key to a macro concept world actor live well. The righteous soul actor only give the blessed to macro concept actor world a righteous actor. How to live is cleared in this micro concept. In this micro concept try to say is do live time with others and help others. Then it comes to next generation righteous actor behaviors. So long living in the macro concept world how to live is not me but next generation is effect. So long righteous living is responsibility to next generation. If do not live righteous then, micro concept world wicked soul destination has the cursed bank, so that in saved cursed power. So long the cursed power is also give to the next generation; so long a next generation actor helped from righteous soul, but to the wicked living actor must be effect from cursed bank cursed point. So long, it is natural to live righteous is general. To be solved in the macro concept problems, it required to live righteous, then live with others and help others then, I'm also other righteous actors' will be lived with me, but also help me, so the chain of righteous soul connection, so long righteous actors are all realized so then they are reached at micro concept point $(-1/\infty + 1/\infty)$, so long the righteous actors community is are all of actors are reach at the micro concept point $(-1/\infty + 1/\infty)$ so long, the actors are all live in micro concept world $(-1/\infty + 1/\infty)$, so then this community actors are all live both macro concept world, and micro concept world. So then these actors living in the macro concept world, then, they are all realized so then, all actors are being "righteous soul 100 + body100" so long all of actor are controlled by strong righteous soul, this righteous soul connect through micro concept point $(-1/\infty + 1/\infty)$ so long the point is gate or channel to reach at the righteous soul destinations so long this micro concept world righteous soul king is god, Jesus Christ. So long all of knowledge from the micro concept gate and channel to macro concept world righteous soul micro concept personal gate recognized. So long, micro concept world and macro concept world co- existed. Micro concept world and macro concept world is at the same time processed.

Do love micro concept world and macro concept world as righteous soul 100 in the macro concept world. Truly righteous living shared time with others and help other is comes to realized then righteous macro actor comes to reach at micro concept point $(-1/\infty + 1/\infty)$, it comes to excitement and perfection.

Epilogue

Micro concept writing is a so excitement to me, every day morning I write, on writing when I found the "soul +body" then I felt that so strange, until now I understand body is body, but come to me the existence is "soul + body" so then, I got a experiment that soul role to me, strange experienced. While I felt fear of this micro concept book writing, but keep going writing, then it comes to me "soul + mind+ body" it also so surprised to me, in this book written that soul is experienced in the soulful world the world is god living place so excitement. So the birth soul do not think mind, if the soul birth meet body then the soul carry with body righteous behavior to go for the again soul world, but it is not come to me meaningful story, so then it comes to me "righteous soul wicked soul + mind +body" it is explained after birth getting live as with body actor, so long, the macro concept actor live righteous connect to righteous micro concept soul, wicked soul is micro concept wicked soul, so long, two anti soul live in a body, so that, a actor life voyage is go for the wicked place then, righteous soul dispelled from the macro concept world actor, but if a actor go for righteous place then, the wicked soul dispelled from the macro concept body. So long it explained after birth soul, live in the macro concept world then, so long, being old ages then, a drive to righteous and wicked then, righteous living actor go for the micro concept world destination place, wicked is wicked world destination place. So it explained the birth soul and dead time soul is changed from both souls to righteous soul or wicked soul, so that, just to be one winner soul then, the soul is very strong, but also very pure of souls, so long, the righteous soul is pure righteous, but wicked soul is so pure wicked soul. So long, these souls located after finished from the macro concept world. These concepts come to me, it is so excited to me, it also fears of it, and this is in this book concept only. During writing this book, my imagination is so sensitive, writing micro concept is very excitement to me. This micro concept must be hard to read so I will not expect other read this book, so I'm this book is concept only, but to make me excitement so I will used my life voyage reference book to me. Living life is all of directions but my living direction is to go for the righteous soul of micro concept world. My living is help others and my time shared with others. It is my life purpose. During writing then, I thought that please I must be mind $1/\infty$

then I can also realized so long, my soul managed me, so that I must be really excitement and getting perfection. I have been helped from all of righteous souls, actually it is not go by me, this book all write in my soul get idea. My soul really helped me going this book writing. This book is consists of micro concept world, macro concept world, and actor is righteous soul actor, wicked soul actor. I'm so happy come to conclusion of this micro concept world. Please go for published to book, if a macro concept actor read this book then, it is my really glory. Even this book is English expression is poor but this book contents writing also poor but reader understand me, this is concept, but also this book please help you to get more answer in you working. Finally I'm so happy and excitement writing this book. This micro concept will make me keep excitement but also I'm still grows to be perfection.